From heaven to earth

GW00546727

13.99

How have Chinese peasants experienced the reforms introduced over the past ten years? Elisabeth Croll, who has frequently visited rural China, has had unique opportunities to study at first hand villages across a wide range of rich and poor regions. *From Heaven to Earth* combines information on events, processes and structures to provide a comprehensive introduction to the study of reform in rural China.

Taking a distinctively anthropological approach to the subject, the author looks behind the simplistic notion of 'reform' as merely a 'return to capitalism'. She discusses the invention and dominance in China of a collective dream in which an imagined future took precedence over the experience of the present, and traces the failure of that dream to its legacy of uncertainty, ambiguity and anxiety. Linking peasants' experiences of revolution and reform to the way they think about time and change, Elisabeth Croll describes development policies, images and experiences. More practically, *From Heaven to Earth* focuses on rural development, emphasizing that the peasant household lies at the heart of recent rural reforms and has replaced the collective as the unit of production. Ethnographic case studies look at family, household and gender relations and throw new light on the relations between state and household giving rise to a new peasant family form, single or two-child families and gender-specific images and experiences of revolution and reform.

The process of reform in China raises questions that are relevant for the study of rural development in general, and this pioneering appraisal provides an invaluable anthropological complement to contemporary studies by economists and political scientists. It will appeal to a wide readership, including students and professionals in Chinese studies, rural development, sociology and anthropology.

Elisabeth Croll is Reader in Chinese Anthropology and Director of the Centre of Chinese Studies at the School of Oriental and African Studies of the University of London. She has written widely on both historical and contemporary China.

From heaven to earth

Images and experiences of development in China

Elisabeth Croll

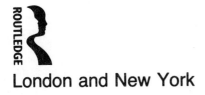

London and New York

First published 1994
by Routledge
11 New Fetter Lane, London EC4P 4EE

Simultaneously published in the USA and Canada
by Routledge
29 West 35th Street, New York, NY 10001

© 1994 Elisabeth Croll

Typeset in Times by J&L Composition Ltd, Filey, North Yorkshire
Printed and bound in Great Britain by
TJ Press (Padstow) Ltd, Padstow, Cornwall

British Library Cataloguing in Publication Data
A catalogue record for this book is available from the British Library.

Library of Congress Cataloging in Publication Data
Croll, Elisabeth J.
   From heaven to earth: images and experiences of development in China/
   Elisabeth Croll.
   p. cm.
   Includes bibliographical references and index.
   1. Rural development–China–Social aspects.   2. China–Rural conditions.
   3. Agriculture and state–China.   I. Title
   HN740.Z9C6324 1993   93–12543
   307.72′0951–dc20   CIP

ISBN 0–415–09746–0 (hbk)
ISBN 0–415–10187–5 (pbk)

We have finally come back from Heaven to Earth.

Focus vision on reality – on having a correct understanding of the national condition.

Renmin Ribao (People's Daily), 18 November 1987

Contents

Preface

Much has been written on China's peasant revolution, less on the peasant experience of reform. It is now thirteen years since the first major reforms were introduced into China's villages, and since that time there have been many shifts and changes in the translation and practice of reform policies so that many of the initial assumptions and judgements made by observers, analysts and participants have been modified over the years. It is not so much that the implications of the reforms for lives, practices and policies have become clearer as that they have become increasingly paradoxical and various. This study is an attempt to portray some of these paradoxes and variations in both their temporal and spatial dimensions.

This book is about images, policies and experiences of development primarily linking peasants' experience of revolution and reform with their conceptualisations of time and change. It combines a study of the images or dreams of development as sets of rhetorical lenses through which peasant populations perceive collective, family and individual experiences, with an analysis of rural development policies and reforms at the centre of which lies the peasant household. This study is about the working and reworking of age-old peasant dreams for sons and land. It is also about the invention and dominance of the collective dream substituting an imaged future for the experience of the present, and the demise of this collective dream leaving uncertainty, ambiguity and anxiety in its wake. The book is also about the new and recent desires which motivate peasant households in China; the new and strenuous demands which are generated by current reforms allocating new responsibilities to the peasant household and family; and family strategies evolved by peasant households to maximise their resources within the context of reformed rural development.

More practically, the study focuses on rural development. In the first decades of revolution, the general interest in development in China was considerable, both because of the form which rural development took and the scale and scope of its development strategies. Prior to the past ten years, development in China was the subject of many studies and books. Indeed China's 'road to development' became a favourite if not somewhat overworked title of several monographs. During the past ten years, however, there has been less interest in China's rural development, partly because the context became reform rather than revolution and the focus domestic, the household or the family rather than the collective, co-operative or commune. Yet it can be argued that the rural reforms in China centring on shifting notions and allocations of social and domestic responsibility are as interesting, as important a context and as relevant as revolution in considering policies of rural development. Moreover, subsequent readjustments, shifting and reshifting responsibility between collective and domestic, have rendered dual categorisations and oppositions inappropriate and inaccurate. The movement from revolution to reform cannot simply be summed up as a movement from socialism to capitalism substituting the household for collective, the market for plan or profit for the common good.

At the heart of the more complex rural reforms lies the peasant household, and this book is primarily about the recent domestication of China's development. The revolution and reform periods in recent Chinese history have brought about shifts in the analytical focus on the peasant household. Previously, from the turn of the century, the small Chinese peasant household was of literary and analytical interest in its contrast with the large rambling courtyarded gentry family with its tens of family members and in its great vulnerability to drought, flood, famine, war and disease. From the mid-century onwards, the analytical focus during the first thirty years of revolution shifted to the relationship between the peasant household and the dominant co-operative, commune, brigade and team within which it was incorporated. More recently, one of the most interesting and important dimensions of the recent rapid and radical reforms in the Chinese countryside has been the interest in and focus on the family or household as an economic, political and social unit ideally reproducing only one child. The peasant household has virtually replaced the collective as the unit of production, consumption and welfare in rural China. To write or talk of the peasant household is to impute some universal significance to domestic institutions as if they did not cover a wide variety of kinship and residential arrangements, the significance of which might vary according to its specific temporal and spatial context and according to member and narrator. Nevertheless, as this book will argue, it is possible to identify a domestic space, domain or arena of relations which constitutes the peasant household and which is the locus of much of the rural development process. Indeed, what characterises the period of reform in the past decades has been the identification of development with the domestic sphere; it is the site where development is produced and re-enacted so that domestic organisation and activity is the centre piece of the rural development plan.

It was the search for appropriate institutions conducive to maximum rural development with equity which led to the constant restructuring of the relationship between collective and domestic institutions and the successive policy shifts affecting the dominance of first one and then the other. Although a major characteristic of the period of reform in the past decade has been the identification of development with the domestic sphere, this does not mean that the village, co-operatives or collective institutions have no part to play. Just as the peasant household remained an important economic unit within the collective during the revolution, policies of readjustment subsequent to reform have supplemented and in some cases substituted domestic organisation and activity with new forms of collective activity in what may lead to important new juxtapositions of domestic and collective institutions. One of my several interests over the past fifteen years has been the investigation of the content of state policy, its channels of communication between state and village and its implementation within the village. Thus this study looks at how China's peasant households have received and responded to startling and shifting policies which challenged pre-existing village institutions, relations, customs and beliefs and norms – some inherited or centuries old and others in place for only a few years or months.

This book aims to attract both the general reader interested in China, in rural development, in gender, in socialism and in poverty as well as the specialist well-versed and experienced in any one of these disciplines or areas. Thus the details of rural policy and their shifts and changes which provide a frame or context for the general reader will already be familiar to many colleagues. For them, I hope the ethnographic case studies will prove to be of value, adding to their own very stimulating work. This study, based on a variety of sources, embraces documentary sources on policy and practice including media and periodical reports, village studies by Chinese and foreign observers and my own field notes as an anthropologist visiting, interviewing and staying in peasant households over the past ten years (see Appendix).

Now that many international government and non-government agencies are establishing both small and large-scale development projects in China, I have frequently been asked to investigate local social environments in its many various regions and to advise on project formulation, establishment and evaluation. These development assignments have provided me with new and perhaps unique forms of access to a range of rural regions from rich suburban villages near Beijing and Wuxi cities and the rich grain lands of Shanxi to the poor and remote Henan highlands, picture-book but steep-valleyed poor Sichuan, poor drought-stricken Shandong highlands and the intensely stunning and stunned stone mountains of the southwestern provinces of Yunnan and Guangxi. These diverse localities were studied, originally between 1987 and 1992, for a variety of purposes, but common to the case studies discussed in this book is a central interest in the peasant experience of reform and the development of village and household economies. These assignments provided special opportunities for data collection on such sensitive issues as economic and social differentiation, welfare, poverty, indebtedness and desires, preferences and dreams. What is especially interesting about many of the questions and dilemmas raised in these projects is that they frequently mirror those facing the Chinese (and other) governments and peoples in their quest to improve rural production, incomes and welfare generally and to develop remote rural regions or improve the livelihood of the poor. This book raises many of these larger issues, but within the context of the local socio-economic and political rural environment of the reformed Chinese village and with particular reference to the rural household or the peasant family. Both my reading and my first-hand experiences over the past few years have provided me with a variety of impressions, insights and hypotheses in the attempt to identify patterns, trends and problems which, limited, tentative and preliminary as many of them are, I have written into this book now both for my own and others' use and to further discussion and debate.

The first two chapters examine the movement from revolution to reform, first in terms of shifts in spatial and temporal images of development from 'heaven to earth' and from the future to the present, and secondly in terms of shifts in responsibility for production, consumption and welfare from the collective to the domestic in what virtually amounted to a reversal of the process of collectivisation. If the rhetoric of reform presented it as a movement for the 'return to earth', the rhetoric of revolution had imaged an ideal of a collective 'heaven', exclusively representing the future and reducing or denying family or individual experience of the present. The first chapter examines the notion of heaven, dreams of heaven on earth (both peasant and Communist) and the language of the dream which, in emphasising heaven and dream, placed the future at the centre of consciousness and privileged it in relation to the present. Chapter 2 documents the reorganisation of agricultural production, the rural economy and rural welfare, and the relocation of responsibility from the collective to the peasant household, and contrasts the new and greater demands placed on the domestic unit with the reduction in responsibility and authority of the village. The peasant experience of development during the recent years of reform has been diverse, and to give some idea of the variety of new economic and political relations within and between China's peasant households and villages, Chapter 3 broadly outlines peasant experiences of household and village reform in nine different localities.

A task as important for anthropologists as investigating ethnographic event and experience is documenting the ways in which the participants themselves represent this experience or think about and conceptualise notions such as production, labour, knowledge, wealth, state, kinships, marriage, gender and future. This study thus attaches importance to peasant representation of experience in all its various facets, and argues that the term 'readjustment' is crucial to understanding changes subsequent to reform that have taken place within China's villages and households. It argues that if the process of reform originally emphasised and favoured household responsibility and autonomy at the expense of the village and its cadres, subsequent processes of readjustment negotiated in the interests of resource management have emphasised and reinvested responsibility in the village and strengthened its corporate economy and polity. Chapter 4 examines readjustments in the distribution of the most important of these responsibilities to do with the management and cultivation of the land, the provision of pre- and post-production services and enterprise development which have proved beyond the capacity of the individual peasant household. This chapter argues that the higher the village income, the more developed the village resources, responsibilities and services, the greater the interdependence between household and village and the more unified the economic and political management centring on the village with greater cadre authority.

If the processes of readjustment have underlined shifts in responsibilities, management and authority to village cadres, relations within the village and between village and state have also undergone major changes, so that authority within the village is not so singularly invested in the cadre. Chapter 5 suggests that readjustments in economic relations between village and household have led to more intricate and symmetric negotiations of power and knowledge in the village, with households exercising greater agency and cadres simultaneously subjected to new checks and balances deriving from new information networks and instituted sanctions including the media and law courts. This chapter argues that it is one of the major characteristics of rural reform that, in the construction and negotiation of local knowledge, peasant households are no longer so encapsulated by the village that incoming information can be so exclusively managed by cadres although knowledge of the village is still almost exclusively constructed for official purposes by local cadres.

Central to the success of reform has been an increase in incomes, consumption and welfare of peasant households. Initially, the association of riches with reform was such that one of the most important questions in the first years of reform was whether the government could satisfy the rising expectations it had set in motion at the outset of reform. Chapter 6 discusses how, officially and in the popular imagination, the numbers of newly rich became the chief rationale for and criteria in measuring the efficacy of the reforms. It looks at income rises and differentials within villages and between villages, and shows how applause for the rich has been increasingly matched with concern for the poor. Within poverty alleviation programmes there has been a readjustment in provisioning from the general to the targeted and of priorities from relief provision to income generation. This chapter looks at poverty alleviation programmes in the poorest villages and the introduction of the development project, a concept imported from the international development agencies during the reform decade and, as a bounded space, perhaps as important to peasant households and villages as the much publicised special economic zones.

All these reforms generating new demands on the peasant household have in turn had repercussions for its size, its structure and its meaning and for family relations. From the first days of reform the response of the peasant household to the new demands, responsibilities and opportunities was very much dependent on the numbers and skills of its labourers. Chapter 7 examines the various strategies deployed by peasant households to increase rapidly their labour resources, and suggests that their limitations have not only encouraged new exchanges of labour between households but also led to the formation of a new family form, the aggregate family, which both acquired the resources and escaped the disadvantages of the single, larger, complex household. This chapter examines forms of economic association and co-operation between closely kin-related households within villages and the new investments in links with households, and particularly affinal kin, outside the village. It argues that, while it is important to take account of the continuing corporate qualities of the peasant household, it may well be that it is this aggregate of households with its spatially extended networks which becomes as important a unit of analysis in the future.

In addition to redefining relations between households, the new reforms have had repercussions for relations within households, particularly gender relations and those between generations. Chapter 8 focuses on sons as family successors, and suggests that one of the single most important family preoccupations of the reform years in China's countryside has proved to be the continuity of the family line. For generations, sons bridging ancestors and descendants signified the unbroken continuity of the family, so that without sons there was deemed to be no family future. However, if dreams of sons and more sons continued into the present, they were also threatened by the introduction of increasingly stringent birth-control policies which, culminating in the single-child policy, were to cut short dramatically age-old dreams of sons or even perhaps of one son. The single-child policy is without doubt the most unpopular government policy of the reform decade, and this truncation or abandonment of age-old dreams of family and future did not take place without a struggle between family and state. Chapter 8 examines six phases in its short ten-year history which mark the government's repeated readjustments to the policy to make it operable by altering the formulations and the means by which it was communicated and implemented.

Chapter 9 focuses on daughters, who, promised 'half of heaven', continue to be objects of discrimination and sometimes even denied the earth as a result of the one-child policy. Despite forty years of revolutionary promises of equity and privileged entitlements to the future, the age-old contrast remained: if sons were for continuity, daughters' lives and dreams were fashioned out of uncertainty and discontinuity. This chapter looks at the discordant and competing messages which daughters received from family and state, first discussing forms of family discrimination culminating in the increase in female infanticide during the reform years, and then state programmes of equity summed up in the concept 'half of heaven'. It suggests that the notion of heaven, implying investment in the future, may never have had the same meaning for female as for male, largely because of a female-specific concept of time deriving from women's anticipation of and experience of marriage. If, before marriage, the present was shadowed by uncertainty, discontinuity and dislocation but coloured by dreams of an unknown husband and images of a limitless future, in the years following marriage women uniquely lived the future as imaged, visualised or dreamed. The study argues that it was this foreshortening or 'early arrival of dreams' not shared by males which had important implications for female conceptualisations of and investments in both present and future and may have differentiated male and female experience of revolution and reform. Indeed, it is the discontinuities and uncertainties which daughters continue to experience in marriage and their implications for a female-specific conceptualisation of time which mark the nearest parallel I can think of in considering the rupture, discontinuity and uncertainty experienced generally by the population in the movement from revolution to reform. Chapter 10 summarises the major changes in image and experience incorporated within the shift from revolution to reform and to readjustment or the collectivist past to the consumerist future by looking at expressions of individual and family aspiration. In discussing the benefits and losses associated with reform, this final chapter suggests that 'living the earth' without the security and certainty of an imaged or chartered 'future', 'dream' or 'heaven' to frame, define or contextualise experience has constituted a major characteristic of the reform years in China.

Acknowledgements

In undertaking this study I would like to acknowledge the help of the following institutions, organisations and persons. I would like to thank the Leverhulme Foundation and the School of Oriental and African Studies, whose financial support made the research and writing of this book possible.

Various international and non-governmental organisations enabled me to make the field visits to China. These included NOVIB, IFAD, the Ford Foundation, FAO and the World Bank. In China, I received much help from various host organisations, including the Ministry of Agriculture, the Institute of Sociology of the Chinese Academy of Social Sciences, the Poverty Alleviation Bureau and the All-China Women's Federation. For aid with my work in China, I would like to thank Mary Ann Burris, Paul Cadario, Meng Fanxi, William Hinton, Howard Johnson, Nick Menges, Lee Travers, Alan Piazza and Zhang Ye, as well as many local cadres, who were unstinting in their assistance.

I would like to express my thanks to the Centre for Cross-Cultural Research on Women, Queen Elizabeth House, University of Oxford, under the directorship of Shirley Ardener for giving me the opportunity to give the Ward Lecture in October 1990, an occasion which stimulated some of the overarching ideas for this book. I would like to thank David Parkin for his reading of the manuscript and helpful suggestions.

To Nicolas and Katherine I offer my apologies for having less time with them than I would wish, and to Jim Croll I offer my thanks for his help during times when I was away in China.

This book has a very general dedication: to all those working for a better earth both within China and beyond. More specifically, its writing owes much to the ideas and stimulation of my colleagues in the Department of Anthropology at the School of Oriental and African Studies, University of London: in particular Richard Fardon, Mark Hobart, Deniz Kandiyoti, David Parkin, John Peel, Stuart Thompson and Andrew Turton; its writing also owes much to the support of colleagues and friends in Anthropology and Asian Studies at SOAS and elsewhere: in particular to Helen

Callaway, Wynn Chao, Monik Charette, Felicity Edholm, Maxine Molyneux, Tony Saich, Olivia Harris, Simon Long, Nanneke Redclift, Rupert Snell, Gordon White, Frances Wood and Elizabeth Wright, who have all been generous with their time in Beijing and/or in London.

Introduction

Chapter 1

Imaging heaven
Collective dreams

The peasant experience of reform is rooted in the peasant experience of
revolution. To attempt to encapsulate peasant experience of either is a
daring act, given both the diverse regions of China and the twists and turns
in the policies of each over time. It has become commonplace, in an age
of reluctance, to fix definitions and limit categorisations, to emphasise that
there is no single representation or overview sufficient to capture the
variety of experiences at any one historical moment. Moreover, the very
concepts of revolution and reform are now recognised to have a variety of
meanings for different persons, platforms and periods and are themselves
an acknowledged part of folk and analytic vocabularies of social and
cultural construction. As analytic categories, revolution and reform are
important and convenient labels for the analysis of certain events, processes
and perceptions, but we are now all aware that how these changes are
perceived, measured and analysed depends not only on observable altera-
tions in structures, institutions and relations, but also on the interests of
the analysts and their ways of seeing and writing![1] Whether the movement
from revolution to reform in China is perceived as enlightenment or as
betrayal very much depends on the perceptions and point of view of the
analyst, which may or may not take account of the perceptions of the
participants whose ideas, norms and values, making up constructs of
revolution and reform, constitute the essential other voices in the understanding, interpreting and recording of events and experience.[2]

In the China of the revolution, perhaps more than in most societies, the
participants' own utterances, be they visual, verbal or written, were
consciously invested with imported meanings and messages representing
or even substituting for the voice of experience. The rhetoric of revolution
imaged an ideal or a collective heaven, largely represented the future and
minimised or denied family or individual experience of the present. The
rhetoric of reform was thus to become a movement for 'returning to earth',
'focusing on reality', or for emphasising experience and the present. In
looking at 'ways of seeing' and of representing experience during the
revolution, it is perhaps appropriate to begin with the eyes. What was

immediately striking to the observer of pictorial representations of the eyes, be they on poster or billboard, in paintings or in films of the first thirty years of the Chinese revolution, was their gaze, the stare of clear, bright, shining eyes, as if fixed and stretched, they focused pointedly on some distant object – undefined, as if beyond the horizon. They overlooked the foreground as if it was of no importance, and blurred it frequently was in these representations. It was as if there was a clear, bright, shining, distant, dream-like landscape which was the focus of the long-sighted distancing eye.

If we turn to the semantic equivalent or the language of this long-sighted and distancing eye, then for the first thirty years it seemed as if language was also fixed, removed and bounded with a limited repertoire of vocabulary available for expression. It was as if the foreground of immediate experience was blurred, masked and confined by words effecting a rhetoric which primarily referred to and defined, not the direct and immediate experience of the body and its senses, but something outside and beyond the immediate – most often a distant image or dream of the future. At best this image or dream framed or encompassed and gave meaning to the present; at worst it bounded or imprisoned the present by denying the evidence, validity or legitimacy of direct and immediate experience and observation by inhibiting its articulation in language via both speech and the written text. The role of language and rhetoric in prescripting and representing experience has been discussed at some length in anthropological texts,[3] and in China, more than for most societies, there were discrepancies between image or rhetoric and sense or experience which were commonly denied or at least minimised in the constantly changing various and complex relationships between peasant images and experiences of China's revolution.

If we bring together visual and verbal representations into a single state of being, which I have termed 'the rhetorical glaze', then our attention is drawn to its single articulated focus – the collective image or dream into which all permitted pictorial and semantic expression was almost exclusively channelled in an attempt consciously to capture or colonise the consciousness. This chapter first examines briefly the establishment of the rhetorical glaze as the dominant lens through which the Chinese population expressed their aspirations and perceptions of the present and the future during the first thirty years of revolution. It also discusses the growing discrepancy between rhetorical representation and experience prior to the introduction of the reforms which led to the demise of the collective dream with the substitution of experience for image and of present for future as the focal points of attention, policy and aspiration.

At the centre of the rhetorical glaze lay a publicly articulated collective dream which for the individual or the group also denoted representation or image in the mind, perhaps vaguely defined but nevertheless greatly desired. For generations, peasant householders in China had dreamed of land, sons and security of person and property. If a household dreamed of many sons, it also dreamed of owning land sufficient to support many sons. Those without either dreamed of both, those with a single son and a little land dreamed of acquiring more, and those with surplus wealth invested in land and sons. Representations of these desires had long featured among peasant Utopian or millenarian aspirations and platforms in the rich heritage of Chinese peasant rebellions whose conceptions of heaven were inherited anew by each generation of villagers. To solicit the support of the peasants, their dreams of land, stability and security had been incorporated into the popular platforms of political movements from the widespread Taiping (Heavenly Kingdom) peasant rebellion of the mid-nineteenth century to the nationalist movements of Sun Yat-sen and Mao Zedong; the latter, of peasant background himself, wrote extensively of the dreams of poor and landless peasants. One of the most important platforms of the Communist Party was the redistribution of land and property belonging to landlord and rich peasant to the poor and landless. For twenty years the promises of the Communist Party coincided with the dreams of the majority of China's peasant households: dreams of heaven on earth.

IMAGES OF HEAVEN

'Heaven' was a term, concept or name that had a multi-faceted history in China and a tradition of thought, imagery and vocabulary which asserted hope for an era of harmonised and equalised unity, of heavenly order on earth, through a sudden but prophesied change.[4] The concept differed from that deployed in Judaeo-Christian and Islamic notions in that, para-doxically, while it was other-worldly and outside of everyday experience, it was central to this-worldly imagination in that it neither offered or made promises of an after-life nor had any transcendental significance. Rather, it was a state attainable on earth. Much, although not all,[5] of this idea of heaven as the earth's other was a necessary part of the construction of the dream and perception of the future. If meanings depend on or are often born of contrasts, then the most significant contrast was that between heaven and earth, and out of the scarce resources and vulnerable conditions of the Chinese earth was born the image of heaven.

Although symbolically and practically it was the earth which was the most durable source of food, wealth and security, for centuries Chinese farmers had lived precariously on the margins of subsistence suffering insecurity of life and property in the face of climatic uncertainty and scarcity of cultivable land. For the majority who had little or no land and had to pay exorbitant land rents, borrow at high interest rates against their land or in extreme circumstances sell their land to survive, it was not surprising that equitable, sufficient and secure land resources were for dreaming. Heaven then was differently characterised – by limitless possibility, by prosperity, plenty and profusion and by equity in distribution with equality and security for all. The contrast between heaven and earth partook of that most fundamental of contrasts between yin and yang so that heaven was mostly associated with yang's light, positive, strong, bright and open qualities. Moreover, to bring about heaven on earth required a mediator, and all Emperors and potential rulers had long fostered the dream of heaven on earth so that knowledge of heaven and its mandate underlay claims to their rule. The mandate of heaven, source and symbol of power, uniquely conferred authority and legitimacy of rule on Emperors and latterly on political parties. Like its predecessors, claims by the Communist Party led by Mao Zedong to embody the will of heaven, to divine the future and to facilitate the potent dream bestowed by both Chinese tradition and Marxist text underlay power and justified their revolutionary government on behalf of the people and their desires.

In addition to representing desires, the dream can also be seen as a potent means or mechanism of adaptation promoting toleration of the present by compensating for its shortfalls. In Chinese Buddhism tradition- ally, dreams of individuals were perceived as excursions of a duplicate soul into regions otherwise unseen. Moreover, the bliss of regions unseen, the imaginary regions of heaven, were popularly thought to represent or encode the collective future so that heaven also became the landscape or map of the future. Thus the saying: 'Heaven sees only what is distant.' Conceptualisations of time and the relation between peasant cyclic and imposed linear time with its implications for the separation of past, present and future has been the subject of anthropological interest for several decades.[6] In China, the emphasis on heaven as opposed to the earth, the dream as opposed to experience, placed the future at the centre of consciousness and privileged it in relation to the present. After 1949, 'Look towards the future' was the essence of countless slogans. Privileging the future functioned to shift attention away from that present and make that present more tolerable. The denial of importance to the present except as an extension of the past and *en route* to the future was already an integral part of Chinese cultural constructions of and reckonings of time,[7] in which it was primarily conceived of as a moment merely successor to a long past and anticipatory of an endless future. One of the first Europeans to reside within a large Chinese household has described how the keeping of time and the recording of event reduced the import of the present, emphasising its ephemeral place between the long narrative of the past and the blank scroll of the future.[8]

This liminal state was reinforced by Marxist theory, in which the present was largely conceptualised as a state of transition to a socialist future or as a state to be transformed and translated, and incorporating the notion of a trade-off between the present and the future with rewards or gratifications deferred to the future which both gave explanation for and legitimised the deprivations of the present. To make the present more tolerable, slogans such as 'Three years of hardship for a thousand years of happiness', common in the first revolutionary years, reiterated the message that tomorrow would always be better than today. In practical terms, this deferral of gratification largely meant delayed consumption not just of the conspicuous kind but also for comfortably meeting basic needs of much of the population. Some ten to fifteen years ago, much of my work was based on a single question: need it be so difficult for planned economies to provide sufficient and accessible food supplies for family nourishment? It seemed even then that consumption was an underdeveloped area of concern and investigation in the European and Asian planned economies, which similarly almost single-mindedly focused their energies on production to the exclusion of consumption. Recent events in those planned economies, and particularly in the Soviet Union, with headlines such as 'It began with a dream and ended in a stampede in the shops', have borne out this asymmetry and its price. If dreams of the future legitimated present deferment by providing imaginary means of adaptation, then it was but a short step from image or dream as compensation to image or dream as substitution for experience.

The process whereby imaging became a substitute for living, which it can be argued increasingly occurred in China's revolution, primarily took a form of visualisation as if what was imaged or envisioned was already in a state of being. Thus the present was not only perceived through the eyes of the future, but the present began to be experienced as if it was the future. Perhaps this kaleidoscope of perceptions was also encouraged by a central feature of Chinese language or the collapsing of time, for there is little formal significance given to tense or clear delineations of past, present and future.[9] The same first European ethnographer residing in a Chinese household was intrigued to find that a century past or a century in the future was not considered 'far off' in a language that had no tense and in which ordinary speech could tell of an event centuries ago as casually as an incident within the very hour.[10] Several decades later a foreigner privileged in conversation with Mao Zedong spoke of 'losing all sense of time in his presence' – as events of the last century, this century and the next were 'criss-crossed' with those of yesterday and today.[11]

What is distinctive to this process of imaging in China in the first thirty years of its revolution was its self-consciousness. Indeed, one of the factors distinguishing the Chinese revolution was the importance attached to consciousness in introducing and maintaining social change which reflected the quite central belief in China that ideology and organisation could serve as substitutes for the development of material forces, at least within certain limits and until material conditions allowed for a further development of the economic base. Each individual's thought and act was to be consciously pondered and their own and relational meanings were to be made explicit via a process of consciousness-raising, which was a state requiring constant and extensive monitoring of thoughts, words and acts. The processes of consciousness-raising and 'thought reform', its more concentrated and intensive form, were above all attempts to instil ways of seeing and ways of speaking so that the thought of individuals became indistinguishable from the message of their environment.[12] However, in order to effect this consciousness-raising and thought reform, it was also necessary to singularise the message of the environment. The exclusivity of message and its imposition were largely attempted by the establishment of a new rhetoric.

THE RHETORIC OF HEAVEN

The first step in capturing the consciousness of the Chinese population was the creation of a new language incorporating new names and categorisations which denied existing deprivation, hierarchies and individual interests separate from those of the collective, which were assumed to be homogeneous. The new language was one that celebrated change and achievement, assuming the formation of heaven on earth and the future in the present, so that the very appropriation of this language of celebration became a form of celebration in itself. In this sequence, it was a short second step to the exclusion of other semantic variations, in rhetoric and in text, so that the language of celebration subsequently became the only language in which discourse was officially permitted. This is not to suggest that this language entirely encompassed everyday consciousness or to ignore divergences, complexities, ambiguities and subtleties in individual thought and reflection that were sometimes concealed by conceptual and semantic masks and ritualised expressions – all forms of coded communication. Indeed, many were the personal strategies for coping with the discrepancies between linguistic expression and experience, including blocking, compartmentalisation and diversion. However, only in the past few years, with the new publications of biography and autobiography, has the extent to which retreat into memory, private fantasy and even loss of memory and person become a publicly acknowledged feature among the generation most intimately involved in thought reform, the intellectual parents of today's articulate younger generation. What was more important for all the population, including peasants, was that it was only recitations of the collective rhetoric, future or dream that could be publicly articulated in codes of speech and texts and, frequently and increasingly, throughout the first thirty years in private spaces.

Perhaps symbolic of the exclusivity of message was the single, uncontrollable loudspeaker beaming official messages into every village square, street and household which even for the fieldworker gave new meaning to the saying 'I cannot hear myself think'. Simultaneously too, it was the very appropriation and near monopoly of the language and rhetoric of celebration and its separation from and eventual denial of experience which disguised the relevance and rendered the very language of experience irrelevant. As the poet Gu Cheng said of the restrictions on his senses and words:

My shadow
is twisted
I am trapped in a landmass.
My voice is covered with glacial scars.
Only the line of my gaze
is free to stretch.[13]

The substitution of dreaming for experience is exemplified in the words of the woman peasant painter, Li Fenglan who, in depicting a profusion of colour, products and people in a perpetual harvest, displayed all the hallmarks of the dream in her paintings. Describing her source of inspiration as based exclusively on her own experience – 'I only paint what I see' – she went on blithely unaware of the shift.

In fact I don't paint things I see, but I paint them from my dream, often I dreamed of them when I came home from the fields a bit tired. My dreams are mostly in colour . . ., one must rise above what one sees . . . Now we are happy, but I am happiest when I pick up my paint brush.[14]

It is these ways of seeing and speaking, at a distance, which made the elicitation and understanding of experience as opposed to image particularly difficult and hampered the task of both Chinese and foreign analyst. For foreign fieldworkers there were severe constraints surrounding entry and time in the field, where there were also the problems associated with the existence of an explicit, well-developed masking rhetoric which was more concerned with what 'ought to be' rather than with what was, a state which anthropologists of the status of Lévi-Strauss have identified as one constituting one of the most difficult of barriers in ethnographic enquiry.[15] In China during these years, even the simplest of enquiries elicited a coded or rhetorically bounded response. Few informants used the word 'I', thus denying individuality of experience or emotion that was not generalised into the range of permitted responses. The very language deployed bounded their experience and reflexivity, and the official certainty that rhetoric expressed experience also rendered any internal Chinese sociological or anthropological investigation of structures, institutions or relations superfluous. The disciplines of sociology and anthropology in China were either disbanded or confined to narrow fields of investigating non-Han 'others' for close on thirty years.

The very purpose of capturing the consciousness was to generate a collective will for social change so that the planned implementation of the dream became an end in itself, generating agency and a collective will. Constructions of knowledge and their relation to power and agency are important topics of anthropological debate,[16] and it can be argued that the very concept of 'revolution', and especially of China's 'continuing revolution', can be seen as a sustained act of will to change the earth in order to pattern heaven by perpetually remaking the environment and person against adverse material conditions and by leaping historic stages through catapulting landscape and person into the future imaged after the notion of heaven. The Chinese revolution in the countryside can be conceived of as an act of will in the interests of realising a future based on, but not entirely embracing, the dreams of the peasantry. If the population took the holistic approach advocated by combining the actions fanshen ('to turn over') and shenfan ('to dig deep') – both popular notions within Chinese villages[17] – then would they not be capable of the most radical and sustained change? Achieving the goal of long-term, radical and continuous change, however, was often referred to as the most magnificent feat ('the sky is high and all must be willing to fly') for a population not experienced in exercising such sustained agency.

Nobody could have been more aware of the contrasting history of obedience and acceptance of fate than Mao Zedong when he stood on the rostrum in Tian Anmen Square in 1949 and asserted that 'the Chinese people, one quarter of humankind have now stood up'. Above all, he was ascribing agency to the population at large who henceforth were to 'master' rather than to 'follow' fate. Mao Zedong frequently charged that the Chinese people were its most precious resource and that the key to a new future lay in mobilising their inexhaustible creative energies. This shift of agency was novel, and phenomena such as the mass line, the mass campaign and mass movement were all acknowledgements of the power of collective agency[18] and were designed to generate the collective will in order, as Mao often said, to 'paint the most beautiful pictures on a blank sheet of paper'. Perhaps symbolic of this shift was the reversal in the relation of person to landscape in Chinese paintings after 1949. Hitherto landscape had dwarfed person; henceforth person dwarfed the landscape; while, in folklore, the foolish old man who removed a mountain was no longer so foolish but a model like other superheroes for emulation. Henceforth, heaven or the future was to be accessible to all and, above all, the future belonged to those who struggled for the attainment of heaven on earth. In particular, it was the previously disadvantaged, the rural, the poor, the peasant and the female who had a privileged claim or entitlement to the future: 'You too can have a share in the future', or 'even chicken feathers can fly to heaven':

The poor want to remake their lives. The old system is dying. A new system is being born. Chicken feathers really are flying up to heaven. In the Soviet Union they have already got there. In China they've started their flight.[19]

THE DEMISE OF THE DREAM

After thirty years of entitlement to an imaged heaven, it is possible to identify a single symbolic moment of visible rupture in 1976 when it became evident to both participants and observers that the dream had lost much of its potency rhetorically to mask, unite and generate collective will. Like all moments, however, it was born of a growing mood – in this case of falling expectations. After thirty years of effort, the gap between dream and experience or heaven and earth did not seem to be narrowing; rather, the dreams of the future or of heaven seemed as far away as ever if not increasingly remote. As dreams of future prosperity receded, austerity in the present became increasingly defined as a virtue in order 'to preserve the strength of plain living and hard struggle'. Two decades of aspiring to heaven rather than resourcing the earth had left the rural economy desperately short of material and technological inputs. The dream seemed to have failed to sustain development which in bankrupting the present in favour of the future perhaps marks an interesting reversal of the platform for sustainable development – that is, against bankrupting the future in the interests of the present. By the mid-1970s, deferred gratification seemed to have become a permanent state, showing little or no movement, little or no observable transition, and no improvement in the realisation of expectations, so that the rhetoric of wealth, equality, participation and transition seemed emptied of meaning, with the dream increasingly emptied of substance. The prolonged present, as it was experienced, made the future more difficult to image. As one young woman lecturer reported to a fellow foreign student, she was the child of her father and 'my father knows it is foolish to hope for the early arrival of dreams'.[20] The prolonged split separating dream from experience and the continuing denial of experience reduced the very potency of the dream to raise consciousness and command support.

Even the original image had faded to a point at which, although continuing to be expressed, it no longer motivated co-operation or generated will. In its presence there was increasingly a shifting, distancing or avoiding of eyes in mutual embarrassment which we now know from recent autobiographies published in China also characterised internal interpersonal exchanges as well as those between Chinese participant and foreign observer. For the fieldworker, discrepancies between representations and experiences or between 'depiction' and 'doing' became more apparent in stark exchanges contrasting the rhetoric of 'what we have' and 'what we never do' with the observation of 'what was not had', 'what we had done that very morning' or were even doing at that very moment. The degree of discrepancy between the rhetoric and experience of equality, well-being and improvement at the time of rupture is the subject of much economic argument,[21] and there is likely to be much more debate on the achievements and shortcomings of the communes and the extent to which they facilitated rural development and the fulfilment of peasant dreams of prosperity. Although the rejection of the collective dream for potentially and practically improving and sustaining standards of livelihood was rooted in the economic, as important as analysing economic variables is the study of the political and social rituals invented in support of the dream – which it can and will be argued also came to debase the currency of the dream itself.

Throughout the revolution and particularly during the Cultural Revolution (1966–76), the rituals in support of the dream, or cycles of rectification and purification, largely took the form of criticism campaigns of structures, hierarchy and undue rewards all conceived of as impurities in the present with the potential either to pollute the dream or to inhibit the future implementation of the dream in its pure form. Perpetual campaigns were designed to bring the deviant present into line with the purity of the future, cleanse the present and at the same time reassert the dream. Indeed, the concept of continuing revolution can be seen as an endless succession of ritual cycles of rectification and purification. However, evidence from villages has subsequently suggested that such campaigns frequently and increasingly had a sub-text and were utilised not so much in the interests of achieving or maintaining purity as for the manipulation of patron–client relations within and outside of the village.[22]

As the dream of the future increasingly became a resource underlying personal and factional claims to authority and for manipulation of knowledge in the service of personal political interests, it seems that the resource itself had become increasingly debased in the negotiations and contests for local power. The consequent generation of gossip, rumour, suspicion, tension, competition and conflict created divisions in interpersonal and intergroup relations that fragmented the local village population, in anticipation of which, or in the presence of such disruption, villagers frequently turned their backs, closed their doors and withdrew into the negatively sanctioned domestic or private spaces of the village, thereby reducing the collective will on which local collectives structured their productivity and participatory politics largely rested. In the pursuit of individual or factional interests, images of the future and heaven receded as village relations were disrupted in cycles of power play and score settlement between competing individuals and interest groups. Although individualism and collectivism are more interdependent than frequently presupposed,[23] individuals in China frequently felt themselves divorced from collective performance, which ultimately threatened the existence of the very collective structures – the team, brigades and communes themselves – and contributed to their rapid disaggregation following the death of Mao Zedong in 1976.

Indeed, the moment of rupture was hastened when the dream lost its architect and its prime facilitator in the person of the Emperor-like figure of Mao Zedong who, it is now known, had lost some credence in his final years. At first he was followed by a succession of leaders who attempted unsuccessfully to inherit his mantle, and the moment of explicit rupture between the rhetoric and experience probably came with the downfall of his supporters, collectively known as the Gang of Four, in 1976 which was the occasion of unexpected celebrations during which it was reported that not a bottle was to be found in the shops! However, so complete had been the rhetorical mask that the euphoria of this celebration and the speed of subsequent change took observers, analysts and perhaps even participants by surprise. The movement from revolution to reform dates from 1978, with the embarkation of a new set of policies marking the onset of radical rural reforms framed by a shift from the aspirations of heaven to the problems of the earth.

RESOURCING THE EARTH

The promised land of modernity was to be firmly of the earth: as headlines in *Renmin Ribao* proclaimed: 'We have finally come back from Heaven to Earth' or 'Focus vision on reality'.[24] Aspirations to modernity had less to do with rhetoric, will or intentionality than with the generation and supply of inputs, commodities and services. Overall, the aim of reform, also called 'socialist modernisation', was to turn China into a powerful and modern socialist society by developing four sectors of the economy: agriculture, industry, science, and technology and defence. Within the sphere of production there was a shift in economic priorities so that the development of agriculture, light and service industries were newly accorded a high priority. The relationship between capital accumulation and construction and consumption was adjusted in favour of giving priority to consumption and raising living standards. The measures to achieve modernisation were designed to proceed at a rapid pace with the avowed aim of catching up with European and North American economies by the end of the century. To this end its constituent programmes emphasised the importance of material resources, professionalism, skills, scientific and technological research, profitability and the operation of economic incentives in the planning, management and expansion of production and particularly agricultural production.

Only by accelerating the development of agricultural production and achieving agricultural modernization step by step can we enable the peasants who constitute eighty per cent of our country's population to become well off. Only thus can the rapid development of the whole material economy be promoted.[25]

In 1978, the government set in motion new rural economic reforms which were designed to alter intersectoral relations in favour of agriculture; separate economic and political authority; redefine responsibility for and expand and diversify agricultural production; and alter the balance of production for the plan and for the market and public and private forms of resource allocation. Above all, the reforms signified a shift in responsibility for production and reproduction.

Part I

Reform: household and village

Chapter 2

State policies
Revolution, responsibility and reform

The first reform signifying the movement away from revolution and laying the foundation for subsequent reforms was the redistribution of responsibility for production from the collective to the peasant household in what virtually amounted to a reversal of the original process of collectivisation. In defining and evolving new institutions and balances in the distribution of collective and domestic responsibilities appropriate to a socialist contract promoting economic development and equity, China first attracted attention because of the scale and scope of the collective process, the means by which it reduced the responsibilities of the individual peasant household for production and reproduction and the redefinition of the household in relation to other economic and socio-political institutions. It was the continuing search for appropriate collective and domestic institutions beneficial to production, consumption and welfare which lay at the basis of its cycles of distribution and redistribution of responsibility, first in the name of revolution and then of reform.

The term 'responsibility', perhaps more than many other terms, is chameleon-like in that with a variety of incorporated meanings its specificity is mostly captured by the attributes of the speaker and by context. Responsibility may be acquired or required, and however it might be allocated, assumed or imposed, appropriated or volunteered, its meanings can be variously defined as claim, obligation, duty or gift. That is, responsibility involves an exchange that may simultaneously endow, enact, enable and entitle and which is rarely equal in authority or permanent in form and content. Rather, its devolution or distribution involves agency and the exercise of power with shifting contests and alliances and arenas demanding constant negotiation and renegotiation between agents with differentials in authority, resources and sanctions between object and subject. Responsibility is also about ability to respond, and it is these complex notions of responsibility and its distribution and redistribution between state, the collective, the community or the village and the family, the household or the individual which lie at the basis of development strategy. In China, successive policy shifts in the distribution of responsibility between the collective and domestic effected the dominance of first one and then the other although not in either case to the exclusion of the other.

REVOLUTION AND THE COLLECTIVE

First, after 1949, the government initiated a process of collectivisation which established an agricultural sector independent of individual small-holdings, reduced private property and socialised the means of production and reproduction in order to establish first the co-operative and then the commune as the unit of production combining economic and political responsibility and authority.[1] During land reform in the early 1950s, the Communist Party fulfilled its long-standing promise to redistribute a certain amount of land and tools of production to poorer peasant house-holds before embarking on a number of programmes designed to collectiv-ise the land and other means of production, collectively organise or manage agriculture and many other subsidiary occupations and substitute collectives for households as the main units of production, distribution and consumption. In 1958 the process of collectivisation culminated in the establishment of the rural people's communes which were designed to substitute fully for the peasant household as the basic unit of production and reproduction in the countryside. Responsibility for much of produc-tion was delegated to its constituent brigades and teams which also had responsibility for accounting, planning and distribution, while the larger communes retained overall responsibility for production, for economic relations with the state, for projects of capital construction and for the ownership of industrial and processing plants. Thus the collective, usually the production team or sometimes the production brigade, was the important unit of production with minimal responsibility devolved to the household.

The communes were more than just units of production, for they were also designed to take responsibility for much of the reproduction, including the consumption and health and welfare of their members. Initially the communes were charged with socialising domestic labour and the establish-ment of community services such as dining rooms, child-care, laundry, food processing and other services, which would mean that a large part of consumption would no longer take place by or within the individual household. For instance, with the establishment of community dining rooms foodstuffs were to be purchased, distributed and processed not by the household (as had been the case for centuries), but by the community, which was henceforth to assume primary responsibility for the sustenance of its members. Large numbers of these services were established in 1958 and 1959, and it can be argued that no post-revolutionary state has initiated such an ambitious programme to socialise domestic labour and substitute the individual peasant household as the chief unit of reproduction.

However, although this large-scale experiment in socialising domestic labour had ended by 1960, the collective remained responsible for meeting or subsidising the basic needs of those with no or reduced labour power and no other means of family support. The production team absorbed all village residents, regardless of their labour power, into the collective labour force in some capacity or another, so that they all earned work points, the value of which was simply calculated by dividing the income of the production team by the total number of work points earned. Thus the collective subsidised the household in its care for their dependants and, in addition, the collectives were encouraged to establish nurseries and kindergartens, arrange care for the elderly and offer maize grinding, noodle processing and other food-processing services. All these services reduced the responsibilities for reproduction of the individual household.

When the dominance of the collective was assured, the demise of the peasant household as an economic and socio-political unit of import was assumed once it was rendered largely invisible by the novel and larger collective unit. Henceforth, most of the analytical focus concentrated on the structure, responsibilities and relations of production appropriate to collective forms of production rather than relations and exchanges between the collective production unit and the individual peasant household, its family members and kin groups. Yet investigations into peasant experience of revolution suggested that, despite state policies to the contrary, the peasant household had remained an important economic unit within the collective and a much underestimated and under-studied fourth tier of production, consumption and welfare within the commune.

Within the commune, production brigade and production team, the basic unit of residence and domestic organisation remained the peasant household (hu), which was made up of a number of kin relations bounded by a common budget and a single cooking stove.[2] The policies of collectivisation had the effect of reducing the land component of the individual family or jia estate and the economic basis of the individual peasant household. Nevertheless, collective economic organisations still demanded that peasant households continue to mobilise their resources in order to meet their community responsibilities and find a solution to a number of organisational problems; namely, production and the transformation of materials for consumption. The peasant household was itself still a productive unit albeit somewhat reduced in scope, and it was also the primary unit of consumption and welfare. In addition to contributing labour to collective production units in the field, in animal husbandry and in subsidiary occupations in return for grain and a cash income, the household itself was still an important economic unit in the private and domestic sector, where much of the production of non-staple foods for subsistence and exchange still took place.

Meat and vegetables had to be produced and cooked, food salted and preserved, children cared for and most clothes and shoes sewn and laundered. Despite collectivisation, these private and domestic responsibilities continued to service and maintain the peasant household as an economic unit utilising family, capital, labour and other resources. Although it was never more than a subsidiary unit when compared to the collective, it was a more important unit of production and consumption than analytically acknowledged and one whose resources could be further tapped in the interests of the nation's economic, political and social development. The government took advantage of these resources after 1978 when responsibility for managing and cultivating land was dramatically shifted from the collective to the peasant household.

RESPONSIBILITY AND THE DOMESTIC

The reversal of the process of collectivisation was primarily a consequence of the contracting out of land and production quotas to the peasant household, which brought about the simultaneous decline of the collective and the emergence of the peasant household as the dominant economic, political and social unit in the Chinese countryside. The reorganisation of agricultural production was effected by the rural production responsibility system, a major new reform introduced in 1978. Originally the rural responsibility system had merely aimed to introduce a new form of management in the collective sector, reduce the size of the labour group and provide incentives to promote production and link reward more directly to performance.[3] Initially it was not intended to either increase the autonomy of the peasant household as a unit of production or so radically alter its relationship with the collective and extend responsibility for production to all households throughout the country. Rather, the responsibility system had been primarily conceived as a means by which the production team might enter into a variety of contracts with a small labour group, individual labourer or household which imposed new sets of rights, obligations and responsibilities for production on both parties. For instance, the party contracting with the production team might range from the small work team or peasant household to an individual, and the degree of responsibility assigned to them might range from responsibility for individual production tasks to responsibility for the entire production process based on allocated lands with payment negotiated according to the demands of the labour process or according to output. What was common to these varieties in responsibility systems was that the production team was to remain the overall unit of production, planning, management and accountancy and maintain its former economic and political controls.

The government had also originally anticipated that the type of responsibility system instituted in any one region would be determined by the fertility of the area, its natural assets, the degree of mechanisation, its proximity to markets and its pre-existing levels of livelihood. Where conditions of production were large in scale and highly mechanised and commune members already had a high standard of living, as in the suburban communes surrounding the cities and the rich arable areas of the eastern seaboard, then the government had recommended that the production team contract out agricultural tasks to small work teams. In intermediate areas less naturally endowed, which were described as neither rich nor very poor, the production team was encouraged to contract land and output quotas to individuals, and only in poorer inland and infertile areas was land to be contracted to the peasant household and payment to be negotiated according to output.[4] However, far from constituting such a graduated continuum, it became increasingly apparent that the distribution of land to the household with payment made according to output had taken place over most of China. At the end of 1982 it was reported that 79 per cent of China's production teams had adopted this system; a year later, at the end of 1983, it was estimated that in 98 per cent of China's production teams, land had been contracted out to peasant households.[5]

LAND RESPONSIBILITIES

In the most common form of the responsibility system to emerge, 'baogang daohu' (concentrating everything with the peasant household), the village government contracted out land and production output quotas to each household. The household was thus allocated land, draught animals and small- and medium-sized equipment. Land was allocated to the household on a per capita or per labourer basis, taking account of quality. Land was either divided into portions of good, average and poor lands and supposedly equally distributed to each household;[6] alternatively, adjustments were made to size of allocation so that the poorer the land the larger the plot. In areas of mixed terrain and fertility, responsibility lands allocated to households were likely to be fragmented, and the landscape frequently assumed an appearance not unlike that of the strip farming of the European feudal manor now referred to in China as 'noodlelands'. For the long-time air traveller in China there is no greater difference than the contrast between the large square fields and the numerous, narrow, multi-stripped and shaded landscape which is perhaps also symbolic of changing mindscapes before and after the reforms! A survey of 1983 estimated that the average land areas were likely to be subdivided into as many as eleven to fifteen pieces in highly variable hilly areas.[7] In villages, the land might be not only subdivided according to fertility, but also according to use or types of crops cultivated, with the main divisions between grain and cash crops. Households might therefore have received an allocation of 'food grain' land, responsibility lands for grains and cash cropping and, in addition, fodder, forest, orchard or waste lands for exclusive use by each household. Furthermore, if the different types of land were allocated on a per capita basis, there might be differentials in the household allocations according to the number of workers, the balance of male and female members, the labour capacity of its members, and due to changes in household composition. Past experience in the allocation of private plots and urban housing did suggest that, although in practice reallocation was supposed to take place according to the changing composition of the household, readjustment in land allocation would be difficult to achieve. Thus the amount of land to which a household had access was likely to be somewhat static and its ability to meet demand very much dependent on the land–person ratio of the region and changes in household size as well as the quality and management of the lands themselves.

The quality and management of the lands was very soon perceived to be linked to definitions of tenure and ownership. Although it was officially stated that land was to be redistributed to the peasant household on a per capita basis and for a period of time, in practice the peasant household gained *de facto* long-term control over the land. Even the contracts blurred the terms of time-use. To reassure peasant households that the land would remain in their use for a period worthy of improvement and long-term investment, the government in 1984 extended the allocation to a maximum of fifteen years and much longer, perhaps fifty years, for waste and marginal lands which required substantial investment to bring them into production or to increase yields.[8] However, informally in villages the allocations of land were frequently and increasingly referred to as 'permanent', 'for the long term' or 'for ever'. Thus instead of working collectively owned and managed land according to collective plans in return for work points calculated in terms of grain and cash income, the peasant household had immediate access to and a degree of control over a piece of land which it could to all immediate purposes call its own. Moreover, the peasant household was to be permitted in its turn to sub-contract out its lands in return for annual cash payments or payments in kind. However, the reallocation of land to peasant households after an interval of nearly thirty years was not an unconditional act of beneficence on the part of the Chinese state. Rather, the acquisition of land by the peasant household was one side of a contracted exchange between state and peasant household which shifted new and additional responsibilities to peasant households.

RESPONSIBILITY AND PRODUCTION

The reallocation of land and responsibility for its production demanded that the peasant household also took responsibility for all field management from sowing to harvesting in order to produce sufficient crops to fulfil production quotas set by the state, its own subsistence, fodder for its animals and a surplus for the market. At first, following the initial allocation of responsibility lands, the household contracted to grow specified crops and, after allowing for state taxes and quotas, retained control over the balance of at least some of the lesser crops. However, in 1985 the government abolished mandatory purchase and state monopoly of the major crops and henceforth households could either take out production contracts with local grain bureaux or produce exclusively for the market.[9] At the time it was anticipated that the market would soon become one of the main determinants of the types and amounts of crops purchased and act as the major redistributive agent.[10] In the meantime, land/grain contracts with the grain bureaux were very often similar to those formerly negotiated between the village government and peasant household. The main difference was that henceforth only a portion of the household's land crops might be covered by the responsibility contract. Thus the new responsibility system increased the autonomy of the peasant household and provided it with a greater number of options in deciding what crops to cultivate, in deciding how to dispose of its surplus, or indeed, in theory, in deciding whether to grow crops at all! Responsibility for production not only made greater demands on the peasant household to cultivate the lands intensively and carefully, it also encouraged the peasant household to diversify its activities to include other agricultural and non-agricultural activities on and off the farm.

The diversification of the rural economy, one of the major new agricultural reforms, was implemented in order to broaden the previous and narrower emphasis on grain production and develop animal husbandry, cash cropping, industries and commercial activities within the rural economy. The government thus revised the former slogan of 'taking grain as the key link' in favour of effecting 'the all-round development of agriculture', and it did so most especially in areas where natural conditions favoured cash cropping, forestry, animal husbandry, fishing and other activities. New policies aimed at abandoning the traditional small-scale rural economy undertaken mainly for subsistence in favour of diverse, specialised and commodity production:

> The experience of many years has proved that we can never extricate ourselves from self-sufficiency or a semi-sufficient economy if we simply rely on tilling the land, concentrate all labour power in the fields and have all 800 million peasants growing food crops.[11]

DIVERSIFIED PRODUCTION

To encourage households to develop their own sidelines in addition to, or instead of, agricultural fieldwork, production teams contracted out most former collectively owned animals, poultry, fisheries, orchards and small rural industries to individual households which, as for land, were both responsible for production and remunerated according to output. More important than the contracting out of former collective sidelines, however, was the new development of diverse on- and off-farm sidelines by the peasant household itself. Previously, household or domestic production based on the cultivation of the private plot, the raising of domestic livestock and the provision of handicrafts, small goods and services had proved to be an essential although controversial source of non-staple food and cash income.[12] From the late 1970s, however, the government not only legitimised and stabilised this sector, but also it actively encouraged the expansion and diversification of domestic sideline production by the household. In the initial search for every available means to expand the rural economy it was clear that domestic sidelines constituted one of the most immediately expandable areas of the economy. Domestic sidelines not only had the advantage that their labour and capital were chiefly provided by the individual peasant household, but that, at little cost to the state or the collective, they provided quick returns, rapidly increased supplies of food and small consumer goods for subsistence and for exchange, and made available raw materials for industry. Moreover, they provided employment for surplus labour, the numbers of which were increasing in the countryside: 'in the full development of the individual industries of thousands upon thousands of peasant households, the surplus labour of thousands and thousands of individuals will be absorbed'.[13]

To encourage the peasant household to increase the production of domestic sidelines, government policy enlarged private plots and abolished restraints on their use. According to official figures, the area of private plots increased by 23 per cent between 1978 and 1980, with the area allotted to private plots accounting for 5.7 per cent of the arable lands in China in 1978 and 7.1 per cent in 1980.[14] A State Council directive in March 1981 raised the maximum allowed to 15 per cent of the arable lands, but this was only deemed appropriate in areas where the per capita land ratio was relatively favourable. In addition to private plots, private fodder and waste lands were also to be allocated to peasant households. Gradually, though, with the extension of the contract system it was less possible to regulate or separate out domestic sidelines from domestic production. All production became domestically organised, and under the contract system, once production quotas for raising animals, cultivating vegetables and fruit and producing small goods were met, households retained control of the surplus. Alternatively, goods were not subject to contract purchase and were entirely sold in the market place. To provide an additional outlet for sideline products and an incentive to peasant households to produce a surplus, rural fairs or markets were established where goods, foods, local handicrafts and daily necessities could be exchanged between the producer and purchaser at a negotiated and agreed price according to local supply and demand.[15] After a period of absence, villages were again astir at dawn as a steady stream of peasants took their chickens, ducks, eggs, tobacco, pigs and vegetables in variable quantities by cart, bicycle, basket or shoulder pole to the peasant markets held in a nearby village, town or even city. Markets ranged from small, daily affairs with just a few peasant vendors sitting on the roadside beside bundles of produce, to the large, crowded, periodic, rural markets held every ten days or so and the large, daily, free markets on the outskirts of cities attracting hundreds of buyers and sellers. It became one of the joys of countryside travelling in the early hours of a Sunday or market morning to pass the steady stream of market traffic with their assortments of produce and goods for sale, to stroll and peruse the market stalls, to turn unexpectedly a country corner and find an isolated donkey market with each donkey tied patiently to a tree around a central clearing or to happen upon a large, central, exotic, herbal market with lines and lines of open sacks of herbs of every conceivable hue and texture.

In addition to the revival of local handicrafts, the production of foods and small goods for the local market, the government also encouraged the home-based production for export by distributing materials for handicraft goods and organising for the production and purchase of finished articles according to fixed schedules, quality and quantities.[16] Provincial administrations began to negotiate contracts directly with foreign agencies to buy these goods, and in a few localities the government formed special economic zones where joint Chinese and foreign capital established enterprises to distribute raw materials to peasant households for processing and to purchase the finished product.[17] In villages, women were again frequently to be seen in groups or in their doorways stitching the most intricate and delicate of piece-work for the export market. In southern and richer regions, the putting out of handicraft, sewing, printing and weaving for production within individual households or in small factories became widespread. Moreover, the aid of international, national and non-governmental development agencies began to be solicited to advise, fund and expand new agricultural activities for domestic and foreign markets.

As a result of these policies encouraging the diversification of domestic sideline production, the household once again became the substantial producer of goods for subsistence and exchange. After five years of rural reform, the majority of peasant households had begun to diversify their activities so that it was estimated that some 85 per cent both cultivated responsibility lands allocated to them by the village government and undertook a variety of domestic sidelines ranging from vegetable production, the raising of livestock and the production of handicraft goods to the provision of services for their local community. In typical mixed-economy peasant households, members produced grains for subsistence, for the government and for the market and also produced vegetables, pigs, poultry and handicraft products of their own use and for the local or export market. The mixed economy household still produced for subsistence although it was increasingly likely to generate a major cash income from its sideline production out of which it purchased an increasing proportion of its daily needs. In a new and increasingly important development, peasant households also began to specialise in some form of commodity production based on agricultural or non-agricultural activities.

SPECIALISED PRODUCTION

As part of the rural economic reforms, the government encouraged the specialisation of commodity production so that there was an increasing division of labour between regions, villages and households[18] in order that units better suited to forestry, animal raising or production of cash crops, such as sugar cane, flowers and vegetables, 'should not necessarily try to achieve self-sufficiency in grain much less produce commodity grain'.[19]

> The rural economy is now being transformed from a self-sufficient and semi-self sufficient economy to a commodity economy, and the business of engaging in specialised jobs and in a multiplicity of occupations besides farming and socialised production has developed in varying degrees.[20]

The introduction of specialised households marked the beginning of a new type of household economy – one that was 'small and specialised' as opposed to one that was 'small and complete'.[21] A rural household was defined as specialised if it was a family-managed unit characterised by specialisation in product or service furnishing a set proportion of production or income. In practice, within a village it was simply the size of an operation that determined its categorisation, so that in some localities a household might be 'specialised' if the main labour force worked or managed some form of specialised commodity production which furnished upwards of 50 cent of the household's income.[22] In other localities, it was simply the number of rabbits, poultry or other products which determined its classification. In 1984 the government permitted the subcontracting of responsibility lands between peasant households, so that specialised households engaged in non-agricultural pursuits could subcontract out their lands to neighbouring peasant households in return for payments in cash or kind (usually grain). The proportion of specialised households by region was likely to be higher in coastal plains and hills and in localities where the average arable land per capita ratio was low. At the beginning of 1984 it was estimated that between 34 and 35 million, or 13 to 14 per cent, of all peasant households specialised in activities other than crop growing and that in some provinces this proportion had risen to 17 per cent,[23] setting an important trend for the future. The government has anticipated that in the future as little as 30 per cent of China's 800 million peasants will be engaged in crop cultivation.[24]

In regions where there were numerous opportunities for off-farm employment outside of agriculture, farmers entered full-time employment as wage earners at the same time as they remained village residents and part-time farmers. Such regions tended to be adjacent to towns and cities, although the rapid development of industrial, commercial and service enterprises within small towns has caused an increasing number of peasants to commute from their village on a daily or weekly basis. In these circumstances, either the members of the peasant households remaining in the village would undertake field cultivation and domestic sidelines or, alternatively, if all adult household members commuted or were otherwise employed, then after work or on their days off they would pool their labour or tend their lands and animals. Interviews in some of these suburban households in late 1984 revealed that household members in the small towns or cities commuted weekly to help those back home on the farm with the cultivation of the responsibility lands in return for a share of the produce. Only in the evenings and on Sundays could small family groups be seen hard at work, planting, watering, weeding and harvesting in a new phenomenon in the Chinese countryside – the development of part-time farming.

RESPONSIBILITY AND PRODUCTION

The allocation of responsibility to the farmers for their land and for on- and off-farm production demanded that the peasant household provide or arrange for their own agricultural inputs, raw materials, capital, transport, storage and processing facilities and marketing information and management. These were new demands on the peasant household, which had all formerly been the responsibility of the collective, and moreover these were all areas where the infrastructure was poorly developed and constituted a past weakness of the rural economy. The development of sideline or specialised production by the individual peasant household meant that it had to invest newly in fixed assets and acquire small and medium-sized means of production. Anticipated and actual demand by China's 200 million peasant households at once created major changes in the rural market for small-scale agricultural equipment and machines, including irrigation pumps, fodder-crushing plants, equipment for raising livestock, transport vehicles, storage buildings and means of processing handicrafts. It was estimated in 1984 that a peasant household embarking on production expansion set aside upwards of a quarter of its income for the purchase of capital goods and fixed assets.[25] By the end of that year it was estimated that on average households possessed productive assets worth ¥579.45 (yuan) at cost value, which represented an increase of 24 per cent over

1983.[26] According to the same survey, the average cost value of machinery for agriculture, forestry, animal husbandry and fishery owned by peasant households had risen by 59 per cent in 1983; machinery for industry and sideline undertakings owned by each household rose by 43 per cent; and means for transport rose by 52 per cent. The cost of extending the productive capacity of each household was high.

If the farmers were also to be responsible for the disposal of their products, be they crops, sideline goods or animals, then they needed to procure the means of transport to take their produce to market and or to the factory for processing. What initially fascinated rural travellers was the ingenuity and variety of vehicles ranging from home-made modes of transport of all descriptions from donkey carts, bicycle trolleys, sidecars on vintage motor bikes to factory-produced small and large tractors. Once households were responsible for their own profits and losses, there was a direct correlation between meeting these demands and their incomes. If responsibility for procuring pre- and post-production inputs and services constituted new and complex demands on peasant households, so also did those for providing for consumption and welfare.

RESPONSIBILITY AND CONSUMPTION

The individual peasant household became responsible for meeting the basic needs of all its members, a task it had only previously partially fulfilled within the collective structure. The distribution of grain by the production team to its member households no longer took place, and the household was itself responsible for producing, disposing of and/or procuring its own grain. It also continued to provide for its housing, non-staple foods, clothes and other basic necessities and to take primary responsibility for the economic support and welfare of its dependants (its young, unemployed, elderly and disabled or otherwise handicapped members). With the reforms, those unable to work fully or partly had either to be incorporated into the income-generating activities of the peasant household or supported by the peasant household rather than the collective.

For many peasant women, though, there were new and substantial improvements in the conditions in which they served, and in particular cooked for, the household as a result of peasant investment in new housing, new cooking stoves and water pipes. The present leadership also expanded the production of appliances such as washing machines and refrigerators which substantially reduced the labour involved in domestic servicing, but it was unlikely that their use would extend beyond the richer rural regions for some time. The production, purchase and processing of the wider variety of foods for consumption alone took up to three to four hours per day, in addition to the continuing demands of laundry, household cleaning and child-care.[27] In 1981, it was estimated that in most rural areas less than 25 per cent of pre-school children had nursery places, although a larger proportion attended kindergarten for a slightly older age group.[28] Even in a much proclaimed rural model county, child-care facilities accommodated only 54 per cent of infants and toddlers.[29] In rural areas, therefore, the care of pre-school children was still likely to be the primary responsibility of the household. The same was true of the elderly for, except in a minority of well-favoured counties, there were few alternative provisions for the care of the aged. Those still eligible for the 'five guarantees' of food, clothing, medical care, housing and burial benefits[30] or direct state support in meeting basic needs were the childless elderly, the widowed, orphaned children or those who had no labour power or no other means of family support. At the beginning of 1984, the government undertook the first-ever survey of those eligible for relief, which revealed that there were nearly 3 million persons, including 2.6 million elderly people, nearly 200,000 disabled persons and 150,000 orphans qualified to receive the five guarantees. For the rest of the population, the economic support and welfare of dependants continued to be the responsibility of the peasant household. Indeed, the new Marriage Law in 1980 and the new Constitution in 1982 both emphasised the duty of the younger generation to support their elders.

Overall, then, the complexity and range of new production, consumption and welfare responsibility allocated to the peasant household had quite dramatically increased the demands on the individual peasant household. As a consequence, it had become a much more important and complex unit, either already engaged in or planning to be engaged in a number of wide-ranging and diverse income-generating activities or specialising in some form of commodity production. If the demands on the peasant household had increased as a result of rural reform, so also had its autonomy and its control over land and farm production, with the net result that the economic relationship between the peasant household and the village had been redefined, although as much because of reforms at the village level as of the peasant household.

REFORM AND THE VILLAGE

One of the most important components of rural reform was the separation of political and economic authority at the local level and the emergence of new political and economic institutions reducing the authority of the village collective. Indeed, after the establishment of the production responsibility system, the local separation of political administration from economic management was designated as the second most important of the rural economic reforms. In the new Constitution of 1982, the government reformed local political structures by substituting new township and village institutions for the commune, production brigade and production team and by redefining the scope of their authority and controls. The government expected that within the village a new division of labour would emerge in which local political institutions remained in control of the local economy and were responsible for guiding, planning and managing its development, but no longer directly participated in production. New forms of economic organisation based on local corporations, co-operatives and economic associations to expand production, develop the commodity economy, and service economic enterprises were to be managed by peasant households either individually or jointly in a new two-tiered system of local economic management. In this new two-tier system, the individual peasant household was to be responsible for the development of its own economy and the management of its own productive operations, while the co-operative or economic association would manage production services and enterprises that were beyond the capacity of the individual peasant household. However, the government also anticipated that, in the longer term, with increasing productivity, diversification, specialisation and the development of the commodity economy, co-operative forms of unified management would come to predominate over the individual household management.

The reforms that separated political and economic authority and introduced new local political structures below county level included the establishment of the township (formerly the commune), the administrative village (formerly the production brigade) and village groups (formerly the production team).[31] The new township governments were set up to assume the government and administrative functions formerly vested in the commune. The commune had been characterised by a clearly defined hierarchical, single line of command combining political and economic authority. The collective structure, with its three tiers of commune, production brigade and production team, had almost entirely encapsulated the peasant household and the village economy, and the co-ordination of political and economic authority had meant that the peasant household had very little independence within or outside of these structures. The former incorporation of peasant households into these large village production units, with exclusive control of resources and the means of production, meant that, although their very solidarity might derive from and draw on kinship and neighbourhood ties, there was little institutional competition to the collective from the family, kin and village. Within the collective, the peasant household had little or no access to alternative production resources and inputs apart from those generated and distributed by the collective, and in politics the peasant household had very little independence within or outside of the collective. New townships governments were to replace the people's commune governments, whose all-inclusive range of functions and direct responsibility for production had been criticised by the reformers as an inefficient and institutional obstacle to the development of the rural commodity economy.

The new township government was responsible for the administration of political and social affairs and for that of overall government and county plans for the local economy. Under the direction of the township head and two executive heads, it had offices to manage markets, disaster relief, public security, welfare, health, culture and education. Although the township government was charged with using economic, legal and other necessary administrative methods to guide and plan the economic development of the whole township, it was expressly discouraged from undertaking economic activities and from interfering in production and management activities of individual household and larger enterprises. The township constituted the lowest level of the formal local government administration hierarchy, and its officials, appointed and paid by the state, usually numbered some ten to twenty cadres who were responsible for administering the affairs of the township, including its constituent administrative villages.

An administrative village – like its forerunner, the production brigade – was an administrative subdivision covering a geographical area made up of one large or several small and natural villages comprising between 200 and 400 households. Each administrative village, governed by a villagers' committee whose members were recommended or elected by the villagers and approved by the township office, was not a formal part of the government administration in that its members were not employees of the state but were rather part-time local leaders. The Constitution defined the villagers' committees as 'mass organisations of self-management',[32] which managed the public offices and social services of the village and helped the local government in administration, production and construction. A village committee was usually made up of five persons, including a head or director, two executive deputy directors, an accountant, and a woman in charge of women's affairs. Unlike the township and county, each officer had multiple tasks and duties that might include the implementation of county or township policy, advising farmers on the development of their economic activities, taking charge of village construction work such as irrigation, forestry and roads, mediating in disputes and overseeing the welfare of the poorest peasant households. Most of the members of the village committee expected to work one month a year on village affairs, and they were usually paid ¥10–20 a month to compensate for their loss of production time. This sum was paid from village committee funds which were managed by the village accountant and derived either from direct annual levies on member households, calculated according to household size, or proceeds from a portion of the village's income from enterprises or cultivated land set aside and cultivated on a sharecropping basis for this purpose.

The village committee was responsible for co-ordinating the activities of its constituent village groups, each averaging between thirty and fifty households and 100 and 150 persons. As for the former production team, whether the village group coincided with a natural village very much depended on settlement patterns and the size of individual villages. The leaders of village groups were elected or recommended by constituent households, and each village group also had access to the services of an accountant for the management of its funds. They also received a monthly sum, perhaps ¥6–9, to compensate for the loss of production time. The main functions of village group leaders were to acquaint villagers with government policy, to mediate in disputes, to be acquainted with the conditions of each member household in order to help them solve problems, and to advise them on the development of their incomes by disseminating information and technologies. The leader also arranged for each household to contribute labour for construction of village or township projects such as planting trees or developing roads, irrigation works or other community needs.

New local and village institutions had been redefined in name and function so as to exclude direct responsibilities for and participation in production, but they were still expected to control the development of the local economy. A report in *Renmin Ribao* on political power at the grassroots level outlined the limits to the economic responsibilities of the local political organisations:

> To guide and manage the economic work of the township is an important power bestowed on the township government by the law. The township government should use the economic, legal and necessary administrative methods to manage the economy of the whole township and serve the development of commodity production, but should not interfere in, undertake or even replace the specific production and management activities of economic organisations.[33]

In addition to and alongside this political restructuring and the establishment of new local political institutions, the government also advocated the establishment of new village economic organisations, including companies, associations or co-operatives.

VILLAGE ECONOMIC MANAGEMENT

When the first steps were taken to separate local political and economic authority, reform was expressed largely in terms of simply 'stripping' the communes of their governmental and political functions and leaving them as economic entities responsible for organising production of local enterprises still collectively owned and managed. Gradually, however, the economic role of the commune declined as collectively managed enterprises were frequently contracted out to individuals or small groups of households and made responsible for their own profits and losses. The commune, instead of assuming new economic responsibilities in the wake of de-collectivisation, gradually diminished in importance so that the very use of the term passed from the local rural vocabulary. Instead, governmental policy directed attention towards a new, two-tiered system of economic management that combined individual management by the peasant household with co-operative and unified management of the larger services beyond the capacity of the individual household. The main aim of the second tier of economic management, comprising economic companies, associations and co-operatives, was to support and service the peasant households in meeting new economic demands and needs which had expanded on an unprecedented scale and required new skills, resources and facilities not only quite outside its previous experience but also frequently beyond the capacity of the individual household to provide. In recognition of this new situation in the villages, the government had encouraged the pooling of existing resources by households to combine and organise new economic associations and co-operatives. These were intended to service the peasant households, especially those specialising in commodity production, and thereby facilitate production and, more particularly, ease circulation, distribution, transport, storage and marketing.

At first, many of the new economic companies were established by communes or production brigades before their demise in order to take care of the capital resources previously accumulated and operated by the collective. Many local resources – irrigation canals, plant protection units, agricultural machinery, seedlings and storage and transport facilities – were transferred to company ownership, and maintained and operated by a staff for whose services and inputs peasant households paid a fee. From various provinces, it was reported that communes and production brigades had established service companies to deal with irrigation, agricultural machinery or artificial insemination or establish supply and marketing companies to make various inputs – such as fertiliser and seed – widely and easily available to peasant households.[34] At first, communes and production brigades administered these companies and received a portion of the profits; gradually, however, such companies began to manage their own operations independently, with staff and local peasant households sometimes taking shares in these corporations or companies and sharing in the profits. In addition to these independently operated companies and corporations, the government also encouraged peasant households to set up their own economic associations and societies to serve their own production needs.[35]

These economic associations might be formed when peasant households combined to purchase an animal, a piece of machinery or other capital equipment, which they then jointly owned and operated. Alternatively, a group of households might employ personnel to perform certain specialist services on their behalf. For instance, reports on the establishment of economic associations often quoted a sequence of events initiated because individual households experienced many difficulties in developing a new or specialist economic activity. They might spend much time and energy on searching for raw materials, acquiring new skills or obtaining market information in selling their products. Sooner or later a number of these households would come together to appoint and send buyers and sellers to search for raw materials and markets and import technicians to help them improve their knowledge and skills.[36] In yet another sequence of events, households might combine to invest in a small industry or a service centre in which they either merely owned shares or they operated jointly by pooling their labour and resources. One of the main characteristics of these new co-operatives and associations was said to be their 'spontaneous association and voluntary participation'.[37]

In encouraging new forms of co-operation and unified management of certain production services in the village, the government took great pains to persuade peasants that the new economic forms of co-operation were very different from those operating within the former three-tiered commune system. For example, an editorial in *Renmin Ribao* reiterated that these new economic organisations and co-operative systems were entirely different from former collectives:

> First, it is not a highly centralised organisation that integrates government administration and the management of the organisation into one, but a pure economic organisation; secondly, the establishment of these organisations does not mean an amalgamation of private property but, under the prerequisite of affirming household management, these organisations promote co-operation with regard to certain economic items, certain kinds of production, or certain technical links in accordance with the desires of the masses; thirdly, peasant households may voluntarily join or withdraw from these organisations, and the higher authorities never issue any orders to the lower levels for the establishment of these organisations; and fourthly, these organisations are established in accordance with local conditions and the demands of local peasant households. The practice of 'demanding uniformity in everything' or 'trying to find a single solution for diverse problems' is avoided.[38]

By the end of 1985 it was estimated that there were 480,000 new economic associations, mainly engaged in industry, transportation and construction, commerce, catering and other service trades, which together employed a total of 4.2 million employees and netted ¥13,300 million.[39]

The government forecast that these new forms of economic co-operation would emerge spontaneously to dominate economic management in the countryside as a result of a three-stage cycle of rural development: the introduction of the responsibility system and the contracting out of land, the diversification of the economy and the development of specialised commodity production; the concentration of land use and the development of agricultural and non-agricultural specialised households; and new levels of co-operation between households based on a mutual need for production services and on increasing specialisation and the division of labour.[40] Simultaneously, in 1985, the government also forecast a decline in household production responsibility and management, with new shifts to village co-operation and unified management and to a commodity economy.[41] In sum, it was clear from the explicit aims and objectives of China's reform programme that the government expected new patterns of economic and political relations to emerge in the villages, redefining the relations between village and peasant household and between peasant households. How peasant households and villages experienced these reforms is the subject of the next chapter.

Chapter 3

Peasant experiences
Household and village development

If at the macro-level, reform, as had revolution before it, became synony-mous with state-planned economic and socio-political development, national policies of reform remained – as does perhaps all development rhetoric – a somewhat idealised, generalised and opaque set of prescriptions which were communicated through the administrative hierarchy to the village. How such state policies, be they of revolution or reform, define, modify or translate into village practice is a subject of abiding interest to social scientists. To provide some insights into village policy, programme and experience of reform, and to take account of particularities of place, occasion and circumstance, nine case studies have been assembled from diverse regions of China to document, quantitatively and qualita-tively, village and household practices to do with land, labour and income-generation.

HENAN, 1987

The first village studied, Village A in Luoning county, Henan province, was located 90 kilometres south of the famed historical city of the thousand Buddhas, Luoyang. The village was set upon highland slopes, with snow reminiscent in freezing mid-February of European alpine regions, with conifers, stone bridges and bouldered stream beds; without snow the higher slopes were denuded to a bare brown and yellow flattened pene-plain with high plateaux and valleys stretching as far as the eye could see. The small village was perched on the edge of highlands near the small township settlement whose sparse market lined the only winding tarmac road with dirt and walking tracks to the right and to the left leading up to highland villages and small hamlets of but two to three or four households. Among the various villages and hamlets studied, one had thirteen house-holds, whose clay and brick houses were variously perched on or caved in the steeply climbed slopes. There were no village-owned buildings, enter-prises or amenities of any kind, with local opportunities for employment outside of the family farm rare.

Most of the households were made up of four to five persons, parents and their children, and only in the few larger households of between five and seven persons did three generations reside, with only one having two married brothers co-resident (Table 3.1). In households only those too young to attend school or those 'too old to work', or over seventy years of age, did not directly contribute to the domestic economy, which was almost exclusively based on land and the raising of animals. The working of the land continued to take most of the farmers' time, much as it had for their ancestors, but now, with reform, both arable and pasture lands had been equitably distributed to households according to the number of persons resident at the time of distribution. The average per capita allocation of arable land in this mountainous village was only 0.3 mu, and already in 1987 there were a number of irregularities in allocations resulting from changes in household size (Table 3.2). In all those households cultivating less than average amounts of cultivated land, brides had married in and there were young children of one to two years of age who had been born since the distribution of land. Pasture lands were more evenly distributed and averaged 7.5 mu but with similar anomalies due to marriages, births and deaths. There was no sign of any subcontracting of lands by peasant households; rather, peasant households referred to the land as 'theirs' albeit somewhat nervously, given the 'newness' and recent 'twists and turns' in government policy. Families relied exclusively on these land allocations to provide for their own subsistence, for meeting crop quotas due to the state and for animal fodder. Families cultivated the land themselves, but crop type was still determined by a detailed village plan with annually allocated production quotas for crops.

The crops cultivated by the farmers included winter wheat, maize and beans, with winter wheat the most important in terms of total output, subsistence and sale to the state (Table 3.3). On average, 80 per cent of the wheat cultivated was used for family consumption, which in 1987 amounted to an average of 421 jin per person, just above the 400 jin defined as the poverty line in China. In addition, maize sufficiently supplemented the wheat to raise all village households above the official subsistence line. The beans produced by each household were a mixture of black and soya beans and, like the maize, were used for seed, animal fodder and sale to the state. Each household sold a portion of its produce to the state, which ranged from 12 to 38 per cent of its wheat crop plus a small proportion of its maize and bean crops. The wide variations in quotas sold were linked to the quality of the land and therefore to both expected and actual yields. The average number of jin of wheat produced per mu was a low 171 jin and, for all crops, 221 jin, but there was a wide range in productivity per mu ranging from 72 jin to 235 jin of wheat per mu and 109 to 282 jin per mu, respectively. These differentials in yields may in part have been due to varying quality of land, but they could also be directly correlated with the amount of fertiliser purchased and applied per mu, the number of cattle raised, and therefore the quantity of animal manure, and with the age, experience, skills and income of the farmers. In the households with the lowest crop yields, there was frequently evidence of some physical or mental incapacity among the members of the family labour force.

The main sideline production activities of the households were chickens and cattle, with pigs lying a poor third (Table 3.4). This is in marked contrast to most regions of China, where pigs are the most important of sidelines so that the pig is often nicknamed 'the peasant's bank'. The raising of animals was mainly the work of the women, including cattle raising, which was the most important economic activity of the households after land cultivation and at the centre of plans to expand peasant household economies in the future. In 1987 there was a total of twenty-nine head of cattle and the number of cattle per household averaged two and ranged from one to four. There were no households with no cattle; a third of the households raised one head of cattle for draught purposes, and no households raised as many as five head of cattle and could therefore be categorised as specialised households. Most of the households had received one head of cattle in 1980–81 when the cattle formerly owned by the production team had been distributed to members of the village group. Although households had not directly paid any cash for these animals, they were very well aware of the value of the animals they had received, which ranged from ¥200 to ¥400 per head. A minority of the households had purchased a head of cattle from the free market, but these were most often draught cattle. Few households had sold any cattle in the past few years, although one had sold the beast distributed to it by the collective and bought an animal of superior quality. Almost all the households with more than one head of cattle had bred the calves themselves over the past few years. Most households did not anticipate selling any cattle in the near future; rather, they preferred to build up their herds, and only those with one head of cattle largely for draught purposes anticipated selling and buying another sometime in the near future.

For each household the annual costs of raising their cattle included the value of the grass, which was gathered after the wheat harvest and stored and cut for winter feed; maize and beans, which were mixed to form high-quality or 'fine' cattle food; and the smaller cash sums allocated to disease protection, insurance and medical expenses. Each household in the village group had joined the local veterinary station based in the nearby township and paid an annual sum of ¥1 per head of cattle for disease prevention. The average annual cost per head of cattle, calculated in kind and cash, amounted to ¥84.7, and for all households the raising of cattle imposed considerable demands on family labour partly because of the lack of amenities and because of the way cattle raising was organised within the village. For instance, water had frequently to be carried some distance before it could be fed to the cattle; the grass cutting in the summer and the mixing of fine-quality winter feed were labour-intensive, especially for the female members of the household; and because summer mountain grazing of animals was undertaken on an individual basis, one household member, usually the young or the old, was required for long hours each day. It was estimated by households that the raising of cattle took tens of hours per week, and much of this was the five hours required daily for feeding and watering in the winter and grazing in the summer, plus the five to six hours weekly required for cleaning stalls, water carrying and cutting of cattle grass. These inputs were required even where a household had only one head of cattle, and households with few members found it difficult to combine these demands with those of general agriculture fieldwork and any other sidelines.

Households undertook a small number of non-agricultural sidelines, including the provision of specialist services such as carpentry, house-building, flour milling and oil processing (Table 3.4). There were also three households where young men hired out their unskilled labour to neighbours or the township government on a part-time piece-work basis. The number and types of sidelines were very much dependent on the size of the household labour force and its material resources. The households in which there were no or few sidelines were without exception those which had no adult women with full labour power or those where there was some illness or hardship. Those with an above-average number of sidelines included the fortunate few who had inherited a walnut tree. In two of the households young men had acquired building and carpentry skills which were much in demand, and two households had decided to invest in machinery to either mill flour or process oil from rapeseed even though this had meant borrowing heavily in order to do so.

The main sources of household income in the village were the crops cultivated on the responsibility lands so that cash incomes mainly derived from selling wheat quotas contracted to the state (Table 3.5). In this village, no household sold wheat on the free market although this may be because the previous year's drought had reduced the crop harvest. In this year of comparative scarcity, the average cash income and value of crops derived per mu was ¥47 or so, and most of the households earned around this average figure. The households with the highest income per mu from crops (households 6, 7, 8) all had numerous adults and, especially, adult sons working in the fields. For example, household 6, with the highest income per mu, had three adult members and no sidelines and thus concentrated its efforts on cultivating crops. The two households with the lowest per capita incomes from cropping included the household with low capabilities and the household which had a lower per capita land ratio as a result of the recent marriage of one of its sons and the birth of their child. An important source of cash income for farmers was sidelines, the most common of which was the sale of eggs, and several of the households sold walnuts. Households with the highest cash income deriving from sidelines in the previous year had either sold a pig (household 1), had special resources in the form of walnut trees (households 8 and 9) or had skills such as carpentry (households 3 and 9), housebuilding (household 12) or capital assets in the form of machinery for food processing (households 11 and 13) (Table 3.6). Those households with few sidelines and which also had sufficient or surplus labour hired out their labour to compensate for lack of sidelines. In the poorest household (household 2), the adult male hired himself out for twenty-five days a year to neighbours to do heavy agricultural work, for which he received ¥1 a day. Most of the neighbours thought that this was a kind of 'aid' given by neighbours rather than a commercial transaction. In household 13, a second young adult son worked at the grain-store bureau of the township for approximately ten days per year. In the household which earned a high ¥100 from hiring out its labour, there were no other sidelines, and father and son were hired by neighbouring farmers outside of the village to pack tobacco (at ¥0.50 per packet) for more than one month a year each.

Altogether, the per capita total income calculated in cash and kind from all sources of income averaged out at ¥197; cash incomes constituted only ¥85 per capita, which was lower than the average for the county and province in which the village was located (Table 3.7). What was most surprising, given the small size and compactness of the village, was the considerable range in income within the village – per capita it ranged from ¥466 to ¥74 in cash and kind, and from ¥351 to ¥17 in cash. The differentials could be correlated with the number of adult members, their mental and physical capacities and the special skills and assets of the household. However, even the poorest householders identified the increase in their cash incomes as the main change in their lives following rural economic reform. They acknowledged this even though cash expenses were greater than cash incomes so that almost all households had annual deficits and accumulated debts. The two most important annual cash expenses were for fertiliser and for food and clothing (Table 3.8). The expenditure on food and clothing amounted to very little, for the diet was mainly grain-based. The almost complete absence of vegetable cultivation was accounted for by the topography and climate; there were also few signs of vegetables for sale, or preserved or stored. Very few households consumed the eggs they produced, and although there was some pork for sale in the markets, it was of low quality with a high ratio of fat to meat, and there was little evidence of its large-scale availability. Except for the poorest household, then, the range in per capita daily living expenses was not large and, given that the figures are estimates, too much should not be read into these differentials. In only one household, that of the village group leader, was there a cash surplus for the previous year and no debts incurred. He was the major exception, in that he had lent ¥200 to friends and neighbours to help them meet costs of marriages. In contrast, almost all households had cash deficits at the end of the year, and the households with the largest deficits were those which had some kind of extraordinary expense associated with housebuilding (4 and 8), health (5, 6, 7, 9, 11, 12 and 13) marriages (6, 9 and 10), special infant foods (13) and the purchase of capital assets (11 and 4).

All but two of the households had debts, with the average debt amounting to ¥395 per household and repayments rare (Table 3.9). Loans had been taken either from the bank or from affinal kin or the kin of wives who lived some distance from the village. The advantage of family loans was that no interest was charged and kin were usually somewhat relaxed about its repayment. Half the households had borrowed from the bank, given that they had no richer relatives to help cover deficits in living expenses and costs of fertiliser, new housing, machinery and weddings. One of the largest and most recent expenses and cause of debt for nearly all households, including the poor in the village, was a new or repaired house. One of the most immediate and lasting of impressions is of the speed with which new houses were built from the foundation to the roof, almost within forty-eight hours. In all the poor and very poor households there was evidence of long-term or severe medical problems associated with the physical or mental incapacity of a family member and giving rise to costs and debts the scale of which was only matched by those incurred by marriage.

Several families of sons in the village had paid out ¥500 or so for new clothes and adornments for the bride at the time of betrothal and another ¥500 for feasting. This was the largest form of debt for households with young adult sons, and one measure of the prohibitive costs of marriage in the village was the older average age of marriage and the number of young unmarried adults between twenty and thirty years. At the time of the interviews half the numbers of this age group in the village were not yet married, although they did constitute the younger members of that age cohort. Family investment was very much directed towards consumption, but, in two of the thirteen households, investments had recently been made in capital assets for productive purposes. As families acquire new houses and repay their housebuilding debts, it may be that there will be greater investment in productive items. However, given that the costs of marriage are an enormous item in family expenditure and given the numbers of young persons in each household in this village coming up to marriageable age, the capacity of the households to invest in alternative assets and sidelines is likely to be inhibited unless there is some rapid development of the peasant household economies.

Hopes for the future primarily rested on the expansion of cattle raising, but if cattle raising was to fulfil the hopes and expectation of local villagers, a number of problems would have to be solved, the most important of which was the quality of the pasture lands, which had been denuded and eroded over the years. It became clear that any improvement of the pasture land would require its reclassification from land which could be continuously used, 'taken from' or extracted from, to land deserving of investment, inputs and fertiliser, much like arable lands. As yet, very few households had experience of sown grasslands, and almost all expressed some degree of surprise that inputs such as fertiliser might be applied to sown pasture lands. A lesser problem had to do with the distribution of pasture land which was according to persons rather than animals, which had led to anomalies whereby larger households with just one head of cattle had two to three times the pasture land available to the large number of cattle owned by smaller-sized households.

The future expansion of cattle raising was also dependent on the availability of labour, fodder supplies and capital. Already the shortage of labour meant that few children attended school, and of those who did most had to leave school early and for the duration of grazing seasons (Table 3.10). The commercial development of cattle raising required that peasant households develop new strategies, either in accumulating and allocating savings or in taking out loans to purchase cattle. However, any attempt to establish credit schemes would have to take into account the annual cash deficits of each household, the dearth of savings and the degree to which indebtedness was already common among peasant households in these mountainous villages. Nevertheless, in these poor mountainous villages, the peasant households were basking in their new cash incomes, low as they were, and their hopes for future wealth largely centred on the expansion of cattle raising – they could almost see the herds of cattle, the meat-processing factories, the trucked meat exports and their new-found wealth and well-being expanding indefinitely into the future.

SICHUAN, 1988

In southwestern Sichuan province, seven villages were studied in Ya-an prefecture a day's car journey south of Chengdu city and located on high, tree-covered and rocky slopes and in deep ravine valleys. Although they were close to Ya-an city as the crow flies, their very inaccessibility along high, winding treacherous dirt roads lent new meaning to the term 'remote'. In each village, between twenty and sixty households clustered in a natural (as opposed to administrative) hamlet in which nestled natural wooden houses whose aesthetic design, carved decorations and thatched roofs, below which dried grasses, straws and sticks were heaped to the low eaves, epitomised for the traveller the purity of natural wooden beauty and quite belied the poverty within. The most conspicuous material object was the harnessed back-basket with its own style distinctive to each valley and a symbol of the carrying culture of the region – a culture in which everything produced and consumed, from baby to food, fodder to piglet and fuel to quilt, was back-carried. In these steep-sided villages even the pasture was daily brought to the penned animals by the basketful. It was as if the basket was just another article of clothing slipped on and off with as much ready grace as a jacket – but much much heavier. The houses sheltered families with an average size of 4 to 4.6 persons in the valleys and 5.3 to 5.6 persons in the higher mountainous villages. The sample households ranged from 3 to 6 persons (Table 3.11). As in Henan, the narrow range of income-generating activities and the absence of village amenity and enterprise was immediately observable. Land was scarce in this ravined region, pigs were few, and the keeping of goats, rabbits and cows was a relatively new and as yet minor activity. Again as in Henan, the remoteness of the villages and the absence of nearby industrial and other forms of employment meant that there were few opportunities for continuous employment outside of the family farm. Prior to the recent expansion in animal husbandry both men and women had worked full-time in the fields.

In this populous province, the per capita allocation of arable land hovered around a low 1 mu per person, and in the seven villages, allocations of arable land ranged from 0.8 mu per person in the valleys to 1.5 mu in the highlands (Table 3.12). Among the sample households the per capita arable land allocations ranged from a low 0.5 to a high 2.2 (Table 3.13). Variations in the per capita allocations were due to marked topographical gradations in land quality and difficulties in keeping pace with changes in household size because of births, deaths and marriages. For instance, in the household with the lowest per capita arable land allocation, two daughters had been born since the distribution of lands. The distribution of pasture lands, mostly of natural grasses and trees in the seven villages, ranged from an average of 0.4 mu per person in a lowland village to 5 mu in a highland village. In the sample households, the distribution of pasture lands ranged widely from 0.25 mu per person in the valley to 5 mu per person in the highlands. This highland village was one of the few in the region where animals were to be seen grazing. In one anomalous case, a household had received less land than their neighbours first because of physical disability (not uncommonly found due to accidents in these steep-sloped lands) and later because of advanced age. With the exception of one village, the distribution of vegetable lands was more equitable, ranging from 0.10 to 0.15 mu per person in the villages. Households cultivated a variety of vegetables, including green beans, eggplant, cucumber and chilli peppers, with the majority cultivating sufficient vegetables for their own consumption. Just under one-third of the sample households produced vegetables for the market, and whether they did so very much depended on their distance from the market and labour resources. There was little sign of any subcontracting of lands by peasant households; indeed, in one village a labour-short household had allowed 1 mu of its land to lie idle because of a rule prohibiting subcontracting for more than one year. With few exceptions, land was a scarce resource, and villagers cultivated their lands intensively and carefully relying solely on the crops they cultivated for their own subsistence, for animal fodder and for meeting the tax quotas set by the state.

The crops cultivated in Ya-an prefecture were rice, maize, wheat and rape, with some soya beans interspersed. In two of the more remote highland villages, maize was the sole crop; in a number of the lowland villages, between one-third and half of the arable land allocation was of rice paddy. The average yields produced per mu in the villages ranged, for rice, between 500 and 1,800 jin per mu (Table 3.14); for maize, between 280 and 500 jin per mu; for wheat, between 300 and 400 jin per mu; for rape, between 50 and 180 jin per mu (Table 3.15). These differences were accounted for by differentials in the location, topography and climatic conditions. The differentials in yields between sample households, however, were only in part due to the quality of land, for they could also be directly correlated with the amount of fertiliser per mu purchased annually by the household, the number of livestock raised and supply of animal manure, and with the age, experience, skills and initiative of the farmers. Of all the subsistence grains produced, rice was the most important and an average 80 per cent of the rice produced was for consumption and some 20 per cent delivered to the state as tax quotas. The wheat produced was also divided between human consumption and delivery as tax to the state. The maize was mainly used for fodder, with the remainder divided between tax deliveries and human consumption. Each household delivered a certain proportion of its rice, wheat and maize to the state, and all of the villagers were said to produce sufficient grains for the consumption of their members (more than 400 jin per capita); in the villages that did not produce any rice, maize was exchanged for rice at a ratio of 8 to 5. In all the villages, grain was very precious and its use calculated carefully, for households were likely to have a deficit rather than a surplus at the year's end. Not only were production costs for grain high, but also the shortage of grain affected the raising of livestock. One of the attractions of goat and rabbit raising in this region was that they consumed less grain than pigs and could eat the plentiful grasses of the highlands.

Sideline activities were almost entirely based on livestock, including pigs, poultry and either goats or fur or meat rabbits, or cows. Just as the main determinants of the crops were terrain and government policy, so the main types and numbers of livestock raised in each village were the products of government policy and the availability of resources (Table 3.16). The main determinant of the numbers and types of livestock in each sample household (Table 3.17) was first the availability of credit and only secondarily the number of labourers and livestock facilities of a household. Those with sufficient labour resources did not necessarily raise more livestock, although households where there were no or few animals were labour-short. Both men and women villagers thought that new demands took up slack labour rather than imposed extra burdens. In one village it was estimated that, at that time, households utilised an average of 250–300 labour days out of a possible average of 600–700 labour days available annually. Almost all adult labourers in each village worked on the family farm with the labour days demanded for cultivating paddy rice, maize, wheat, rape or other miscellaneous grain on each mu of arable land estimated to be 115, 135 and 150 days respectively, with variations according to the topography, the amount of rice paddy, and the distribution and shape of the fields. In the village requiring an average of 150 labour days per mu, the arable land was steeply sloped and the plots small and scattered. If it was assumed that households farm 1 mu of land per member, then the labour days would be multiplied by 4.5, which gave a total of 1.5 labourers per household per year which was just manageable for a two-labourer household with dependants and left substantial resources of labour in households with more than two labourers (fifteen of the twenty-two in the sample). If the household owned or hired an ox, the number of work days demanded of the household was almost halved. However, the major problem determining the livestock raised was not labour but the access of the household to seasonal or short-term loans for funding the acquisition of livestock, amounting to ¥50–60 for a piglet, ¥50–70 for a goat, tens of yuan for several rabbits or hundreds more for a dairy cow. Although nearly all households raised pigs, only a varying proportion of the households in the seven villages had so far been able to take up new livestock occupations – for dairy goats the proportion was 58 per cent and 61 per cent; for fur rabbits, 82 and 15 per cent; for meat rabbits, 3 and 7 per cent; for dairy cows, 3 per cent.

Almost all households except those very short of labour power (household 4) raised a pig or, more usually, two pigs – one for sale and one for consumption – although the most cited advantage of pig raising was the production of manure. The pig consumed also constituted a major source of meat for households that otherwise ate little meat, while the pig sold provided a small cash income, although profits from pigs were considered to be minimal after production costs were deducted (Tables 3.18, 3.19). In addition, the labour required for cutting and collecting grass, for mixing food and cleaning was estimated to lie between two and four hours daily depending on the distance of the pasture lands. Raising a pig to its full potential weight, requiring grain and concentrated feed for several months, was considered to be a very expensive business and there was much shaking of heads at the small profits to be made. Hopes for future prospects all centred on the expansion of other livestock raising, and the villagers had all enthusiastically embraced the idea of raising meat and fur rabbits, goats or cows because of the higher level of profits, the lower costs of production and their grass-eating habits.

Goat raising was the most important new sideline in two highland, sloped villages nestled among dark green ravines and rocky outcrops. In one village, 61 per cent of the households had taken up goat raising since 1983, and in another, where goat raising had only begun in 1987, 55 per cent had already taken up goats with alacrity. It was a popular income-generating activity in these villages largely because of the availability of natural pasture, which made it easy to obtain grass. In 1988, the average size of household herds ranged from four to seven goats, and the cost of purchasing and raising a goat included the price of a kid goat (¥50–70) or a milking goat (¥150–200); concentrated food which ranged between 180 jin (¥54) to 300 jin (¥94) per goat; and ¥10 for inoculations, medicines and artificial insemination. Initially, funds were also required for the construction of a goat pen which, for an average household herd of four to five goats, cost ¥120. There were few savings accumulated by village households; thus in one village a loan of ¥900–1,000 had on average to be borrowed to cover the initial costs of purchasing four to five grown goats and a goat pen. In return, it was estimated that a dairy goat produced 4 jin of milk per day which was sold for ¥0.26 per jin, and that if a goat yielded between 700 and 1,000 jin of milk per year then it earned the household between ¥182 and ¥260 per year, which, after deduction of production costs, provided a net profit of approximately ¥100 per goat per year. The labour inputs required in keeping an average goat herd of four to five goats amounted to four hours per day including the collection of grass (two to three hours), the milking of the goats undertaken by the women once a day (one hour) and the daily dispatch of the milk which was collected on the highway between 7 and 8 a.m. each day (15 minutes). The periodic cleaning of the goat pens was largely undertaken by the men of the household.

As for dairy goats, it was the higher level of profits, lower costs of production and their liking for grass which underlay the attraction of fur rabbits in two of the villages. Fur rabbits had the added advantage that the initial outlay was less, in that an infant rabbit cost ¥30 to purchase and its pen ¥12–15 to construct. The cost of raising a rabbit each year amounted to ¥24–26, including ¥21 for feed (richer households bought concentrate and the poorer households ground maize mixed with wheat bran). Monitoring the health of the rabbit and inoculations cost an average of ¥3–5 per rabbit each year. Compared to other animals, little labour was required by households to raise the fur rabbits: householders estimated that one full-time labourer could maintain forty to fifty rabbits a year and that a household with fiive to ten rabbits required one to two hours daily. The fur was cut every three months and sold as cut – that is, not sorted or graded – either to the county government or in the free market. Except in the busy farming season when the county office sent somebody to purchase the fur, the farmers preferred to sell their fur in the free market where fur was purchased by 'middlemen' from southern China, and in particular Zhejiang and Guangdong provinces, for ¥2 per jin. The annual income from each rabbit amounted to ¥30–35 in that each rabbit produced 1 to 1.2 jin of fur each year, but the farmers had already experienced large fluctuations in the market price of the fur, which had ranged from ¥20 to ¥45 per jin over recent years. Despite these worries, farmers were adamant about the advantages of raising fur rabbits, and, given the enthusiasm for raising fur rabbits, what was surprising was that not more villagers raised rabbits. In one village one-quarter of the households had not yet raised rabbits, and in the other only eight (15 per cent) of the fifty-two households raised rabbits, with an average of three per house-hold. Most of these households had taken an average-size loan of ¥50 for one to three years at 2.6 per cent and also raised cash from selling vegetables or eggs to supplement the loans in order to purchase both male and female adult rabbits so as to begin breeding their own rabbits. Those without rabbits were said to be too poor to even join the long queue for loans or to accumulate the savings themselves.

The raising of meat rabbits was only a very recent activity in two of the villages, and so far very few households had participated in this new income-generating venture. None the less, there was much enthusiasm expressed for raising meat rabbits by the villagers, who were convinced that it would become their most important economic activity even though, after only five months' experience, it was still too soon to take full cognisance of the costs of raising rabbits. The initial costs were low, for the price of each four-to-five days' old rabbit weighing 1.5 jin for fattening was ¥3–4 and the cost of a breeding rabbit weighing 6 jin was ¥17. Most of the rabbits were home-bred, from the male breeding stock costing ¥50 each and female breeding stock costing ¥20. A pen for keeping two to three rabbits cost ¥12–15, and the costs of raising the rabbits over three months totalled ¥5–7, including the purchase price of ¥3, the value of the grain, ¥2–3, and ¥0.6–1 per inoculation. The daily labour inputs for an average number of ten to twenty rabbits amounted to two hours per day, including one to two hours for feeding and cleaning by the women of the household. The fattened rabbit was usually sold to the state when it weighed 5–6 jin, which earned the household ¥6.8–10.8 per rabbit (¥1.3–1.8 per jin). The main attractions of rabbit raising were said by the villagers to be the short 'raising' cycle of three months and the 'high' profits, although it had to be admitted that these might not turn out to be so high after the subtraction of production costs.

Despite the low initial outlay, households in these poor villages still needed loans to get started, and only a very small proportion of households in the two villages had so far received loans to raise rabbits. In one village, only seven of the 204 households raised rabbits, making a total of 120 rabbits (an average of seventeen rabbits with a range of ten to twenty rabbits); in another village only one of the forty-two households had received a loan to raise ten rabbits and in a third village nineteen, or 7 per cent, of the households presently raised 100 rabbits between them. Although all but the poorest households had applied for loans, those successful had been selected because, it was said, they were better educated, better trained and had the facilities and the labour resources to keep rabbits. So far, the only limit placed on increasing rabbit raising in these villages was the availability of funds, for there was no lack of supplies of rabbits or skills as more than 200 householders had attended training courses. The villagers were sure that rabbit meat was growing in popularity. Certainly, the newspapers were exhorting their readers to eat more rabbit meat, and it has to be said that I was given enough rabbit stew to last a lifetime! However, it may well be that the high expectations for rabbits will be misplaced given that any rapid development in rabbit raising will cause difficulties in creating a large enough domestic market or processing facilities for the coveted foreign market. Already some years previously, they had had to abandon the unsuccessful raising of fur rabbits.

In the lowland villages, raising dairy cows was the most important goal of peasant householders, who thought that it required no special farming skills, did not require off-farm labour, made use of plentiful grass supplies, took advantage of the villagers' proximity to the town market and generated higher profits than any other alternative economic activity. However, it was the most expensive activity to take up in that a milking cow cost ¥3,000 and a calf ¥700. The cost of keeping a cow was estimated to be ¥530 per year, made up of ¥480 (3,000 jin of maize at ¥0.15 per jin, which was a subsidised price available to those selling milk to the state), and ¥50 for carbon, calcium, salt and inoculations. Another expense was artificial insemination, which cost between ¥40 and ¥120, depending on whether the service was state- or privately provided. It was estimated that the demands on labour for cow raising amounted to 4.5 hours daily. In return. the average yield of a milk cow amounted to 8,000 or 10,000 jin which. at ¥0.27 per jin, meant that households received ¥2,160–2,700 or ¥1,500–2,000 net income after the deduction of production costs. However, in 1988 only ten of the 340 households in one village raised a total of sixteen cows, with thirteen households raising one cow and three households raising three, four and two cows respectively. Dairy cows had been introduced into the village in 1981 and, since that time, most households owning dairy cows had either bought or bred their own calves, which only produced an income after 2.5 years. Dairying in the village received a boost when a nearby state dairy farm was disbanded, thus providing an opportunity for the households to purchase cows at ¥3,000 and calves at ¥700 each. To purchase these, five households took loans equal to two-thirds of the value of the cow, and five had loans equal to the total value of the cow at 2.6 per cent from the Help the Poor Fund to be repaid within seven to ten years. As in other villages, the main obstacle inhibiting expansion was the lack of credit, for there was said to be no problem in procuring cows or calves from a number of sources including nearby dairy farms and state farms sponsored by the Agricultural Ministry. Although there remained the problem of fodder, the villagers hoped to overcome these problems in the near future, and indeed there were expectations that eventually the village would become richly 'specialised' in raising dairy cows.

For all households, the most important factor limiting the expansion of economic activities was the shortage of capital. Many households already borrowed each year in order to raise pigs and to purchase fertiliser, and in most of the villages there was little credit available for additional activities (Tables 3.20, 3.21). Although there were supposed to be special sources of credit in this poor county, most households had applied unsuccessfully for credit and few had the opportunity to accumulate their own savings from income. The remoteness of the villages and the absence of nearby industrial and other forms of employment meant that in most of these villages there were very few opportunities for continuous employment outside of the family farm. There were some intermittent contracts for cutting stones and building roads, and some villagers utilised their carpentry or masonry skills to supplement the family income. Whereas in one of the villages it was estimated that 50 per cent of the households earned some off-farm income in this manner, in others only one or two such cases were reported. In the sample households there were only two examples of off-farm labour: in one household one of the sons had emigrated to far Fujian province on what seemed a semi-permanent basis, and in another, the elder son, a senior middle-school graduate, had become half-time village accountant. Given the narrow range of economic activities, the main sources of cash income in the villages were few and uniform. In kind, households consumed the grains and vegetables they cultivated and varying amounts of the pigs, chickens and eggs they produced. Cash incomes were commonly derived from the sale of poultry products, rapeseed and pigs, with perhaps one of the following: goat milk, rabbit fur or rabbit meat or dairy milk and some small off-farm income. The per capita gross income in the villages (¥200) was low in comparison with the average per capita net income in the same year for Sichuan province (¥338) and China (¥420), with the considerable variations between the villages due to differing crop yields, proximity to markets for vegetables and availability of credit for livestock (Table 3.22). The villages where less than 10 per cent of the households raised livestock other than pigs had the lowest per capita incomes. The village where 60 per cent of the households raised goats had a higher than average per capita income, but here the households grew only maize and no cash crops such as rape, which generated a high proportion of the cash incomes in other villages. As might be expected, the average incomes of the lowland village in close proximity to the Ya-an city, with some of its households raising both goats and cows, were higher than in the more remote villages.

The range of incomes between the sample households was also wide and similarly caused by variations in location and in access to credit and only less directly by variations in labour resources (Table 3.23). For the twenty-two sample households, the gross cash incomes were low, with five earning between ¥50 and ¥100; four earning between ¥100 and ¥200; and one household earning ¥374 per capita in 1987. The per capita range of cash income was wide, between ¥0 and ¥374, and within each of the seven villages, differentials between the richest and poorest households amounted to sums of ¥43, ¥128, ¥55, ¥78, ¥56, ¥65 and ¥195. The most important sources of cash income were from pigs, which were raised by all but one household; poultry and vegetables were common but less important sources of income, and it is a measure of the scarcity of cash incomes that most of the eggs produced were sold rather than consumed. For the fortunate few households with access to credit, either goats, fur rabbits or dairy cows constituted an important source of income. Overall, income depended on the quality and quantity of each household's labour resources, the range and scale of their economic activities and their access to credit. In their evaluations of their own economic situation, villagers were more aware of the rises in their incomes than of the parallel rises in the costs of production, even though their annual cash expenditures, including production costs, totalled more than their incomes, so that few households had savings and indebtedness was widespread.

The annual cash expenses of peasant households could be divided into the costs of production, which included inputs and farm implements and the cost of consumption, that commonly covered grain processing, fuel, medical and school fees and daily living necessities amongst which were clothes (Table 3.24). The costs of production were high (Table 3.25), taking up 50–60 per cent of the total annual cash expenditure of a household, with the cost of chemical fertiliser constituting the largest single item of cash expenditure each year for all villagers. Within the villages there were very wide discrepancies in the value of the fertiliser applied per mu, which ranged from ¥0.4 per mu to ¥80 per mu. These discrepancies, while they may be related to the quality of lands and the number of alternative sources of livestock manure, were most directly related to the income of the household. For example, the household spending a low ¥4 per mu on fertiliser was also the household with the lowest per capita income; likewise, the household spending ¥80 per mu had one of the highest per capita incomes of the sample outside of the lowlands. Not only were the production costs high, but production costs had also risen at a higher rate in recent years than rises in incomes. For instance, in one village, the costs of production had risen to the extent that average farm profits had been reduced from ¥55 in 1983 to ¥12 in 1987, which suggested that over the five years increases in production costs had cancelled much of the rise in cash incomes.

The items of consumption were quite standard in the households, embracing food, clothing, fuel, school and medical expenses, with variations according to the age and health of its members. There were fewer durable items of consumption to be had, given the absence of electricity. In several of the villages, the total cash expenditures of households were substantially affected by fuel costs, especially where households commonly used between 1 and 4 tons of coal per year at the price of ¥30 per ton. However, they saved on labour in the collection of firewood, which in many villages took one day every three to four days, but this was an ambiguous advantage in a region labour-rich and cash-poor. Primary-school fees were usually ¥30 per year except in the remotest of villages, where teachers were employed by the villages themselves at a cost of ¥20 per year. Middle-school fees cost a high ¥40 per year and double this amount when students were required to board, and it was these costs which were said to be the main factor preventing children staying in school (Table 3.26). Medical expenses varied widely, but for those with elderly grandparents co-resident, medical expenses could substantially affect the size of household debts and the credit-worthiness of the household. Because on average the cash expenditures incurred by peasant households each year totalled more than the average cash incomes, very few (at the most three to four) or no households had any savings. In the majority of the villages a high proportion, between 63 and 88 per cent, had loans either borrowed from friends or relations or the rural credit co-operative (Table 3.27). None of the sample households had any savings, and they all had loans from the credit co-operative or from friends and relatives amounting to more than ¥1,000 (14 per cent), ¥300–700 (34 per cent) or less than ¥200 (50 per cent), which were mainly used for fertiliser (45 per cent), pigs (54 per cent) and special livestock loans (Table 3.28). Although a high proportion of the village population had loans and the average size of debts ranged between ¥30 and ¥1,000, the number and size of the loans were lower than they might have been because of the shortage of credit available. Those without loans or with small loans frequently said that they had or would have applied for loans or larger loans from the rural credit co-operative and or relatives and friends if funds were available. Despite the all-important shortage of credit, however, the villagers were generally optimistic. Even the poorest cited the rise in incomes and living standards as the most important difference in their lives since the reforms, and they were uniformly very hopeful that in the future the availability of credit would permit them to raise livestock; indeed, for most their future hopes lay almost entirely on that most risky of animals – the rabbit.

BEIJING VILLAGE, 1990

The Beijing village was nestled in tall fields of maize some 25 kilometres southeast of the capital city off the main highway to Tianjin. Its location in a county which has been designated a satellite city of Beijing had many important implications for the intensive suburban development of the village. Indeed, it was presented by its leaders as a 'half-way' urban–rural village linking or combining to an unusual degree both industry and agriculture. Its location and connections with Beijing city certainly enabled it to enjoy many advantages in establishing alternative economic opportunities to land cultivation and agriculture. Its mostly new whitewashed and low spacious houses with central heating, high-quality furniture, colour television and a refrigerator had walled courtyards sheltering flowers and vegetables exhibiting an air of well-being which perhaps reflected the wealth of this suburban village. After a decade of reform, village income in 1989 was more than fifteen times that of 1978 (Table 3.29) with three-quarters of it deriving from industry (Table 3.30), which now provided employment for two-thirds of village labourers (Table 3.31).

There was a total of 470 households in the village, with a low average size of 2.8 persons, mostly made up of two labourers and one child and sometimes elderly parents. This, reflecting the average younger age of the village, was probably due to a number of factors including strict family-planning policies, the migration of younger working-age persons into the rapidly expanding village enterprises and the establishment of separate nuclear households on marriage, which is more an urban than a rural practice. More than half the village population of 1,339 persons were waged labourers in a variety of village enterprises, and the incomes of most households were made up of factory wages and sometimes a small number of domestic sidelines including pigs, chickens and calves. Less than 10 per cent of the village households still contracted land. The village had a total of 3,180 mu of flat fertile land, mainly made up of grainlands (1,275 mu or 40 per cent), double-cropped with winter wheat grown between October and June and maize from June to September. The remainder was divided between orchard (900 mu or 28 per cent), forestry (750 mu or 24 per cent) and vegetable lands (8 per cent). The distribution of the grainland first took place in 1979, and thereafter there were several shifts in the numbers, parties and arrangements in contracting land.

In 1979, when the rural production responsibility system was first introduced, 280 labourers in the village contracted land; by 1980 the number had decreased to 150. After 1981, land contracts were taken over by the agricultural machinery team until 1985, when the land was once more contracted out – this time to forty villagers. Thus in the space of a few years, those contracting grain lands had been reduced to one-seventh of the original figure, a decline which largely correlated with increasing mechanisation. Whereas by hand it had previously taken one labourer to cultivate 3 mu, it soon took one labourer with the appropriate machinery to work 30 mu of land. Each of the forty contractors had an average of 30 mu of land with a range between 25 and 50 mu depending on land shape, distance from the village and soil fertility. The contracts required that a fixed yield of grain, 450 jin per mu in 1990, be sold to the state, which was almost half the average yield of 860 jin produced per mu. For the 450 jin quota, the contractor was paid a fixed state price of ¥0.3 per jin; the extra jin produced were usually sold to the state at the higher price of ¥0.56 per jin. From the contractor's gross income, the costs of seeds, fertiliser and machines had to be subtracted. Most of the planting, spraying, watering, harvesting, drying and storing of grains was mechanised and undertaken by the agricultural machinery team, so that in the contract for the land the farmer undertook to provide such hand labour as required and pay a fee per mu to meet the costs of seed, fertiliser, herbicides, chemicals, irrigation and contributions to the cost of agricultural machinery. The village provided all these services and paid the land, energy and water taxes, the costs of irrigation and more than half the costs of operating and maintaining the farm machinery.

One agricultural contractor, a married peasant woman fifty-two years old, contracted 43 mu; her main work on the fields consisted of supplementary watering, cutting wheat, choosing young maize plants and applying fertiliser to the maize. These tasks took approximately 120 days a year, and were concentrated in busy planting and harvesting seasons when family members also provided help. Outside of busy seasons, one labour day per week was said to be sufficient to cultivate the fields. The hire of the agricultural machinery team's labour amounted to ¥27 per mu per year for ploughing (twice a year), planting, spraying and harvesting, so that she only had to undertake the weeding. She was given a contract quota of 450 jin per mu for which she was paid a fixed state price of ¥0.3 per jin or a total of ¥135 per mu; she usually sold the extra 410 jin produced per mu to the village at a higher price, the bargain price of ¥0.56 per jin or for a total of ¥229.6 per mu or a total of ¥15,678 for 43 mu. At the end of each year, she paid the village for the production inputs and services which she had received. Thus the land contractors did not have responsibility for supplying the inputs so onerous and worrying a burden for farmers in many other regions; they only supplied minimal hand labour and their incomes were several times higher than that of others in the village. This combination of features had led them to be dubbed the 'new landlords' of the village. To reduce the privileges of the contractors and increase the profits of the village, in summer 1990 the agricultural machinery team was once again about to take over the land contracts. It will pay its members wages and bonuses out of the profits on the same 2:4:4 basis as the village industrial enterprises: 20 per cent of the profits pays the bonuses and supplementary wages of team members, 40 per cent is allocated to the team accumulation fund for investment in the expansion and improvement of the team's assets and 40 per cent is paid into general village funds.

The orchard and vegetable lands were to continue to be contracted out to farmers. The orchard lands were carved out of the poorest grain land in 1987 with sixteen persons taken out of grain production and transferred to the orchard and forestry. This land was not subdivided, and the varieties of plum, peach, apple, pear and apricot trees, grape vines and poplar trees for building materials planted between 1986 and 1988 were tended in common. The heavy work was also performed by machines, although the pruning, tending the soil around the trees and the fertilising and spraying of the trees were still undertaken by hand. In 1989 income from the fruit trees yielded ¥27,000 and was divided between wages, bonuses, production costs and improvements and village taxes. It was planned that the income from the orchard would increase to ¥1.5 million in 1995. The vegetable lands (255 mu) were divided among forty-two persons who each had approximately 6 mu on which they grew cabbages, eggplant, cucumbers, tomatoes, squash, pumpkin, beans and radish. The parcels of land were cultivated individually, and most of the vegetables were sold in the free market by the vegetable growers, who also retained sufficient for their own household's consumption.

If in 1980 the majority of the labour force was employed on the land, by 1990 just 30 per cent of the labour force of the village remained employed in agriculture, including forestry, the orchard and animal husbandry and in the farm-machinery team. Village households engaged in very few other agricultural activities, so that there were only a small number of households specialising in raising cows (nine), pigs (four) and sheep (two). A number of 'commercial' households purchased goods for resale mainly in open-air village stalls and shops; two households in the village had members who undertook repair and maintenance work, and there were a number of individual entrepreneurs, mainly young men who were contractors in construction, transportation or had a rare technical skill. More than two-thirds of the labourers in the village were employed in the seven factories of the village established during the previous twelve years.

The establishment of manufacturing enterprises had been the most important single development in the village and had provided employment for displaced agricultural labour. Beijing factories had rented land from the village and established satellite factories or subcontracted portions of the production process to factories utilising the cheaper labour of the village. In turn, the village benefited from the investment, technical advice, steady supplies of raw materials and markets in partnerships which were of mutual advantage to city and village. The history of the village clothing factory, which was established in 1984 as a result of the increasing interest and demand for clothes, is an interesting example of the importance of such city–village links. For the first three years the factory, with some forty-six workers, was in some difficulties due to lack of skills, technology and market information. It was not until 1987, when the Beijing municipal government attempted to increase supplies of clothes to meet new consumer demand and encouraged city factories to invest, expand and contract out production to countryside enterprises, that the clothing factory received technical help from a large clothing factory in Beijing. As a result, the clothing factory expanded its labour force to 172 workers and imported a production line from Japan and made substantial profits. Its annual income of ¥17,272 million in 1990 was twenty times its initial income six years previously.

Another village factory, the electric and porcelain factory producing porcelain fuse boxes of all shapes and sizes, was established ten years earlier as the first factory in the village. Originally, the Beijing Electrical Facilities Company had a small subsidiary factory in Beijing and, wishing to expand, established and supplied the village factory with raw materials; each year it purchased ¥1 million worth of goods from the factory, leaving the enterprise the easy task of finding an alternative outlet for another ¥1 million worth of goods. The modern colour printing factory was one of the most successful of the village enterprises, with an annual income of ¥2.1 million in 1990 and a permanent contract to produce books and calendars on very high quality glossy paper imported from Germany. These could frequently be seen in peasant households which, not surprisingly, used these pictorial calendars as very superior wallpaper!

The bookbinding factory, with an income of ¥500,000, was established in 1988 to undertake the service work for the colour printing factory. It had been established as a social service factory employing more than 50 per cent of handicapped workers, thus enabling it to enjoy 50 per cent tax exemptions. Recently, however, for tax reasons, these handicapped workers have been transferred to the more profitable colour printing factory.

The Fine Chemical Factory is the most recently established factory in the village, and in 1990 was not yet in full production. It will manufacture chemical dyes, printing chemicals, chemical waterproof coating and glue for trademarks; all are relatively scarce products in China. The factory was aiming at the export market and it benefited from its inclusion in the Beijing Municipal State Plan, which entailed advantages for its investment, production and marketing strategies. There was still a shortage of labour for the factory, with more than thirty workers needed to operate it at full capacity.

Most school leavers entered the village enterprises, and in this village it was reported that 100 per cent of school-age children attended junior middle school and a high 40 per cent went on to senior middle school. In 1990, of the twenty-two junior middle-school graduates, seven went on to senior middle school and the rest nearly all took up employment in village factories, where they received some vocational training (Table 3.32).

During the years of reform there had been a rise in per capita incomes in the village from ¥162 in 1978 to ¥1,579 in 1989, which placed this village well above the average for China and among the richest of suburban villages in north China (Table 3.29). Within the village those without full labour power earned a few tens of yuan while some of the richest individual entrepreneurs were reported to earn upwards of ¥30–40,000 each year. Outside of these extremes, there were wide differentials between those contracting the land and other occupational categories. Agricultural contractors generally earned upwards of ¥10,000 net from their land which, higher than for most groups in the village, was one of the reasons why they seemed prepared to give up their contracts with less reluctance than might have been anticipated. They had been so obviously privileged within the village and earned their incomes so easily that such an inequality could not be reasonably sustained or defended even by the contractors themselves. Those who cultivated the vegetable lands worked very hard to earn an average of ¥5,000 per year. In contrast, those in other agricultural occupations earned closer to the average wage of the members of the agricultural machinery team, ¥2,490, while the workers in the orchard and forestry earned an average low income of ¥1,250–1,300 per year, a sum which was expected to improve when the fruit trees begin to produce. The wages in the factories averaged around ¥2,000–2,500, which included bonuses and was almost always earned through piece-work. Each month the workers were paid a fixed amount and then their salary was adjusted at the year's end out of enterprise profits.

The average income of village households was reported to be ¥5,000–6,000 which, for the majority, was usually made up of little more than two sets of wages. Household incomes, however, ranged between ¥2,000 and ¥20,000 per annum. At the lower end of the scale there were ten to twenty or so households earning around ¥2,000 because they were weak in labour power, lacking in technical and other skills and were perhaps incapacitated in some way. At the other end of the continuum, in one of the richest households, the husband, an agricultural technician, earned ¥9,700, while his wife, an agricultural contractor with 40 mu of land, earned ¥10,000. These differentials did not take account of the thirty to forty individuals engaged in transport and construction and earning a high ¥30,000–40,000 per year. In the sample households, the highest earners were those contracting the responsibility lands who earned upwards of ¥12,000 net per annum from their lands alone (Table 3.33, households

1 and 6). The poorest household was made up of young parents, with a young son, each earning just over ¥2,000 per year in enterprises. All of the households had a cash surplus of several thousand yuan at the year's end and in recent years, most had spent many thousands of yuan on the highly fashionable intricate, multi-coloured room-length sideboards, a colour television and central heating. Large cash expenses included housing improvements, rebuilding or refurbishment and marriage, which cost between ¥5,000 and ¥8,000, and the majority of the households were saving up for one of more of these extraordinary expenses. With few households undertaking their own productive activities, most of their surplus income was used for items of consumption – both for daily needs and extraordinary expenses.

In the future, the village planned to combine agriculture, forestry and orchard in a reorganisational move which it expected would increase agricultural income to ¥4–5 million per year and would only require the management and labour of a minimal number of persons. There were also a number of plans to develop village enterprises: the clothing factory was to begin to initiate its own designs; the colour printing factory was to use four-colour printing techniques instead of two and also produce to its own designs; the paper box factory was to expand into plastic bags and packaging; and the dyeing factory was to modernise its techniques to use a wider range of cloths and more permanent colourings. At the same time there were plans to establish new enterprises, including fruit processing and men's suit manufacturing, whose explicit aims were to provide further employment for those displaced on the grain lands and in the orchard. The villagers had every reason to be pleased with their experience of the reforms and every hope that, with the village's plans for the reorganisation of agriculture and expansion of industry and services, their already high standards of living would continue to improve.

SHANXI, 1990

The Shanxi village was built of yellow, hard-baked clay and was divided into new and old settlements located on the inland loess plateau in south-east Shanxi province. The centre pieces of the older settlement were a crumbling, stilted village stage, now piled high with stacks of straw, and an old, elaborate clan temple which, once the production brigade head-quarters and soon to be a food-processing factory, perhaps aptly illustrated the passage of space in time. The well-trodden lanes between the houses have primitive village pumps and worn stone grinding-posts long in place and, together with the still small and previously bound feet of the black-velvet-hatted elderly ladies and the swarthy-lined and turbanned heads of the old men, gave an appearance of timelessness not so obvious elsewhere. The old clay houses were small and neat, dark and tight in contrast to the grander, high-storeyed, windowed and greybrick, green tiled houses of the newer section of the village. The village was hidden from road view by the high sorghum and maize, and, with the tall poplared straight roads, the landscape was strangely reminiscent of summer in France, even to the extent that it has the odd distant spire reaching to the sky – unusual in China but evidence here of the decades of northern European missionary activity before 1949. Although the village was some distance from any major town or city, it was located near a main highway and had ready access to Changchih town and its neighbouring mining settlements, which provided markets for its agricultural produce.

The village economy continued to be dominated by agriculture, with 85 per cent of the village income still derived from agricultural activities in 1989 and the major portion of that income (53 per cent) deriving from the grains (Table 3.34). The gradual rise in total income of the village over the previous ten years (Table 3.35) could be closely correlated with the rise in income from grains, which reflected increases in grain yields per mu due to improvements in inputs, mechanisation and practices such as ploughing in the stalks and raising the organic content of the soil (Table 3.36). After 1984, an increasing proportion of village income derived from vegetable and mulberry cultivation. The village population, evenly divided between the age groups made up 370 households, with an average of 4.5 persons who were mainly engaged in agricultural activities specialising in grain production, vegetable cultivation, sericulture or animal raising.

The village had a total of 5,442 mu of land, of which 3,883 mu, or more than 70 per cent, were allocated to grains – mainly maize, wheat and millet (Table 3.37). The rest was allocated to a number of cash crops, including vegetables (300 mu), orchard (500 mu), forest (270 mu) and mulberry (330 mu). All the lands of the village were contracted out to households, with the grain lands subdivided into two categories: just less than 60 per cent were 'responsibility lands' (2,283 mu) subdivided between a number of contractors; while the rest, food-grain land (1,600 mu), was distributed on a per capita basis to each household so that each family member received an average of 1 mu of land (0.8 mu if such land was closer to the village and 1.2 mu if the land was poorer and some distance from the village) on which to grow grain for their own consumption and as fodder. The responsibility lands were distributed on a per household rather than individual basis so that each of the eighty contracting households was allocated parcels of land according to the number and sex of its labourers, with each receiving between 15 and 20 mu depending on the fertility of the land and its distance from the village. To calculate the land allocation, the labourers within the household had been assigned labour points, which were totalled and divided by ten to calculate their portions of land. Male labourers received 10 points and 10 mu of land, while women were rated between 5 and 8 labour points and received 7 mu of land: a system which seemed to be unnecessarily complicated and certainly discriminated against women. The cash-crop land was distributed to a number of households on a per labourer basis, with households receiving either an average of 5 mu of vegetable lands, 5 mu of mulberry lands or 10 mu of fruit-tree lands. With the increase in yields in grain, 25 mu of the responsibility grain lands had been taken out of grain production and transferred to sericulture, vegetable or the orchard. Simultaneously, thirty grain-land contractors had been transferred to the cultivation of cash-crop lands.

According to village cadres, this village did not divide its responsibility lands until 1983 or some time after the rest of the country, and then it had soon became apparent that one of the weaknesses of the distribution of land into individually managed strips of 'noodlelands' was its repercussions for mechanisation. Given the flat grain lands, the village evolved a double management system known locally as 'double level development' in which the village took responsibility for supplying the inputs such as seed, fertiliser and chemicals, the machine planting, sowing and harvesting and the sale of grains, while the contractors remained responsible for the hand cultivation processes and daily management of the land. The village had a farm machinery team of twelve members and a number of machines for planting, sowing, harvesting, spraying herbicides, short-distance transportation and chopping, threshing and turning maize stalks back into the soil.

The village printed coupons worth ¥1 and ¥10 which were delivered to the contractors in the spring of each year, and the contractors, when the tasks were undertaken, paid the farm-machinery team with the coupons, the value of which had been calculated by the village according to the costs of services. These normally amounted to ¥16 per mu for all the work per mu per year for all crops. Because this price did not meet the total mechanisation costs, the village continued to provide a subsidy to the land contractors. They also benefited from the village's responsibility for inputs, as these were periodically in short supply and there were difficulties in obtaining good-quality seed, fertiliser and diesel oil. The village either had to have resources to pay a higher price for high quality, store some inputs ahead of time, or have the necessary connections (guanxi) to enable a steady supply and good quality. The village also paid for transportation and other costs and usually purchased input requirements a year in advance. Many of the farmers pointed with great satisfaction to the following year's stores of fertiliser located in the village, and without doubt the village was much better placed than the individual farmers to have access to funds, connections and supplies. As for the farmers, there was also an incentive to manage their land well, for, if yields rose above 800 jin per mu, the surplus could be sold in the market or to the state by the family at a higher price.

There were 335 labouring households in the village, with a total of 737 labourers (Table 3.38). Most of the younger members of the village proceeded to junior middle school either in the township or the county, and each year about half the junior middle-school graduates entered senior middle school (Table 3.39). The remaining graduates were employed in the village enterprises or on the family farm. Senior middle-school graduates were either given jobs that required some skill, including driving tractors, planting seeds, scientific work such as tests on soil structure, or joining the army. The majority of labourers worked in one-activity households, perhaps primarily grain or sericulture, although there were also some households which were more mixed in economy. Households were categorised according to main occupation or activity furnishing the majority of income. In 1989 per capita income in the village was ¥750, which marked a rise of more than ten times that of 1978 (Table 3.33), and in 1989 the average household income was estimated to be ¥3,400 with a range between ¥2,300 net and ¥10,000 net, with the lowest-income households working the land and one of the highest engaged in chicken raising. The village leaders thought that there were no large differentials between either rich and poor households or agriculture and industrial labourers, for they had taken some steps to allocate land and enterprise jobs in the village evenly. For instance, if a household received grain responsibility lands, its members were not eligible for employment in village industry or for allocations of cash-crop land.

The majority of village households cultivated grain, and the eighty households which contracted grain land earned an average of ¥7,833 per household after paying the expenses of the inputs and for services provided by the village. In the case of maize, the sum of ¥75 per mu – made up of fertiliser (¥50.5), seed (¥1), chemicals (¥4), farm machines (¥16) and land tax (¥4) – was subtracted from the income of the farmers. For wheat, the costs the contractors paid to the village were higher, at ¥90 per mu. This was made up of fertiliser (¥50), farm machinery (¥20), seeds (¥15), land (¥4) and chemicals (¥1). In addition, the contractors also paid the village a hidden subsidy of ¥59.45 per mu for maize and ¥39.18 per mu for wheat to the village. These subsidies came about because a certain fixed quota of grain was purchased from the contractors at an artificially low price and was then sold by the village to the state at a higher price. This village paid almost half the price fixed by the state for after-quota grain, a practice which was said to be acceptable to the farmers of the village because they produced much higher yields than the fixed quotas per mu which could still be sold at a much higher price in the market. Their income already amounted to ¥200 per mu, which was higher than that of many villagers, and moreover the subsidies were used to establish organisations, education and other services of benefit to the farmers. The sample households contracting grain (households 1–3) contracted 20–30 mu of grain lands on which they cultivated wheat and maize (Table 3.40). One of the households with 30 mu of land produced 1,450 jin of maize, which earned ¥450 gross per mu, and ¥300 net per mu after the payment of ¥150 fees for fertiliser and machinery. The farmer said that he did not worry about these costs for he thought that he did not have sufficient education or knowledge to assume this task and thus was happy to leave these responsibilities to the village. He also sold the surplus grains from his food-grain lands after taking sufficient wheat and maize for household consumption and more than a 100 chickens. Another farmer, who cultivated 20 mu of grain land, said that he had no idea of the cost of inputs because he 'just pays for these with his produce'. He produced 24,000 jin of maize, 18,000 jin of which went to the village for inputs, taxes and quota grains, and the other 6,000 jin was sold on the free market. He also produced 2,000 jin of wheat and 1,000 jin of maize on his food-grain lands. The wheat was for the family's own consumption and 1,000 jin of maize for feeding pigs and chickens. The grain-contracting households usually worked 190 labour days per mu per year, and the number of labour days was decreasing with increasing mechanisation. Most of these households also cultivated their food-grain lands, raised on average three pigs per year to sell and for manure, and raised twenty or so chickens, partly for selling and partly for eating; perhaps in the slack agricultural season they also undertook sideline activities such as selling vegetables or raising additional pigs. As in Beijing village they constituted the privileged members of the village.

The vegetable households each contracted 5 mu of vegetable lands and cultivated a variety of vegetables including eggplant, cabbage, tomatoes and cucumbers. Each vegetable grower was responsible for selling his own vegetables and either taking the vegetables to nearby cities, coalmines or factories, or, alternatively, middlemen, frequently from these and places farther afield, purchased the vegetables as they were harvested for sale elsewhere. It was estimated that each mu of vegetables required thirty days of labour per year, and that incomes ranged between ¥1,000 per mu for the most skilled growers to ¥500 per mu for those less skilled. In one household with four adult labourers (household 4), all members minus the sixty-one-year-old grandmother cultivated the vegetables. They had a total of 3.9 mu on which they grew cabbages, chilli, potatoes, cucumber, tomatoes and garlic, and food-grain lands of 6 mu. The grown son sold the vegetables in nearby villages and estimated family income to be ¥600 gross per mu, a net income of ¥500 per mu or a total of ¥1,950 in 1989. Each orchard household contracted 10 mu of land, and without any mechanisation the fruit trees at present necessitated 100 labour days per mu. In 1989 the income to be received from each mu was ¥300, or ¥3,000 in total, as the trees were young and not yet producing fruit although the orchard was said to be progressing well and there were plans to mechanise production.

Sericulture households contracted out 5.5 mu of land and earned between ¥300 and ¥600 per mu. They cultivated the mulberry trees, which took about thirty labour days per mu per year, and sold the silkworms for ¥6 per jin to the village silk thread factory. The mulberry trees had been supplied by the village, which had invested in and organised the establishment of sericulture. In one household (household 5) which had writhing silkworms actively munching the mulberry on every conceivable surface including under the bed, the family cultivated 2.7 mu of mulberry, which took the wife thirty-seven labour days a year. The gross income of ¥1,700 to ¥1,900 was reduced to a net income of ¥1,500 to ¥1,600 after subtracting the costs of production, which included ¥32 for four beds of silkworm eggs which came from a county-managed worm egg-hatching station some 10 kilometres distance from the village, ¥20 to buy chemicals to reduce disease and ¥135 for village taxes calculated at 3 per cent of this family's income. Each family paid a percentage tax appropriate to the number of mu of land and according to their income. There was a short-fall in production of silkworms and the village still had to buy in silkworms, which was said to be illegal. To expand the factory to its full capacity would require another 22 mu for mulberries, making a total area of 500 mu.

The animal husbandry households specialised in raising chickens or pigs and, to a lesser extent, ducks or cows. It was estimated that they earned a high net income of ¥10,000 or so, and they were said to have no problems with inputs in that they used their own maize and mixed their own feed using fish-bone powder, maize and beancakes and vitamins. Apart from the small costs of feeding, their production expenses might include the cost of the young animals, disease protection and some small transportation costs. The households did not contract to produce, for there was said to be a ready market in the nearby city of Changchih, factories and mines. The village arranged for the regular transport of eggs to these markets, or individual producers might use their bicycles and arrange for their own sales. One very successful chicken-raising household (household 6), which had begun three years ago with 100 chickens, had expanded to 500 in the second and 700 in its third year. In 1982 the village helped some households to learn to raise chickens in order to encourage individual household enterprises and set up a village chicken farm managed by one household to act as a model for the village. This household had used its savings to purchase 500 chicks, of which 200 had died: it had spent ¥200 for each of three cages (¥600), making a total of ¥900 initial investment. One chicken fed on 70 jin of feeding material, mainly millet, in a year, and the family spent ¥38 on feed, coal, veterinary fees and electricity. Each chicken produced approximately 550 eggs in one year, or 28–30 jin, which made for an average gross income from eggs for one chicken of ¥55. After subtracting the expenses, it had a net income of ¥17 per chicken, or a total of ¥8,400 in 1989.

There were a number of enterprise households which undertook small production operations that were not based on the land or animals. These included grain processing, concrete roof-plates and bricks and tiles. They usually had some kind of contract with the village to produce the goods or services for its members. These households numbered about fifty, and had an average annual income of ¥1,589 per person, with a range between ¥1,250 to ¥3,000 per person. For instance, one family set up a small grain-processing factory in 1985 (household 7). They spent ¥5,000 on establishing the enterprise using their own savings, a ¥2,000 loan from friends and relatives, and another loan of ¥300 from a local credit agency, all of which had already been repaid, as the enterprise was increasingly successful. The work was undertaken at night by the daughter and the mother partly because there was no electricity supply to village households in the daytime. Earnings in 1989 from this source amounted to ¥3,000 or so, although neighbours and cadres thought this to be a less than honest estimation of family income from grain processing.

The non-agricultural enterprises in this village were few, and ranged from those which were small and managed by one or several households to the larger, collectively run factory enterprises. The most important of the former, based on households, were the small tiles and brick enterprise established in 1986, grain processing established in 1987 and the concrete roof-plates enterprise established in 1987. The tiles and brick factory seemed to be made up of a number of contracting households sharing a large open-air site but each responsible for a product or process. One of the contractors for tiles had established his family enterprise two years earlier when he took out a contract with the village. In his enterprise there were five persons: two brothers and himself, his neighbour's son and a technician from Henan province with the requisite skills whom he had invited to join him. The raw materials for the enterprise were derived locally from what looked like arable land despite assurances that it was local waste soil, and the 'high-quality' tiles were sold to the villagers and to neighbouring villages within 30 kilometres. He reported no shortages of materials or inputs and his enterprise was less reliant on electricity than others and therefore was not affected by its erratic supply. He had no problems with the market, and his enterprise had advance sales and payments, which was not surprising given the plentiful housing and other building projects in the area. However, there might be a more limited market in the future once housebuilding in the village slows down. The income of the household from the enterprise was ¥6,000 per annum, and in the winter months (January, February and March) its members cultivated vegetables, which earned an additional ¥2–3,000 each year.

The most important collective enterprise, the silk thread factory, had been established very recently, in 1988, and had only came into production in 1989. The idea for this factory originated with the recent production of mulberries which had only been grown in the village since 1983. The village invested ¥150,000 in the factory for machines, boiler and pipes, and they had received technical help from the provincial silk research institute. They now processed all the silkworms produced in the village, although these by no means fulfilled the capacity of the factory. The workers, all young girls with an average age of seventeen years, were not yet very experienced. To see them standing in long rows with hands permanently in the boiling water removing the thread from the cocoon was very reminiscent of old photographs from Shanghai silk factories in the early decades of this century. The factory had no fixed contracts for selling its silk, but there was a good market, with much of the silk sold to the arts and handicrafts factory in Jiangsu province. The inferior graded silk was sold for silk quilting, and the waste as chicken feed. The first year after its establishment, the net profits of the factory were ¥40,000 after payment of salaries. At present, the income of the workers was a low ¥1,800 (¥60 a month plus an average of ¥70–80 (¥30–95 range) bonus a month). The girls were paid by piece-work – ¥3 for every jin of thread. They worked a six-day week and every ten days had one day off because of absence of electricity. There were plans to expand production by improving the skill of the workers and increasing the supply of raw materials in order to earn capacity profits estimated to be ¥360,000 per annum.

The sample households had per capita incomes ranging from ¥440 to ¥3,375, which represented the large differentials of the village. The sample households with the highest incomes cultivated grain and raised pigs and or chickens. One household with a low per capita income cultivated vegetables, and the poorest household in the village had an absent father who only remitted ¥1,200 a year, and three sons still all in school. None of the households needed help from the village and most had savings, although some had short-term debts incurred to meet the costs of a new house, a marriage or some consumer item. Most of the households had very definite plans for their savings, which included both items of production and consumption. One household had purchased a television set and an elaborate sideboard, and had constructed a courtyard during the previous year. They were saving to establish a family chicken enterprise, as they said they had surplus grain with which to feed chickens and because they had observed the successful examples of chicken raising already established in the village. They had also visited the chicken-raising family in the village (household 6) who had told them there were not yet sufficient eggs produced in the region to meet demand. They had investigated the costs, and anticipated spending ¥3,000 on three cages of chickens; thus this household needed ¥1,000 for preliminary investment in one cage of ninety-six chickens to begin the cycle of producing grain for chickens, chickens for eggs and meat and manure for the grain lands. The household already raising chickens did not care to save; rather, they preferred to invest in the expansion of their chicken raising. The household head said: 'I save my money in chickens.' His previous investment of ¥3,000 had earned ¥7,000 the last year and he planned to raise 2,000 chickens the next year and 5,000 the following year, for he thought it was lighter work than cultivating in the fields. Many of the sample households were saving for new houses, which in this village cost around ¥15,000 each, for family weddings which were expected to cost ¥5–6,000 and for furniture. The villagers not only borrowed from but also lent substantial sums to friends and relatives.

The villagers were appreciative of the increase in their village and per capita incomes, the quality of their livelihood and the development of village facilities. The diversification of the village economy largely rested on household rather than village enterprises, and in many households there needed to be more investment and training in the most appropriate utilisation of local resources and enquiry into potential markets. The leaders had made plans for future village developments, some based on agricultural on-farm developments and some off-farm and collectively operated. The chief characteristics said to distinguish this village from others were the separation of wheat and maize cultivation, cutting stalks into the soil after harvest and the extensive utilisation of farm machinery. Many villages were said to be interested in following this model, and it was estimated that a total of about 1 million mu in the province had followed their example so that substantial time was taken up with the reception of visitors from other parts of China. It was planned to alter the present cropping patterns in order to either cultivate three crops of wheat, soy beans and maize in two years (or, more ideally, five crops in three years) and the village was already experimenting along these lines on 80 mu with a mix of wheat, maize and soya beans. It was planned that, as mechanisation displaced labour, and land contractors were reduced by half to some forty households, those not cultivating grain land would be transferred to mulberry lands which would have been expanded from 200 to 500 mu. This would have the advantage of increasing the supply of silkworms for the factory production of silk thread. In 1989, each orchard household managed 10 mu of fruit trees but, as the trees grew older and bore fruit, each contracted parcel of land was to be reduced to 3.5 mu as more labour was required. The village might then encourage some households producing vegetables to transfer to the orchard and the production of fruit. Finally, in a major new development, it was planned to import a silk commodities production line to weave the silk thread already produced in the village. On the whole, these villagers felt themselves to be busily engaged in their domestic mixed-economy activities and fortunate in their plans for the future.

SHANDONG VILLAGE A, 1991

Shandong village A is a small settlement in Shandong province made up of a number of mud-walled lanes, with each household having a high natural-wooden and gated doorway, and which in March still had its colourful red New Year posters which added a touch of brightness to the brown of the clay. Although the village was not far from the city of Zhucheng, it was entirely rustic with houses surrounded by clusters of crafted haystacks all with their distinctive circular plaited hats topping the rounded piles of straw. Surrounded by fields as it was, the village also benefited from its close proximity to one of Shandong's fast-expanding open cities with a population of more than a million and growing foreign and export markets. Although the city had no direct rail links, it was at the junction of a good highway system with ready access to a number of seaports. The village itself was not large, with 259 households and a total population of 1,052 persons reasonably evenly distributed between male and female and the different age groups. The average size of a household was 4.6 persons, with a range from one to eight persons. The village was reported to have a stable population with little movement of persons in or out of the village and a rising income the sources of which were mainly agricultural (Table 3.41).

In 1990, agriculture continued to provide more than 90 per cent of the village income, of which income cotton and grains made up more than 79 per cent (Table 3.42). Consequently, of the total number of labourers in the village (425), more than 86 per cent, or 348, worked in agriculture (201 males and 167 females) (Table 3.43). Each household in the village had a land allocation on which it cultivated both cotton and grains for sale and for consumption. The cultivation of cotton was labour-intensive and, in most households, family members cultivated cotton and in slacker seasons or spare time raised animals, cultivated vegetables or drove tractors. Only a minority of the villagers were categorised as 'non-agricultural', and they were employed in enterprises for making clothes, agricultural processing, building, transportation or services. It was estimated that there had been no major changes in the proportions of the village population working in the non-agricultural and agricultural sectors of the village; rather, the major change had been the expansion of sidelines by farming households so that many households had diversified their economies. The per capita income of the village was ¥1,000 in 1990, which was almost fifteen times that earned in 1978 (Table 3.44).

The steady rise in village income since the reforms was marked by major increases in 1983 coinciding with the distribution of responsibility lands, and in 1987 with the change-over to wheat and cotton intercropping, which led to an increase in the number of mu devoted to cotton (Table 3.45), and in grain and cotton yields (Table 3.46). In 1990 the lands of the village totalled 2,600 mu, which were divided between pure cotton (200 mu), wheat and cotton intercropped (900 mu), wheat and maize (1,100 mu), orchard (120 mu) and vegetables (80 mu). The total sum of 2,400 mu grain and cotton lands were divided between the households according to two sets of calculations. All persons in the village received 0.5 mu of land, called food-grain lands, which amounted to 526 mu of the village land; the rest, 1,874 mu, was distributed as responsibility lands to households on the principle of 40 per cent according to number of persons and 60 per cent according to number of labourers per household. That is, 40 per cent or 840 mu was distributed per person, making a total of 0.7 mu per person per household, while 60 per cent or 1,260 mu, was distributed exclusively to the labourers at 2.8 mu per labourer. A full labourer was defined as a male aged between eighteen and fifty-five years and as a woman between eighteen and forty-four years. Each woman, however, was only worth 0.7–0.8 of a full labourer, and as such only received 70 to 80 per cent of the male allowance. To take a hypothetical example, a household with four persons of whom one was a full labourer would receive 2 mu (four times 0.5 mu) of food-grain lands, 2.8 mu (four times 0.7 mu) responsibility lands and 2.8 mu (one labourer) making a total of 7.6 mu. The average amount of land received by a household was 10 mu, and only one family fully taken up with business had no responsibility or food-grain lands. Since there was very little difference in quality of lands, families received one or two blocks of land on the understanding that the higher the quality of land, the less land and the greater the social benefit payments due to the village. On the food-grain lands the household paid agricultural land tax of ¥3 per mu; on the responsibility lands, the household paid a number of taxes and levies including ¥3 per mu land tax, quota grain amounting to 60 kg per mu of wheat and 45 kg per mu of cotton sold to the government and ¥52 per mu cash for social benefits. These were made up as follows: education, ¥18; family planning, ¥1; army families, ¥3; public health, ¥2; transportation and maintenance, ¥1; militia drills, ¥0.5; social security, ¥1; for irrigation, ¥20; and the remaining (¥5.5) service fees, for village government and social welfare for the old and sick. Each household paid ¥52 per mu, or roughly the equivalent of ¥40 per person.

Although the food-grain and responsibility lands were managed by individual households, it was the village committee which decided the crops, the production timetable, the irrigation and mechanisation. It also provided a number of services, including the supply of production materials such as seed, fertiliser and chemicals and ploughing, drainage and planting by machines, which were all paid for by the households. For instance, the farm mechanisation team of the village was made up of four persons who provided services for ploughing, harrowing, harvesting, planting and shelling, maintained the machines, obtained diesel oil and arranged for and managed the irrigation system. The team, operating two large tractors made a charge for these services. For the ploughing, harrowing and irrigation, the village provided the machines, and each household paid ¥6.5 per mu service fee; planting of wheat also cost ¥1.5 per mu, and in 1990 the harvesting of wheat by reaper cost ¥2.5 per mu. During busy seasons, the villagers grouped into temporary mutual aid teams to make maximum use of the nineteen tractors owned by individual families and in which there was an informal system of payment from the team to the tractor-owning household.

The cultivation of cotton was labour-intensive, and it was estimated that the number of labour days required by cotton was forty-five per mu. Before mechanisation it took sixty labour days, and the reduction in labour days in cotton from sixty to forty-five took place with the mechanisation of spraying, which saved some fifteen days. The reduction in demand on labour permitted the expansion of household economic activities, including chickens, food processing, vegetables and various types of business. It was expected that with more machines, labour days would be further reduced by about 60 per cent to fifteen to twenty or so. A few households in the village specialised in fruit and vegetable production. The orchard (120 mu), established five years previously in 1987–88, was divided between nineteen households which tended fruit trees – mainly hawthorn and peach – and which only in the present year bore fruit. Most of these nineteen households had less responsibility lands than others in the village, and they were also charged ¥200 per mu social benefits compared to the usual ¥52 to offset the greater income expected from the orchard. The vegetable lands, 80 mu, were distributed so that each household received approximately 0.3 mu on which to grow vegetables, mainly cabbage, eggplant, chives and beans for their own consumption and for sale on the market. Additionally, an increasing number of villagers were taking part in a number of newly established activities in the village, including shops, marketing, selling vegetables, food processing, mushrooms, weeds for antibiotics and rabbit and chicken raising for consumption and for sale on the market. Many of these activities could be adjusted to the demands of the slack and heavy farming seasons, and were thus appropriate in a situation where there was little full-time surplus labour due to the labour-intensive demands of cotton. Most of the younger members of the village graduate from primary school and go on to attend junior middle school before working on the family farm. Although it was estimated that some 50 per cent of these students go on to attend senior middle school, Table 3.47 suggests that the proportion was lower, and there is reported to be an increasing trend for middle-school graduates to move into agricultural technical occupations, enterprises and industry.

This village had thus chosen to combine the major development of family enterprises with only the minor development of village enterprises. The majority of households thus concentrated on the cultivation of the land and developing other subsidiary economic activities. The balance between farming and other economic activities for each household was variable, with some households placing primary emphasis on farming and others primarily operating an enterprise. In the eight sample households, the main family enterprises were tractor driving, vegetable cultivation, tailoring, raising chickens and professional work (Table 3.48). All the households except one, which was fully given over to managing a machine-part shop, cultivated cotton and grain and raised pigs, which furnished a varying proportion of their incomes. The sample households earned an average per capita income ranging from ¥700 plus to ¥10,000, which makes the sample average higher than that for the whole village, which was reported to be ¥1,000, although of a similar range (¥800–10,000). The highest incomes were earned by those in business and enterprise, especially those to do with machine maintenance and poultry farming. Families with the lowest per capita income had fewer sidelines, but the village leaders thought that the differentials between most village households were not wide. After the deduction of production and living expenses, all the families had surplus income from the previous year, with some of the households having savings of as much as ¥30,000. Most had savings of more than ¥10,000 unless they had recently had an extraordinary expense such as the building of a house, purchase of a vehicle or the marriage of a son, and all were saving for a specific item or occasion such as a tractor, vehicle and a plough or a son's marriage. Most households had family plans for the expansion of their sidelines either immediately or as soon as grown children left school and augmented the family labour force, be it in bricklaying, chicken raising or some other activity. These family plans were encouraged by the village leaders who planned to provide support for family enterprises through the collective provision of services rather than developing their own village industries.

The village leadership planned to continue to combine village and family enterprises in the future, with most support to be provided for family enterprises through the collective provision of pre- and post-production services including the provision of larger machines less suitable for family operation and ownership. The village was paying particular attention to transportation and marketing services – that is, off-farm services for on-farm activities – with the aim of procuring stable markets, facilitating transportation and food storage and raising family incomes. A model for future village development of family operations was the poultry-raising enterprise. This had been jointly developed by a Zhucheng city foreign trade company, the village and family households, with the foreign trading company providing the supplies, chickens, feed and market, the village providing housing and equipment and the family supplying the labour. Originally, in 1985, the foreign trading company had approached the village and, after a shaky start, poultry raising was expected to be one of the stable and increasingly profitable activities in this region, which was already exporting one-quarter of all China's chicken meat, much of it to Japan. Local production was expected to increase from 6,000 tons in 1990 to 10,000 tons in 1993, and the expected profits to be had from feeding chickens were high, for there was little investment demanded from the household and no worries about marketing. Furthermore, the manure could be used in the fields. This complete service system, which solved the problems of supplies and marketing from 'tail to head and from head to tail', was known locally as 'the dragon service system'. Such an encapsulated enterprise was deemed a very suitable family activity in a village where most of the economic expansion was taking place at the household level, largely because of demands of cotton cultivation on labour which were unlikely to be reduced in the near future. According to villagers, plans for diversification of domestic sidelines with collective support were popular, their incomes had already risen and, if their past experience was anything to go by, they could look forward to the promise of 'a bright future'.

SHANDONG VILLAGE B, 1991

Shandong village B was located 15 kilometres from Longkou city and seaport which was also an 'open city' with a population of 600,000. However, although the city had a number of foreign ventures, the village was not thought to benefit especially from its proximity. With some resemblance, rather, to a town, Shandong village B consisted of a main paved street lined with shops, offices blocks, factory compounds and large, many-storeyed houses with elaborate twin-lined gateways stylistically and colourfully tiled, which all contributed to its urban ambience. Certainly the village had urban pretensions, judging by a wall mural in the main street portraying the village progressing towards the future as an urban street with urban facilities. The village had a total of 905 households, with a small average size of 3.36 persons and ranging from one to seven persons. The total population numbered 3,042, with almost half the population in the labour force (1,350). After a slow start there had been a steady rise in the contribution of industry to the village income (Table 3.49), amounting to more than 60 per cent in 1990 (Table 3.50), and in 1990 the majority of the labourers in the village worked in the village enterprises (Table 3.51). Household incomes derived from a variety of sources including the land, animal raising and, most importantly, factory wages.

The total area of land in the village amounted to 4,215 mu, which was divided between wheat and maize (1,900 mu), wheat and peanuts (400 mu), beans (300 mu) and pure peanuts (200 mu). There has been intercropping of wheat with maize and with peanuts since 1976, and the yields of both grains and peanuts have increased as a result (Table 3.52). The village has a two-field system of land distribution: on the one hand the food-grain lands were distributed on a per capita basis so that almost all persons in the village received 0.5 mu, on which they grew maize and wheat according to the village plan. Each family cultivated and harvested its own piece of land and paid the village ¥6 per year for its use. The rest of the grain land (1,515 mu) was distributed among the 166 farmers of the village who each received an average of 7 mu of land with little variation in size. Where food-grain or responsibility lands were variable in quality, the taxes on the land were adjusted accordingly so that those farming the more fertile lands paid higher taxes. The farmer was responsible for producing a combination of wheat and maize or wheat and peanuts in accordance with the village plan, and the village was responsible for arranging the supplies of fertiliser and chemicals as well as village machines to plant, harrow and irrigate the grain lands. The individual labourers paid for these services and also paid an agricultural tax of between ¥13 and ¥15 per mu depending on quality. In 1989 the costs of production, including fertiliser, chemicals, seeds and machine use, ranged between ¥64 (maize), ¥75 (wheat) and ¥99 (peanuts) per mu (Table 3.53). The village leaders said they had no trouble in procuring supplies of good seed, fertiliser and chemicals from the neighbouring city factories and service stations. The village owned a number of caterpillar tractors and trucks, which were used by the agricultural machinery team; in addition, twenty families in the village each owned a 20 hp tractor and a small number of implements, including ploughs and wagons. The families mainly used their tractors for field transportation work and made use of the village machine service to cultivate the crops. The mechanisation team consisted of thirty-four members who were divided into several groups to take charge of irrigation, maintenance or field services.

Each labourer supplied the village with 600 jin of quota grain (90 per cent in wheat and 10 per cent in maize), for which he received ¥0.267 per jin for wheat and ¥0.167 per jin for maize. Since the normal yields in this village were 690 jin per mu for wheat and 804 jin per mu for maize, the labourers either consumed or sold the remaining produce on the market at higher prices. Farmers usually produced 268 jin of peanuts per mu; 80 jin of this was due to the state, and above-quota produce was either consumed as oil or nuts by the household or sold on the market. It was estimated that the annual average income for each farmer from 7 mu of land amounted to ¥1,500. On the 1,200 mu of orchard lands, apples were the main fruit produced, along with smaller amounts of pears, grapes and apricots. There were 150 orchard workers who were divided into five groups, each responsible for approximately 240 mu of the orchard land. Their wages were calculated according to output, and each received approximately ¥2,000 per annum. On the vegetable lands, approximately twenty-five growers cultivated 1 mu, on which a wide variety of vegetables (especially tomatoes) was grown for sale in the market. The growers paid the same taxes on their land (¥13 per mu) as others and worked very intensively to earn approximately ¥4,000 per annum.

The agricultural labour force had been gradually reduced from 1,350 labourers ten years earlier and 450 five years earlier to 200, including thirty-four members of the agricultural machinery team. This reduction in numbers working the land was largely due to the mechanisation of ploughing, harvesting, sowing, shelling and spraying of crops. Before mechanisation, the cultivation of wheat and maize required sixty labourers per mu; after mechanisation, intercropped wheat and maize took 29.15 labour days, wheat and peanuts 33.2 labour days and pure peanuts 25.6 labour days. With further mechanisation, it was expected that the cultivation of the crops would take between four and six labour days. Finding alternative employment for those displaced from the land was not a problem given employment opportunities within and outside of the village. A significant number of village labourers (230–250) worked in enterprises outside of the village, and, since the end of 1990 in a reverse trend, the village had been recruiting labourers from outside the village for its expanding industries. There was said to be a shortage of village women workers between eighteen and twenty-five years, and the towel factory had recently employed fifty female workers in this age range from outside the village. Each year most of the young persons of the village are recruited into village enterprises after graduating from junior middle school (85 per cent) as only 15–20 per cent of the eighty to ninety village junior middle-school pupils pass the entrance examination to senior middle school (Table 3.54). Most senior middle-school graduates also work in village enterprises, although they are often later recruited into management positions.

In 1991 there were six main enterprises in the village, most of which had only recently been established. The bath towel factory was established in 1987 and the work force had already expanded from 100 to 160 persons. Formerly there were a number of smaller towel factories in the village which had been amalgamated once stable markets, including city department stores and provincial textile departments, were assured. The factory had recently expanded its machines from twelve to thirty-six, and there were plans to produce its own raw materials and dyes. The factory was said to be fortunate in that it had a number of contracts with textile factories in Shandong and other provinces which supplied raw materials and stable outlets. In 1990 the income from the towel factory was ¥3.329 million and the average salary ¥1,800–1,920. The less successful plastic factory, established in 1972, was the oldest enterprise in the village and, although it had thirty-five workers and an annual output of ¥0.65 million, there had been a steady decrease in the demand for its main product – plastic pipes – which was largely due to the increased competition from new rural enterprises which had contracts with chemical factories to supply cheap raw materials. The factory could not now offer its products at a competitive price on the market and the average wage was a low ¥1,600 per annum.

In contrast, the insulation factory was the pride and joy of the village. Established in 1986 with twenty-five workers, it was originally based on a family enterprise in the village which had developed to a stage where it needed more investment, work force and skills than the family could provide. It took some time to get established, but its income had risen since it had received some help from a technical expert from Shanghai. The value of total output was ¥0.25 million in 1989 and had doubled in 1990 to ¥0.5 million. In 1991 it had 100 workers, and there were plans for the factory to produce its own raw material although research had shown that it would require investment of ¥5 million. This factory, one of three of its type in China, had links with large factories in cities in other parts of China, and it was hoped to expand to produce output worth ¥3.5 million in 1991 although the current average wage was ¥1,600 per annum. In another case, the village hardware shop found that it had a good market for rubber and plastic goods and was thus encouraged in 1985 to establish a rubber and plastic enterprise to produce these goods. The factory began with eighteen labourers and in 1990 had a labour force of 115, with an output worth ¥0.5 million in 1990 and an average wage of ¥1,700 per annum. The most popular of its products were truck batteries, and the factory had many regular customers in Shandong and neighbouring Hebei province.

The high-tensile fibre factory, which was established in 1975 with twenty-five workers and an annual output of ¥0.3 million, had eighty-five labourers and an output worth ¥0.7 million in 1991. The factory, one of the first of its kind, was established largely due to the efforts of one much-travelled villager with extensive contacts who had introduced the idea into the village, and another villager who, working in the Wuhan iron and steel factory, established contacts and links between the two factories. The average wage was ¥1,700 per annum. The building materials factory began in 1983 with around twenty-seven workers producing ¥0.13 million output; in 1991 there were forty-five workers producing floor tiles with an output of ¥0.3 million. It was started when a villager visited Shenyang city and made an investigation into and formed links with a building factory to establish markets. The factory did not find it difficult to procure raw materials, it had received appropriate technical assistance from Shenyang and it had established a number of links with building companies in neighbouring cities which provided for regular customers.

In this fast-expanding village, per capita income had risen gradually over the past ten years and in 1990 the per capita income of the village was a high ¥1,222 (Table 3.49). There was not a great variation in the cash annual incomes earned by village labourers in agriculture (¥2,000), the orchard (¥2,000), the agricultural machinery team (¥2,200) and village enterprises (¥2,000), although vegetable farming, which usually entailed help from other family members, earned a high ¥4,000. The estimated average cash income of households in the village was ¥4,000–5,000 per annum with variations largely related to the number of labourers and especially factory-worker members rather than any other factor. In this village, family enterprises were rare; much more common was a mixed economy household with a variety of sources of income deriving mainly from a combination of agricultural activities and enterprise salaries. In the sample households, the main sources of gross household cash incomes, ranging from ¥1,161 to ¥2,667 per capita, or ¥4,050 to ¥20,710 per household (Table 3.55), were grain, pigs, vegetables or orchard and the salaries of enterprise workers. The proportion of income deriving from agriculture was low and the number of persons in each household employed full-time in agriculture was small, although most enterprise workers helped in their spare time with the cultivation and harvesting of grains (a light task now that machines undertook most of the work) and with the raising of animals.

The expenses of the households were mainly divided between the costs of production – which, for most of the households, were low, given that they only cultivated food-grain lands and raised a pig and chickens – and the costs of meeting daily needs. All the households had a cash surplus at the end of the year ranging from ¥1,400 to ¥10,000, which was added to the family savings to be used for extraordinary expenses. The village leaders estimated that 90 per cent of the village households had savings, and most of the sample households had plans to save for children's marriages (expected to cost ¥5,000 each), their children's higher education, house repairs or improvements or a consumer item (usually a refrigerator). Several of the families had built new houses or refurbished their houses in the past few years, which had usually necessitated a loan from a relative, since repaid. Apart from one family, which was saving for a share in a tractor, no family had any plans to save for production items or to establish or expand family enterprises as they all expected to be fully employed in agriculture or in enterprises.

In planning the future growth of its economy, based on the expansion of its enterprises, village leaders thought that, although the village income had risen over the past ten years, it was still not as high as it might have been and suffered in comparison with increases in other villages. There had been a village meeting in 1990 at which there had been some village criticism of the leaders who themselves admitted that they had been hesitant in supporting the new policies for many years. They had not been sure 'what was right and what was wrong' and therefore had not adhered closely to new government policies to expand village economic enterprises. They thought that 'if they retained a small boat, they could turn it around more easily than a large boat if there was a change in policy'. They now acknowledged that 'a large boat could steam ahead despite strong winds from any direction', and on this basis they had made new plans for 1990 to develop the orchard and expand enterprises, which involved making new investments of up to ¥5–6 million. They aimed to help present enterprises expand their range and number of products to include both traditional and popular products as well as highly fashionable products and those of high quality. To make up for their slow beginnings, the village leaders planned to double the income of village enterprises in the following year and again to double this sum the year after that. Following some dissatisfaction at the slow start to development, these ambitious plans had the enthusiastic support of the villagers, who now had higher hopes than previously for the future.

WUXI VILLAGE, 1991

Wuxi village, 10 kilometres from Wuxi city, did not have the clustered shape of a village; rather, its large square houses, mostly of two if not three storeys, were placed in right-angled lines leading off a straight vehicular track. The houses themselves rose perpendicularly in sharp straight lines out of a flat landscape of rice and vegetable fields in what had virtually become an untidy rural suburb amidst startling urban settlements and industrial development. The village was located in one of the most advanced of China's industrialised counties and it certainly benefited from its easy communication with Wuxi city – an important centre in the flows of information, goods and contacts between the village, city, province and foreign lands. The village had developed a number of flourishing industries and in 1990 they provided 98.5 per cent of village income (Table 3.56). This large urban village had 595 households, with an average size of 3.75 persons, and the population amounted to 2,234 persons with more than half – 1,288 (58 per cent) – of the village population of labour age. Only 10 per cent or 130 persons in the village remained in agriculture or agricultural enterprises (Table 3.57). The rest of the working population were employed in waged labour in the village enterprises (63 per cent), in enterprises outside of the village (20 per cent) or in services and handicrafts (7 per cent). Apart from a very few households which worked in agriculture, most of the households were made up of two or more labourers whose wages constituted the entire or major source of household income.

In the village there was a total of 1,470 mu of farming land, 95 per cent of which was used for cultivating grains (Table 3.58), mainly wheat and rice which were used to provide for the consumption of its members, approximately 500 jin per capita per year, and for payment of quotas due to the state. The village also had 15 mu of fisheries. The grain lands, first distributed in 1981, were ten years later divided into two main categories: food-grain land (1,085 mu or 77 per cent) and responsibility lands (320 mu or 23 per cent). The food-grain land was divided by the total population so that all persons had 0.45 mu of grain land and fodder land ranging from

0.035 to 0.036 mu per person. There was little difference in the quality of the grain lands, and the food-grain land was usually farmed in one or occasionally two blocks of land. Each household paid the village ¥22 per mu land tax for the use of the food-grain lands, for fertiliser (estimated to cost ¥44.83 per mu for wheat and ¥35.24 for rice) and for the services provided by the agricultural machinery team which undertook most of the farmwork (¥84.6 per mu). The 320 mu responsibility lands were divided into three parts: 150 mu collective farm, 150 mu shared between two households and 20 mu temporarily cultivated as food-grain lands. When the land was first divided in 1981, the 550 mu of responsibility lands were divided between 450 households, but several major changes in 1985 and 1986 resulted in the cultivation of responsibility lands by just two households. Each of these households had gradually accumulated more and more land, in a block each of 90 mu and 58 mu respectively, in order to facilitate mechanisation undertaken by the farm machinery team; it was thus frequently said that these lands were 'managed' rather than 'farmed' by the two households.

Mechanisation had played an important part in village development, with all households taking advantage of the comprehensive services provided by the agricultural mechanisation team of sixteen full-time members. These included ploughing twice a year for rice and wheat (¥10 per mu), harrowing (¥2.6), plant protection including cost of chemicals (¥20), field drainage (¥14), field irrigation canals (¥3), covering wheat after planting (¥2), seeds for those not using their own seeds (¥8), fertiliser transportation by the team paid for by the village at harvest (¥15) and rice transplanting, 60 per cent by the team (¥10), all making for a total of ¥84.6 per mu. The villagers themselves spread the fertiliser, did some weeding, levelled and cleared the land and dried the grain after the wheat and rice harvests, which was estimated to amount annually to five labour days per mu for wheat and nine labour days for rice. The yields on the food-grain land were on average 1,000 jin per mu rice and 450 jin per mu wheat, with the yields from the responsibility lands a little higher due to a subsidy of ¥100 per mu for additional fertiliser and other inputs. The two households cultivating responsibility lands also paid ¥22 per mu as land tax, but the village had also reduced its service charges for them so that the harvesting of wheat cost ¥12 instead of ¥15 per mu and plant protection ¥15 instead of ¥20. They also had the advantage that the village teams serviced their lands first. They estimated to take five to nine labour days per mu for wheat and rice respectively; and for help in the busy seasons, they hired the labour of either relatives or friends or from outside the village. Their quota grain had amounted to 1,100 jin per mu, after which they could dispose of the surplus as they saw fit, but in 1991 this quota had been raised to 1,200 jin per mu so that they were not unduly advantaged in terms of income.

One of the households consisted of a couple, each of whom was fifty-eight years of age, who cultivated 40 mu (now 58 mu) of farming responsibility land, a task which they reckoned took 150 labour days between them. At busy seasons they hired labourers who came from other provinces and were looking for short-term work, which cost them approximately ¥2,000–3,000 per year. The costs of production included the village machines at ¥70 per mu (or a total of ¥2,800), fertiliser and chemicals at ¥80–90 per mu (or ¥3,200) and village tax of ¥22 per mu (or a total of ¥880), making a grand total of ¥6,880. In 1990 they produced 16,000 jin of wheat, all of which was sold as quota grain to the village at ¥0.26 per jin, thus contributing ¥4,160 to their income. Of the 44,000 jin of rice produced, 5,000 jin were for their three pigs, 800 jin for their own consumption and 38,200 jin were sold at ¥0.40 per jin, or a total of ¥15,280. The farmer constantly referred to 'managing' the fields, and said that he did not find the farmwork too demanding, for his main work included pulling the weeds, spreading the fertiliser and draining the fields.

In the second household cultivating responsibility lands, a slightly younger couple in 1990 farmed 72.5 mu: 70 mu (now 90 mu) responsibility lands and 2.5 food-grain lands. They said that they worked most of their time on the land, although they also hired labour and tended their 129 pigs. Altogether they estimated that the 72.5 mu required 122 labour days per year. Their production costs (¥16,474) included fertiliser amounting to ¥80 per mu (or a total of ¥5,800), tax at ¥22 per mu (or ¥1,599), agricultural machine use at ¥70 per mu (or ¥5,075) and ¥4,000 for hired help in busy seasons. They produced 31,175 jin of wheat, of which 30,000 jin were sold as quota grain to the village at ¥0.27 per jin (or ¥8,100), 500 jin were used for consumption, and the remainder were used for seeds and feeding pigs. Of the 76,125 jin of rice produced, 47,000 were used as quota rice, earning ¥12,690 (¥0.27 per jin), 4,000 for consumption and 25,125 jin were sold in the market for ¥0.42 per jin, making a total of ¥10,552. Altogether, the household earned a gross income from grains of ¥31,342 which, after subtracting the production costs of ¥16,474, made for a net income of ¥14,868. Although both families had among the highest per capita incomes in the village and had both recently increased the size of their responsibility lands, they were also well aware that there were plans for their lands to be taken over by the village and incorporated into the collective farm. They said that they were not unduly upset by this prospect as they knew their incomes were high and they had already made the most of their high incomes to invest in expensive new houses and consumer items.

The collective farm, recently established in 1989, was 150 mu in size and was cultivated by eight contract labourers who each managed a number of mu and in return received a wage plus a bonus calculated according to output. The village paid the production costs, which were deducted from the profits after each harvest. One of the young contract workers was aged thirty-three and a mother, who, formerly an employee in the glove factory, had chosen this occupation because her parents-in-law had recently died, leaving her with no care for her two small children. She only provided the labour, and the contract she signed with the collective was based on 'three fixes and one flexible': that is, the costs of production were paid by the village including machines, tax, fertiliser, irrigation and power fees, making up a sum of ¥200 per mu. The agricultural output due to the village was fixed at 1,200 jin per annum (40 per cent wheat and 60 per cent rice), and the village had fixed the salary of the contract worker at ¥150 per mu. She could therefore expect a salary of ¥3,000, which was not dissimilar to the wage of an industrial worker. If she produced more than the fixed quota, she would receive a bonus commensurate with the surplus produced. The land was intensively mechanised, so she expected to be able to cultivate the fields without any help, and, to add to her income, she had begun to breed more than thirty piglets a year. The contracting-out of collective farmland was an experiment which had only been in operation for one year, but already it was planned that all the responsibility lands would be incorporated into the collective farm within three years. The village had taken this decision so that the village, rather than individual households, might benefit from the profits. Within the existing system, the farmers achieved high yields and high incomes, but they did use the surplus as they pleased and mostly for consumption, hence little profit had been reinvested in agriculture or in other activities to the benefit of the village. Now that most of the villagers were employed in enterprises, the incorporation of the responsibility lands into a collective farm would directly reduce the incomes of just two households and at the same time provide employment for a number of contract labourers in the village.

There were few agricultural enterprises in this village, but one of the most important was based on the mulberry lands (53 mu) which were managed by one household, and the others specialised in pig raising, with each having more than thirty pigs. Pig farmers received from the village a ¥15 cash subsidy as well as ¥5 per pig from the township and county to encourage pig raising, but because these subsidies had encouraged over-production, the market for pigs in 1991 was 'not good'. One household made up of an elderly couple raised 150–170 pigs per year for slaughter, together with eleven hogs and five sows. The pigs were sold at around ¥280–296 each, with a profit of ¥50 on each after meeting production costs amounting to ¥110 for the purchase of the piglet and ¥136 for feeding materials purchased from the feeding materials company. This household had expanded its pig raising in 1983 when it became a 'specialised pig-raising' household; until 1988 it had responsibility lands which members said they had not minded giving up once they had an alternative activity. There was a village orchard, 12.7 mu of peach trees and grape vines, which were tended full-time by an elderly couple. They supplied manure, pruned, loosened the soil and produced 8,000 jin of peaches and 2,000 jin of grapes for sale in the farmers' market. Their gross income from these two fruits was ¥8,300, but the production costs amounted to ¥3,000 made up of ¥8 per mu inputs, tax at ¥22 per mu and ¥2,000 for the hiring of casual labour during the fruit-picking season, when students, young persons and part-time labourers were paid ¥4 each day. Finally, there was also a fishery which employed three labourers.

Very few of the village labourers continued to be employed in agriculture. Rather a high percentage worked in industry either within or outside of the village. There was thus some mobility in and out of this village, 262 (or 20 per cent) of whom worked in the township (112), in the city (41) and in business services and private enterprises outside the village (61), and 48 worked in the enterprises of neighbouring villages. There was also some movement of labour into the village. By 1990, 101 labourers, some of whom were technicians, had been recruited into a variety of village enterprises, including forty-six labourers with special technical skills who worked in the glove-knitting factory. Most of the village labourers were employed in one of the nine enterprises, which had almost all expanded to constitute a very important component of the village economy (Tables 3.59 and 3.60) and an important source of employment in the village. The dyeing and chemical factory which was established in 1977 with fifteen labourers had 400 employees. It had expanded in 1983 when it acquired an international export market and links with chemical and dyeing factories in Jilin, Dalian, Wuxi and Shanghai. The drying lacquer and soft-drink machinery factory was established in 1975 with seven persons, and by 1990 it employed 180 persons after developing links with the Nanjing Light Industry group machine factory in 1987, which had led to rapid expansion. The boat-building factory was established in 1985 with nineteen labourers and had since expanded to eighty labourers. It was now a joint venture with Jiangsu and Wuxi shipbuilding factories, supplying spare parts for them and for the market.

The spare-parts textile factory began in 1985 with eleven labourers; in 1990 it had sixty workers, expanding as its links with Wuxi textile factories were formalised. The iron-casting material factory began in 1958 and had developed from ten to twenty-five workers because its products had such a good market that there was said to be no need for a permanent contract with a link factory. This factory only developed after 1984 when the factory head was changed, technical expertise increased, the market enlarged and the factory expanded. The aluminium alloy factory was established in 1986 with eight workers, but once links were established with Wuxi interior decorating factory and the Wuxi building design academy, its work force expanded to thirty persons. The concrete pipe factory opened in 1986 with seven workers, and in 1991 it had twenty-five in the labour force. Again, as for the iron-casting materials factory, there was said to be no need for contracts as there was a good local market for simple pipes for irrigation. In 1989, an engineering mechanical facility factory had been established with three to four persons in the work force and in 1991 they still only numbered ten. This factory was identified as the least successful factory of the village, largely because its links with a Guangxi provincial factory which had been set up by a relative of one of the villagers were unstable due to some readjustment within that factory. The glove factory opened in 1985 with sixteen persons in the work force. At first it had a contract with a factory elsewhere which was unsatisfactory and did not give it a sufficient market, but since 1990 links have been developed with Wuxi city textile factory and the work force increased to forty members.

In most of these factories it was linkages and contracts for materials and markets which were important to the growth of the enterprises. Some of these links were initiated by the factory/village and some by the customers searching for a market or product, some were established through relatives or friends, and others were said to be due solely to the quality and demand for the product. The village leaders set great store on the importance of information and the need to go outside of the village to acquire linkages and contracts. Given that each of the surrounding villages, townships and counties were also developing small, medium and large enterprises, their assessment of the importance of information and links making for steady supplies of raw materials was certainly correct. The enterprises were also important in providing employment for school leavers. Most of the young persons of the village attend junior middle school, with a quarter going on to senior middle school (Table 3.61). In 1990, of the forty junior middle-school pupils graduating in the village, ten passed the examination into senior middle school and almost all the rest were recruited into the village industries, with a few going on to technical school. Of the six or seven who graduated from senior middle school, one went on to university and the rest were recruited into technical positions in the village.

Per capita income in the village had risen tenfold over the previous ten years to a high ¥1,430 in 1990 (Table 3.56). The average labourer's wage was ¥2,000–2,500, with the lowest labourer's wage (¥1,000) for enterprise apprentices and the highest (¥20,000) for a private business entrepreneur. In addition to enterprise wages, which constituted the sole or major source of household income, households also earned small amounts from raising pigs or selling surplus food-grain, with a few households specialising in one activity or another. The sample households had per capita incomes ranging from ¥1,000 to ¥5,000 (Table 3.62). Those with the lowest per capita incomes had one rather than two full-time workers and worked in agriculture (although not on responsibility lands) rather than industry, whereas the highest per capita incomes of the sample households derived from cultivating responsibility lands. Most of the households had substantial surplus cash at the year's end ranging from ¥2,000 to ¥12,000, and all the households had elaborate plans for the future. Without exception, the households had saved or were saving for extraordinary expenses, including new or refurbished houses, marriage (which was expected to cost ¥10,000–20,000) and expensive consumer items (such as colour television sets and refrigerators). The few agricultural enterprise households (over-represented in the sample), such as the pig-raising household, were planning to expand their income-generating activities. Households with waged labourers and only very minor sideline activities were not planning to expand these, for they had neither the spare labour nor any interest in so doing. Any debts accrued by these households were caused by the heavy expenses of housebuilding, and loans from relatives and friends were gradually repaid.

The village planned to pursue present trends of growth and expansion in the future. It was expected with further mechanisation that labour days in the fields would be further reduced from five to 2.5 (wheat) and nine to four (rice) per mu, with a corresponding rise in yields. The labour saved was to be employed in an expanding and improved set of village industries. Given that the village was located in one of the most industrialised counties in China, it was not surprising to find that the village leaders were greatly committed to further industrialisation, that they had the support of township and county governments and that the villagers were anticipating further enjoyment of the combined benefits of urban incomes and durables with rural housing space and food supplies.

YUNNAN, 1991

The Yunnan villages were nestled in forested mountains in the east of the province near the Guangxi border; some were only accessible by mud road in dry weather, and then for the majority of the villagers only by foot or, for a privileged minority, by mule. Others villages could only be reached by a foot track. The houses were mostly of yellow clay or mud with natural wood beams and thatch, picturesque on the outside, but so very poor and dark and sometimes chokingly dusty within. Because there was little in the way of furniture, bedding, clothes or food beyond the barest of essentials, it was usually a case of crouching or sitting on slabs of wood a few inches off the ground, making this stay and these interviews physically very taxing. There was no drinking water in the vicinity of the village for much of the year, when villagers had to trek four hours to and from the nearest source of water sometimes twice a day. There was no electricity in the village, and some of the villagers were so poor that they could not even afford the sticks, paper or matches to light their way from house to house after dark. The villages were located in one of the poorest 273 counties of China, defined because their per capita income was around or below ¥150 and grain consumed per person less than 400 jin per annum. In one village of 533 persons, 35 per cent of the population were Yi and Miao nationalities (Table 3.63), and although this was often given as an explanation for poverty in the region, it is important to emphasise that the terrain, inaccessibility and resource base was such that any inhabitants would have difficulty in developing household and village economies. More than half of the ninety-seven village households had practically no cash income, and the lack of cash to purchase even the most basic of necessities was the most oft-cited characteristic of the village. For those with a small cash income, the sources of cash were few, for the households commonly farmed only a small portion of land and raised a few animals, for there were sparse opportunities for employment off the farm.

The village, in common with other poor, remote and mountainous villages in this region, lacked available flat arable land; of the 540 mu of cultivable land available to the village, about half was categorised as 'flat', with the remaining sloped, sometimes steeply (Table 3.64). In the village the per capita allocation of arable land amounted to around 0.5 mu, which, for a high proportion of the village households, was not enough to permit the cultivation of sufficient yields to supply 400 jin of grain per person per year. The flat arable land yielded around 400 jin per mu and, despite the scrupulous cultivation of maize on the high slopes, the yield on these slopes amounted to a bare 100 jin per mu. Maize was the main crop, together with a very small amount of wheat, but with yields of the latter so low (around 30–50 jin per household), many of the households said that they had given up planting wheat. Six per cent of the grain produced in the village was used to pay agricultural tax, 4 per cent for quota grain paid to the state and 90 per cent was used for consumption. It was estimated that the per capita output of grain was 433 jin, of which the per capita consumption of maize was 391 jin. However, at least half of the households in the village were short of grain for two to three months in the year, and the poorest households were short for four to six months of the year.

A sample of eight households representing a range of incomes and embracing both the richest and poorest households revealed that half of the households had less than 257 jin per capita for consumption and that two-thirds had grain shortages of between two and six months a year (Table 3.65). These shortfalls were generally due to lack of cultivable and especially flat land, but they were also due in some cases to the increasingly uneven distribution of land in the village because of changes in the composition of each household. Indeed, there was hardly a household that had the same number of persons as in 1982 when the land was originally distributed, and so there were wide variations in the land held per capita in 1991. The sample households ranged between per capita allocations of 0.625 mu and 1.25 mu. The poorest households in the village were those whose land allocations were grossly inadequate to support family members.

For instance, there were reported cases in the village where five persons were living on one person's allocation of land, or less than 1 mu. In one of the village hamlets, three of the four poorest households had land for one person supporting a large household – in two cases, of five or more persons. In the first household, the second son divided from the main household taking his portion of land; since that time he had married and had three children, so that five persons now had to be supported by his land. In the second of the poorest households, it was the daughter's original portion of land which was required to support her household and three children; and in the third household, the first son originally had land for his wife and son, but after his first wife died, he remarried and had four more children, so that by 1991 land for three persons was supporting seven persons.

In addition to cultivating grain, most households raised a few animals which, in the absence of alternative economic activities in the village, assumed prime significance in determining the wealth, cash income and welfare of peasant households. Animals were the most important single source of cash income and also for savings for extraordinary or unexpected expenses. However, their numbers were not plentiful, and it might be said that they still constituted a scarce and vulnerable resource. The type and number of animals in a household was the most cited measure of wealth in a village and was officially used to categorise households into three groups – 'poor', 'very poor' and 'not poor' (Table 3.66). Those households with a number of animals were 'not poor' and those with few or none were 'very poor'. Chickens were the most numerous of domestic livestock kept in the village (3.5 per household), followed by pigs (2.6) and cattle, horses or mules (1.4). Poor households found raising animals a problem because of their difficulties in providing cash to purchase the animal, housing space for animals and the labour required for obtaining fodder, which, in the absence of any surplus grain supplies, had almost all to be collected from the mountains. What was also very noticeable was the high death rate of animals, with chickens and pigs particularly at risk, and which was exacerbated by the almost complete absence of animal husbandry and veterinary services.

Household 1, 'not poor', raised one head of cattle (draught), five pigs and twenty chickens, of which seventeen had died during the year. It sold one of the pigs for ¥150, which it regarded as a poor return for the amount of work, especially fodder collection, involved in its raising. Household 2, also 'not poor', raised four cattle, seven to eight pigs and no chickens, for they had all died the previous year. This household had sold two pigs for a sum of ¥560 and one head of cattle for ¥260. Household 3, 'very poor', raised just one piglet which it had killed at the New Year; all its chickens had died. Household 4, 'not poor', raised two head of cattle, one of which it had sold for ¥280. It had also raised ten pigs: three pigs were killed for feasting as payment for help with housebuilding, and one sow and six piglets were all sold for a total of ¥60. The household raised ten chickens, although neither the chickens nor the eggs had been sold in the previous year. Household 5, 'poor', raised one head of cattle, purchased a horse for ¥160, and of the five pigs raised in the previous year, three had died and one was killed, leaving just one live pig. Of the chickens raised last year, thirty died and ten were sold for ¥7 each. Household 6, also 'poor', raised two head of cattle, one adult and one young, three pigs which all died, and twenty chickens which also all died. Household 7, 'very poor', sold its one head of cattle to repay a long-standing debt, it exchanged its pig for grain, and its eighteen chickens all died. Ten eggs were sold at ¥0.25 each. Household 8, also 'very poor', acquired one head of cattle as a loan from the village; one horse was sold to repay an outstanding debt; one pig was given to the household by a distant relative; the chickens also donated by relatives had all since died.

Unless a household could raise a pig to adult weight, the returns were not considered to be 'good', and, given the high death rate and vulnerability of chickens and pigs to disease and the absence of veterinary services, this seems to have constituted some feat. Despite the risks, animal husbandry continued to be popular, for it was one of the very few means of generating wealth and formed one kind of security. There was, and there was seen to be, a direct correlation between the number of animals and the cash income and wealth of a household, with the animals themselves not only used as a way of accumulating wealth, but also as a means of exchange for grain and labour between neighbours and relatives and for repayment of debts. If the range of on-farm opportunities for income generation were very limited, so also were the off-farm opportunities to earn an income in the village.

There was no collective enterprise in the natural or administrative village, and even in the township the proportion of population employed in enterprises outside of agriculture was small. The only individual enterprise in the village was a grain-processing household, which undertook to process wheat or grind flour with machinery that had been previously operated by and was now rented from the village. After meeting the costs of processing, the rent of the machine (¥30) and the oil (costing ¥44 per month), the income of the household was not high given the low costs for the service (¥1.2 per 100 jin), and because many of the households were so poor they did not have the cash to pay. The household estimated that it made a profit of between ¥100–200 per annum, although their neighbours thought that this sum was an underestimation. The lack of opportunities to earn a cash income in the villages privileged those on a monthly salary, including the administrative village cadres (average ¥50) and schoolteachers (¥50–120), whose regular state incomes placed them in a different category from the rest of the villagers. It was the woman schoolteacher who lent small sums of cash to her fellow villagers and assumed some responsibility for their welfare. The other source of off-farm income was the remittances of family members temporarily or permanently absent from the village. A few of the adult males left the village for one to two months during the annual slack seasons, mainly to undertake terracing and other construction projects within the township or county. A few households had younger members working outside of the village who sent back remittances supplementing the family cash income, and in one unusual instance a young couple working outside the village had managed to save and borrow ¥5,000 to contribute towards the cost of the only new house in the village.

In the absence of a wide range of opportunities to generate a cash income, the average per capita income in this poor village lay just on the poverty line, at ¥150, which was lower than that of the administrative village and township (Table 3.67). The proportion of households categorised as 'poor' whose average per capita net incomes were less than ¥150 was 56 per cent (fifty-four) and fifteen were categorised as 'very poor' with no or a very low cash income. Poor households had in common a low per capita arable land with a shortage of grain and few animals, and they frequently suffered a shortage of labour through premature death, physical illness or disability and mental incapacity (Table 3.68). The range in per capita incomes was from nothing to ¥227 in the natural village, and in the sample households between ¥6 and ¥108.5, with the main differences caused by the number of pigs and cattle raised and sold, whether a household cultivated and sold rapeseed (although no household earned more than ¥55 from this source) and whether they received remittances from outside the village (Table 3.69). Only one or two of the poorest households were eligible for relief in the form of cash, clothing, grain or grain subsidies, and the largest cash expenses each year for those house-holds not eligible for relief grain was the purchase of the grain during grain-short months. Other basic cash expenses included clothing, salt, cooking oil and kerosene, which in the poorest households were all in short supply.

Those categorised as poor but with small cash incomes invested in piglets and other animals; those not so poor additionally purchased fertiliser. Other cash expenses included education fees of ¥11–12 for each of the two semesters. In the sample households the major cash expenses ranged from those affording only few yuans' worth of salt to those which could afford ¥71 for fertiliser, ¥283.5 for grain and school fees for three children (¥66) (Table 3.70). In addition to the ordinary cash expenses to do with living and production, there were periodic extraordinary expenses including medical expenses, and marriage (¥500). Because these regions were mountainous, remote and poor, which made for difficulties in living, including the carrying of water and firewood, girls were reluctant to marry into these villages, a factor which raised the payments to the bride's family and hence high costs in relation to income. The price of coffins averaged ¥300, and under the village eaves these were frequently stacked awaiting their elderly occupants. Many households went into debt to meet these extraordinary expenses.

Only a very few households were estimated to have any savings, for there was seldom any surplus cash left at the end of the year; rather, 'poor' and 'very poor' households commonly incurred debts to meet the ordinary expenses of purchasing necessary grain, while even households categorised as 'not poor' incurred debts to meet the costs of extraordinary occurrences such as illness, marriage and death. The sources of credit to meet these expenses were mainly relatives, neighbours and friends, and most commonly the wife's mother, who lived in another village. In order to repay debts, a household often raised an extra pig specifically for this purpose. Not all debts were repaid, and, interestingly, some members of the present generation had inherited debts from generations past which were still due for repayment. In one household interviewed there was still an outstanding debt of ¥70 incurred by the father's father in the 1970s; in another household the son had not yet been able to repay his inherited debts of ¥700–800 incurred by his now dead father, who had borrowed to build a new house. In the sample households there was a range of debts. Household 1, 'not poor', had no savings, for a son had married the previous year and, to meet the expenses of ¥1,000, ¥500 had been borrowed from a sister-in-law, of which ¥200 had so far been repaid. Pigs were being raised to pay off the remainder. Additionally, some years ago, the mother had been ill and the costs of her hospitalisation had amounted to ¥800, ¥600 of which had been borrowed from her brother, which had taken five years to be fully repaid. Household 2, 'not poor', had no savings and no debts. Household 3, 'very poor', had no savings, and this year the son had borrowed ¥30 from the village schoolteacher to purchase a piglet to raise. He planned to repay her when the pig was sold.

In household 4, 'not poor', the daughter and son-in-law had saved and borrowed their contribution of ¥5,000 to the cost of the newly rebuilt house the previous year. In 1982 the father had borrowed ¥500 to purchase a head of cattle, which he had since repaid. Although this farmer had no outstanding debts, he did not think of himself as solvent as he had put all of his money into the house and was consequently having difficulties in raising the cash to purchase fertiliser. Household 5, 'poor', had no savings and no debts. Household 6, also 'poor', had no savings, but the mother had borrowed ¥100 from her sister at the New Year to cover living expenses. Household 7, 'very poor', had no savings, and the husband had borrowed ¥500 in 1984 to get married, which he had come to think of as a poor investment since his unseen wife had been retarded. In order repay this debt he had sold a head of cattle the previous year. In the past year he had borrowed ¥70 to take his child to hospital; the child had died and the funeral cost ¥20 (a loan which he will have to repay sometime). According to neighbours, this household had perpetually borrowed small amounts from other villagers to purchase grain and other daily necessities. Household 8, also 'very poor', had no savings and was in receipt of a loan for ¥120–130 which it was not expected to repay. This household had sold its horse the previous year to repay a debt of ¥150 to a relative who had needed the money quickly. This household had received several animals from relatives who did not expect repayment given that the household ordinarily had no cash income.

Perhaps the most important factors determining the income, well-being and welfare of individual households, in addition to land allocations and the number of family members of labouring age, were the health and capacities of the labourers. In the village there were more women in the labouring population than men, which reflected the higher proportion of women in the village population and the high death rate among males around forty years of age who were said in the village to suffer 'rapid death' (Table 3.71). Generally, there was a shortage of labour largely because water, firewood, vegetables and fodder had to be collected and carried some distance, but households most at risk were those which suffered a shortage of labour due to premature death, non-marriage and mental incapacity. The very poorest households in the village had all suffered chronic disease, premature death or mental incapacity, or had a high number of either elderly or young dependants. In the sample households, health profiles revealed that few households had escaped illness and death.

In household 1, of five persons, and 'not poor', the mother had suffered a serious illness some years before but had recovered in recent years. In household 2, of ten persons, and 'not poor', there had been no serious illness in recent years. In household 3, of two persons, and 'very poor', the widow was in a constant state of ill health with an eye problem. In household 4, of seven persons, and 'not poor', two boys and a daughter had died: one son had died three days after birth from tetanus – he had been carried to hospital, which would not accept him once he was diagnosed as having tetanus; another son, three years old, died in hospital probably from pneumonia; the seven-year-old daughter also died from pneumonia, apparently 'very fast', before a doctor could be consulted. In household 5, of six persons, and 'poor', there had been a series of 'small illnesses'. In household 6, of six persons, and 'poor', one child of two years old had died rapidly within two days of falling ill with high fever; the husband had a persistent cough and was ill with frightening stomach cramps every two weeks during which 'he seemed to die'. He had not consulted a doctor for some years but took herbal medicine, though some years earlier he had consulted a doctor at the county hospital, a visit paid for by his brother. In household 7, of four persons, and 'very poor', one two-year-old son had died from dysentery after a visit to the township hospital; the mother was mentally incapacitated and not in good health, and one of the daughters was also mentally retarded. In household 8, of four persons, and 'very poor', both parents were mentally incapacitated. Eight children had been born and five had died. This was not the only case in the village where such a high proportion of children in one household had died. In one other household, four of the children died at birth and one died when she was two years old; the mother had perpetual illnesses and an eye problem for which she had once received medicine ten years earlier at the township hospital, but to no effect.

With health profiles such as these and a paucity of resources and services in this isolated and remote village, the villagers felt that they had experienced very few changes in their activities and lifestyles in the previous few years. After a number of years of little change, they were more hopeful that poverty alleviation programmes, much talked about locally, would bring about improvements in their livelihoods. They felt their hopes had some foundation now that the village had recently received some help to begin a well-building programme. This help, from a foreign non-governmental organisation, had taken the form of dynamite for blasting local rocks and the provision of cement. The men of the village were all busy building wells with much touching intricate care and attention, in the hope of improving their water supply in the near future. Without this sign of a more hopeful future, making for much busy activity and community enthusiasm, the morale in the village would have been much lower and hopes fewer.

GUANGXI, 1991

The two Guangxi villages, made up entirely of Zhuang and Yao nationalities (Table 3.63), were located in the stone mountains, a line of tall, almost perpendicular, stark stone with high, zigzag rocky tracks and narrow, stony paths winding perilously around steep mountain sides to villages tucked away in dips, valleys and basins. The houses were made of wooden slatted sticks built high off the ground on stilts, flimsy at best and bare or treacherous at worst. The houses were nestled among luxurious foliage worthy of sub-tropical tourist brochures and quite belying the very remote, isolated and poverty-stricken villages that they were. Above all, they were quite inaccessible. One could only be reached along a dry-weather track of such perpendicular peril that I refused to let the jeep take me on a second visit; the other could only be reached by climbing high, steep mountain paths 18–24 inches wide along which all goods had to be back-carried in and out of the village. The inexperienced clamberer could. only marvel at the inhabitants' bare-footed dexterity on the sharp stones and their practised eye for such precarious heights, sometimes demanding the use of all four limbs. These villages were typical of a region in which more than 80 per cent of the natural villages could not be reached by road. Neither of the villages surveyed had electricity, and in one of them, the source of water was one hour's walk from the village. In the other there was, unusually in this region, a source of drinking water within the village. In almost half of the villages in the region, drinking water had to be carried over 1 kilometre of rocky terrain. Each village had a small number of households, usually thirty to sixty, which were even more poverty-stricken than the previous villages in Yunnan province. They all had little land, very few income-generating activities and almost no cash income.

In both villages studied there was only a very small portion of flat arable land, less than 15 per cent, and that lay at the bottom of such high-steeped basins that farmers had to clamber down almost perpendicular slopes to till the land, or alternatively, given the scarcity of flat arable land, climb to the tops of the almost perpendicular mountains to find cultivable patches between high, rocky outcrops where even just one plant might be placed. In the villages the average per capita allocation of cultivable land was 1 mu or less, with the per capita allocations of flat land ranging between a low 0.5 and 0.11 mu per person (Table 3.64). Here again changes in household composition had led to an increasingly uneven distribution between households. Despite scrupulous cultivation of maize, the yields in the stone mountains averaged 200 jin per mu, with 150 jin per mu in the highlands and 300–400 jin per mu in the flat lands. In the stone mountains, the average amount of grain per capita for consumption was a low 221 jin per mu, and in the absence of sufficient grain for consumption the state had waived grain taxes and quotas. Even so, all households in the two villages were short of grain for several months, which constituted a considerable handicap given than the staple diet was coarse grain porridge and wild vegetables. In the region, roughly 80 per cent of the households were eligible for relief grain, with the remaining number permitted subsidised grain.

The cultivation of small amounts of land was the primary occupation in the village, and in the absence of alternative economic activities, animal husbandry here also assumed prime significance in determining the cash income and welfare of the peasant households. As in Yunnan, the type and number of animals in a household was an important gauge of wealth in a village, and was used as a measure to categorise households as 'not poor', 'poor' and 'very poor'. Many households in the administrative village had no animals or only raised chickens (Table 3.72). In one of the natural villages there were thirty-seven households raising seventeen cattle, twenty-eight goats, twenty-five pigs and a number of chickens, with a high proportion (27 per cent), or ten, of the households having no animals. In four random households of this village, one 'poor' and one 'very poor' household had no livestock, a third, 'very poor', had a share in a pig supplied by the widow's sister, and a fourth household, the richest in the village, raised one small pig which it sold for ¥150, eight goats of which it sold one for ¥20, and fifteen chickens from which there was no income. In another of the natural villages of fifty-three households there were thirty-four cows, three goats per household, 140 pigs distributed among thirty-three households and 126 chickens, or two per household. Some households raised no animals, and again there was a direct correlation between the wealth of a household and the number of its animals. In three random examples, one relatively well-off household purchased one head of cattle the previous year for ¥170, raised two goats and raised two small pigs which it purchased the year before for ¥30 each. It sold one pig for ¥200 and raised two hens. Another household, 'poor', raised two goats and one hen and chickens, ten of which it sold for ¥6 per chicken. A third, a 'very poor' household, raised no animals.

In each village there was an extra and sometimes extraordinary economic activity which gave the villagers a source of cash income. In one village, rare lizards were collected and sold at ¥6, each furnishing one of the most important sources of village income, and in another village, tung-tree oil and seeds produced a cash income. The poorest households, without these assets or activities, resorted to the collection of firewood for sale in the market, the collection of mountain weeds and the weaving of the odd bamboo mat. There were no collective enterprises in any of the administrative villages studied, and even in the townships, the proportion of population employed outside of agriculture was less than 2 per cent and then they were employed in service activities such as building construction and transportation rather than enterprises. Again, as in Yunnan, one of the highest and most regular of cash incomes was the monthly salary paid to administrative village cadres (average ¥50) and schoolteachers (range ¥50–120), which privileged them above the rest of the villagers. A small cash income might be earned during slack seasons by the males of the households who left the village for one to two months a year for a variety of destinations, including the township, the county town and other mountainous regions in order to participate in terracing and other construction projects. These movements were not organised by villages or townships; rather, individuals looked to their own initiative for road building, stone breaking, building construction or the collection of water, firewood and field construction in other villages. The income derived from these activities was very variable. On average, men brought back ¥20–30 after working for twenty days or so at ¥15–18 per day, although some brought back no cash, for they had either not found work or only sufficient to pay for their board and food while outside the village.

All the households in the administrative and natural villages within the township were categorised as 'impoverished', in that 100 per cent of the population had a net income of less than ¥150 and 400 jin of grain. They were subdivided into 'poor' and 'very poor' households (Table 3.66). As in Yunnan province, poor households had in common low per capita arable land with a shortage of grains, few animals and less labour with a cash income of less than ¥150 net per capita. The 'very poor' households had a per capita land ratio higher than the average in the village. They frequently suffered a shortage of labour through premature death, physical illness or disability, or mental incapacity, which was especially a problem where water, firewood, vegetables and fodder all had to be collected and carried some distance to and from the village. There was a higher proportion of dependants in the stone mountain villages, and there was a significant difference between the proportions of males and females who made up the labouring population (Table 3.71). As in Yunnan, this was the result of the higher death rate among males around forty years old who were said in the villages to suffer 'rapid deaths'. The 'poor' and 'very poor' households in the village commonly suffered a shortage of labour due to premature death, non-marriage and mental incapacity, or had a number of small children. In the two villages studied, the poorest households were reported to be those where either the adult male or female had died leaving a widowed partner and dependent children, either young in age or disabled. In one such household of three persons, a father had died and a child was handicapped; in another, the single occupant was dying, and in a third, of four persons, two children had died of pneumonia and dysentery and the mother was chronically sick. In poor households there was much illness and sickness, some of which was chronic and had lasted several years.

The average per capita cash income in these poor villages was around ¥70–80 (Table 3.67), which was lower than the average (¥188) for the township, a figure which included the value of grain consumed as well as cash which, in the poor villages, was so little that even basic necessities were beyond the reach of villagers. There was a paucity of furniture, bedding, clothes and food other than the most basic, and even medicines were beyond the reach of the households. The villagers reported that 'the main problem for all the poor households in the village was lack of cash income'. The cash incomes of eight sample households displayed the paucity of resources. In household 1 of seven persons, and 'not poor', the cash income was ¥200 derived from tung oil, fruit and the sale of bamboo sheets; while in household 2, 'poor', the household earned ¥200 – all from tung oil. The cash income of household 3, with three persons, and 'very poor', was a low ¥30 earned from tung seeds, but even so it earned more than household 4 of one person who, with no cash income at all, was totally dependent on relatives for support. Household 7, with seven persons, was the richest household in the village, earning a high cash income of ¥1,214 from the sale of a pig (¥150), ¥500 from tung oil, ¥20 from its goat, with the remainder (¥564) made up of the salary of the father, who was the village leader. In another village, household 5, of five persons, and 'not poor', earned ¥490 from collecting lizards (¥240) and from the sale of a pig (¥200), and ¥50–60 was earned by the father when he worked out of the village for a couple of months. Household 7, of four persons, was 'very poor' with no animals and no cash income, despite the fact that the father had left the village to find work. He had returned after earning only enough to cover his expenses. Household 7, of four persons, and 'poor', earned ¥200 by collecting and selling firewood and ¥60 from the sale of its chickens.

The largest cash expense for those households not eligible for relief grain was the cost of their grain supplies to cover grain-short months. In one administrative village of 298 households, 130,000 jin of subsidy grain was sold to the village at the subsidised rate of ¥0.19 per jin, which averaged out at a cost of ¥82.88 per household. Other basic cash expenses included clothing, salt, cooking oil and kerosene, but there was little evidence of any of these in the poorest households. Some of those households categorised as 'poor' had sufficient cash to invest in piglets and other animals, but no household in these stone villages purchased fertiliser. Other cash expenses included educational fees amounting to ¥22 per year, and in addition there were extraordinary expenses requiring cash sums which households had to meet from time to time, including marriage, medical expenses and death. In the stone mountain villages there were reported to be no savings, for at the end of the year households did not have surplus cash which could be carried over into the New Year, let alone be accumulated over any period of time. 'Poor' and 'very poor' households commonly incurred debts in the ordinary course of each year, while all households incurred debts to meet the costs of illness, marriage and death. The only sources of loans to meet these expenses were relatives, neighbours and friends and again especially the wife's mother, who generally lived in another village but within the same township. Most debts in the stone mountains were left unpaid.

As in Yunnan there was a direct link between the poverty of the household and the health of its members. The main diseases in the village were malaria and stomach diseases, from which there were many deaths. Many children died from tetanus and dysentery, and those who were not ill were so malnourished that they were several years older than their size would suggest. In the villages a high proportion of men were reported to die prematurely from hepatitis. A spot check of four households revealed the following health profiles. In one household of nine persons including seven children and categorised as 'poor' there was no serious illness. Interestingly, the younger children in this household, at home on their own, did not want to let the 'foreign doctor' into the house because they were afraid that she was the doctor who had come to give them their inoculations! In the second household of three persons, 'very poor', the father had died, one child had also died and another was handicapped. In a seven-person household, 'not poor', the elderly grandparents had recently been ill, and in a fourth, of one person, 'very poor', the woman was dying on the bed at the time of my visit after having been ill for the best part of fifteen years and more seriously so with liver disease for the previous two months. In another administrative village, thirteen children aged between a few months and twelve years had died from dysentery and pneumonia the previous year. Again, the men of the village were said to die at an earlier age than the women, from liver disease. In one of the small natural villages, five children had died of pneumonia the previous year and there were obvious cases of severe malnutrition in the village. Again, a spot check in three households showed that in one household of five persons, 'not poor, there had been no serious illness; in a second household, of four persons, 'very poor', two children had died of pneumonia and dysentery and the mother was chronically sick; while in a third household, of four persons and 'poor', the mother was chronically ill, sometimes bedridden, from a respiratory ailment and the father had a long-term back problem due to an earlier accident.

As in Yunnan, the villagers were hopeful that the poverty alleviation programmes recently introduced by the government would bring 'development' to their villages. Quite how this hope would be realised and what form this help would take was hard to ascertain, although many local aspirations centred on animal raising. Without the well-building programme of the Yunnan village, there seemed little activity to break the eerie 'stillness' of the bare and timeless cycle of poverty and death, albeit within a spectacular and luxuriant setting.

What is immediately observable from this case-study approach is the diversity in village experience of reform. Underlying the diversity is variation in location – ranging from suburban villages near large cities, rural villages on plains and hills to remote and high mountainous villages – with consequent variety in resource base, accessibility and policy implementation. Much of this diversity can be assembled via the collection of comparative quantitative village, farm and enterprise data, but what is as interesting to the analyst is the congruence in perceptions or features common to how villagers view policy, event and situated practice and think about or represent their experiences both among themselves and in conversation, interview, letter or newspaper report. In the villages, perceptions of both practice and expectations of reform centre on three 'hot topics', involving major divisions between household and village in relation to the distribution of resource, information and reward. One of these – and they are all discussed in subsequent chapters – was the distribution of responsibility for land and pre- and post-production services, including the provision of agricultural inputs which could make or break peasant experience of reform. In these discussions, frequently arousing strong emotions, the concept most frequently deployed was that of 'readjustment' (or tiaozheng), which was conceived of as almost a third stage of development following on from revolution and reform. A second 'hot topic' was that of cadre–villager relations and the definitions and measurement of cadre authority and agency, which were very much about both the management of information and how local knowledge is constructed and negotiated within the village and between village and state. Another 'hot topic' in the villages has been the rising differentials between rich and poor. Discussions of income generation and differential touch on concepts of reward, hierarchy and incentive, and have commonly structured villagers' perceptions and representations of their experiences and expectations of reform.

Part II

Readjustment: the village

Chapter 4

Resource management
Land, service and enterprise

In the first years of reform, the balance of production responsibilities so favoured the peasant household that it had seemed that one of the most likely repercussions of reform in the countryside would be fragmentation of the village as its corporate identity, politics and productive capacity declined. Given the reduction in the political and economic role of the production team, brigade and commune, it had seemed likely that the peasant household would become more autonomous and less dependent on village facilities and village government. If the household no longer found it so necessary or so advantageous to focus on relations within the village collective in the search for raw materials and markets, then its attention would be directed towards the elaboration of its own networks of relations and alliances outside of the village. Indeed in the mid-1980s, I went so far as to write that the weakening of village organisation and the fragmentation of village cohesion might be designated one of the most significant changes occurring in China during the first reform years. If this seemed an appropriate conclusion to draw, even as late as 1987, it was shaken by later field studies which suggested that the village economy and polity have again been strengthened and that the balance of responsibilities between household and village are no longer so asymmetric. Increasingly in the village studies, the term 'readjustment' (tiaozheng) was used to refer to more recent changes in the distribution of economic and political responsibilities between household and village. If the process of reform originally encouraged household responsibilities, subsequent processes of modification reinvested responsibility in the village for the management and cultivation of the land, the provision of pre- and post-production services and enterprise development.

LAND MANAGEMENT

The relationship of peasant to land, be it in terms of ownership, management or cultivation, has long been a most important determinant of peasant livelihood and security and peasant representation of government. In peasant rebellions, revolution and reform, programmes of land reform, collectivisation and decollectivisation had been central in soliciting peasant support and underlay their experience of revolution and reform. Thus the new production responsibility system has been both popular and productive, but it has not solved all the problems to do with land. For villagers, as for government spokesmen, land remains 'the principal issue in China's rural areas'.[1] For government spokesmen, 'the success of China's farm production is very much dependent on the development of a rational land policy';[2] for villagers current fears include decreases in available arable land, lack of investment and inputs and the disadvantages of the small-scale plot for large-scale farming. In a country where arable land is already scarce, the continuing shortage during reform is a serious matter. Between 1981 and 1985 it was estimated that cultivated land decreased at an annual rate of 7.38 million mu, so that the per capita share of cultivated land dropped from 1.52 to 1.4 mu and to even less than 1 mu in one-third of the provinces,[3] which can be mainly attributed to the expansion in village and township enterprises and housebuilding. The use of arable lands for these two purposes is immediately observable as is a third – its use for burial grounds.[4] For many years, on long train and car journeys, I have observed the common placing of raised burial mounds in the midst of, and often taking a goodly portion of, the farmer's small arable plot or narrow strip. Its placing may be due to the choice of the most auspicious geomantic site, but it is also so that, for the villagers, the placing of ancestors' graves constitutes the most permanent symbol of *de facto* ownership.

It was quite clear that there was a direct relationship between land ownership, tenure and management and investment in maintaining the fertility of the soil.[5] Simply put, unless peasants were guaranteed long-term use, they would not sustain or improve soil fertility, although with diversification of domestic economic activities, land frequently became a less important component of the farm economy and repository of scarce inputs.[6] Moreover, the bid to mechanise agriculture and improve crop yields had drawn attention to the constraints of the small size of peasant plots. To solve each of these problems there were periodic media discussions calling for clarification of the relationship between peasant and land, its ownership, management and cultivation.[7] In most of the villages I have studied over recent years (which includes many more than the nine case studies), land remained the major resource of most peasant households, but there were continuing major changes in the relationship of peasant to land.

In villages, land was variously categorised and allocated to peasant households as responsibility lands for grain or cash crops, as food-grain lands for subsistence, and as fodder, forest or waste land. Land might be the sole, the primary or a subsidiary resource within the peasant household economy, depending on the degree of diversification. In the majority of the rural villages, each household cultivated its small parcels of land intensively and carefully, relying on its crops for subsistence, animal fodder, and for meeting agricultural tax and quotas contracted to the state and for sale in the market. The contribution of the land to the peasant household's cash income, over and above subsistence, taxes and crop quotas, was largely dependent on the number and range of alternative economic activities undertaken by the peasant household. In regions with few alternative activities, and particularly in poor and remote regions and in specialist grain-production villages or households, income from the land furnished the most important source of cash income. For the mixed economy household, however, land was usually only one of a number of sources of cash income, and for those in waged labour or entirely taken up with alternative economic activities, income from the land had become minimal or non-existent. It can be said that with increasing diversification and development, land became a less important resource for the individual farmer in terms of income generation, although it remained the most important source of food and fodder.

The amount of land distributed to each household was primarily dependent on the land resources of the region and per capita ratios. In many regions of China, arable land was sufficient to provide plots of the size and quality necessary to provide for the full subsistence of its members and more. In other regions, land was scarce and of such poor quality that plots were barely capable of providing for subsistence. Within villages, the initially equitable distribution of land has been eroded as original allocations have increasingly failed to keep pace with changes in household composition. The poorest households in villages were frequently cited as those whose land allocations had to support more persons than had been originally reckoned. For instance, daughters married into other villages, where they received no land, continued to be supported by their natal household's land allocation which may also have its own new members to support. There were few examples of land redistribution between households perhaps because there is some tension between the arguments favouring equity for redistribution and permanence for long-term investment. In most of the villages, the farmers talked of 'their' land and seemed to feel reasonably secure in its continued use. For village leaders, it seemed more important to foster security of tenure rather than embark on a redistribution exercise. Some villages have reduced these tensions or even avoided the problem by readjusting responsibilities for the land, not by redistributing land from household to household but from household to village.

Originally, and still in the majority of China's villages, the household cultivated and managed its lands or at least a portion of its lands in keeping with the production plan of the village decided according to contracted quotas. However, in an increasing number of the more developed regions, the village has gradually taken over much of the cultivation of the land using machines or a village team of contracted labourers, although the land may remain demarcated, contracted and managed by individual households. In yet another variation, where the topography and crop type favour mechanisation, responsibility lands may be both cultivated and managed by the village. Where cultivation was largely mechanised, the process of readjustment followed a common sequence. First, where production was wholly or primarily mechanised, farmers might hand-work the remaining production tasks, bear the costs of village services and generally manage the cultivation and disposal of the crops. Gradually, however, the demands on peasant labour were so reduced that soon only a few households contracted out, cultivated and managed the responsibility land. In these villages, the agricultural mechanisation team almost completely farmed the land at a subsidised cost to the contracting household which, after subtracting machine costs from production costs, still earned a much higher income – sometimes several thousand yuan higher – than village enterprise workers. To permit the village to accumulate the profits from the land and to reduce increasing differentials between villagers, village committees ended responsibility land contracts with individual households and either contracted the land out to the agricultural machinery team (Beijing village) or established a collective farm employing individual farm labourers (Wuxi village). In either case, it was the village which assumed the costs of production in return for control of the profits, and the contract labourers were paid a wage and, as an incentive, a share in the profits. The rest of the profits accrued to the village rather than to the individual household. In this respect the introduction of the 2:4:4 principle in some of the more developed villages was identified by villagers as representing a major turning point, for agriculture was thereby categorised alongside other enterprises adhering to the principle of 20 per cent profits to the individual, 40 per cent to investment and development and 40 per cent to the village for services. This new system was said to mark not only a shift in responsibility, but also in the distribution of rewards and incentives which, in order to meet the combined goals of efficiency and equity, invariably favoured the village.

Where responsibility lands were reclaimed by the village, the response of household contractors was mixed. Where households contractors had constituted a minority in the village and combined very high incomes with very little labour (and were sometimes described as 'the new landlords'), villagers generally thought that the village was right to take over the land, acquire the profits and reduce income differentials. The few households that had continued to contract out the land were, not surprisingly, not so favourable in their response, but their reluctance in accepting the change was somewhat mollified by the fact that they had enjoyed large incomes and accumulated savings for a number of years enabling them to have built superior houses and furnished them lavishly. Where large numbers of households in the villages had surrendered their land contracts to the village, it is important to note that in each case they had retained their per capita allocations of food-grain lands, which, although they too might be mechanically cultivated by village teams, were still managed by households whose subsistence grain and fodder supplies were thus individually assured. That this is an important practice, both practically and symbolically, can be seen from the few villages of my acquaintance (not included in the case studies) where land has been entirely removed from the villagers.

In Chanping county, some tens of kilometres from Beijing, where I stayed in May 1989, village land had been reduced or lost in three villages which had been quite randomly selected some ten years previously by Beijing University for demographic study. In the mountains near Beijing, the farmers in one village were exceedingly angry at the depletion of their land resources and the changes in the land contracts issued to them. They had expected to keep their original responsibility lands, but had found that after some investment and improvement, some 30 per cent of the best of the village's flat arable land was to be used for a through railway line to Japan. As a result, not only had they lost valuable land, but they also suffered the daily indignity of watching coal being transported to Japan while they suffered continuous power cuts! The village had accepted a cash sum in compensation, which it had mostly used to fund a new kindergarten, but this did little to assuage the unhappy farmers. The older generation, in particular, worried that without the security of land there would be nothing to keep their sons in the village. In a second village, the land resources had been reduced from 300 to 30 mu as factories and housing had gradually encroached from the local town into the nearby countryside. Here alternative employment in town factories somewhat compensated for the loss of land, although here too there was some residual insecurity expressed about its permanent loss affecting the welfare of future generations. In yet another village, near the Ming tombs, almost all the land had been taken for a tourist golf course, and although villagers had been compensated for its loss by having their household registration changed from rural to urban residents with concomitant pension and grain ration benefits, they could not wholly rest easy knowing that their sons and sons of sons would be deprived of a landed source of sustenance should future conditions change – and, as they said, shifting government policies were something with which they all were familiar! Thus after ten years of reform some variation in the distribution of responsibility for land between household and village has emerged. If in all but a minority of villages studied, readjustments between peasant and village over land had taken place relatively amicably and did not seem to pose undue worries in the village, the same could not be said about inputs, the supply and costs of which openly worried the farmers and imposed a sometimes intolerable burden upon their resources.

PRE-PRODUCTION SERVICES

Along with readjustments in the distribution of responsibilities for the cultivation and management of land there have also been readjustments in responsibility for the provision of pre- and post-production services. There is little doubt that one of the most important repercussions of reform was the generation of a complete new set of demands on the peasant household, including the procurement of raw materials, production inputs, technical knowledge, capital, transport, storage and markets. These were all demands which had formerly been the responsibility of the collective and which now openly posed difficulties for households, given both their inexperience in such matters and the weakness of the service infrastructure. In anticipation of these difficulties, the government had early encouraged the establishment of economic associations, companies and co-operatives to support and service the peasant households, but what was increasingly clear from the village studies was that unless the village itself had assumed responsibility for the supply of pre- and post-production services then their provision was difficult, reduced or absent and both peasant incomes and morale suffered. Once individual households were responsible for their own profits and losses, there was likely to be a direct correlation between meeting these new demands for information, production inputs or services and their incomes. To take the obvious example of fertiliser, which was the most important of inputs in maintaining and improving per unit area yields, the village studies frequently showed there to be a direct correlation between yields, fertiliser administered per mu and incomes. The complaint most often heard in the countryside was of the short supply and poor quality of fertiliser, and the press has repeatedly taken up the cause on behalf of farmers, in recognition that 'chemical fertiliser markets in many localities are in a mess and a major factor adversely affecting agricultural production and standards of social conduct'.[8] The greatest disapprobation is reserved for 'fertiliser rats', or those who create disorder in the market and resell chemical fertiliser at high profits. For households in most regions it was one, and sometimes the most constantly expensive item, of cash expenditure in each year's household budget. As the village studies also showed, poor villages or poor households with low cash incomes often made do without fertiliser or went into periodic debt to procure supplies.

During my first village studies in Henan (1987) and Sichuan (1988), farmers had openly worried about supplies and costs of fertiliser, with many incurring debts in order to procure inputs, but it was not until a subsequent visit to a number of mountain villages in Shandong province (not those included in the case studies) a year or so later that it became clear that problems with the supply of inputs were not only the focus of discontent in many villages, but also constituted an important measure of peasant experience of and attitude towards rural reform. In these mountain villages, not only did the majority of households not have sufficient cash to purchase fertiliser, agro-chemicals, seed and other inputs each year, but they were also the most common reason for households borrowing either from the rural banks or from kin and neighbours. In each of the several villages studied, at least half the households, and in some villages upwards of 80 per cent of households, had taken out loans ranging from ¥100 to ¥1,500 for agricultural inputs, including fertiliser and chemicals for wheat, maize, fruit trees and for concentrated feed for pigs and cattle. Many had experienced difficulties in repaying their loans, and the poorest peasants with 'no ability to repay' were frequently in a position where they had accumulated such debts that they could not continue to take out loans for agricultural inputs. In these circumstances the returns from their lands were increasingly meagre, and many of the farmers interviewed complained bitterly about the costs and difficulties of obtaining supplies of fertiliser and feed. They felt these new responsibilities to be particularly heavy, and indeed this 'heavy burden' was perceived by many of the poorest villagers to outweigh any of the advantages of reform. Several of the poorer farmers openly expressed a wish to return to collective farming for the simple reason that the village had previously taken responsibility for procuring agricultural inputs. It was clear that unless there was some outside intervention, these poor and very unhappy and discontented villagers were caught in a downward spiral.

In contrast, it was a welcome change to visit subsequently a number of richer villages where the assumption of responsibility by the village for supplying inputs, particularly fertiliser, had transformed the experience of reform for peasant producers. There were fewer worries expressed, and the farmers and producers did not feel the same anxiety about supplies and costs – indeed, some were quite nonchalant: did not the village take care of this problem and just deduct the costs from their output at harvest time? The salience of this was brought home to me in the Shanxi village, which, still mainly reliant on income from grain and, interestingly, also a pioneer in ploughing the maize stalks back into the soil, was also heavily dependent on chemical fertiliser to maintain the high yields. The village cadres, in order to play safe and ensure supplies, accumulated sufficient fertiliser a year in advance, which, stacked neatly under cover but visible to all in the village, had become a symbol of assurance and stability welcomed by the households. This was fortunate, for this village also had a storehouse full of grain from the previous year which it had not been able to sell given the lack of capacity, storage and distribution facilities in the province.

Alongside periodic reports of farmers in various regions of China not being able to sell their grain,[9] there have been more reports expressing fears about further falls in the area of grain lands and in grain supply. This shortfall is largely due to the low purchase price of grain and high costs of inputs which discourage farmers from cultivating grain and encourage them to cultivate cash crops which give higher returns.[10] There have been several rises in grain purchase prices, and there were no complaints spontaneously voiced in the villages about the prices paid for grain. Where the majority of villagers no longer contracted responsibility lands, it was the land contractors who still earned the highest incomes. In the better endowed villages too, farmers also enjoyed lower prices in the purchase of fertiliser and other inputs, although, in these circumstances the village frequently paid the farmers a lower price than the state and used the difference to subsidise the costs of production and add to village income. This practice was defended by village leaders because grain farmers already enjoyed the highest incomes in the village. In many of the villages studied, grain lands had been reduced in favour of orchard, forest, vegetables and mulberry, but these deductions in land allocation had generally been compensated for by increases in yields per mu. If the demand for pre-production services and their costs especially vexed farmers in villages where they were still entirely dependent on their own initiative and individual networks, problems of prices and markets for crops and other goods were newly encountered by both individual farmer and village alike.

POST-PRODUCTION SERVICES

Newspapers report instances where farmers have encountered marketing problems due to poor information and their misunderstanding of supply and demand, causing them to be unable to sell their products either due to over-supply, falling prices or insufficient quotas on purchases. Year after year there are reports that contracts to purchase grain and promises to purchase agricultural sideline products remain unfulfilled.[11] Neither the state nor the market always fulfilled this promise. For example, farmers in Shanxi province were reported to have begun breeding long-furred rabbits whose fur was in great demand, with supply and marketing co-operatives, foreign trade companies, state-owned commercial departments and middle-men all competing to purchase their product. Other farmers observing this demand applied for loans to take up rabbit breeding so that increased output of rabbit fur decreased the demand and with it the price, so that the following year the farmers found themselves having to kill the rabbits for meat.[12] From other provinces, too, came reports of local farmers planting crops or raising animals at the behest of township, county and provincial bodies only to find that supply and marketing co-operative purchases fell short of production, and because farmers had no means of selling, storing or processing their products much went to waste.[13] In such cases, farmers were reported to be loudly protesting: 'How can it be regarded as a commodity economy where there is no market for principal farm and sideline products?' or 'We cannot grow things that can make money and what we have grown is worthless.'[14]

One of the most bitter interviews I have ever undertaken was in a household in a village near Beijing in 1989 which, on the brink of bankruptcy, exemplified a common sequence of events in villages where the production by an individual household of a new item in great demand was expanded and copied by other households, only to find that in emulating the original success, they had flooded the market. The farmer interviewed had developed and specialised in raising chickens from the early 1980s, and subsequently established a large and successful chicken farm with some 1,000 chickens so that by 1984 his had become an envied ¥10,000 household. His success was short-lived, for first the costs of chicken feed rose, supplies dwindled and its quality declined. Secondly, he was not only left with rising costs and poor stock, but once other neighbouring farmers in the village had copied his successful example, the local market was flooded with eggs resulting in falling prices and baskets of eggs left unsold. He had tried to travel to more distant markets where eggs were in short supply, but had been fined for illegally crossing provincial boundaries to sell his produce. At the time of my stay in the village, there were hundreds of undernourished, bedraggled and smelling chickens, a rusting small truck once used for transporting eggs and eggs piled high to be fallen over in every corner of the home. I was only too well aware that two to three years previously this household would have been presented as the local success story; now this failing enterprise had resulted in a great deal of bitterness and resentment which, for lack of other targets, was primarily directed towards village cadres, who, it has to be said, were, unusually, nowhere to be seen in the village during my visit of several days. Not only was the farmer bitter, but the family also seemed at a complete loss to know how to deal with their situation.

In great contrast was the popularly dubbed 'whole dragon service' or the 'head to tail and tail to head' service made available to the villagers raising chickens in Shandong village A which had been negotiated between a Japanese foreign venture, village cadres and households to guarantee the capital, inputs, labour supply and a market. In this most comprehensive service of my acquaintance, the villagers were provided with the chickens and the feed by the company; the village helped with the provision of coops and veterinary services and the households provided the labour, with the grown chickens purchased by the company. Thus it was that within my most recent experiences, the most stable, assured and contented villages were those where the village had assumed at least some of the responsibility for pre- and post-production inputs and services, thus reducing the burden on individual peasant households. The most unstable, anxious and discontented villagers were those where the farmers continued to have sole responsibility for processing inputs, production services and markets. It was also the case that, in these latter villages where inputs were scarce, farmers had to pay the most for the inputs and services, thus adding to their already heavy burdens. Indeed, the costs of inputs and services, the scarcity of inputs and services, and the fees, levies and charges which the scarcity imposed upon peasant households was in shorthand form increasingly referred to in the villages and in the national press as the 'peasants' or farmers' burden'.

Following on from the first few years of reform, when the distribution of land and price rises of agricultural products benefited and were seen to benefit the peasants, there have been increasing acknowledgements in the press and in villages that problems in the supply and rising costs of inputs had adversely affected or in some cases even reversed the benefits of the early years. Even for those with substantial and rising cash incomes, the scarcity and rising costs of farm inputs over the years meant that any assessment of rising incomes was quite misleading unless it took account of these factors which in some villages had cancelled out rises in income. Time and again this had been the case in the various village studies of household budgets, and a survey conducted in 1988 of a sample of 66,982 peasant households in 846 counties had confirmed this as a national trend. The survey had showed that peasants' cash payments grew faster than cash income, and that their payments for production expenses grew faster than payments for daily consumption. From January to September of that year, peasants' per capita cash payment (exclusive of payment for savings and loans) was ¥392, ¥84 more than for the same period the previous year. Of this amount ¥117.86 went to defray production expenses – an increase of 31.5 per cent over the same period the previous year – while ¥238.87 went to defray daily living expenses, an increase of 26.6 per cent.[15] However, the scarcity and costs of inputs was not the only constituent of the 'peasants' burden', for increasing publicity has been given to the growing number of periodic and annual levies which peasant households had to pay for services. There were interview references to fees for hydroelectricity, water and roads, crop protection, charges for anti-epidemiology for livestock, technical services and for social services, some of which were mismanaged or non-existent. There have been suggestions in the media that nationally both the number of fees for services and their total sums are increasing. It was estimated in 1988 that during the previous three years, the average per capita burden of services for the peasants had risen at an annual rate of over 20 per cent, far exceeding the 7.5 per cent annual growth in peasant incomes.[16] In some regions the deductions are reported to be forcibly and simultaneously administered by the grain management bureaux at the time of grain purchases, so that in these cases the reckonings are such that peasants are left with no income from grain at all. The media have drawn attention to the serious damage which the imposition of these burdens have, not just for peasant income, but also for their attitudes towards reform and social stability. Certainly, the most unstable and most openly rebellious villages of my recent acquaintance were those where the number of levies and fees exacted had reached double figures, and, with few returns and little thought to their effect on the incomes and attitudes of the villagers, there was an underlying and seething resentment focused on these exactions. One of the problems is that there is frequently a chronic shortage of funds at the middle and local administrative levels so that all bodies are looking to the villages to make good the shortfall.

Whether it was for supply of inputs or services, in no cases of my acquaintance had the households themselves got together to form an economic association, co-operative or company independent of village cadres, who, if successful in facilitating the procurement of inputs, pre- and post-production services and credit, provided a service that most individual peasant households could not begin to match. Moreover, in the village studies there is an important correlation between the provisioning of pre- and post-production inputs and services for agriculture and the development of industrial enterprises and village income.

VILLAGE ENTERPRISES

The establishment of village enterprises has long been identified both nationally and in the village as the most important income-generating rural activity. Government leaders continue to emphasise it as the 'pillar of the rural economy'[17] or the 'key to rural prosperity',[18] and their efficiency in promoting the local production of goods, providing local employment for surplus labour and servicing the needs of the rural population has been well-documented nationally and is evident in the village studies. The degree to which enterprises have become an integral and important part of the rural economy was underlined when many were pre-emptorily closed or threatened with closure at the turn of the decade because of government policy, with the result that village incomes were reduced, village employment threatened and many peasants were forced back to the family farm.[19] In the village studies in 1990–91, most of the village enterprises had recently expanded or were at least stable, and the villagers observed there to be a direct correlation between rising village income and the development of village enterprises. In contrast, in the most remote and poorest villages there was a complete absence of any enterprises and an almost non-existent village income; in less remote and poor villages, there might be one or at the most two small enterprises and low levels of village income, and in the richer and richest villages there were both profitable enterprises and high incomes. Many of these latter villages were favoured by their proximity to cities and larger towns, although small-town expansion throughout China has also encouraged their surrounding villages to follow suit. Where township and county cadres have encouraged village enterprises to establish links with larger factories guaranteeing raw materials and markets, village income has been unusually high.

In Wuxi village, where village income totalled ¥54.60 million, with 98.5 per cent (¥53.8 million) deriving from industry, village income had risen in 1987 once industries had dramatically expanded as state policy towards village enterprises had been sufficiently clarified to encourage new initiatives and linkages by township, county and city governments. For example, the city had sent a team to investigate links and contracts with enterprises in Shenzhen Economic Zone. Village leaders had had no hesitation in travelling far and wide in their search for materials, markets and technical innovations through establishing contracts and links with large city firms, heavy industries and research or technical institutions. However, as the history of enterprise development in Shandong village B illustrated, villages which had less encouragement from higher administrative levels and less confident leaders had an even more hesitant start. Although there, village income had risen gradually from ¥3.02 million in 1981 to ¥11 million in 1989, it was not as high as it might have been or (much to the chagrin of villagers) as high as in other neighbouring villages. Because of this dissatisfaction, there had been a village meeting in 1990 at which there had been some outspoken criticism of the village leaders. The village leaders themselves admitted that they had been hesitant in supporting new policies favouring enterprise development, as for many years they were still not sure 'what was right and what was wrong' or, as they rather graphically put it: if they 'retained a small boat, they could turn it around more easily than a large boat if there was a change in policy'. Only later had they come to acknowledge that 'a large boat can steam ahead despite strong winds from any direction', and on this basis they had made new plans to expand their enterprise production to include 'highly fashionable items of high quality' as well as the conventional and popular items. As a result, there had already been a rise in village income of some ¥5.17 million between 1989 and 1990. Some of the poorer more remote villages, in which there was still no enterprise development, represented enterprise development as a panacea to all ills. They frequently expressed interest in building food-processing factories before they had either the animals or the facilities for livestock raising! In the poorest and most remote villages where there were no roads, water or electricity it was difficult to anticipate what form enterprise development might take in the immediate future, although it was central to the development agenda. For the villages rich and poor, enterprise development constituted the most observable measure of development and immediately expandable source of village income.

VILLAGE INCOME

If the correlation between village income and enterprise development made the establishment of village enterprises a popular priority in the villages, it also led to much debate about the balance between the development of individual or household-based enterprises in relation to village-operated enterprises.[20] Private and individual household enterprises were also officially encouraged, with examples of households or individuals who, from tentative beginnings, had successfully generated an income of thousands or even tens of thousands of yuan and cited in stories circulating in the media and by word of mouth. In almost half of the village studies, there were instances of enterprises established by individual or small groups of households which by 1990–91 earned the highest incomes in the village. For example, one household in Shandong village A built up a substantial family enterprise in the purchase, distribution and retail of machine spare parts. The head of the household was originally a purchaser for the agricultural machinery station in a nearby city, but once he heard of the change of policy to expand private enterprise he applied to take over the village shop, and stocked it with machine parts for agricultural machinery – mostly small tractors, threshers and flour-milling shellers. From small beginnings, it expanded into a flourishing business employing four family members to serve customers from 'nine counties and nine cities'. He earned a gross business income of ¥1 million with profits of ¥40,000 in 1990. The most surprising feature of the household was the low taxes which the household paid to the village, amounting to just ¥40 per person per year, or a total of ¥160. Thus its contribution to village income was small compared to that of an equivalent village enterprise; the advantage of village over household enterprises was that profits accrued to the village rather than to individual labourers or households.

Most of the village enterprises interviewed were established through the initiative of village committees which had provided a loan or grant for the initial investment and appointed a manager to establish, maintain or expand the enterprises and be responsible for their profits and losses. Occasionally, a small private or individual household enterprise already well-established, but not successful enough to invest further and expand, had been taken over by the village, which then managed its expansion on the same basis as other village enterprises. For all village enterprises, profits were divided at the year's end and distributed between bonuses for the manager and workers in the enterprise, investment in the maintenance and expansion of the enterprises and village funds. As the village studies showed, the proportion of profits allocated often took a 2:4:4 ratio: two-tenths for bonuses, four-tenths for investment and four-tenths for village funds. If the most important source of village income was the village enterprises, then the most important differentials in village income were between villages with and without enterprises. The presence of profitable enterprises furnished village funds, contributing not only to the establishment of pre- and post-production services, but also to the provision of social and welfare services and the authority of village cadres.

Where the village had a stable and rising income generated by its agriculture and industry, then it usually invested part of these profits in the establishment of facilities for education, health care and welfare. In both education and health there was a shortage of state funds, so that villages generated funds to contribute towards the cost of facilities and personnel. Except in the very poorest villages which had received extra help for the development of schools, there was a direct correlation between village funds and levels of education and health care. In the richer villages, Beijing, Wuxi, Shandong and Shanxi, it was reported that all children attended primary school, and, with the exception of Shanxi village where 75 per cent of village pupils go on to junior middle school, all the children in these villages proceeded to junior middle school. A smaller proportion, ranging between 20 and 50 per cent of junior middle-school pupils, passed the entrance examinations to enter senior middle school. In the poorer villages not subject to special state funding, some children did not attend school at all, only a small proportion of the children graduated from primary school and an even smaller number went on to enter junior middle school. In Henan, the majority of the village children had not attended school for more than two to three years, and of the teenage children aged between twelve and sixteen years, none was in senior middle school, only one had graduated from junior middle school, one was a graduate from primary school, and four had dropped out of primary school. Four more were still attending school and of these, three had started late; of the seven children not yet attending school three were of primary age. In the poorest Yunnan and Guangxi villages what was interesting was the presence in even the smallest, most remote natural village of a yellow clay school of poor fabric, few classes, few facilities and of dubious standard, but nevertheless a school, with teachers, half to three-quarters of whom had vocational training and more than half, sometimes rising to 100 per cent, of whom were more often than not paid high wages by the state to teach in these remote and very poor villages. After a number of campaigns in these poorest regions to encourage minority nationalities and especially girls to attend school and measures to encourage teachers to stay in these remote villages, a surprisingly high proportion of children, generally upwards of 90 per cent, entered primary school, although the drop-out rate was high after one or two years and only a small proportion graduated, with an even smaller proportion going on to junior middle school. The high drop-out rate was largely due to the costs of schooling, which rose sharply after the first couple of years of primary schooling when pupils frequently had to attend boarding school, to family discrimination against girls and to widespread failure to achieve the required examination standards.

The provision of health was also largely dependent on the income generated by the village to furnish it with facilities. In the richer villages there were clinics, doctors with more than bare-foot training and medicines. In Shandong village B, the village doctor had learned much from his grandfather, who had also been a doctor in the village. He had subsequently received formal training and certificates and had practised in the village for over twelve years. He had an income of ¥4,000, which mainly derived from the village income and from small payments made by the villagers for treatment. Frequently, too, these richer villages were within vehicular proximity to a township or county hospital which had frequently had more sophisticated facilities for X-ray, diagnosis and operations. In the poor and poorest villages there were very few facilities, and it was often said by the villagers that 'the destiny of the sick was death'. In the poorest villages there was usually access to a doctor within the same or a neighbouring village (sometimes some distance) with a rudimentary three months' training who, in some regions, received an allowance from the county hospital of ¥10–15 a year or in other regions received no remuneration. This remuneration was in stark contrast to the wages of teachers and was not enough to permit them to practise fully, as they had also to cultivate the fields, raise animals and carry water or firewood, which took them into the fields and sometimes beyond 'not of help distance'.

The poorest villages were distinguished by the absence of clinics and even medicines, because it was said that the doctors were too poor to provide them, the villagers were too poor to pay for them and the village had no funds with which to provide a subsidy to pay for clinics, medicines or to help the villagers meet the deposits and fees demanded by township and county hospitals. One of the practices which villagers said deterred them from making the arduous journey to such hospitals was the prohibitive deposit demanded of them, usually ¥50–60, on arrival at the hospital. In the poor remote regions, the township hospitals had little or no equipment – perhaps a stethoscope and thermometer – and in the more fortunate an ancient X-ray machine; most of the buildings were dilapidated and there were few personnel with anything but the minimum of training. In these circumstances even villagers who had the stamina or the money to attend their township or county hospital were reluctant, and they only visited hospital in the most extreme of instances – a situation which had led to the common association of hospital with death. Most villagers interviewed in the poorest remote villages had never had any treatment beyond that of their village doctor; hence the depressing health profiles in the households interviewed in Yunnan and Guangxi. In contrast, in the Henan village, the village was within a day's journey of the county hospital where provincial investment had provided equipment and services out of the ordinary. Villagers who had health problems said that they frequently bypassed their village doctor, of whose training they were somewhat scornful, in favour of the 'more modern' treatment of the county hospital.

Unusually for rural villages, but increasingly common in the high-income villages of the city suburbs, there were also village provisions for the retired, the handicapped and a system of maternity benefits in Beijing and Wuxi villages. In Wuxi village in 1990 when the profits from industry were higher than ever and contributed ¥0.53 million to the village funds, ¥0.47 million was used for agricultural investment and ¥0.06 million was allocated to welfare, including public health (¥25,000), single-child family benefits (¥20,000), investments for those over sixty years of age (¥13–15,000), aid for retired village cadres (¥3,000) and help given to those households in difficulty (¥3,000). A large sum, ¥15–20,000, was spent on village buildings and the village environment, and ¥25,000 was given to the primary school. In Beijing village, where there was a considerable amount of village industry, retired persons in the village each received ¥10 per month to help with their living expenses, ¥1 for every month they had worked in the village labour force and ¥5–10 per month if they had held a position of village responsibility. Three- to six-year-old children attended kindergarten, in which tuition, books and materials were all provided by the village. Very unusually in the countryside, women received full salary for forty-five days after giving birth. In contrast, in the poor villages of Henan, Sichuan, Yunnan and Guangxi, there were no services which were provided from village income, for the simple reason that there was little or no village income available, let alone generated for allocation to aid and welfare.

VILLAGE GOVERNMENT

If the degree to which villages were able to provide pre- and post-production services and education, health and welfare benefits for their members could be directly related to village income, and if enterprises were the most reliable source of income and profits in a village, then management of enterprise profits and village income also constituted one of the most important sources of authority in the village. The more resources to be managed, the more services generated, then the greater the need for village management. Village cadres thus had a vested interest in generating resources, income and profits, the management of which underlay much of their continuing power in the village. In villages without resources, incomes and profits, cadres had little but their tenuous position in the lowest echelons of the administrative hierarchy to maintain their authority. In villages where there were resources to be developed and maintained, cadres had moved into a new position mediating as brokers between village members and those outside the village in the interests of generating stable supplies of inputs and markets for output. One of the greatest changes since the reform has been the attention drawn to the measure of political skills of village cadres and particularly to economic skills or their 'business' acumen by villagers. Even in relation to foreign researchers there has been a marked change in their demeanour from that before the reforms: they had much time to sit and talk while the village economy largely continued to run itself; after the reforms, however, they seldom had the time just to talk unless they were officially involved in the visit and it was likely to generate resources.

Although in theory political and economic affairs were to be increasingly differentiated with a division of labour and authority, both political and economic activities continued to be combined, co-ordinated and jointly managed. The village studies showed that this continuing correlation of political and economic authority was largely effected by the duplication of personnel on the various committees of the village. A study of village government in the villages showed that in all case studies there were two to three leadership bodies in the village sharing in the joint management of political and economic affairs. The first was the Party Branch, which was made up of Chairman and between three and six Party members of the village, depending on the village size. It was usually responsible for discussing and implementing Party policy in the village. The Party Secretary was, without exception, identified as the main leader of village develop-ment, and the Party leadership group was perceived as the main decision-making body in the village. The second leading group in the administrative village was the village committee, which consisted of the head of the village, representatives of constituent natural villages or groups within a large village, the Secretary of the Party leading group and representatives from the Women's Federation, the Law and Order group, the village militia and the Youth League. The village committees outlined their main responsibilities as mediating civil disputes, solving practical welfare problems and supervising family planning.

In less developed villages, these two committees exclusively managed the political and economic affairs of the village; in richer villages with numbers of enterprise resources there was often additionally a third village body, usually known as an economic co-operative organisation or economic association, which was made up of village leaders and the managers of agricultural and industrial enterprises of the village. In the Beijing village, for example, the economic co-operative organisation was made up of a manager charged with responsibility for agriculture including grain lands, forestry, orchard and animal husbandry, and a manager in charge of industry responsible for liaising with the village factories. Each occupation group in the village also had a team leader who was responsible for liaising with this economic co-operative organisation, which was charged with organising production, channelling information and procuring the appropriate inputs and markets that enabled it to acquire a comprehensive knowledge of all that happened in the village and to take all the major decisions in the village.

A feature common to all the villages was that, although these two to three village organisations might be separate organisations with specifically defined responsibilities, their personnel overlapped so that in effect it was the same few persons meeting under different headings, or 'wearing different hats' as it is often said in the villages. In Shandong village B, for example, the government of the village was divided into two main groups. The Party Branch was made up of seven persons, who were proudly presented as all having junior middle-school or higher education and an average age of only forty-three years! Its main functions were to carry out Party policy in the village, and its seven members included the Party Secretary, who took responsibility for the village, three Deputy Party Secretaries, each taking responsibility for either political work, village enterprise or village committee work, and three members in charge of Party work, Party propaganda and Party policy respectively. Because the village had three hamlets there were also four 'responsible' persons, all Party members, one each for the three hamlets and one for all village enterprises who also met frequently in the Party branch. The village committee, much larger, was made up of thirteen persons all of whom had more than junior middle-school education and an average age of forty-four years. There was one director who took care of all the work in the village, two deputy directors who took charge of agriculture and industry respectively and ten members who took responsibility for youth, women and children, militia, village security, civil affairs and welfare. There was a substantial overlap in personnel in that the director of the village committee and the Party Secretary were the same person and five of the Party branch officers also served on the village committee.

In Wuxi village, the village organisation was made up of three leading groups which were presented in the following order: the Village Integrated or Complex Company, which was made up of four persons – a general manager, a deputy manager in charge of agriculture and agricultural enterprises, a deputy manager in charge of industry and the accountant for the village. The deputy manager of agriculture liaised with the agricultural technical group, the agricultural machinery group, agricultural enterprises, the irrigation group and the plant protection group. The deputy manager in charge of industry liaised with the managers of the nine village factories. The Village Integrated Company had been established in 1986, and its four members were responsible for developing the economic development of the village in line with Party policy, for improving the livelihood of the villagers and for providing services for their benefit. The village committee was made up of the village director and four committee members who were each responsible for safety and mediation, social benefits and civil affairs, women and family planning and public health and the management of lands. As in other villages, there was an overlapping membership with a few persons on all three village committees. For example, the general manager of the company was also the Party Branch Secretary; the deputy manager of the village company in charge of industry was also the Deputy Party Secretary; and the deputy manager of the village company in charge of agriculture was also a member of the Party Branch. The most important persons in the village were the Party Branch Secretary, the village committee director and the managers of the company who, together holding a number of overlapping posts, constituted the main *ex officio* policy- and decision-making body.

What the village studies showed was that there has been some readjustment in the relationship between household and village, with households remaining more dependent on the village than originally anticipated mainly because many of the new reform demands made on them were simply beyond the capacity of each individual peasant household. Generally, the higher the village income, the more developed the village resources, responsibilities and services, the more unified the economic and political management centring on the village and the greater the cadre authority. It seems that villages have not been so fragmented by individual household interests as originally anticipated, as households and cadres continue to have a vested interest in generating and maintaining village resources, income and services. Without these, peasants' own incomes, livelihood and welfare were that much poorer and cadre authority that much less. If the initial processes of reform favoured the authority of the peasant household by placing new resources within its control, it has been increasingly evident that processes of readjustment have underlined the responsibilities, management and authority of village cadres. However, as the next chapter will argue, the relationship between cadre and villager is not so asymmetric now that village and household are incorporated into multifarious networks which extend far beyond the village.

Chapter 5

Information networked
Cadre, knowledge and agency

Although there has been much analysis of the present and potential repercussions of rural reforms for peasant household and village economies, there has been less attention given to the political implications which the reforms have had for the relation between village cadre and peasant household. Yet, from the early years of reform, it was apparent that there would be important shifts in the form and content of this relationship following the introduction of the responsibility production system and the separation of political and economic authority, both of which favoured an increase in the autonomy of the peasant household. In the early years there was some evidence to suggest that peasant households themselves had perceived the balance of power in both production and reproduction to have altered very much in their favour. In one village, where peasants were reprimanded after they had bared the fields of topsoil to make bricks for house construction, they remonstrated that 'now the land has been contracted out for use to the peasants, anyone else can mind their own business'.[1] Peasants countered the single-child family policy with a similar argument: 'Since they now cultivated the land, ate their own grain and brought up their children on their own, there was no need for the state to bother about their child birth.'[2] Arguments such as these and subsequent modifications to unpopular state policies in areas such as family planning supported the view that there had been a decline in cadre authority in the village and, by implication, in the power of the state. It seemed as if the process of reform had set in motion a rapid and radical reduction in cadre and state authority in China's villages. Studies in a number of villages since these early years, however, suggest that, although there have been significant changes in the relation between peasant household and village cadre with a reduction in the power of the cadre and an increase in the bargaining position of the peasant household, these shifts are far from signifying the dramatic decline in state power anticipated by many, including myself, in the early years of reform. Rather, subsequent readjustments in the economic relations between village and household have led to more intricate and symmetrical negotiations of power and knowledge in the village, with both cadre and household incorporated into new information networks and subjected to new checks and balances in the exercise of agency.

The subject of cadre–villager relations and their redefinition during reform has been much discussed in the media. As one typical recent report suggested, now that rural cadres are engaged in market information, commoditisation and business management rather than in calling meetings and allocating tasks to local farmers, 'the problem of relations between cadres and the masses in the rural areas had become a hot topic for many people'.[3] There have been cases of tension and conflict between cadre and villager reported in the press, where cadres have attempted to implement unpopular policies such as grain procurement and family planning, some of which have culminated in violence against cadres. The non-fulfilment of promised services and markets have also been cited as the cause of friction in cadre–villager relations. Cadres in Henan and Anhui who were interviewed in one rural survey on 'grassroots work' attributed strained relations between cadres and villagers to 'imperfect and unstable policy', 'to the different interpretation of policy by cadres and villagers' and, thirdly, 'to the problem of workstyle of some cadres'. However, the villagers interviewed in the same survey also stressed that

> though we curse and fret, we surely do not want to return to the old days. Now, we have more freedom. We are now free to choose to till the land, work for other people, or do business. We now dare to speak our minds and air our grievances. There was no such freedom in that era of the big collective.[4]

The survey concluded that new relationships between cadre and villager were evolving, but what is more interesting is not so much public acknowledgement of the shift from relations based on command to negotiation, but that such relations should be investigated at all and reported on 'as a hot topic'.

In the village case studies, the form and content of cadre–villager relations was much talked about. In Henan, local cadres said they were looking for new ways of relating to villagers now that they felt they could no longer directly impose authority and had fewer sanctions given that the villagers had more economic autonomy. Recent experience had suggested to them that they would have to negotiate with the villagers rather than issue orders as before. It was no longer sufficient that their authority rested on the support of the state administration. Gone were the days when a personal record of revolutionary activity several decades old was sufficient to ensure co-operation. Before the reforms, I vividly remember the retort of a village cadre in my hearing to a criticism that he might not be doing his job properly: he had nothing to fear, for had he not joined the revolution in 1943? Cadres could not cite such a revolutionary pedigree today and expect it to have such effect. Since the reforms, cadres in the villages have been well aware that it was their initiative and competence in providing practical services for the villagers that determined their authority rather than their position *per se*. It is true that such a brokerage position is still frequently dependent on contacts and favours from superiors in the administrative hierarchy, but contacts and favours from others might be as useful. One of the most popular cadres I have ever encountered was an ex-army officer, who had worked in the provincial capital where he had been a basketball player of some note; these were occupations and activities that had allowed him to build up a wide network of useful city contacts which he had subsequently utilised to maximum effect and the lasting gratitude of the villagers. In many villages, local cadres have been praised in my presence for their encouragement, service and solicitude, and their popularity has been evident in our household visits. In other cases, cadres have been criticised in my hearing for not sufficiently facilitating the development of the village or household economy. In one or two villages, cadres have been criticised for 'living too well' and for accepting bribes in their brokerage role. In one or two villages, the cadres have been absent because reputedly they were 'too busy' or because it was soon evident that their inability to look after the villagers' interests was such that they dare not set foot in the households!

What stimulated discussion of cadre–villager relations was the access of villagers to comparative knowledge facilitated by the new multi-faceted flow of information between households, villages, cities and capital which, more than any other factor, has undermined the empowerment of the village cadre with important consequences for the rule of village cadres. The most important change affecting the relationship between cadre and villager, and one that marked one of the most significant of breaks between revolution and reform, was the elaboration of multi-faceted and facilitated channels of information which have increasingly incorporated household and village into broader political and economic networks, alliances and structures. Indeed, it might be argued that one of the most significant repercussions of the decade or so of reforms has been the emergence of the peasant household from its encapsulation within the village and of the village within collective structures. During the revolution this encapsulation had been primarily achieved by the management of information between household, village and state, with the subsequent bounding or enclosure of village populations.

REVOLUTIONARY ENCLOSURE

During the thirty years of revolution, information had been one of the most scarce of resources largely because there had been a singular identifiable and centralised source of information – the state. Within the state structure, the flow of information and command operated vertically, with each administrative level having full policy and operational control over the units within its jurisdiction. The lines of vertical authority along which information flowed coalesced at the local level to constitute both a singular channel of information reaching the village and a single line of all-inclusive authority and extensive control embracing the village. At the local level and within the village, information was communicated to village cadres who were neither salaried officials nor members of the state administration nor even outsiders, but were both resident and working members of local production units who were usually 'recommended' by both local state cadres and villagers to manage the internal affairs of the village and represent it in its negotiations with the state. The state set great store on the oral abilities of village cadres who, as 'insiders' or members of the local population, were considered to be particularly well placed to cultivate close face-to-face ties with local populations and involve them in their own government, production and revolution. This was important, for the purveyance of information during the revolution was primarily directed towards the achievement of goals which were revolutionary in their scope, embracing as they did change of village institutions, relations, normative and belief systems, and were a challenge to conventional village notions of privilege, hierarchy, kinship, family property and privacy. In theory, distinguishing features of village government were the emphasis placed on policy communication and popularisation and the symmetrical ascription of agency to cadre and villager alike. The 'mass line' allowed for the symmetric two-way flow of information 'to and from the masses' in the formulation and implementation of policy,[5] and the mass campaign aimed at involving local populations in their own consciousness raising, persuading them to participate voluntarily in the implementation of new policies (see Figure 5.1).

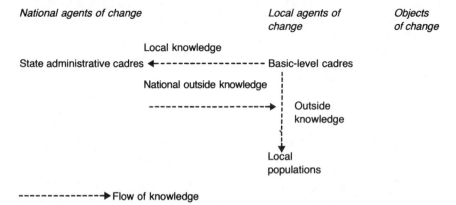

Figure 5.1 The mass line in policy formulation and implementation

In practice, village cadres, as representative of both state and village, found themselves positioned with difficulty between state and village, or 'facing both ways'. During the revolution, village cadres became increasingly identified as the chief representative of the state or 'outside' cadres or 'the higher-ups', as they were often referred to collectively in the village, and they became increasingly privileged persons in the village as outside knowledge or information originating outside of the village became increasingly scarce. There were few alternative channels of communication reaching the village, for only government and Party-sponsored newspapers and periodicals reached the village and these not always so. There was no television and few radios and the most common medium of communication within the village was the ubiquitous loudspeaker. Moreover, with prohibitions on mobility and movement, local populations were more confined to their villages than ever before in Chinese history. Apart from the exchange and movement of women in marriage, and in the absence of markets, fairs, temples and a job market, there was little movement of persons of even the most temporary kind, so that few peasant households had continuous ties outside of the productive unit. The scarcity of information in the village and the singularity of its source not only privileged the cadre, but also resulted in the encapsulation of experience and enclosure of interpretation. Villagers could only 'know' the local, explain the local and interpret the local in terms of the local, for there was little or no knowledge of other local experiences beyond those modelled for emulation by which to gauge or measure their own experience. One of my many clear memories of village visits before reform was the clarity with which villagers could describe their own local experience, their goals and practices, and articulate the rationales for their activities, but they very clearly had no idea how similar or different their experience was with regard to that of other villages in the neighbourhood, in the next valley or elsewhere. Able to acquire only the most general knowledge of other experiences and thus unable to relativise their own experience, villagers were placed at a disadvantage in their relation to village cadres with their privileged information and outside knowledge (see Figure 5.2).

One example which stands out for me as capturing the bounding of the pre-reform village and the hierarchical and asymmetric relationship between cadre and villager derives from a popular prize-winning novel entitled *A Small Town Called Hibiscus*.[16] The author, Gu Hua, reveals time and again the privilege accorded to those in receipt of outside information. In one incident, a young village leader was selected by county officials to travel northwards to visit a distant model commune. On his return from this unusual journey, he was sought out by village cadres and villagers alike, who were all eager to learn of his 'outside' experiences:

'Secretary Wang! Seems you travelled thousands of li (miles) by special car and train, and ate special grub for a whole month . . . Now that

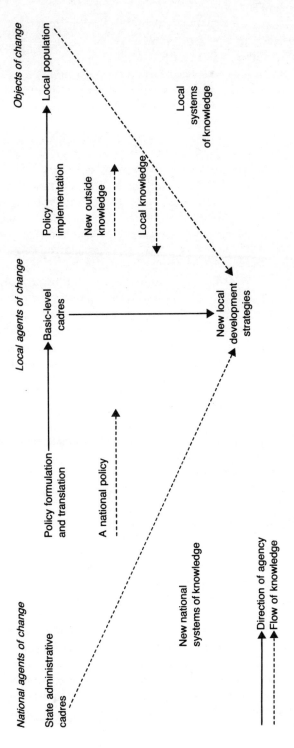

Figure 5.2 Patterns of policy implementation

you've been all that way, seen so much of the world and brought back valuable experiences, you must tell us all about it.'

He had indeed observed and learned of much that was new:

'Rich experience. Enough to last us for several lifetimes. Including something we'd never even heard of. If I hadn't seen it with my own eyes I'd never have dreamed of it.'

He couldn't wait to show off his new knowledge and new ritual skills to the villagers and within a few hours of his return he had called the villagers to a meeting on the old stage of the market place where, brilliantly lit by a paraffin lamp, he reported on his new experiences:

'I've just had the honour of going north to gain experience with the delegation from our country and district. We travelled thousands of li (miles), spent over a month. Dazhai (production brigade) is a red banner for the whole country, a model in agriculture. People from all over China and abroad are learning from it. Dazhai has lots of valuable experience . . . Up here in the mountains we don't know about that. But now I've brought you word of it and I'll show you what it means.'

The villagers were intrigued and mystified by his demonstration of the morning and evening rituals which involved various physical gestures, special handling of the little red book and accompanying recitations. Local cadres, also amazed, relayed the details of these rituals to higher state cadres who in turn recognised that the distant origins of these rituals made them an important and new innovation in the region the neglect of which might lead them into trouble. They therefore invited the young man to pass on his 'travels abroad' experiences to other communes and, in receipt of privileged knowledge, the young man became a privileged person received and sent off in a jeep in style with firecrackers, drumming and gonging and, treated to more chicken, duck, fish and meat than he'd ever seen before in his life.[7]

During the thirty years of revolution, information had been one of the most scarce of resources, so scarce that it can be argued that its passage primarily constituted political patronage and underlay guanxi (relationships) and the exercise of power, in that communication of knowledge constituted one of the most important of gifts or favours underlying patron–client relationships. If information bestowed privilege and conferred agency, then information could also be managed and manipulated first to establish hierarchies in the village and then to redefine those hierarchies at will. It can be argued that it was the exclusive receipt of outside information or knowledge by the village cadre and the consequent generation of ignorance among those in the village not receiving that information which had underlain the power of village cadres and the development of asymmetric and hierarchical relations between cadre and household during the revolution.

During the revolution, state cadres continuously communicated new forms of outside knowledge and new policies, either to village cadres or sometimes to other individuals or groups within the local population who had been selected as appropriate recipients of such knowledge and information and to take the lead in criticism campaigns. Privileged information communicated to them either took the form of details of imminent policy changes and new ritual skills or advance knowledge of the types of social behaviour and social practices to be selected as objects of criticism in the frequent campaigns of rectification and purification which had become an institutionalised part of the political process in the 1960s and 1970s. The aim of the state cadres in transmitting this new knowledge was to place village cadres or another recipient individual or group in a privileged position *vis-à-vis* the rest of the local population, given that the limited transmission of outside knowledge had the effect of generating new spaces of ignorance and therefore disadvantage within the village (see Figure 5.3). Again, a passage in the same novel by Gu Hua indicates the shifting lines of knowledge and ignorance during such campaigns. During the feasting and merriment celebrating the building of a new house, certain of the more astute villagers observed that one of their members who was usually at the centre of such festivities was unusually quiet and subdued. The villagers wondered if 'he was envious, very busy and preoccupied or unusually worried about something'. Another much more disquieting possibility that occurred to the canny was that 'he had some inside information, and knowing what was brewing, was on his guard'. After the event it did emerge that he had already been warned of a coming campaign directed against new riches and conspicuous consumption, of which celebrations, feastings and new houses were obvious examples.[8] However, although state intervention in successive cycles of rectification and purification was represented as in the interests of achieving revolutionary purity, at the local level it seems that the manipulation of information in these

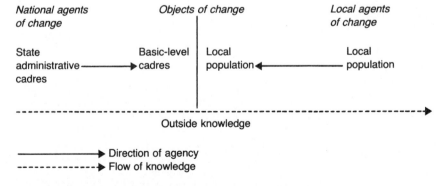

Figure 5.3 Mechanisms of purification and rectification

periodic campaigns was used to generate and settle disputes between competing individuals and interest groups in a manner akin to such other phenomena as witchcraft and sorcery common in other societies.

Where knowledge had been limited to forewarning of political campaigns, and rectification campaigns had come to take the form of cycles of score settlement and factionalism quite outside their official and public terms of reference, they had quite disrupted the implementation of the very development policies and programmes they were designed to purify. There is some evidence to suggest that it was the constant intervention of outside agencies and the negotiation of knowledge and ignorance which had the effect of fragmenting the local population, undermining the very solidarity of collective structures upon which the implementation of state policies rested. By constantly generating new patron–client relations within the village and by introducing and privileging new outside knowledge, the definition of agency and the spatial boundaries between ignorance and knowledge in the village were constantly contested or in a continuous state of flux. Such shifting processes of intervention by the higher-ups generated much rumour, suspicion and divisions in interpersonal and intergroup relations within local populations, thereby reducing the village solidarity on which collective structures and productivity largely rested. Theoretical studies of collective organisational structures and their productivity have suggested that the evolution of a structure and a system of incentives which enabled collective action to extend the domain of individual action and yield organisationally optimal outcomes was ultimately dependent upon personal relationships between members of the group.[9] However, this behavioural approach to productivity usually centred on examining and defining appropriate 'work' relationships of production, and did not extend to include other aspects of political and interpersonal relations. So, while most attempts to explain the recent rapid and radical disaggregation of collective structures in rural China concentrated on examining shortfalls in economic performance, resource allocation, economic incentives and pricing policies, as important a factor may have been their association with constant and unpredictable forms of political intervention. It is interesting to conjecture that initially, after 1976, it was not the constraints of the collective structures themselves so much as the divisiveness and intra-village struggles generated by the singular channels of information and manipulation which affected interpersonal and intergroup relations to such a degree that one of the elements underlying the initial popularity of reform was independence from village affairs previously exclusively managed by village cadres.

INFORMATION AND AGENCY

The most important change in the first years of reform was the multifaceted and facilitated movements of persons and information. Village persons increasingly began to move in and out of the village, if just to visit the revived local market. In the remotest of mountain regions, one of my most memorable sights was of the weekly winding files of men, women and children wending their way to the local Saturday market with perhaps a few eggs, a bundle of wild vegetables or firewood or, unusually, a small wicker bound piglet for sale, and then a few hours later their return with perhaps a bag of grain, fertiliser or a small piglet. The periodic markets breaking many a long journey are a sight to behold with their colourful crowds chatting seriously in small, tight groups gathered or crouching around the makeshift stalls or clustering at low teahouse tables to eat seriously. Markets are of course about more than just the purveyance of foods and goods. Before 1949, it was at these markets that goods, information and daughters were exchanged with news, rumour and gossip relayed to those remaining in the village. Now these markets once again fulfil such functions for the local village populations. Further afield, villagers move outwards from the poorest to the richest villages in search of contract work, raw materials, markets and wholesale goods or to visit kin, and to the nearby township and county towns, and perhaps to cities. If the cut-off in mobility was one of the single most important features of the revolutionary countryside, the movement of persons was one of the most novel features of the newly reformed countryside – so much so that I have always thought that if I had to identify the most significant new item of personal property, then it would have to be the suitcase or travel bag! There is no more potent symbol of reform signifying the new mobility, a trend which can be testified by all those who have attempted in recent years to purchase rail tickets, navigate the large crowded railway stations and travel in carriages and buses piled high with people and goods.

One of my own first and favourite experiences, which graphically signalled the implications of the new mobility and networking of alliances for distant villages, was an encounter I had in the mountains of Henan in 1987. For some hours I had been walking the mountains with a county cadre from village to village; it had been a hard trek with arduous climbs, but the feeling of being high and away from it all and experiencing an isolation and intimacy of village contact denied to the vehicular demar-cated the experience from the ordinary. My initial surprise and even chagrin at eyeing across one valley a large black official limousine which had dared to penetrate the seemingly inaccessible was only overcome by my curiosity at its origins and errand. What I discovered was, I felt, immensely symbolic of the new times. Inside the clay house high on a promontory and on the outskirts of a small cluster of such houses sat several men from diverse destinations talking and drinking. Joining them, I soon learned that the son of the household was on contract work building hotels in a tourist city more than half a day's car journey away. He had befriended the engineer on the building site, and together they had come

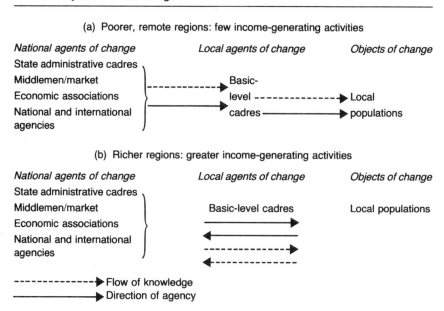

Figure 5.4 Mechanisms of post-reform brokerage

by means of the large black limousine to the village household where the engineer was about to install a wind generator, making it the first household in this mountainous region to have electricity!

In the multiplying sources and channels of information (see Figure 5.4), peasant households now have access to a choice of media, which makes a welcome change from the sole loudspeaker. There is an increasing number of houses with television, colour or black and white, radio and cassette players, and on one memorable occasion a video-recorder was to be seen. Radios and television sets are to be seen even in villages where there is no electricity. Frequently I have counted tens of batteries stretching the length of the table on which the radio or television was set, or a television set in place awaiting a supply of electricity. Access to television and radio networks are likely to bring important and substantive changes into villagers' lives; as one television owner said, 'it feels as if the distance between the world and myself has been shortened'.

Another of the important changes to be observed in households now is the number of written materials, including technical books – how to grow rapeseed, recognise diseased crops, raise chickens or care for rabbits and so on – perhaps a novel or two, and or a number of current newspapers or periodicals may be lying around or even standing in for wallpaper! Markets and township book-stores too have stocks of booklets on planting crops, raising livestock and producing handicrafts, ranging from those in the simplest of language and many pictures to the more sophisticated and technical. The new economic demands on and responsibilities of peasant households have altered the content of outside knowledge so that it is more technical, and villagers recognise the necessity of acquiring or improving their technical skills if they are successfully to operate profitable, income-generating activities. In all the villages of my acquaintance, meetings and training courses to purvey such information were well attended, and booklets and technical newspapers with items on production and how to expand domestic sidelines make for popular reading in households, many of which now subscribe to these publications. Popular reading demands literacy, and it is the demand for information which has reinvested a new interest in and concern for literacy. Illiteracy is designated the main threat or barrier to modernisation. It is estimated that some 20 per cent of the population over the age of fifteen years is still illiterate or able to read fewer than 500 characters (the proportion rises to 35 per cent if the half-literate population is included) with 95 per cent residing in the countryside and 70 per cent female.[10] The government launched anti-illiteracy campaigns in 1982, establishing local classes and special schools in villages, and in 1990, the government stated that it aimed to eliminate illiteracy among 71 million young people and adults between the ages of fifteen and forty and to have eliminated illiteracy and semi-literacy among people forty-one or older by the year 2000.[11]

In 1990 I conducted a study of literacy, reading materials and sources of information in four villages, which, within an hour or two's vehicular distance from an 'open city', but poor and located in the dry highland mountains of Shandong province, had approximately a third of the population officially categorised as illiterate. Although it was estimated that in each village about 20 per cent of the households had no person who could read and write, interviews in households revealed that a high proportion of the adults over the age of thirty had received less than five years of primary schooling and could not easily read or write. More than half of the adults were primarily reliant on oral sources of information, including village broadcasts, village meetings, village leaders or on family members who were literate. The village broadcasting systems were arranged so that there was also a speaker in each house, although each household also had its own switch. The broadcast was the most common source of information on agricultural, technical and other matters – including my own visit! However, it was such a common background feature of village life that, in the words of several villagers, they 'had heard but not heard' its messages. There were frequent meetings in the village to impart information – about once a fortnight in the less busy agricultural seasons – and these were either general multi-topical meetings held by the village leaders which were somewhat compulsory or more specialised but voluntary and addressed by visiting technical experts. Many of those interviewed had attended such a general or specialised meeting within the previous few weeks and learned of the spring planting schedules or fruit-growing techniques. For the not literate the most important source of information was either the village leader, who visited and talked with them individually, or the literate members of their own household. Apart from one old father who could never understand what his son read to him and much preferred a visit from the village leader, most householders who had members of the younger generation with sufficient schooling to enable them to read newspapers preferred this method of receiving information. I suspect this was because they could interrupt to request repetition and explanation, for nearly all of those who totally relied on the oral seemed to have a problem with their memories, finding it especially difficult to retain the technical details and in some cases even the simplest of messages.

Among both illiterate and literate there was evidence of a substantial demand for information on potential income-generating activities, detailed technical knowledge and general information on the world outside of the village. Many of the households subscribed to newspapers, but found the costs of purchasing their own booklets prohibitive. Instead, they borrowed newspapers and booklets from the village committee collections, which operated a loan system. In one poor and quite underdeveloped village some of the loan materials were quite encyclopaedic, offering some 500 pages of guidelines on how to choose, establish and develop family production sidelines. In the households there were substantial numbers of copies of the local scientific and technical newspaper, which was commonly read aloud for its instructions on how to manage their crops, raise rabbits, plant fruit trees or water melons. The second most common periodical was the *Shandong Law and Order Journal*, which a number of peasant householders subscribed to and apparently read with great interest. I have to confess that it took me a little while to realise that not all householders were in training to become lawyers; rather, they avidly read the details of law cases as a wonderfully rapid means of keeping up to date and out of trouble! Other reading matter included popular novels and magazines on 'life', which were lent and borrowed within the village, although it has to be said that reading was only a favourite pastime within a small minority of the households, with most villagers preferring a game of cards to reading. However, even in these relatively remote and poor villages, the demand for information and knowledge was far from absent, and this was so even though they did not have the advantage of radio and television now so common in much of the country.

There is still a wide range in the channels of information reaching the villages of my acquaintance, from the multi-media links of television, newspaper and radio to the single telephone, and not even that in some of the more remote villages. In the Guangxi villages and some Yunnan villages the only telephone was in the township, several hours' walk away. In one larger Yunnan village, which was also the headquarters of the administrative village, there was a single, antiquated telephone whose shrill old-fashioned bell could be heard in the village from time to time signalling a communication. In the Sichuan highland villages there were also no telephones, and communication was by word of mouth. Within such villages the pecking order for 'knowing' and closeness to cadre was important: in one village, for example, the first and only person to have heard of and taken advantage of the new opportunities for credit was the brother of the village cadre. As he was recounting to me his unusual activities in a crowded room, I was suddenly alerted to a facial likeness between the two men, and asked the farmer whether he was by any chance related to the cadre. There was much merriment and nodding of heads at the exchange, which elicited the response, 'You know China very well!' On another occasion I trekked the mountains with a very popular cadre who, unusually tall and charismatic, brought information and inputs and facilitated contacts and services to the remote and scattered cattle farmers. On an unexpected visit, he would hail the villagers from the top of the valley, and one by one they would welcome him to their households with drinks and gifts while there was much talk of 'foreign affairs' beyond the village. In contrast, in Wuxi village, the most industrially developed of all the villages in the case studies, it was quite apparent that villagers were well informed about technical, national and international matters. In recording the enterprise histories it was very noticeable how much their expansion rested on the multiple contacts of both villager and cadre outside of the village. As the leaders themselves said, the secret of their success had been that they had gone out beyond the village and obtained the best information. 'Information', they said was the 'light to the wealthy way' in that it could be likened to a lighthouse so that 'no information meant no light and no light meant no direction'.

If knowledge was no longer so privileged so too was the content of knowledge more varied. Knowledge has less to do with campaign, criticism and contest between personalities and patrons than with the political beyond the village and the technical. Knowledge of national and international political events is much more widespread, although this is not to suggest that its presentation may not be biased. Many of my recent travels have coincided with reasonably accurate reports of the dramatic events in the Soviet Union and Eastern Europe, and even in remote counties and townships there were animated discussions as to the significance of these events for China. One in particular, in one of the more remote corners of Shandong province, ended unusually with loud voices, red faces and food quite ignored. Technical information, too, was much more accessible, although examples drawn from the village studies suggested that villagers still took some persuading to adopt new technical practices. For instance, in the Beijing village a new sprinkler irrigation system had to be introduced gradually because of village reluctance. At first, only half of the land was mechanically watered, so that the farmers could see for themselves that the maize grew more quickly and ahead of schedule, which gained the village time in planting the winter wheat. In case the sprinkler system failed to work, all the supply ditches, trenches and channels were retained for the first couple of years. Experiments conducted during the gradual changeover from ground to sprinkler irrigation had showed that, with the sprinkler system, the wheat yield rose by 32.8 kg per mu. Moreover, the new system also saved water by 70 per cent, loosened the soil and removed less groundwater. While with groundwater one person might irrigate 4 mu per day, with a sprinkler two persons could water 15 to 18 mu in one day. Once the farmers saw the advantages for themselves, the remaining ditches, channels and trenches were levelled and cultivated, increasing the village grain lands by 11.2 per cent. In Shanxi village, new machines were greeted with more than a degree of ambivalence. When a new machine for harvesting sorghum was promised one afternoon as an experiment in mechanical harvesting, between the morning promise and the afternoon arrival of the machine, not a single field of sorghum was left standing. It had all been harvested in the intervening hours, for did not machines have eyes? These examples notwithstanding, the most noticeable feature of the reform countryside does remain the demand for technical information, its practice and the association of information with agency. The 'peasants' or 'masses' are now represented as farmers and entrepreneurs, both categories with an agency observably different from the amorphous categorisations of the past.

INFORMATION AND SANCTION

One of the interesting repercussions of this incorporation into news and information networks was the bargaining power it potentially gave to the villagers in their negotiations with the village cadres. No longer did cadres have a monopoly of outside knowledge nor was their outside knowledge so singular and therefore they as messengers so privileged. Plural sources and channels of information were not only less manageable and open to manipulation by local cadres, but the villager also had recourse to a number of higher authorities and a number of approved sanctions against the exercise of undue cadre authority, thus reducing the previous asymmetry between village and cadre. As the Deputy Director of the Sociology Institute of the Academy of Social Sciences stated in 1987, the farmers should be permitted to have more decision-making power, to acquire the means to protect their interests and aspirations, and channels should be established for farmers to voice their complaints to the authorities.[12]

One of the most important of these channels was the media, and especially the press. In this respect my favourite such story, perhaps because of its novelty, is one which I like to entitle 'The Peasant who

Called a Press Conference',[13] which, for me, has all the attributes of a watershed. A village farmer in suburban Beijing held a press briefing at his house on 13 May 1988 criticising the local government for unilaterally scrapping a land contract and forcibly taking back his contracted land. He asked the journalists present to uphold justice and safeguard the peasants' legitimate rights and interests. Showing the reporters a contract stamped with the red seal of the villagers' committee, the farmer recounted the details of the contract for 45.5 mu of barren land which had required inputs amounting to several thousand yuan. The contract had been broken before the due date by village cadres on the pretext of developing agriculture on a fairly large scale.

The reporters present asked a number of questions of the farmer: 'Did the village consult with you and get your consent before it terminated the contract?'; 'Did you have other sources of income from industry or sideline occupations?' and 'Had you been given another piece of land?' To the latter question, the farmer replied: 'I do not want other land. I want to till the land I have contracted. The contract clearly states that it is good for three years. Why did they unilaterally scrap the contract before its expiration? According to *Required Reading for Specialised Households*, a book I have kept on government policies, this should not happen.' The reporters also talked to township cadres who said that 'The contract has been nullified, not scrapped, because we want to develop agriculture on a fairly large scale and fulfil the annual target of wheat growing acreage. There is nothing wrong with what we have done!'

One reporter asked: 'When the township decided to terminate the contract, did it ever consider giving compensation to the contractor for the investment he has put into it and other losses he has suffered?' The Deputy Secretary said: 'Developing agriculture on a fairly large scale is a national policy that will unavoidably put some peasants in a disadvantageous position. The farmer has received income from contracted land. He did not suffer any economic losses. If the township sympathises with him, it may give him some compensation; otherwise he cannot get any.' A reporter then quoted Premier Li Peng who said that in development of agriculture managed on a fairly large scale, 'We must not rush headlong into mass action, issue arbitrary orders, and spoil things by excessive enthusiasm', and the central authorities Document No. 1 of 1984 which clearly stipulated that the contracting of land should run for fifteen years. When asked, 'What do you think of these things?' the township cadre said nothing. The report concluded by stating that more than ten reporters from *Renmin Ribao, Xinhua News*, the central TV station, *Jingji Ribao, Fazhi Ribao* and *Beijing Fazhi Ribao* had attended the press briefing. Admittedly, as the report made clear, it had taken a certain amount of panache for an individual peasant to call a press conference, which suggested that the press was still more of a potential than actual form of recourse, but it is still surprising to long-time observers just how many grievances and complaints make it to the pages of the press.

Even more important and perhaps potentially more reliable than the press is the introduction of an alternative system of appeal or recourse to the law courts newly available in some developed regions and accessible to villagers in taking up cases against cadres. According to one survey of farmers in the rural suburbs of Shanghai, almost a quarter of farmers thought that a lawyer's office in the neighbourhood was more important than a good local leader; only 19 per cent thought the opposite; and the majority presumably thought that both were desirable.[14] In one or two villages, there have been complaints that the rule of law was not yet strong enough, and in another one or two villages the *Law Journal* was a popular read. Certainly in the press there have been a number of instances in which farmers were reported to have sued cadres for breach of contract. One such case, in which a Chinese farmer sued county cadres, 'created a stir' when the Wenzhou Intermediate People's Court opened a hearing on 25 August 1988.[15] More than 1,000 people were reported to have crowded into the county movie theatre where the hearing was being held, while hundreds of others stood outside, 'keenly aware that the event itself was quite as stupendous as any outcome'. In this case, the plaintiff, a sixty-one-year-old peasant, accused the county government of demolishing parts of his private houses. In 1985, he had allegedly built a three-storey house with official approval; however in July 1987, some 300 people, led by county officials, demolished the structures alleging that he had not received a building permit and had built his house on a dike, thus violating water conservancy regulations. The indictment was read by the farmer's son, who said that many of their relatives and friends had tried to persuade them to drop the suit, convinced that ordinary people could have no hope of winning a case against officials. However, his father had insisted on maintaining that the common people's right to sue the government was guaranteed by law.

The defendant, a county official, claimed that the county government and the Communist Party committee had been opposed to his appearing in court as a defendant, but he said, 'I made my own decision'. The magistrate was quoted as saying, 'The defendant is not necessarily a criminal. I am willing to contribute my bit to the development of China's legal system.' The presiding judge told reporters that the court had not met with any administrative interference so far, although there had been controversy over whether to accept the case. He went on to describe the plaintiff's determination to solve the dispute through legal procedures as 'right and normal' and expressed appreciation for his courage. 'This shows that the people's concept of law is undergoing a change', he told reporters. The hearing lasted more than five hours, until almost 10.30 in the evening, and four days later the court announced its judgment in favour of the local government by ruling that the demolition of the farmer's home was a legal and correct act, whereupon the farmer and his lawyer said they would appeal to the Provincial People's Supreme Court. The villager lost the case, and the newspaper report suggested that this was still a brave and unprecedented attempt to counter a cadre decision, but again the presence of procedures for redress and their reporting is an important indication of the new plurality of authorities in the countryside, placing new checks and balances on the rule of village cadres which lead to more symmetric relations between villager and cadre in the exercise of agency.

One area where there continues to be asymmetry in the relationship between local cadre and villager is in construction of official representation of village affairs or experience. The writing of reports which pass up through higher administrative levels, amounting to a great lattice of reports, is still the prerogative of local cadres, who almost exclusively report on the village for 'outside' administration and government. If the channels of communication into the village are now multifarious, official channels from the village remain narrow and hierarchical given that the prerogative to construction of knowledge invokes acts of power. This is not a new situation for, during the revolution, village cadres, as both agents of the state and villagers, frequently found themselves in the difficult if not impossible position of having to reconcile differing expectations, as they were expected to implement novel or even unpopular state policy at a rapid pace. Studies of policy implementation at the local level frequently concluded that during the revolution new political, social and economic practices were evolved which represented significant departures from previous customs and practices, concessions to the new policy and, very importantly, an adjustment to the local physical and economic environment.[16] For instance, new structures might coincide with long-established village hierarchies, customs might be only partially transformed, older categorisations might be tacitly relabelled and kinship elders permitted to influence village affairs unduly but via new and permitted mechanisms. However, local modifications to national policies might be omitted from or only partially reported in cadre reports on village affairs, or frequently new terms might be simply redefined by village cadres to fit local practices. What was common in the villages was that the changes instituted fell far short of the all-inclusive goals of the state for radical social change, and in periodic assessments of the progress of revolution, what increasingly dismayed the state was the slow pace of change in the villages which was increasingly attributed to the failure of village cadres to communicate and implement national policies correctly at local levels. This common slippage in local reporting has continued into the reform years.

In studying villages, it is my custom to conduct interviews at all the higher administrative levels, from county, through township to administrative village, about the village studied. Frequently there is some discrepancy between official representations of village affairs and popular experience recounted in households. This discrepancy is not so much due to dishonesty as to the desire to present a semblance of orderly, efficient and satisfactory policy implementation discriminating in favour of a positive example. In one recent and glaring example of neat reversal, what was officially reported to be 'efficient, speedy and amicable' village resettlement to make way for a new road or 'pathway to the future' became, in the words of villagers, harshly imposed chaotic relocation in return for 'a great wall' in their village. What is still missing from official reports is ambiguity of village experience, and it is this discrepancy between the image of official reports and village experience which has frequently given rise to 'hot' discussions of the relations between cadre and villager in the past ten years. Another area of debate which has also been designated a 'hot topic'[17] of the reform decade has been the rising differentials between rich and poor, a subject on which both official and popular representations coincide.

Chapter 6

Income generation
Riches, poverty and projects

Initially, on the eve of reform and after the long years of the revolution and its promises, it was the association of riches with reform that sold the idea of reform and acted as an incentive to those about to undertake and live the reforms. One of the most important questions of the decade was whether the government could satisfy the rising expectations it had set in motion at the outset of reform. It seemed as if this was more than possible in the first years of the decade, for one of the most important and much publicised repercussions of the early years of reform was the dramatic increase in cash incomes and standards of living of peasant households. Indeed, throughout the countryside, a combination of economic reforms and new pricing policies caused the largest overall rise in peasant incomes since the 1950s.[1] The number of newly rich, and in particular 'ten thousand yuan', households became the chief rationale for and criterion in measuring the efficacy of the reforms and not only in the popular imagination. Officially too, the association of riches with reform permeated government reports, policy documents and speeches, and constituted the overriding criterion of success. For example, a major policy document in 1984 openly stated that the main criteria for judging the 'correctness' of new agricultural policies was not whether they furthered socialist or national development but whether they enriched the peasants rapidly.[2] 'Get rich quick', 'You too can become rich' and 'Riches for all' became the gist of many a popular saying and official slogan encouraging the emulation of the 'ten-thousand-yuan' rich households. Significant and sometimes dramatic rises in the national per capita peasant income were widely celebrated in the first few years of reform.

There are certain problems associated with calculating national average per capita peasant incomes to do with sampling techniques and the definitions of and categorisations of income, be it gross or net, cash or kind. Thus figures commonly understated real income levels in that on-farm consumption of self-produced grain was valued at below market price and on-farm consumption of other self-produced foods, such as vegetables, might be discounted. Nevertheless national surveys, although they should not be taken too literally, did illustrate the important general trend of rapidly rising peasant household cash incomes in the first few years of reform. One survey of 22,000 households in 589 counties undertaken in 1982[3] showed that the proportion of peasant households earning a cash income of between ¥200 and ¥500 annually had risen substantially from 27.4 per cent in 1978 to 66.5 per cent in 1982 (see Table 6.1). A more detailed study[4] suggested that, on average, per capita income between 1978 and 1982 had more than doubled or had risen from ¥133.60 to ¥270.11 (see Table 6.2). Lee Travers made adjustments to these figures to compensate for the bias in the selection of households, and his revised figures showed a less dramatic but still significant rise in income, from ¥108.24 in 1978 to ¥165.96 in 1981.[5] In 1983, another sample survey of 30,427 peasants in 682 counties spread over twenty-eight provinces revealed that average annual income per capita had risen to ¥309.80, which marked an increase of 14.7 per cent over 1982, when the average per capita income (¥264.30) was just below that of the previous survey – although, like earlier surveys, it did not take into account the simultaneous rise in prices.[6] After five years of reforms, a more sophisticated survey of farm households conducted in 1984 did take price rises into account. It calculated that, although the average per capita income reached ¥355 in 1984 and represented an increase of 160 per cent over 1978 per capita income, the percentage rise would be reduced to 100 per cent after allowing for price rises.[7] By 1985 the average per capita net income in rural areas had risen to ¥397.60 from ¥133.57 in 1978, representing an increase of 197.6 per cent. After deducting factors caused by price hikes, the actual growth rate was estimated to be 132.4 per cent.[8]

Although analysis suggests that rises in peasant incomes were not always as high as officially represented if they took account of the simultaneous rise in prices, they were nevertheless very significant and much talked about both within and outside of China. In the richest and in the poorest regions, official reports and rich and poor householders identified the rises in cash incomes and improved quality of their livelihoods as the most important single change in peasant lives, with an almost immediately observable increase in available foods, goods and services, contributing to an impressive humming and purposive bustle of economic activity and evident well-being in accessible villages and households. 'Ten thousand yuan' households were selected as official models for emulation, and almost without exception it was the specialised households which earned the highest incomes over the first five years. Indeed, an early survey suggested that one of the strongest correlations was to be found between the wealth of the peasant household and the degree to which it had diversified its activities into sidelines. As Table 6.3 shows, only 20 per cent of the total income of the richer specialised households derived from field cultivation, while poor peasant households relied on the land for more than

65 per cent of their income.[9] Most of the newly rich households were also large, had higher levels of education and were more likely to be inhabited by cadres or ex-cadres of production brigades or communes, or some young educated persons and former members of the army, or of those groups who already had some experience in management, in developing their own networks of communication or in acquiring technical or specialised skills.[10] Those who achieved such riches found themselves the centre of much media and village attention and applause, with their life-history rise to riches a much-cited source of local pride.

My most vivid and memorable example of local pride in the early years of reform (1984) was in a village a day's journey from the large central city of Wuhan on the Yangtze River. It was a large village set along the banks of a tributary river with small, compact houses set in low rows with one outstanding exception: standing at the centre of the village and two storeys higher than its neighbours one newly built house provided a startling contrast. Unlike its neighbours, its courtyard was high-walled, and within the shining green-tiled interior courtyard was an elaborate stone fountain whose stream was turned on and off as visitors proceeded through gates much in the style of a Jacques Tati film. The village cadres were very familiar with its exact mechanics, and seemed completely at home showing off this large, airy house with six rooms which uniquely included a bathroom and a modern, large, well-stocked kitchen. The house was a prime example of the new conspicuous consumption and was certainly much talked about by cadre and villager. More than any other attribute of reform, the presence of such new riches was reassuring, providing evidence of the efficacy and early success of rural reform.

If the presence of the rich and advocacy of riches continued to be reassuring, it was also clear that in the course of reform, rises in incomes, though still increasing, were levelling out with the annual percentage rises reduced in comparison to the early years. This was so nationally in these latter years – whatever the actual levels of per capita net income calculated (see Table 6.6) – and at the village level in most of the case studies. Moreover, the costs of inputs and other services were increasing, which also reduced rises in net incomes by as much as a half, a discrepancy which had led *Renmin Ribao* to conclude in 1987 that nationally 'rocketing prices had resulted in greater losses than gains for peasants'.[11] Certainly, price rises of inputs had offset the gains in many of the poorer villages, leaving some households with an annual deficit and accumulating debts. Nevertheless, if it remains one of the achievements of the reforms to have brought about increases, and sometimes very large increases, in average peasant incomes over the first ten years of reform, it is also clear that the overall trend in rising incomes was accompanied by rising income differentials between rich and the poor. In the first years of reform, analyses of trends in average per capita incomes between regions and provinces showed that the range in average provincial incomes was quite substantial.[12] In 1982, peasant incomes were estimated to range from ¥174.50 (Gansu) to ¥381 (Guangdong) (see Table 6.4). Not surprisingly, the highest average per capita peasant incomes for single counties were to be found in the rural suburbs of the largest municipalities of Beijing, Shanghai or Tianjin cities, where the average per capita peasant income soon exceeded ¥500. Other provinces with high per capita peasant incomes ranging between ¥400 and ¥500 were Jiangsu, Zhejiang, Guangdong, Shandong, Liaoning, Jilin and Heilongjiang, which all lay along the northern, eastern and southern coastal regions. In these coastal provinces, where the commodity economy was earlier more developed, the annual average per capita income in 1984 was greater than ¥400, while in the hinterlands the average was nearer ¥300.[13] Within provinces too, there were wide variations in per capita income which could be roughly correlated with the natural endowments of the region. In Anhui province, for example, economic development was very uneven, with those on the plains earning an average per capita income of ¥304 compared to ¥275 in the mountains and ¥239.40 in the hills.[14] In Shaanxi province a survey of peasant incomes in 1983[15] showed a greater difference of ¥67 per capita between plain and mountain (Table 6.5), and in the poorer western provinces with more extreme variations between mountain and plain, the differentials were likely to have been even wider.

That not all peasant incomes had risen at the same rate and within the same time period and that some incomes had hardly risen at all was increasingly both officially and popularly acknowledged. Whereas during the revolution, the rhetoric of equality had camouflaged very considerable disparities and differentials, the reform government officially anticipated in 1982 that reform would widen income differentials, with 30–40 per cent of peasant households becoming rich, 40–50 per cent achieving considerable improvements, while only 15–20 per cent of peasant households with little or no planning or business acumen would continue to encounter difficulties in meeting basic needs.[16] The government, also forecasting that within any one community it was likely that on average richer households would earn two to three times the income of poorer households, seemed prepared to tolerate these rising differentials as one of the inevitable consequences of permitting greater household control of production and in the interests of providing material incentives to promote production. It is officially acknowledged in the Chinese media that there have been increasing differentials over the reform period,[17] and within villages in many different regions of China and over most years during the past decade my own interviews with villagers both rich and poor suggested that the popular view was of wide and increasing differentials. The poorest village households have uniformly noted that though their incomes had risen, they too felt that the gap between them and their richer neighbours had widened considerably since the early years of reform.

VILLAGE DIFFERENTIALS

Village studies suggest that, while income increases might be slowing down, differentials were not lessening and that they were still wide, both between and within villages. The average per capita cash incomes of the sixteen villages featured in Chapter 3 showed that four had an average per capita income below ¥50, three below ¥100 and four below ¥200. The remaining five villages all had an average per capita income higher than ¥750, with two of the villages higher than ¥1,400; the highest was the suburban village near Beijing with an average per capita income of ¥1,579. Even allowing for the two- to three-year interval between the first and last study, the highest village per capita income was thirty times that of the poorest. Within villages the differentials were also great. The study of an entire small mountain village in Henan province in 1987 had revealed the extent to which differentials could demarcate peasant experience of reform despite any outward appearances of equity or even uniformity of house, yard and furnishings.

The average per capita cash village income was ¥85.20, or ¥413 per household, which was lower than the average per person (¥114) and per household (¥600) for the county and than the average of ¥104.70 per person and ¥550 per household for the township in which the village was located. Within the village, per capita income ranged from ¥17 and ¥351 per person and ¥105 and ¥1,405 per household which, constituting wide differentials by any reckoning, could be most directly correlated with family labour resources, their physical and mental capacities and their education and skills. The number of adult male workers tended to determine the quality of field cultivation and crop yields, and the number of adult females determined the number and types of sidelines. In the richest household in the village earning a cash income of ¥1,405, or ¥351 per person, there were four persons (two adult labourers and two children) with average land resources, twenty-eight chickens and one head of cattle. They also undertook food processing, which alone earned an annual income of ¥1,200, and this made it the only household in the village to earn a substantial cash income from sidelines and only one of four households who earned any cash income from the provision of services or handicrafts. In contrast, in the poorest household in the village, there were two adults and four children, of whom only one was still dependent. None of the children had enjoyed lengthy schooling, for all had been taken out of school to contribute to the economic activities of the household. There was some illness in the household, but although the household was not labour-short, there was evidence of a general mental slowness and lack of agricultural, technical and managerial skills in it. The yields per mu were very low, so that the income earned through the sale of crops to the state amounted to only ¥50; the household earned ¥30 from the sale of its eggs, and the adult male hired himself out to neighbours to help them in agricultural work for which he received ¥1 per day, or a total of ¥30 per year.

In the township in which the village was located, the richest household was one with ten persons – two parents, a married son and daughter-in-law with their four children ranging in age from ten to three, and another son and daughter neither of whom was yet married. The household had 35 mu of cultivable land on which it cultivated wheat, maize, beans, tobacco and vegetables for subsistence, fodder and sale. It also had 700 mu of pasture land on which it raised fourteen head of cattle and sheep, and a cash income of some ¥3,000, or ¥300 per capita, which was five times the household and three times the per capita average for the township. In contrast, in reputedly the poorest household in the township, a cash income of ¥250 was shared between three persons, including elderly parents and an only son who was mentally incapacitated and whose treatment had cost his parents ¥400 the previous year. With no long-term means of support, these parents had moved to the village of their married daughter to obtain help for themselves and their son in their old age. Although the elderly husband and wife could manage the agricultural fieldwork and the raising of some chickens, two cattle and a pig, they did not expect to be able to continue to support themselves in the long term. Very reluctantly and feeling that they had no alternative but to move to their married daughter's village, they had left their old village, their house, land and friends. Although they had received arable land in the new village, there had as yet been no pasture land available for distribution to them. In the meantime, feeling very much displaced – and indeed it is rare to hear of households moving villages – they grazed their animals on their daughter's and other neighbours' land. The interviews conducted in the 'very poor' households revealed that in every case premature death or poor health, including both physical or mental incapacities, were important causes of low income and/or debt. Premature death or poor health reduced the labour resources of the household and therefore the yields per mu, the number of sidelines and therefore the income of the household, although income was not always a reliable guide to the welfare of a household, as the burden of medical expenses incurred by the prolonged illness frequently left considerable debts.

A year later in studies of income differentials within seven Sichuan villages, also located in poor regions with few income-generating activities, the range in per capita incomes within and between the villages was wide. Without exception, the peasant households with the highest incomes in any of the villages were located on the lower lands and were labour-rich with a high ratio of labourers to dependants. They had a higher than average number of livestock, suggesting access to credit, and there was usually a source of off-farm income, suggesting surplus labour or a skill such as carpentry, masonry or bricklaying. The richest household in the sample was lowland-located, and made up of six persons of whom five were full-time, able-bodied labourers, including a married-in daughter-in-law. The household raised one dairy cow, three milk goats, four pigs and five ducks, all of which – together with an off-farm income of ¥300 earned by the elder son with senior middle-school education as a village accountant – furnished a high cash income of ¥2,245, or ¥376 per capita. They had no savings and still owed ¥500 of a ¥3,000 loan for their cow. The second richest household of the sample, also lowland, had four adult labourers including the fifteen-year-old son who had left school after only three years of primary education, and an eighteen-year-old son who had had five years of primary schooling before taking up farm work. Because their mother and father had both been ill, their labour power was much reduced. The previous year they raised two pigs and four chickens, and their main sources of cash income were rapeseed (¥250) and the sale of fourteen piglets (¥300). However, although the sow had died of disease the previous month, the farmer had high hopes for an increased income in future years as he had just been given a kid goat and a share in a buffalo. He qualified for a relief grant of ¥40, which he used for fertiliser. He owed ¥90 in taxes, ¥300 to the rural credit co-operative for hospital and house repair expenses, and ¥350 to his neighbours for his share of the buffalo.

The household with the third highest income was located in the highlands and was made up of a husband, wife and two young school-age children. The basis of their high per capita income of ¥138 was the sale of a pig (¥175), the high yields and sale of rapeseed (¥225) and a surplus of rice (deriving from the high yield in relation to the low consumption of young sons), which sold in the market for ¥90. He had a loan of ¥250 to help meet the costs of fertiliser (a high ¥324), ¥100 for seed and chemicals and ¥120 for coal to provide fuel for cooking fodder for the pigs and food for the family. His income was the highest in his village but so were his expenses, leading him to think he was only one of the lower-middle income families in the village. The household with the fourth highest cash income in the sample was made up of four persons: parents and adult sons. In the past three years they had raised two goats which between them had produced 1,200 jin of milk, earning ¥312 each year; the sale of a pig each year earned another ¥200. The pigs had been bought from the proceeds of goat milk, but despite the relatively high income, the wife's sickness had cost the household ¥20–30 per month, and with three pigs and two goats, the household was grain-short and had both borrowed grain from friends and relatives and purchased additional grain. Even among the richest households in the sample, expenses matched or exceeded incomes, so that there were few savings, little surplus income for investment and, in most cases, debts.

The four poorest households in the sample all earned less than ¥40 per capita and were located in the highland villages. They were labour-poor, with few able-bodied labourers; their land yields were lower than average; and they raised few or no livestock. In the poorest household of the sample, which earned no cash income, there were three persons: a very slow father, his son of fifteen years who helped on the farm after having graduated from primary school, and a twelve-year-old daughter who looked after the house, having never been to school. The mother had died three years before and, about the same time, the elder son of nineteen years had migrated to Fujian province to make a living. They only cultivated maize, had allowed 1 mu of land to lie idle and raised no livestock. They received relief from the government in the form of wheat flour, rice, fertiliser and living expenses. The father's debts had been cancelled once before and he now only owed 300 jin of maize to a relative. The second poorest household was made up of two young parents with two small daughters who had been born since the allocation of responsibility lands, so that altogether the household only had arable and vegetable lands allocated to two persons. The rice and wheat crops cultivated produced 650 jin and 300 jin respectively, and were insufficient for four persons; some maize was cultivated for fodder. The previous year they had raised one pig, which they consumed, and five chickens, which were sold, as were all the eggs produced. The cash income derived from the sale of rape (¥47) and of poultry/eggs (¥40). They lived abstemiously, but fertiliser took up practically their entire cash income; they owed ¥131, borrowed for purchasing fertiliser and a pig, and had received a ¥30 relief grant.

The third poorest household in the seven villages was made up of three persons: two parents in their fifties and a nineteen-year-old daughter. They also sold rapeseed (¥70), vegetables (¥5) and raised one chicken, all the eggs from which were sold (¥10); they had just begun to raise one pig in the last year largely for its manure. They had debts totalling ¥940, for fertiliser (¥180), and a piglet and house repairs (¥860), borrowed from the bank and from relatives and friends. They hoped to repay these by raising more pigs, hiring out the father's labour (which was very difficult in the remote village) and by raising rabbits. The fourth poorest household was made up of a husband, his rather 'weak' wife and three children, one of whom had left primary school early to tend the three pigs. Since their chickens had died of disease they had raised no other livestock. Although the husband usually sold ten to twelve piglets each year, earning ¥200, he used this sum entirely to purchase fodder grain (¥200) and repay annually repeated 500-jin loans of grain from friends and relatives and to purchase rice for themselves (¥126). He owed grain to friends and, because he still had not repaid a loan for fertiliser and seed borrowed in 1984, he could not borrow from the bank until it was repaid. A few months before, he had applied to take up goat raising, for now that his daughter was helping to raise the pigs, he expected to be able to repay his debt in the near future and thereby become eligible for further loans.

It is differentials such as these, officially and popularly acknowledged both nationally and in villages, which have led to ongoing debates about polarisation of rich and poor in the countryside in relation to reform.[18] How much differentiation is acceptable in the interests of growth and efficiency? Is there a necessary trade-off between 'efficiency versus equity' during a period of economic take-off? Indeed, economists have debated as follows:

> how to balance efficiency and social equity is an important issue in China's economic reform and development . . . Social equity is, in principle, one of the goals of socialism. But, for a long time before China began its reforms in the late 1970s, equity was pursued at the expense of efficiency. As a result, egalitarianism became a common practice. The enthusiasm of the working people was dampened and general poverty and low efficiency became a vicious circle . . . In recent years, a small number of people in both countryside and towns have earned much more than the majority whose income also increased in general. This gives rise to anxiety about the possible polarisation of society into the poor and the rich. However so long as different policies are adopted in different cases, the socialist system can, fundamentally speaking, prevent such polarisation.[19]

While all those debating seemed to agree that the system known in China as 'everyone eating from the same big pot', or egalitarianism, had disadvantaged China, there were considerable problems associated with the increasing polarisation between rich and poor. One means of avoiding the problem but retaining incentives and nurturing the rich was to improve the conditions of the poor, and gradually through the years of reform there has been a shift in focus from applauding the rich to increasing official and popular concern for the poor reflected in new poverty alleviation programmes and development projects reaching the village.

VILLAGE POVERTY ALLEVIATION

Increasingly, alongside the applause for the rich there was a growing official and media concern for the poor of China's countryside, or those who had not and were not in a position to take advantage of new income-generating opportunities. In June 1984, *Renmin Ribao* published a letter written by a peasant from a small village in eastern Fujian province who described how they still lived a very poor life, dwelt in crude houses and fed mainly on sweet potatoes.[20] Thereafter a number of media reports not only highlighted the new economic reforms and the rise in incomes, but also the still 'very bitter' peasant lives in the northwest and southwest, old revolutionary base areas, young, newly developed areas and the border and mountainous regions.

There was a dramatic decline in the number of absolute poor during the first five years, during which time it is estimated that the numbers of absolute poor dropped from 270 million, or 33 per cent of the population, in 1978, to 96 million, or 12 per cent of the rural population, in 1985 (see Table 6.6).[21] Nevertheless, there were also reports from poorer regions that as much as 26.8 per cent of the population still had a per capita income of less than ¥22 per year, and 11 per cent did not have enough to eat.[22] Thus in the mid-1980s there was an explicit shift in official concern from rich to poor regions and poor households, and simultaneously a readjustment in state policies.

The concept of poverty alleviation as a distinctive set of policies specifically to improve the lot of poor villagers was not widely deployed until the middle of the decade. At first in the initial years of reform the government encouraged villagers themselves to provide support for those who required assistance by accumulating public welfare funds for distribution, by arranging for the cultivation of their produce or some form of self-help or community care. One county government in Anhui province was officially praised for developing its own networks for social relief in a 'help-the-poor' campaign when it had compiled a register of the needy and issued them with certificates entitling them to preferential consideration in regard to loans and access to means of production, reduction in medical expenses and free education for their children. Groups of willing cadres and peasants, organised into 'help-the-poor' committees, gave practical assistance to those in their immediate vicinity by helping them either to cultivate their lands or plots or develop their domestic sidelines such as pig raising.[23] The establishment of similar 'help the poor' committees was encouraged,[24] but they implied a degree of voluntarism and self-help which was plainly inadequate when it came to ameliorating poverty on a large scale.

In September 1984, the Central Committee of the Chinese Communist Party and the State Council jointly issued a Circular for Aiding Poor Areas which acknowledged the still great regional disparities in economic development due to the differences in material conditions, natural conditions, employment opportunities and the implementation of the new policies.[25] The report referred to the alleviation of poverty still necessary in remote regions where tens of millions of people were still poor, and that 'their problems of food and clothing had yet to be solved properly' was said to be 'of tremendous economic and political significance'. The report urged Party committees and governments at all levels to take 'positive and effective measures to shake off poverty, improve productive conditions, raise productive capacity and develop commodity production so that these areas could catch up with others'. In practical terms this meant an increase in investment and exemption from agricultural tax for five years to 'help them shake off poverty'. In 1986, in order to co-ordinate, study and supervise the economic development of poor rural areas, the State Council set up the Leading Group of Economic Development in Poor Areas with administrative offices at national, provincial, prefectural and county levels and officers at the township level to identify and organise appropriate forms of intervention in poor regions. In the same year, in the country's Seventh Five Year Plan of National Economic Development (1986–90), the State Council clearly defined the two steps for developing the country's poor areas: providing basic needs and generating a self-development capacity by helping targeted 'poor counties' to set up commodity production bases that relied on local resources and industries.

'Poor counties' were defined as those with an average annual per capita net income lower than ¥150 which, in 1988, totalled 698, and were mainly located in the resource-scarce inland, border, remote and mountainous regions where the poor of China were increasingly concentrated. Although outside of these regions, in otherwise well-off regions throughout the country, there was also a residue of households disadvantaged by high dependency ratios, ill health and other difficulties, the state planned to concentrate its efforts to reduce poverty in these 'poor' counties. The Five Year Plan also signalled a major policy change from state delivery of 'pure' aid or relief, albeit small during the revolution, to income generation with the aim of engendering development rather than dependency by 'gradually helping poor areas to form the capability of self development in introducing a commodity economy, solving the problem of food shortage'. What this meant in practice was the establishment of enterprises, services and associations which would aid poor households and villages by creating employment and the production of commodities with the help of funds, technology, materials, information and training provided by and administered by the Poverty Alleviation Office.

What became clear during the latter reform years was that, despite these policies and strong overall economic growth, little further reduction in poverty was achieved, with the proportion of total population living in absolute poverty remaining roughly constant at 9 per cent.[26] The poverty gap also increased slightly, and not just in the poorest regions, because of sharp increases in food prices and particularly the doubling of the average rural retail price of grain, which placed new pressures on the real incomes of rural poor. Other factors generally affecting rural incomes included the reduction in the growth rate of agricultural production from an average annual increase of more than 7 per cent during the period 1978–85 to about 2.3 per cent during the period 1985–89, and the modest slowing of employment generation from 3.1 per cent per annum during 1978–85 to 2.6 per cent per annum during 1985–89.[27] The slow-down of rural enterprise development during 1989 and 1990 also reduced off-farm employment opportunities and contributed to a more general decline in real rural income in 1989. However, a high proportion of the absolute poor was concentrated in villages in several northwestern, northeastern and southwestern provinces, and in 1989 it was estimated that at least 10 per cent of the rural population in the northwestern provinces of Shanxi, Henan, Shaanxi, Nei Meng, Ningxia, Gansu, Qinghai and Xinjiang, the northeastern provinces of Jilin and Heilongjiang and the southwestern provinces of Guizhou, Guangxi and Yunnan were 'absolutely poor' (see Table 6.7). Including Liaoning (6 per cent poor), and Sichuan (7 per cent poor), the rural poor of these fifteen provinces numbered 53 million people and accounted for 80 per cent of those categorised as poor, making up approximately 50 per cent of the population in these provinces.[28] They were concentrated in deep mountainous regions with poor natural conditions not conducive to development, minority nationality populations, endemic diseases and infrastructural deficiencies including serious shortages of drinking-water supply, and had seen few if any recent improvements in their living standards. The village case studies in Yunnan and Guangxi were located in just such regions.

The provision of relief in the villages took one of three forms, including grain, cash sums or clothes and quilt, for which very few households in each village were eligible (see Table 6.8). It was the responsibility of village cadres, on behalf of the Ministry of Civil Affairs, to decide the households eligible, which usually included the five-guarantee households, elderly single-person households and those with little or no labour power. They numbered on average about twenty-four in each township and two to three in an administrative village of some 200 to 300 households. The number of village households which received cash aid annually was less than 3 per cent, with no household receiving more than ¥10. In two of the Yunnan villages, the two households that received cash relief had no more than a few yuan cash income a year and did not have full labour power. In one Guangxi village where no households received cash relief, a total of twelve, or one-fifth, of the households, were reported to have no cash income at all. The households which were eligible each year for a suit of clothes and a quilt consisted of the five-guarantee households, those with no labour power due to chronic illness and those handicapped. In the Yunnan village, three households received a set of clothes (distinguished by their plain blue and black fabric) and a quilt. In Guangxi stone mountain villages, between 30 and 40 per cent received clothes and quilts, including not only the very poor but also some of those who were categorised as 'poor'. In these villages, the one suit of clothes owned by those in impoverished households were very worn and tattered, and frequently households had no quilts or bedding or they were extremely shabby and torn. The village leader also ascertained each year which households were grain-short, the number of months for which they expected to be grain-short, and the current assets of the household, including labour, animals and cash income. In one Yunnan village, seven of the ninety-seven households (7 per cent) received relief grain, which averaged 20–25 jin per month. Grain-short households not eligible for relief grain, because they had labour capacity, animals and a cash income, were provided with grain at a subsidised price, usually ¥0.19–0.20 per jin for 20–23 jin per grain-short month, or a sum which even those categorised as 'not poor' found it difficult to find each year and considered the costs to pose a heavy burden. In the Yunnan village, one of the largest and richest of the households (ten persons) found it difficult to pay for the grain even at a subsidised price of ¥0.21 per jin compared to the free-market price of ¥0.40–0.45 per jin. This household was grain-short for four months of the year: in the first month, it was permitted to purchase 20 jin per person; in month 2, 50 jin per person; in month 3, 25 jin per person; and 40 jin per person for the fourth month – making a total of 135 jin per person, or 1,350 jin per household. After purchasing this grain for a total of ¥283.50, or ¥28 per person, out of its total cash income, the householders said that they had difficulty making ends meet. Poorer households with less cash income found it even more difficult to meet these costs.

In the Guangxi stone mountains, the proportion of villagers receiving relief grain was higher, which reflected the smaller area and lower quality of the cultivable lands and the fewer assets per household. Households eligible for relief grain frequently required this relief for as many as six months of the year or even more, while the amount of relief grain provided averaged out at 20–23 jin per month per person which the recipients said was not enough because they had little else to eat but wild vegetables. The quality of the relief grain was not as high and there was an observable difference between maize porridge made with relief grain and other home-grown grains. Grain-short households which were not deemed eligible for relief grain (ranging between 35 and 75 per cent of households in each village) were provided with grain at a subsidised price, usually ¥0.19–0.20 per jin for a total of 20–23 jin per month. Households which had labour capacity, animals and a cash income had to purchase their subsidised grain during the grain-short months, and again, even the 'not poor' found it extremely difficult to find the cash to pay for this grain, which amounted to a substantial sum – as much as ¥120–200 per annum. The remainder of the households were mostly eligible for relief grain, and only a few fortunate households in each village were not grain-short or had sufficient income to purchase grain at market prices. In the township as a whole, the decline in proportions purchasing subsidised grain was due to the quality of the grain harvest which, owing to a number of climatic and economic factors, had been somewhat better than in the recent past.

Relief constituted a small part of village poverty alleviation programmes, for their main goal was to increase the supply of grain by providing inputs such as fertiliser, plastic sheeting and seeds, and introduce new income-generating activities, mainly fruit trees and animals. It was the villages which were targeted for alleviation programmes and only then individual households, so that each village had its turn every few years to secure loans for a portion of its households. Loans provided for planting usually averaged ¥45 per mu and were made up of a ¥5 grant, ¥20 no-interest loan and ¥20 low-interest loan. In contrast, loans made for animals or fruit trees were for much larger sums – between ¥100 and ¥500 per household – and usually took the form of no- or low-interest loans. Within villages, the poverty alleviation loans did not aid the poorest or poorer households in the village, largely because either poorer households did not themselves want to take on loans or think that they themselves had the ability to repay following the negative experience of those who had received loans and been left with no assets and large debts, or because the poorer households were not judged credit-worthy by village leaders. So far in the villages even recipient households had not always benefited from previous loans, although it was too soon to judge the efficacy of the programmes. Fruit trees, for example, had not yet matured to a point where they provided an income, loans for planting had been very recent and were not yet due for repayment and in the case of animals, while a significant proportion of the loans had not yet been repaid, many of the animals had died in the meantime. In view of the concentration of loans for planting, the efficacy of the inputs in raising grain yields to the degree anticipated (thereby permitting the repayment of loans) had yet to be tested, and there has to be some doubt whether these loans will be effective in raising yields, and whether, given the present system of rotation, households which have already received loans for planting will continue to purchase the inputs in subsequent years out of their own scarce incomes. There also seems to have been a high degree of failure in recent poverty alleviation programmes focusing on fruit trees and animal husbandry, which suggested that the degree of technical assistance backing loans was lacking.

In Yunnan province, poverty alleviation programmes had been in operation in one township since 1987, during which time total funds of ¥556,800 had been allocated to animal husbandry, planting and processing. These funds had been distributed in the form of low-interest loans (normally 2.88 per cent) made annually to enterprises, village committees and households. Half the funds allocated in 1990 (¥260,000) were retained in the township for enterprises and processing (¥130,000), one-third (¥40,000) was allocated to village committees, and the remaining two-thirds (¥90,000) was loaned directly to households for planting and animal husbandry. The number of township households receiving loans directly for poverty allocation in 1990 amounted to 350, or 5 per cent of all households and 12 per cent of poor households. The average loan received was ¥257, and the households receiving loans were concentrated in the few villages whose turn it was to receive poverty alleviation funds. In one village which received loans for the first time in 1990, 120 or 20 per cent of poor households which also had the ability to plant and raise animals received loans for planting and animal husbandry. The average loan was ¥80; the highest loan amounted to ¥500 and the lowest ¥50. The loans were for two to five years at an interest rate of 2.4 per cent, and of the loans allocated in 1990, ¥5,000 was divided among twenty-five households for raising cattle or pigs, so that each had received credit averaging ¥200. The remaining ¥4,000 allocated to the village was divided among ninety-five households, with an average loan of ¥42 for plastic sheeting, fertiliser and seeds. According to the village leaders, the twenty-five livestock loans were allocated among the eighty poorest households in the administrative village, with the remaining fifty-five 'poorest' households receiving loans for planting. The rest of the households selected for loans were among the 200 'poor' of the administrative village. However, the interviews conducted in the three smaller natural hamlets making up the village suggested that none of the poorest households in the natural village had received loans.

In hamlet 1, none of the four 'poorest' or nine 'poor' households had either received a loan designed to alleviate poverty or applied for a loan, as they wanted the burden of neither interest nor capital repayments. The problems encountered by villagers with previous experience of loans had not encouraged their neighbours to follow their example. Already there were six households which had outstanding loans from another source that should have already been repaid. For example, in one household, which had a low-interest loan in 1986 of ¥1,500 to purchase a horse, the horse died and the family was left with an outstanding debt of ¥1,500. In a second, soldier's household, which had also borrowed ¥1,500 in 1986 at an interest of 0.8 per cent from a special fund for such families to purchase a mule, the mule had subsequently died and left the family with an outstanding debt. In hamlet 2, none of the poorest or poor households had a loan. Again, as in hamlet 1, the experience of villagers in relation to credit had been unfortunate. Two of the fifteen poor households had received loans in 1986 from the Civil Affairs Bureau Department for Animal Husbandry. In these two cases the households had received ¥120 to raise ten to twenty hens as the first step towards developing a chicken farm. Although at first there was some success in hatching chickens and selling eggs, within a short period of time the hens had all died. Again, the other households in the village were said to not be inclined to follow the examples of these two households. In hamlet 3, none of the ten very poor or fifteen poor households had received any loans, and no household in the hamlet had applied for a loan. Again, as in the first two hamlets, there were negative examples within the village. In 1986, a ¥500 loan at an interest of 8 per cent had been given to a household from the Nationality Commission to purchase a cow, but this had died within a year so that the household had been left with an outstanding debt.

In Guangxi province, the poverty alleviation programme had been in operation two years longer than in Yunnan province. As in Yunnan, the main form that poverty alleviation took was the allocation of interest-free loans for planting and, to a much lesser extent, animal husbandry. Of the total funds allocated in one township between 1985 and 1989, 262 or 4 per cent of loans had been allocated to households for animal husbandry, making for an average of ¥214 per household or ¥55,950 in total. In the same period, fifty-five households had received loans totalling ¥10,000 for rebuilding their houses following fire, and the remainder of the households had received a total of ¥281,586, or an average of ¥52 per household for planting. The remainder of the funds had been used for technical training and a television transmission station. Within this township, one administrative village of 298 households first received loans in 1985 and again in 1986 but not thereafter. These were mainly allocated to animal husbandry (16 and 3 per cent) and fruit trees (0 and 9 per cent) in the respective villages (see Table 6.9). The households awarded loans were chosen according to the following criteria: whether they were poor or not; whether they were willing to accept a loan; and whether they had sufficient labour and ability to repay a loan. Of the twenty-eight households that had accepted loans in 1986 to plant fruit trees, twelve had since repaid their loans, and, of the remainder which had not yet made repayments, the loans were said to have helped them increase their incomes but not lifted them above the poverty line. It was said in the villages that these previous schemes for poverty alleviation had not generated much profit and that as a result, new programmes focused on improving maize production by providing plastic sheeting, fertiliser and seeds which, it was anticipated, would increase yields by some 120–130 or even 200 jin per mu. In 1990, seventy households in the administrative village had participated in this new programme, receiving plastic sheeting, fertiliser and seeds to the value of ¥45 per mu which was made up of three sums: an agricultural grant of ¥5, a no-interest loan of ¥20 from the development fund and a low-interest loan of ¥20 at 2.4 per cent. The scheme was too new to ascertain what proportion of households would be able to repay their loans, but it was expected that generally most would be able to repay unless there was flood or drought. Twenty-five of these seventy households were located in one natural village where, after the promotion of the new scheme, thirty of the thirty-seven households in the village had applied to take out loans, and, of these, twenty-five had been selected because of their 'abilities to apply the new inputs and repay the loans'.

In a second administrative village with a total of 263 households, a high proportion – between one-third and half of households – had received ¥10 to ¥13 for fruit and tung trees in 1985 but less than 5 per cent the following year for fruit trees and for both years to raise animals (see Table 6.10). There had been no further loans for three years, but in 1990, 132 or 50 per cent of the households had received loans of ¥44.16 per mu ranging between 0.5 and 2 mu per household for inputs (plastic sheeting, fertiliser and seeds), making a total of ¥5,620 allocated to the village. A higher proportion of the households, 80 per cent, had applied for loans in the hope of producing sufficient grain and generating a cash income, leaving a total of seventy-eight households which were unsuccessful in their application – mainly, it was said, because they did not have 'the ability to repay'. The villagers were reported to be expecting to receive loans again the following year, but this did not seem to be a realistic expectation given the rotating patterns of loans between villages, which meant that this village after an interval of several years had only recently again received loans. In this administrative village it was also reported that, although these previous loans had generated some additional income for the individual households, the activities which they supported had not turned out to be very profitable. In 1985 in one of the natural villages within this administrative village, ten of the households had received a ¥300 loan to purchase cattle. Twenty-five households had originally applied for these loans, but fifteen had been turned down on the grounds that they did not have 'the ability to repay'. Of the households that did receive loans, none of the ten had yet repaid their loans although it was long past due dates of repayment. In 1990, forty of its sixty-three households had applied for and thirty-five, or 55 per cent, of the households had received loans the previous year totalling ¥2,272 or ¥65 per household, for plastic sheeting, seeds or fertiliser; however, none of the poor households visited in these villages had ever received loans.

What the studies of poverty alleviation in these villages suggested, despite its short history, was that improving the lot of poor villages and households was not an easy task given the paucity of resources with which to generate incomes. What little help they had received had not in the past and was not likely in the future to make any real difference to incomes for several reasons. First, although new plastic sheeting, fertiliser and seed might increase grain production to a small degree – and this had yet to be proved on any scale in these regions – they were unlikely to generate much in the way of additional income or employment for the villagers. Secondly, most of the improvements were only available in the form of loans, which penalised the poorest in that it was they who already had debts and were without a guaranteed 'ability to repay'. There was also insufficient technical back-up, especially in crop and fruit cultivation and in animal raising, to guarantee returns on the loans, let alone make repayment possible. Finally, perhaps the most important problem highlighted by these village studies had to do with the very definition of poverty alleviation itself. It had too much of a bias towards the economic generation of income, so that it has to be said that it became very difficult to distinguish between poverty alleviation and policies of general economic development, and between the work of the Poverty Alleviation offices and Agricultural, Industry and other ministries. Moreover, poverty alleviation was narrowly defined and, most importantly, excluded primary health care which emerged as the most important factor hindering labour capability and therefore income generation. It could have been assumed that the provision of a clinic and medicines would have received higher priority than the ubiquitous plastic sheeting! However, if poverty alleviation excluded the care of the body, not so the mind. What was very impressive in even the smallest of these villages was that, despite their poverty, they had a building for a school, a salaried teacher and the majority of village children as pupils at some point in their childhoods. Despite the short stay of many of the pupils, most of whom never acquired or maintained literacy, education had been accorded a priority in poor regions perhaps reflecting cultural inputs into the definition of poverty. As Chinese legend and model has it, it was the educated herd boy who made good and reversed the fortunes of his family. If poverty alleviation programmes were entirely a Chinese government initiative to 'help the poor', a novel and important palliative unique to the reform decade was the rural development project, a concept imported from the international development agencies during the reform decade.

THE DEVELOPMENT PROJECT

Much has been written about the 'Open Door Policy' with its new, geographically bounded entities, the Special Economic Zones, which were designed to utilise jointly foreign and Chinese-generated resources, investments, technology, commodities and markets. What has not attracted so much attention has been the other repercussion of China's 'Great Leap Outwards', or a similar geographically bounded entity, the rural development project, which has much in common with Special Economic Zones and is likely to affect an increasing number of China's villages. The introduction of the development project came about as a result of new agreements between the Chinese government and foreign development agencies. Ten years ago, in a new and surprising gesture after decades of 'self-reliance', the Chinese government both permitted and encouraged international, government and non-governmental development agencies to provide aid for development programmes and later to establish development projects in China. In 1978 the government took the first initiative and sought technical aid from the United Nations Development Programme, and within two years UN development agencies were supporting some 200 projects in China, ranging from installation of computers and training of technicians to improvements in livestock breeding and fisheries. In a short time span, China had transformed its status from an aid donor to an aid beneficiary, or a developing country disavowing multi-lateral aid to one

with the largest number of UN aid projects. China's entry into the
International Monetary Fund and World Bank in 1980 marked another
turning point, and, from that time, China drew important assistance from
those bodies to develop energy sources, railways, ports and telecom-
munications and the expansion of medium- and small-sized agricultural
and other projects.

Simultaneously, China's agricultural ministry and organisations began to
import funds, technology, talent and managerial expertise from the United
Nations and other international organisations, and it has been estimated
that between 1979 and 1986, China's agricultural, animal husbandry
and fishing departments borrowed US$1.28 billion from abroad for the
establishment of 180 agricultural projects including, US$717 million from
the World Bank and the International Fund for Agricultural Development.[29]
Most of these funds were used to cultivate new seed varieties and import
advanced agricultural technology and management, including plastic
covering techniques, mechanised rice cultivation, fish raising in nets
and boxes, animal-raising technology, hothouse cultivation, agricultural
chemicals and remote sensing technology. With foreign co-operation there
have been improvements in rice varieties, maize and wheat strains,
vegetable growing in high temperatures, sheep breeds and cattle breeding
and the manufacture of fertiliser and other agricultural chemicals. Finally,
there have been new opportunities for agricultural technicians to train both
within China and abroad. To help implement these innovations and
generate new resources at the local level, many of these international
agencies, from the large United Nations Food and Agriculture Organisation
to small non-governmental organisations – have established development
projects centred on groups of villages.

The introduction of the development project was a new experience for
government and village alike, bringing them for the first time into direct
contact with foreign personnel and techniques of development. Although
in China, 'outside' knowledge and inputs are usually mediated by Chinese
cadres, project managers and technicians, 'the project' is still a recognisable
space demarcated by the boundaries of special intervention and inputs
made in the name of development via 'outside' help. Because most
projects involve the channelling of extra, and sometimes extraordinary,
resources to the villages within project areas, most recipient villagers said
that they feel privileged in comparison to those outside the project
boundaries, although this was clearly not always so for reasons that will
become clear. Compared to many development experiences in other
societies, however, the role of foreigners is minimised and normally limited
to short periodic visits to do with innovation, advice and evaluation, with
daily local management almost entirely in the hands of local cadres and
locally appointed project directors. Many of these projects have furnished
inputs for improvements in crop production, the expansion of livestock

raising, or establishing and extending handicrafts and industries by house-hold or village and the supply of credit, raw materials, technical training and markets. One project, sponsored by a United Nations agency, was designed to provide small loans to farmers by supplementing pre-existing but scarce government sources of credit to encourage livestock raising. In counties where over half the households were designated as 'poor', farmers already had access to the Help the Poor Fund (HPF), which offered loans at a subsidised rate of 2.6 per cent for production purposes or mainly to support crop growing and livestock raising. A list of eligible households was drawn up by the township office, which decided how many poor families could be supported, and the purpose and the size of the loans. In 1988 it was estimated that because of the shortage of funds only 4 per cent of the households in the townships received HPF loans, the average size of which was ¥400, with approximately 20.8 per cent having outstanding repayments beyond due dates. A loan might also be obtained from the Rural Credit Co-operative for cultivating crops and raising livestock, at an interest rate of 7.92 per cent. The average size of these few loans was estimated to be ¥400, and the time limit was seasonal or one year. For the privileged few, 'luxury' funds at high interest rates provided loans for housebuilding, television and other consumer items. In each of the project villages, one of the most vexed questions was the access of peasant households to credit, which, given the absence of savings and surplus cash, was the most important factor in determining the capacity of a household to take up any new income-generating activities. As Table 6.11 shows, short-term, seasonal loans of up to ¥50–60 for pigs were widely available in the villages, those for dairy goats were more readily available; and for rabbits and cow raising it seems to have been particularly difficult to acquire loans, with the proportions of households in any one village receiving loans for these purposes less than 10 per cent.

In all the project villages, demand for credit far outweighed supply. In most of the villages almost all the households had applied for credit to take up livestock activities (see Table 6.12), and where they had not, they were said to be put off by the long waiting lists already existing in the village and the declining supplies of credit. Of the sample households, all had applied for loans to raise goats, rabbits or cows; ten had taken up new livestock activities within the past five years and all but one household (which had borrowed from friends) had taken a loan from the HPF at 2.6 per cent. Most of the loans amounted to less than ¥150, with those for fur rabbits varying between ¥30 and ¥150 and for meat rabbits between ¥120 and ¥200. Exceptionally, one household, which had taken up large-scale breeding of meat rabbits, had taken a loan for ¥1,400 made up of ¥450 from friends, ¥450 from the credit co-operative at 2.6 per cent and a ¥450 interest-free loan given by the government for setting up rabbit-breeding operations. The single household which had purchased a dairy cow had borrowed ¥2,000 from the HPF at 2.6 per cent. Given the existing shortage of credit supplies for new livestock operations and the intention of the agency in this project especially to improve the incomes of poor households, one of the most important criteria of successful project implementation was the inclusion of poor peasant households. The main criteria employed were said to be need, material resources, knowledge and training, capacity to repay and order of application. A household was said to have the resources to raise livestock if it had the space for and skills to construct pens or hutches and spare labour capacity, including grown-up children leaving school, to take on a new economic activity. In fact, the spare labour capacity in most villages meant that this criterion only ruled out those depleted due to ill health or death, or parents with young school-age children.

Necessary skills and knowledge were, almost without exception, acquired in locally based training courses for those hoping to take up the new livestock, and in all the villages most, if not all, households had at least one member who had previously attended a training course. This factor effectively meant that, according to this criterion, most of the households in a village were eligible for loans. The 'capacity to repay' was an important criterion of credit-worthiness and usually meant that a household already had a sufficient income for subsistence and that it had already repaid any pre-existing loans. It was the operation of this criterion which discriminated against the poorer households of the village, although there was some confusion about whether the loan recipients were more or less likely to belong to the poorer category households in the village. In this respect, there may be some differences between villages, in that some village heads suggested far more forcefully than others that the credit was more likely to be allocated to its poorer category households. In no village was the 'poorer' quantitatively defined in terms of an upper income limit, and the 'poorer' did not include the poorest households. In sum the 'poorer' category seemed to be very loosely defined and, since other criteria were more rigorously applied, some of these conversely worked in favour of the selection of higher-income households.

Frequently it was said that those who applied for loans first were more likely to be successful, and there was evidence of a correlation between timing of application and success, a correlation which favoured households which had prior knowledge of forthcoming loans which they had usually acquired by reading local newspapers, having networks and lines of communication outside the village or by having privileged information from the village head himself. The village procedures for selecting credit recipients primarily involved the village head, who received, assessed and made a preliminary selection of village applications, which were then passed on to the village committee. They made a second assessment and selection according to a quota sent down by the township government, which then passed applications to the rural credit co-operative where the final selection of credit recipient households was made. In one village, for example, forty-two households applied for loans for raising rabbits, from which the village head recommended ten to the village committee. In common, these ten households were educated (junior middle-school level), they were said to have the ability to learn techniques, attend and care for the animals, to be 'pioneers' in this new activity and already to have used this skill to raise their incomes. The village committee, because of the quotas received from higher administrative levels for each village, chose six out of the ten applications to pass on to the rural credit co-operative of which four were selected to receive credit. Where households were encouraged to apply directly to the rural credit co-operative for loans, the co-operative also consulted the village head as the official best acquainted with the circumstances of peasant households.

The investigation suggested that so far in almost all the villages, the poor to lower-middle income groups had not yet been provided with the necessary facilities to take up livestock raising. Given the existing divisions and differentials between villages and within villages and the aims of the agency to help the poor, it would have to target strictly various categories of households if it was to direct resources to the poor. Within counties it would have to concentrate its resources in the highland and remote villages where households had low annual per capita gross incomes and few income generating activities alternative to livestock raising.

Within villages there were three categories of households which stood especially to benefit from such project inputs. The first was poor lower middle-income households for which, without livestock and sufficient labour resources and particularly young persons graduating from school into the family labour force, it was only the absence or shortage of credit which prevented their raising livestock. They were very keen to acquire credit and were even prepared to pay slightly higher interest rates in order to acquire credit, take up new economic activities and increase their income. If funds continue to be scarce, smaller loans might be spread over as wide a number of recipients as possible, and, as far as is feasible, be allocated on a seasonal basis with periodic repayments built into the contract, which would prevent farmers from accumulating debts and help them to take a more realistic view of the profits to be made from these new livestock activities. For another group – poor, low-income households without livestock and with able-bodied but insufficient labour – it was the lack of labour resources which required attention. For the poorer, low-income, labour-short peasant household, a credit system which permitted more than one of these peasant households to contract a joint loan, share in the care of animals and in the profits might be the solution. The third category of households included the very poorest, which not only had insufficient labour resources but also suffered sickness, ill health or disability, and were unlikely to benefit from resource inputs, thus widening yet further village differentials. Only by the incorporation of the incapacitated into small ventures based on secondary or partial labour inputs such as the grading or processing of wool or some other auxiliary farm process or by the organisation of village livestock ventures financed by shares supplied on a credit basis could close-by employment be offered to those with partial labour power. In all the various projects of my direct acquaintance, one of the most difficult questions has been one that is both familiar and difficult, and that is how to generate resources and services to benefit the poorest of villages, or those inaccessible and without resources, and how to benefit the poorest households – that is, those lacking in labour power or without able-bodied members, funds or skills.

In addition to project targeting, a second major problem has to do with the dissemination of project information. International agencies establishing projects in China's countryside have had no choice but to utilise the information and resource channels already available between village, township, town and city. Although no outside agency could hope to establish alternatives which might compete with these, investigation of the distribution of project loans and information showed that it could be the leader's relatives who were not just the first and sometimes only households to receive loans, but that they had heard about the new possibilities long before others in the village. In one project the preparation of a small booklet providing information about the new inputs and opportunities was made a prerequisite to the expansion of the loan programme. This condition was accepted by the Chinese government, and a booklet was written for villagers by me and an economist informing them how to obtain credit via the new mechanisms. It was tested at all levels from officials in Beijing, the province, county and township and in the village households, embracing the old and the young, the literate and illiterate and the rich and the poor. It was a difficult booklet to write in the language of the villagers, and our time and efforts in experimenting, rewriting and testing were not always appreciated by officials, but it was potentially important mainly because it placed a permanent written resource for ready reference in the hands of the villagers and especially the poor, the young and the women. However, if credit and information were important prerequisites to the establishment of new projects, many have been jeopardised by the demands of the international agencies that there be counterpart funding furnished by the government which, in the absence of government funds at the intervening administrative levels, can only be derived from the very villages the agency is intent on developing. If the village has already been subjected to levies in order to counterpart-fund the project, then the expectations of villagers may already have been soured and support diminished because the village has already in fact 'paid' for the project.

In addition to the poverty alleviation programme and the rural development project there is a third option, which is perhaps also the most controversial of the palliatives for reducing village poverty, and that is the movement of population outside the village.

VILLAGER MOVEMENT

In the case of villages in inhospitable regions, development in the village is sometimes deferred or rejected in favour of taking villagers to development by resettling populations in regions with more favourable conditions for development or encouraging labour mobility. In the arid northwestern provinces of Gansu and the Ningxia Hui Autonomous Region there have been some resettlement programmes co-financed by the Chinese government and the World Food Programme.[30] These aimed at the movement of persons from barren and destitute villages without water or fuel to reclaimed and irrigated lands at mountain bases or near the Yellow River.[31] A solution to poverty much favoured by development economists is enhanced labour mobility by lifting previous restrictions on labour movement. In their view, restrictions on labour mobility impose significant costs on the poorest groups in the country, restrict their choices to participate in the growth of the wider economy, and accumulate population pressures on the resource-poor or depleted natural environment. In China, normalising population movements would necessitate training, advice and greater protection and security for migrants than presently received by the 'floating population' – a category of moving persons newly characteristic of the reform decade.

Estimates suggest that two-thirds of the 50 million 'floating population' are presently employed in construction, services or trade on a temporary basis upwards of three months, with 10 million divided between China's twenty-three largest cities, including Shanghai (1.83 million), Beijing (1.55 million) and Guangzhou (1.1 million).[32] Although some of this movement has been encouraged, facilitated and even organised by the Labour Bureaux, by far the greater proportion of these people have moved of their own accord. In the case studies there were the beginnings of movement out of the villages, usually by the adult members, but mostly of a very temporary, seasonal kind. At peak seasons as many as 100,000 rural labourers are reported to pour into Guangzhou daily, and in other regions the sheer magnitude of the numbers 'blindly flocking' to the cities from the countryside has caused much official concern, for there are frequently insufficient water, crowded facilities and reports of disorder on trains and in railway stations where large numbers squat and sleep, thus creating a new category or subdivision of the poor – the 'floating poor', as opposed to the 'fixed poor' of the villages. Whether the poor are 'fixed' or 'floating', the majority of the poor are likely to remain in villages largely because labour mobility rarely involves entire households. If poverty is not to be feminised, development must still be taken to the villages, for it is to village, family and kin that the mobile frequently and voluntarily return; it is to the village that the government encourages the 'floating' to return; and it is in the village that most prefer to stay.[33] Given the choice, even the poorest are heard to say that they prefer not to leave the 'ancestral poverty' of their village in order 'to seek a better life in a strange place away from family and kin'.

Part III

Readjustment: the household

Chapter 7

Aggregation
Labour, family and kin

One of the most interesting repercussions of rural reform has been interest in the peasant household, which has become the focus of attention after an interval of nearly thirty years of revolution during which it was very much shadowed by the commune, production brigade and production team. Much has been made of the new responsibilities, opportunities and demands on the peasant household, but of equal interest are their repercussions for its size, structure, and relations within and beyond the household and for family and kin. The household, or hu, is the basic unit of domestic organisation within the village, and is usually defined as the group of kin relations distinguished by a single kitchen, a common budget and normally, although not necessarily, co-residence. Members of peasant households usually use the term 'household' (hu) for the family members who are co-resident and 'family' (jia or jiating) for closely related members of different households. From the late 1970s the response of the peasant household to the new reforms has been very dependent on its pre-existing resource capacity and, in particular, the numbers and skills of its labourers.

The absence of any substantial inherited or accumulated capital from the period of collectivisation meant that initially the only means by which peasant households were able to establish new economic activities was through savings from incomes of family labourers. The correlation between income and labour resources was not a new characteristic, for even within the collective, the labour resources of a peasant household had been the single most important determinant of livelihood and welfare.[1] Then the peasant household relied not so much on the exploitation of family lands or estates but on the waged and domestic labour of its members to fulfil its obligations to the collective production unit, cultivate its private plot, raise livestock, undertake domestic sideline handicraft production and service family members. The performance of all these activities, be they collective, private or domestic, demanded the maximisation of family labour resources and, because the hiring of labour was prohibited by law, control over family labour underlay economic differentiation within villages. Thus the removal of constraints on family income generation placed greatly intensified rather than new demands on the peasant household. From the very first, it was not lost on peasant households that many new 'ten thousand yuan' households were recognisably larger in size (Table 7.1).[2] Sufficient labour resources enabled a household to diversify its activities beyond field cultivation and into sideline economic activities, which surveys show to have been the most important first step in accumulation and the expansion of domestic economies.[3] Conversely, poorer households most frequently lacked labour power, and interviews revealed many instances where lands were left idle or sidelines dormant through lack of family labour.

In a radical departure from past policy, the government permitted the hiring of labour, but it was such a novel step that initially there seemed to be much uncertainty surrounding the details of the new policy and just how many and in what circumstances a household might employ labourers without being termed 'exploitative',[4] and there is still a wide variation in its practice. In most regions of China, it is little practised, largely because hiring labour requires the generation of surplus income, but in the richest southern provinces, with apparently limitless opportunities for alternative economic activities, it is not uncommon for field cultivation to be almost entirely undertaken by labour hired from outside the village, thus freeing village labour for more lucrative activities. Where there is surplus labour, members leave their villages for short and long periods to be employed as mobile or contract labourers by enterprises and individual peasant households on a daily or short-term basis. There were some instances in the village studies where such labour was hired during busy seasons by households managing orchards, vegetable farms and enterprises. In a few cases poorer neighbours hired themselves out to richer neighbours, but again usually on a daily or short-term basis and perhaps as much as a favour as of necessity. With notable exceptions, the majority of peasant households in most regions are still almost entirely reliant on the mobilisation and augmentation of family labour resources.

FAMILY LABOUR RESOURCES

One of the most immediate means available to peasant households to maximise their labour power was to intensify the demands on existing family labour resources and arrange and re-arrange the divisions and distribution of labour within households. The ending of the collective organisation of labour enabled them to do just this, in that it had obvious repercussions for structuring the working day. In the early 1980s villagers repeatedly and quite spontaneously referred to and welcomed the 'new freedoms' or working methods as one of the most important changes in their lives. They contrasted these with previous practices, in which production team leaders had allocated tasks and their work points were directly dependent on their daily presence in the fields for long, fixed hours whatever the demands of the work. Now peasant households controlled their own production timetables and only worked in the fields when necessary, which left time free for alternative activities. It was certainly evident in conversation and interview that villagers appreciated and enjoyed this new degree of flexibility and control over their own working timetables, although many of them also recognised that what this meant in practice was that they now worked much harder than before. Women, in particular, pointed out that although they had always had to work hard, the recent reforms had made their daily routine even more demanding: 'Though it's hard work, we peasant women have been accustomed to work in the fields since we were children. Women continue to undertake field and household work, but we have become even busier in the last two years.'[5] In post-reform village life there is a very new attitude towards time: as a long-time fieldworker in Chinese villages, I have become only too aware that time is now money and that, whereas in the past, I was surrounded by company who were being paid whether they were in the fields or talking to me, now I frequently find myself in an empty village left in the presence of only the very old and the very young unless prior arrangements have been made or cadre and villager anticipated returns for their time.

That family members of all generations have been pressed into some form of income-generating activity, from grandparents to grandchildren, was evidenced in family interviews when it was made clear that only those not yet in school and those more than seventy years old or incapacitated were described as either 'too young' or 'too old' for work. Even so, the very elderly and those shuffling with perhaps previously bound feet are to be seen in the fields, feeding the animals and tending children or herds. The scale of after-school activities of peasant children has often been recognised as a hindrance to homework, but since the reforms, the drop-out rate in schools has been rising and has been attributed directly to the expansion of peasant household economies and new demands on family, and especially girls', labour.[6] There have also been numerous reports suggesting that child labour has become a worsening problem in some of China's rural areas.[7] A letter published in *Guangming Ribao* in 1988 called attention to the increase in child farmers, workers and pedlars in one county in Jiangxi province, of which 85 per cent were girls. In one township, 181 farmers, 141 helpers in family shops, a quarter of poor peasant construction teams and one-third of pedlars were said to be under the age of fifteen years. The newspaper editor thought that the cause was the farmers' pursuit of quick profits for, as he said, 'while farming makes money, schooling takes money'.[8] In Hebei province, an investigation in nine prefectures and cities found a total of 7,400 child labourers employed by township enterprises aged from eleven years upwards and mostly girls.[9]

Nationally, the Ministry of Labour has estimated that child labourers amount to some 10 per cent of total employees in some rural enterprises and as many as 20 per cent in others.[10] The State Council on Education and other national bodies have also expressed increasing concern about the rise in school drop-outs where children were newly compelled to work in the fields or help their parents operate private shops, businesses and enterprises.[11] A spot check in Guangdong province of 2,940 households was reported as showing that only 71.5 per cent of children between six and seventeen years and only 54.4 per cent of fifteen- to seventeen-year-olds were in school.[12] Maximisation of family labour has not only intensified the demands on family labour but also its control and management into new divisions of labour.

In household interviews each family member had clearly identified responsibilities for specific tasks, and could quite precisely delineate who did what and for how long each day, week or season, although the distribution of labour has become increasingly divided and complex. New modes of remuneration according to output rather than time had fast led to a decline in the demand for field labour nationally, estimated to be a reduction of a third or so over the first five years of reform and then two-thirds, giving rise to surplus labour of some 22 million persons available for alternative activities.[13] In one village report which is typical, seventy persons cultivated 300 mu of responsibility lands in the first year of contract, forty-five in the second and twenty-five by the third year.[14] The village studies of Beijing, Shanxi, Shandong and Wuxi all clearly showed the decline in numbers employed in field cultivation during the past few years. In many regions, much of this surplus labour was likely to be made up of women, whether they were previously the main or auxiliary fieldworkers. By 1981 in one or two counties in Zhejiang province, more than 90 per cent of the female work force had no regular fieldwork assignments, and even in busy seasons, only a small percentage of this work force was still required.[15] In other regions it was the women or a combination of men and women who remained working the fields, but generally the reduction in field labour and farm diversification has caused the reallocation of household labour.

Where households have diversified into animal husbandry or handicrafts or villages into textiles or electronics – that is, into activities traditionally associated with female labour – then men continue to cultivate the fields while women develop new domestic sidelines or enter enterprise employment. Greater female responsibility for domestic sideline production is a reversion to a more traditional division of labour in that the scale of operation of domestic sideline production based on vegetables, animals or handicrafts has long been almost exclusively determined by the availability of female labour. For example, in one peasant household located in the hills of Jiangxi province, the husband and sons between them cultivated 10.9 mu of paddy field, 5 mu of tobacco lands, a joint fruit orchard and

6.5 mu of a small fish farm; the wife, no longer needed in the fields, devoted herself to tending three to four pigs, two litters of young pigs, numbers of chickens and the family vegetable garden, which between them provided a fifth of the total annual cash income of the household.[16] In another example reported in the press, once it became evident that her husband was able to take almost exclusive care of their 6 mu of contracted land, with her help limited to harvesting and planting seasons, his wife began to operate a noodle-processing plant and raise pigs and rabbits, all of which enabled her to contribute several hundred yuan to the household annual income. She thought that her experience was not unusual and that peasant women in China were increasingly turning to side occupations now that they and their husbands did not both have to earn work points in the fields.[17]

In quite another pattern, where male labourers had long been employed in non-agricultural occupations such as heavier rural industries, capital construction projects, mining, fishing or forestry, the proportion of women employed in the agricultural labour force had consequently been much higher, sometimes up to 80–100 per cent.[18] Since the reforms, the diversification of peasant household economies have all broadened the scope of women's income-generating activities, and where it is the women who alone combine land management and cultivation, domestic sidelines and domestic labour, then peasant households have become for all practical purposes female-operated and -managed. It is commonly reported that many peasant households had become 'half-side' families in which husbands worked in occupations other than agriculture or farm work and commuted from the village, whether daily or for longer periods. Combining the management and cultivation of contracted lands and expanding domestic sidelines have increased the demands made upon peasant women who long laboured from dawn to dusk to fulfil collective and domestic obligations. In the first few years of reform, women, and particularly younger women with small children, in half-side households observed that their lives had become much busier, although they also enjoyed higher incomes. One young mother of three small children described how she alone farmed the land and undertook domestic sidelines. Her husband worked as a miner and lived away from the village so that she cultivated 17 mu of land, grew cucumbers, broad beans and tomatoes in her courtyard and raised a pig, three sheep and a dozen or so chickens in addition to domestic chores and minding the three children. She thought that although she had had to work hard in the past, the recent expansion of domestic sidelines had made her daily routine even more demanding.[19] There were thus limits to the intensification and distribution of existing labour resources, emphasising anew strategies to expand family size via reproduction and recruitment.

FAMILY LABOUR STRATEGIES

The reproduction of family labour, although essentially a longer-term strategy, was a time-honoured means of augmenting the labour force of the peasant household and ensuring its future and longer-term fortunes as an economic unit. The continuation of age-old patterns and timing of child bearing suggested that the peasant household still aimed to ensure a plentiful and steady supply of labour by having at least three to four children and timing the births so that potential labourers might enter the labour force at around the same time as the older generation retired. The heightened correlation between household size and income observable in the first few years of rural reform only confirmed customary perceptions 'linking more children with more blessings'. However, any attempt during the reform years to maximise family size by this means brought households into direct conflict with the one- to two-child family-planning policy. Indeed, as the following chapter argues, the simultaneous implementation of rural economic reforms and stringent family-planning policies brought dual demands to bear on the peasant household which have probably never been so conflicting or contradictory as during the first few years of reform.[20] At the same time as peasant parents were prohibited from having more than one or at the most two children, the potential value of family labour resources was increased by the new economic policies. Despite modification to family-planning policies, it can be assumed that the reproduction of family labour is likely to remain restricted, so that households also adopted alternative or additional shorter-term strategies to augment their labour force. One of the most important of these strategies was to continue to arrange for the immediate recruitment of a daughter-in-law.

Peasant households continued to arrange for their sons' early marriages, despite the strictures of the Marriage Law, in order to supervise the recruitment of a daughter-in-law into their household.[21] Because marriage was still largely virilocal in the countryside, parents often expressed their support for early marriage in order 'to drink a cup of tea provided by a daughter-in-law'. This was particularly so when the family's labour had been recently depleted either by death or the loss of a daughter in marriage to another household. That girls of marriageable age had continued to be prized for their labour power was illustrated by the continuing payment of the betrothal gift to the bride's household, which, despite legal prohibition, persisted both openly and covertly as an openly acknowledged form of compensation to the girl's family for both the expenses of her upbringing and the loss of her labour. Many parents informally stated that after years of raising a daughter they ought to be able to get something, 'if not a handsome sum', in exchange, and those who thought the betrothal gift too small complained that they were getting 'a small return for raising and bringing up a daughter'. After 1978, the rising value placed on family labour has been such that the costs of marriage have risen substantially as wife-giving households demand more compensation from those taking wives.

The recruitment of a daughter-in-law usually requires family savings of considerable and increasing sums. In Henan province it was estimated in 1989 that the average cost of a wedding was ¥3,000 and that ¥2.4 billion was spent on weddings in the province each year.[22] In the many villages I have visited, the costs of marriage have rarely fallen below ¥1,000, and frequently they have cost more than ¥5,000, of which at least half was given in cash and kind by the groom's to the bride's household as the betrothal gift. Among the rich, much or all of the gift is returned with the bride as furnishings for the couple's room and eventually separate household; among the poor it is retained by the groom's household to procure a daughter-in-law for its son. Indeed, one common means of meeting the costs of marriage was to marry out a daughter first. The costs of brides required either cash savings or the exchange of a daughter's for a daughter-in-law's labour, meaning in effect that on marriage there might not be net gain, and there were no more disappointed households than those which had failed to realise the expected returns on a daughter-in-law or wife. One of the most disappointed and dispirited farmers I have interviewed had paid ¥500 for a distant bride only to find that she was mentally retarded with weak labour power, as were subsequently several of their children.

Marriage, an essential event in the extension and formation of households, continues to be very much a family affair in the countryside, with parents initiating or at least negotiating its timing and the choice of son- and daughter-in-law. That marriage continues to be a financial worry to the family until the negotiations are successfully concluded is reflected in the decrease in the age of marriage since the onset of reforms to near or even below the legal age of marriage. Investigations by the State Family Planning Commission have shown that early marriages with one or both parties under the legal age of twenty years for girls and twenty-two years for boys have increased and now account for 20 per cent of all peasant marriages, with the number rising to as high as 90 per cent of all marriages in poorer regions.[23] There have also been several recent reports of child betrothals resulting in under-age or early marriage. In Shanxi province, many of those in school were found to be already betrothed;[24] in Gansu province it is reported that young persons are getting married and having children as young as fourteen or fifteen years;[25] and, nationally, in 1987 the average age of marriage was reported to have declined to 23.60 years for men and 21.01 for women – 1.83 and 1.79 years younger respectively than in 1982.[26] In 1989, early marriage was reported to be a 'very serious issue' in the countryside,[27] and one of the reasons seems to be the fear that a suitable bride or an advantageous match at a feasible cost will not be possible if the family leaves it later than others to initiate negotiations. The difficulty in procuring brides in poor regions has also led to a reported rise in the abduction and traffic of young women by those exploiting the demand for brides.[28] Once a household had recruited a daughter-in-law, another means by which a household might take advantage of the son's and daughter-in-law's labour to diversify its economy and accumulate resources was to delay household division.

HOUSEHOLD SIZE AND STRUCTURE

A household might take several structural forms, depending on the number of persons, generations and nuclear units residing within any one household. Analysts usually distinguish three different types: the nuclear unit made up of parents and children; the stem or three-generation household of parents, one married son, his wife and children plus any unmarried sons and daughters; and the larger, complex or joint family household in which two or more married sons, their wives and children reside with the parents. Before the revolution the average size of the peasant household usually numbered between four and six persons, and it had been rare for peasant households to pass through a complex phase for demographic and economic reasons. A key factor in the maintenance of the joint or complex form was the existence of an estate sufficient in size to meet the claims of its numerous members and hence its predominance among the gentry. For the peasantry, the developmental cycle had customarily alternated between the nuclear and stem forms due to the early deaths of the elderly and the rare survival or permanent village residence of more than one son, so that formal household division, or fenjia, was rare among the majority of peasant households.[29] When households had more than one son, their marriages, which were patrilocal in residence, normally occasioned either expansion into a joint household, or, alternatively, they might precipitate household division which commonly took place sometime after marriage, perhaps on the occasion of a younger son's marriage or on successive births.

In revolutionary villages there was a wide range in family size so that concurrently there might be numbers of nuclear, stem or joint family households awaiting division. Expansion of the peasant household into extended or joint form for at least a short stage in its developmental cycle had been encouraged by a number of new economic and demographic features of the 1950s, including improvements in diet, health and general welfare measures, which increased the life spans and the number of surviving sons, who were now more likely to remain in the village because of the cut-off in migration and the expansion of local employment opportunities within the collective. Traditionally, it had been a mark and means of upward mobility for peasant households to expand their size once there was sufficient wealth to support a larger and more complex household.[30] Likewise, the comparatively secure conditions of the 1950s occasioned the widespread development of joint forms, thereby offering a unique opportunity for peasant households to use their temporary expanded labour resources following the marriage of sons so as to increase their income and delay household division until sufficient wealth has been accumulated to divide satisfactorily to the advantage of each unit. In the late 1970s, it had seemed to me that peasant households had become more elaborate in form during the revolution than at any time during the recent past, and that it might be expected that this trend would continue into the reform period.

More than in any other period this century, the majority of post-reform peasant households have expanded their estate to include the lands, *de facto* ownership, residences, enterprises, means of production, livestock and household effects, thus providing a basis for the support of larger numbers than hitherto. Both the removal of one of the most important constraints on family size, the size of the household estate, and the exacerbated demands on family labour could then have ostensibly led to extended delay in household division and the elaboration of greater numbers of peasant households into complex and joint forms. As the Chinese sociologist C.K. Yang suggested many years ago, the Chinese household is like a balloon – ever ready to inflate should the expansion of its economy allow.[31] However, there is little evidence that such an expansion has so far taken place in the past ten years; if anything, there has been a reverse trend, with declining household size. Surveys within villages suggest that the proportion of large and joint households has declined, and a national survey based on the 1982 census also showed a marked rise in the number of smaller one- to two-generational nuclear households with a corresponding drop in the number of larger, multi-generational stem and joint households.[32] In 1985 in Hunan province, it was estimated that 76 per cent of households were nuclear, with four to five members, and that there had been a sharp rise in this number since the introduction of the responsibility system.[33] In 1987 a sample survey of peasant households also showed that average size had declined from 4.41 in 1982 to 4.23 persons, and that households with fewer than four persons were the norm in the municipalities and in Shandong, Jiangsu and Zhejiang provinces.[34] The majority of peasant households had more than five persons, although overall there had been a decline in the number of five-plus households from 46.35 per cent in 1982 to 40.5 per cent, although less than 20 per cent of households had three generations (see Table 7.2).

In the poor, remote and mountainous Yunnan and Guangxi village case studies, average household size ranged between 5.2 and 5.5 persons; in the ten villages in Henan, Sichuan, Shanxi and Shandong (A) the household size averaged 4.5; and in the more suburbanised Shandong (B), Wuxi and Beijing villages, average household sizes were 3.4, 3.7 and 2.8, respectively. In the preliminary census results of 1990, the average family size was estimated to be 3.96 persons.[35] There is evidence of an increasing degree of opposition from both the older and younger generations to complex family forms which were potentially and by reputation more hierarchical, patriarchal and tension-ridden. A number of surveys of young persons in rural areas suggested that they preferred not to become part of a complex household on marriage.[36] There was also some evidence to suggest that, given the substantial degree of servicing required in a large and complex household, some older women advocated early household division. Grandmothers said that they commonly found themselves keeping house for a dozen or so persons, perhaps including two married sons, their wives and children, until it all became too much for them and arguments ensued between them and their daughters-in-law. They looked around the village and saw that other mothers-in-law lived separately from their children and consequently had more freedom, so at their request the household was soon divided.[37] This is an interesting phenomenon, although it is difficult to ascertain its significance in precipitating household division. What is important is that the majority of peasant households in China range between four and five persons, are composed of parents, children and maybe one or two grandparents, and that it is this smaller nuclear or stem unit which had to shoulder new responsibilities and acquire new resources. One means by which they might meet new demands was via exchanges of labour and other resources between households.

INTER-HOUSEHOLD RELATIONS

Several years ago, I suggested that the exchanges of labour between households may have led to a new family form which not only acquired the resources and escaped the disadvantages of the joint family household, but also provided a convincing explanation for the precipitation of family division. If peasant households were dividing sooner rather than later, partitioning was also not as complete as it was in the past when the household was fully incorporated into collective economic structures. In other words, at the same time as a household divided to establish separate cooking stoves – and in many regions the enormous amount of new housing may have encouraged division – it continued to hold some property in common and share in economic ventures which included some form of joint investment and pooling of labour. Additionally, close-kin-related households, which had previously divided, increasingly came together or combined jointly to invest in and develop common income-generating activities. The new and emerging family form was thus made up of a number of households related by close kin ties, which developed new forms of association or co-operation based on economic and socio-political links and exchanges. I termed this new family form, made up of two or more households, an 'aggregate family'. The adjective 'aggregate' seemed appropriate because, despite the fact that families consisted of separate households, it was the linkages or relationships of co-operation and association between them which were of major importance to the analyst. Generally, to take the individual household as the unit of analysis has sometimes encouraged analysts to isolate and conceptualise the household and so minimise the links and exchanges between households; in much of rural China, the important unit of analysis may be not so much the individual household and its structure, activity and boundaries as the aggregate family. The basis for co-operation and association between aggregating households are, first, kinship and proximity of residence and, secondly, the mobilisation of resources to meet new economic and socio-political demands on the household.

The aggregate family is usually distinguished by its close patrilateral kinship ties made up of brothers, fathers' brothers and fathers' brothers' sons; that is, those males descended from a common male antecedent and extending to three or so generations. This co-operative kinship unit clearly corresponds to a group frequently identified by villagers before 1978 and referred to as the 'jiating' and 'zijia' (own family), or 'jinqin' (close kin). My own field investigation in one village in Guangdong province in 1977 had suggested that villagers drew a line between their close kin or jinqin, made up of brothers who had established separate households, fathers' brothers and fathers' brothers' sons, and more distant kin such as fathers' fathers' brothers and their sons.[38] The village itself was characterised by geographically concentrated clusters of agnatic kin made up of these groups of brothers or fathers' brothers. In a Jiangsu provincial village, field investigators noted the emphasis placed on the zijia as an identifiable kinship unit corresponding to a patrilineage of groups of men descended through males from a single male ancestor, plus their wives and unmarried sisters and daughters.[39] Although dispersed among several different households, there was usually a degree of clustering of close-kin-related households which, interestingly, frequently corresponded to the primary unit of kinship co-operation identified by anthropologists in their village studies before 1949. Since that time, and until 1978, it can be argued that the economic and political significance of the relations within this smaller unit were reduced as individual households were more tightly incorporated into larger economic and political structures although they had remained the main focus of various informal economic and ritual forms of co-operation. In contrast, since 1978 in the absence of collective production structures, relations between post-division and close-kin-related households have been reinvested with a new economic and political significance as new demands have frequently proved beyond the capacity of the small individual household. This tendency towards economic association and co-operation between closely related, kin-based units has also been officially encouraged. The government, recognising the limited resources available to the individual households to diversify and expand agricultural and non-agricultural production, has urged peasant households to pool their savings in order to invest in common assets so as to facilitate production, processing and marketing as a first step in a more complex exchange of labour and services. Although to facilitate the entire production process from cultivation or construction to processing and marketing would prove beyond the material and labour resources of the individual household, they might fall within the capacity of the aggregate family.

An aggregate family might simply continue to operate a number of joint ventures which, developed by father, sons and brothers prior to household division, continued to necessitate some common investment and management. Alternatively, one household might initiate an economic activity which became so profitable that kin-related neighbouring households either contributed their resources to enlarging the venture or set up their own parallel ventures involving a certain degree of co-operation in production, processing and marketing processes. Households running successful and lucrative ventures have shown some degree of interest in aiding their kin-related and neighbouring households, for there is some evidence to suggest that those households which rapidly acquired out-standing wealth still feel very vulnerable: 'Although we are willing, we dare not become well off. We fear that if we become well off, we may suffer.'[40] Rather than draw exaggerated attention to themselves as individual households richer than their neighbours, they would sooner forestall criticism and envy and share in or pool resources with close kin or neighbours. Several examples in the village studies show closely kin-related households shared the raising of an animal (one furnishing the capital, another the fodder and the poorest the labour) with all sharing in the profits. This distribution seemed to be a common way of helping poor relations earn an extra cash income. Numerous interviews and press examples show households successfully cultivating mushrooms, raising rabbits or establishing small industries or services and then proceeding to help close kin establish similar ventures or incorporate them into the same venture. The aggregate family might specialise in a single income-generating activity or it might evolve a division of labour whereby one household undertook to cultivate all the lands allocated to the aggregate family, another promoted some kind of commodity production or service and yet another provided transport, technical or commercial marketing expertise so that the member households were to a large degree interdependent and relatively self-sufficient.

In addition to the major economic factors encouraging the development of the aggregate family, membership of the aggregate family engendered a greater degree of welfare, well-being and security based on corporate interests, and claims for mutual assistance replaced that of the collective. In many villages, especially in the early years of reform, the decentralisation of collective management took place at such a pace that collective assets to facilitate community welfare were frequently dismantled and distributed to individual households. There were numerous reports of enterprises, schools, clinics and other such community facilities being dismantled and divided among peasant households, and, although again it is difficult to ascertain the scale, it does seem that the peasant household could not thereafter expect to have the same socio-political support from village institutions. In these circumstances claims and counter-claims of assistance and welfare were more likely to be generated at least in the first instance between neighbouring and kin-related households making up the aggregate family, and only in the absence of this support was the support from other kin, village or the state solicited. It was the aggregate family which was most likely to provide support for the elderly, with each household either making a cash donation or taking it in turn to care for aged members. Similarly, arrangements involving association and sharing by households may be made for the care of the very young, the unemployed, the disabled and other dependants. Relations between member households of the aggregate family were also likely to be expressed symbolically through the common funding of occasions to mark birth, marriage and death ritually. In many respects, the provision of food, services and financial and mutual support in recognition of significant life-cycle events was a tradition unbroken despite revolutionary campaigns to reduce both the significance and 'extravagance' of such ritual occasions. However, as a result of recent increases in income and other resources, families newly welcomed opportunities to advertise their sudden riches and maintain kin ties. There have certainly been numbers of articles in the press criticising the increased waste and extravagance of feasting associated with such events.

It is also possible that aggregate families have become stepping stones for the revival of lineage or clan groups long characteristic of rural and particularly southern China. In the early 1980s, there were reports from southern counties (where traditional lineages were strong) of the common worship of ancestors, claims to lineage land, temples and even the testing of corporate loyalties in inter-lineage feuds usually over graves or water rights.[41] In one clan grave dispute involving the removal of more than 3,000 unmarked ancestral graves on a tract of waste land, some 2,000 people engaged in smashing, beating and looting, causing serious physical injuries to security cadres, policemen and workers, and damage to state, collective and personal property exceeding ¥300,000.[42] Although these reports may suggest cohesion among larger kin groups in limited regions and circumstances, it seems unlikely that larger kin groups will assume the importance of the smaller aggregate family economically, socially and politically in most regions of China. None the less, neighbouring patrilineal kin links are deemed to be a very important resource without which households feel severely disadvantaged.

With such a strong patrilineal and patrilocal bias in favour of male kin relations, it is not surprising to find that affinal links, or links through the wife's kin, have normally taken second place, although recent work on kinship in Chinese societies has suggested that they may have been more important than was previously assumed.[43] Certainly, my own village studies reveal the importance of affinal kin in providing gifts and loans for peasant households. Whether it be in meeting extraordinary expenses or basic needs, it was the wife's kin who almost invariably provided funds. Even if affinal kinship ties may have previously been more important than was generally accepted, they have probably assumed greater significance since the reforms as a potential source of credit and other assistance. Their increased importance reflects one of the most interesting social phenomenon in the countryside, which is the new importance attached to spatially extended networks by households or family aggregates or kin ties beyond the immediate village environs. Early post-reform surveys suggested that the highest rural income earners are usually cadres, ex-cadres, demobilised soldiers, returned students or educated youth, precisely those individuals in a position to cultivate relations and alliances outside of the village which gave them privileged access to raw materials, markets and market information.[44]

It seems that where possible kin ties in cities, towns and distant villages have been activated to facilitate production, processing and marketing, and it has been interesting to note the growing tendency for peasants to establish such links in towns and urban centres. However, because of past restrictions on migration, many households have no existing extensive ties outside the village, and they have commonly newly set out to establish them by several means including the time-honoured device of negotiating the marriage of daughters. The continuing controls over marriage exercised by the older generation in the countryside meant that marriage negotiations could still be employed for these purposes, and there is some evidence that such purposive alliances increased during the first five years of reform.[45] Alternatively, a single household or a group of households might establish one of its members in a local town or even distant city to facilitate access to new resources and market outlets. Migrants might find employment in the expanding number of urban, collectively operated enterprises or might establish their own individually operated enterprises, perhaps processing or marketing goods produced by their kin back home. I used to joke that no urban kin with a ground-floor flat out of whose windows produce or articles could be sold would be left unclaimed by their rural kin! In 1984, I conducted a survey of young tailors in a Chengdu city street, the majority of whom had come from villages of varying distance from the city. Each had been set up with tools of a trade and provided with grain by their families, and some had even had a city house purchased for them with the intention that other family members would eventually join them. Similarly, produce and articles of rural origin were often sold in markets by these 'urban representatives' of a single or group of kin-related village households. Analysing chains of migration will prove increasingly interesting, and it is possible that in the future these inter-familial urban and rural relations will come to resemble the dispersed families so well depicted by Lin Yueh Hwa in *The Golden Wing* for the republican era,[46] and by Myron Cohen in *House United, House Divided* for Taiwan.[47] While both the extended networks and the spatially bounded relations between households have proved increasingly important for the income and welfare of the single household, so the new conditions of commoditisation and their effects have also had implications for intra-familial relations.

INTRAFAMILIAL RELATIONS

While it is important to note the interest of the household in external alliances, it is also important to emphasise the continuing corporate qualities of the peasant household. However multiple the sources of income, members continue to be incorporated into a single budget which is primarily controlled, allocated and distributed according to joint interests. It is still the case that in rural households, individual members pool their incomes unless they are working away from the village for a long time, in which case only a portion of their incomes, after the subtraction of their own living expenses, is remitted and pooled. This pattern of pooling a joint budget from which individual expenses are subtracted differs from that characteristic of urban households, where individuals retain their own incomes and only pool a portion to cover household living costs. It may be that as the opportunities for individual consumption stimulated by the new availability of clothes, tapes and records increase, then family, and especially younger members, may come to question the corporate manage-ment of the household budget which places household accumulation, production and consumption above their individual interests and may even deny them a share. Where they also work in non-agricultural waged employment which may require commuting or periodic mobility, then it may be much more difficult for accumulation to continue to take place at the household level. A new pattern of accumulation may then develop which resembles that characteristic of urban areas, but at present there are few signs of changes in accumulation patterns in village households, which are still characterised by a large degree of economic interdependence between members, although the distribution of authority in this corporate management is not so clear.

The expansion of the household estate, embracing housing, productive assets, tools and other capital goods, has potentially strengthened the authority of the household head, who is officially registered as the senior male – although this does not necessarily mean that he is the manager of the family budget. Frequently, interviews have revealed it to be his wife or elder son who manages the family budget. But whoever 'manages' the household budget, there is likely to be much more negotiation since the reforms, with the bargaining position of each member very much dependent on the division of labour, income inputs and the range of economic activities which a household embraced. In households where both men and women continue to cultivate fields, with few additional economic activities, then it might be more difficult now than during the revolution for women and other family members to identify their share of the rewards. Women's share of the earnings may be more equal now that remuneration is made on the basis of fulfilling output quotas rather than the calculation of individual work points frequently discriminating against women and rewards distributed irrespective of the sex of the producer. Much will depend on their also receiving an equal share of the land, and, as the case studies show, this is by no means always the case. Moreover, women's individual contributions to the household budget may be less visible now that payments due to the household are calculated on the basis of output quotas with no recognition of the number and identity of the family members whose labour contributed to its production. In one respect this may not be too different from past practice, when even though women's work point totals and their value were listed separately, actual payments made for agricultural labour had frequently continued to be enclosed in one envelope addressed to the household head. Where the men and women of the household continue to be mainly employed in agricultural production, it is now the male head of the household who will probably decide the organisation and distribution of labour within the household and receive the remuneration due to it, so reproducing hierarchical relations of authority within the household in production and affecting female shares of rewards.

Where there is a more marked division of labour within the household with gender-separated activities, then it is more likely that their individual contributions are recognised. As sidelines have become increasingly substantial or dominant, women's separate contribution from domestic sidelines has been increasingly recognised by other members of the peasant household. In the past, their scale was so small that they were not so distinguishable from domestic labour and therefore not always even categorised as income-generating. For instance, one grandmother described herself as 'too old to work' and 'only able to do her bit by cooking the meals, taking care of the grandsons and the raising of two pigs and fifteen chickens', neglecting to add that the sale of these pigs, chickens and eggs amounted to ¥300 or just under half of the household's total cash income.[48] However, these definitions have become less of a problem as domestic sidelines have expanded in scale and scope to become the major household economic activity, and have increasingly generated a major portion of household incomes so that, in some richer villages, a skilled women's annual income from sideline activities such as animals and handicrafts has far exceeded that of the fieldworking or factory-employed male. One of the most interesting early effects of the reforms was the increase in economic and social status of agricultural workers. Previously they had been disadvantaged in terms of income and other benefits compared to those employed in rural industry, the army and other occupations beyond the village. Because of the higher prices paid for agricultural produce and the opportunities for combining fieldwork with other income-generating activities, fieldworkers in many regions have generated more income than those on fixed wages outside of agriculture. It is this factor which has done so much to increase the status of the agricultural workers within the village and household, and whether it was the men or the women of the peasant household who were the agricultural workers, this rise has increased their contribution to the household budget and their status *vis-à-vis* other members of the peasant household. This trend has particularly benefited women whose contracted sidelines frequently became the dominant income-generating activity, earning thousands of yuan for the household and providing employment for other family members.

A survey by the All-China Women's Federation published in 1987 showed that 35 to 40 per cent of specialised households in the country and 55 per cent in more developed regions were operated by rural women.[49] One of the first most successful chicken farms in China was established by a fifty-year-old peasant woman fieldworker who used her family savings and a state loan to build a four-roomed chicken house to supply eggs to the nearby market of Beijing, for years habitually short of eggs. Within a year or so she had not only repaid the original loan but she had also earned a cash income of more than ¥10,000 enabling her to expand the enterprise and provide full-time employment for her teenage son.[50] Where the women of peasant households are engaged in agricultural fieldwork or sidelines, then these have virtually become female-operated and -managed households. In one village, as many as one-tenth of the households were for all practical purposes female-headed and -operated, in that the men of the household worked and resided away from the village leaving the farm and other work entirely in the hands of the women, many of whom had to work singlehandedly to make a success of their many enterprises. For instance, one wife with two young children whose husband worked and resided in a nearby town was kept very busy in the fields cultivating wheat (3.5 mu) and cotton (0.5 mu). Because she was on her own she was often to be seen in the fields applying fertiliser, weeding, spraying and doing other jobs while keeping an eye on her children playing nearby. Her high-yielding plot earned several hundred yuan and she also earned a considerable income by raising pigs and chickens. She was very proud of the fact that she by herself had managed the household economy in such a way that it not only supported the family but also allowed them a surplus to accumulate for a new house. In the village as a whole, it was jested that several wives held up not just 'half the sky' but 'all the sky'.[51] As one husband ruefully remarked on his return to help with the harvest: 'Now that she [his wife] handles everything in and outside the house, I've been reduced to her farmhand.'[52]

It has never been clear whether female-operated households have suffered discrimination within villages in, for example, the distribution of resources. This is a question that is often asked, given the degree of discrimination experienced by female-headed households in other agricultural societies. Recently, in an investigation of female poverty, I was particularly interested in the circumstances of female-operated households which were referred to as female-'managed' rather than female-'headed' households. In Guangxi Autonomous Region, it is estimated that a high proportion – 23 per cent of the total households and 2.02 million households out of the 3.3 million or 61 per cent of poorer households – are female-'managed' in that the men are absent or labour-weak. They were considered to be unduly disadvantaged not so much in terms of inputs, information and markets as due to the heavier demands on female labour. The investigation of their conditions by the Women's Federation here was an important initiative, for it is one of the first instances that I know of, in which female-managed households have been a matter for official and specific concern; interestingly, one of the solutions to their problems was the establishment of one-to-one alliances between these and other more fortunate households in the interests of direct co-operation and aid. This reflects the general trend to see the well-being, welfare and the generation of corporate resources of the individual households as ultimately to lie in the extension of alliances among close family and kin groups. Perhaps, then, it is not surprising that one of the single most important preoccupations of the reform years in China's countryside proved to be the continuity of the family line.

Chapter 8

Continuity
Sons, successors and the single child

For generations, fathers and grandfathers had dreamed of sons and grandsons who would support them in their old age, maintain or expand their landholdings and guarantee their prosperity. Above all, sons, betwixt and between ancestors and descendants, continued the family line. Sons were not only for dreaming, for, in very practical ways, they represented survival, prosperity, security and a future. Indeed, without sons there was no future about which to think, plan and dream. For generations in the peasant household, be it large, extended or small nuclear, there had been a traditional birth preference in favour of sons. In turn, the males of each generation were exhorted to have many sons to fulfil their obligations to their father and their father's lineage, or, as a Chinese saying has it, 'to continue the incense smoke at the ancestral shrine'. Of the attributes customarily charged against an unfilial son, the failure to provide descendants was the 'gravest of unfilial acts', and testimony to the anxieties surrounding the disappearance of a patriline were the many social practices and rituals performed to obtain sons and celebrate their arrival into the world. Correlatively, to have many sons was 'the greatest of blessings' because of their potential role as begetters and providers of family income through labour, land and skills. How many times have I sat in households where the smiles gradually broadened and the cheer heightened among both family and observers as son by son was introduced to the 'foreigner'. After the death of parents and grandparents, it was sons, as sole performers of the ancestral rites, who were responsible for the welfare of their departed forebears. It was only sons who were bounded into the chain of generations giving every male of each generation merely a precious title to his body, entrusted as it was to him as the sole link between the past and the future. The first-born son was often referred to as the 'successor' son, and naming practices confirmed that identity primarily derived from place in the chain of continuity conceived in terms of descent order. Simply put, without sons bridging ancestors and descendants and signifying the unbroken continuity of the family, there was no future for the family, for female as well as male members.

The unbroken line of descent may not have exerted so powerful an influence on wives to bear sons, but a woman's prestige in her husband's family undoubtedly and immeasurably increased once she had presented them with a son or sons, who for her were also a source of status and a basis for her individual negotiations within the patrilineal household. In her son or sons, a young wife found her long-term influence and protection, but interestingly studies of family relations have also suggested that women, unlike men, may not have viewed the family as primarily a line of descent encompassing all the members of the household: those dead, those alive and those yet to be born. Rather, they tended to define the family largely in terms of the temporary and contemporary small, trun-cated unit consisting of mother and children, a unity which Margery Wolf has aptly termed 'the uterine family'.[1] However, women too continued to invest in their sons through weaving emotional ties that were not only personal, but also the most important if not exclusive source of security for their old age. For men and women, then, despite differing perceptions of the family, sons as the permanent members of the household were invested in, emotionally and structurally, as a source of security and support in old age. Even if the future were not in jeopardy from lack of a son, there was still uncertainty, because survival rates were always under threat from high rates of infant and child mortality.

SON SURVIVAL

In the countryside before 1949, economic factors and especially access to land and other material resources influenced the birth and survival rates of children within each generation. The scant data on differential fertility in China before 1949 estimated that the number of surviving children in peasant households averaged out at 2.5 or so,[2] with the number of births per couple declining with their resources and social status, and that the survival of just one son to maturity was not uncommon. Surveys showed there to be some correlation between size of farm and number of surviving children,[3] and although it is more difficult to ascertain the number of births, the studies showed clearly that of the children born, many died and among the poor more died. There are no exact figures for child and infant mortality in China before 1949, but most estimates place the rate some-where between 30 and 50 per cent. One study of a rural market town in Sichuan province in the mid-1940s showed that although the average number of children 'ever born' was 4.99, the average number of children surviving was 2.35, or 47.3 per cent.[4] In a Guangdong village, the infant mortality rate showed 300 per 1,000 live births, with the incidence of death bearing more heavily upon the infants of the poor so that poor couples considered themselves fortunate if they were able to raise two children to maturity out of six or seven or even more live births.[5] And in a northern village in Shandong, where the death rate was two to three out of every six or seven children born, the survival of all children born into a household was thought to be unusual, and most couples expected to lose a child or children. Indeed, only if a family lost more than half of its children – for example, three out of five – did villagers think that there must be something larger than fate at work.[6]

In the country generally, the death rate was highest among children under the age of three with a gradual tapering off between the ages of five and ten, so that in most regions the ages of three and ten or in some cases twelve years were celebrated as milestones critical to survival. High infant and child mortality rates meant that only three sons ensured the survival of one to adulthood, and to have three boys, a family would need to have an average of six children – more than most poor households could support. As one old folk saying suggested: 'To feed a family of five a peasant must work like an animal. But even with whipping, an animal couldn't support a family of six.' In contrast for the rich, 'Nothing so much indicated the social status of a household in the Chinese countryside as its size, which is a matter of pride, and especially when it contains a large number of sons.'[7] In sum, before 1949 all the available evidence suggested that a number of economic and demographic factors interrelated to affect the number of children born and surviving within each generation, so that a minority of households with many sons contrasted with the majority for whom poverty and poor health care left only one son surviving to maturity in each generation.

It was during the first decades of revolution that the majority of peasant households came closer to realising their dreams of more sons than they had at any time during the recent past. In the 1950s a number of public health and economic factors – including specific measures to improve sanitation and hygiene and increased stability of food supplies and improved medical services – contributed to a rapid decrease in the malnutrition and epidemic diseases which previously had taken such a high toll of the young population.[8] Improvements in diet, health, preventive medicine and general welfare had all combined to reduce infant mortality rates drastically in the first two decades after 1949. A familiar slogan reflected the attention directed towards infant and child health: 'one pregnancy, one live birth; one live birth, one healthy child'. By 1957 the proportion of child births attended by trained health workers was estimated to have reached 60 per cent or so in rural areas,[9] and most estimates suggest a reduction in infant mortality in rural areas from 250 in 1949 to 40 or 50 per 1,000 during the first decades of revolution.[10]

In the new stability and security of times in the 1950s, children not only constituted a source of personal pleasure, but they also were a symbol of the comparative new-found post-revolutionary wealth and status, and with the prohibitions against the individual and private hiring of labour, became the only means of acquiring wealth and status. In the 1950s and 1960s peasant families saw little need to revise the old adage which equated more children with more blessings. The costs of child rearing in the countryside were relatively small, children were normally allocated a grain ration and their care was shared by family members sometimes with the help of the collective. Within a very short period of time children could contribute to the household economy by undertaking various small and diverse tasks, and eventually they contributed their full labour power constituting the sole form of economic support in old age. Indeed, it was frequently said in the countryside that it was 'better to produce a little flesh dumpling [a baby] than produce work points yourself'.[11] The scarce data on preferred family size suggested an ideal of four to six children, and data on the average family showed that the average number of children born per peasant woman was around four, five or six children which, with a decrease in infant and child mortality rates, allowed for an increased number of surviving sons. In one village which I studied in 1977, an average of 2.5 sons had survived per mother over the age of forty years (when child bearing could reasonably have been expected to have ceased) over the previous twenty-five years. If dreams of sons and more sons had continued and were increasingly realised during the first post-revolutionary decades, simultaneously they were also threatened by the introduction of increasingly stringent birth control policies which, culminating in the single-child family policy, was dramatically to cut short family dreams of sons – perhaps even of one son.

SON PLANNING

At first in the early decades of revolution there were no very specific or clear directions as to the number and spacing of births in birth-control campaigns which primarily emphasised the planning of fertility rather than reduction of births. Thus the campaigns concentrated on delivering contraceptives and other family planning services to couples who had already completed their desired family size. Accounts of family planning in villages during these years illustrated both the advisory and voluntary nature of birth planning which was still defined as a private family matter in which individual couples themselves took their own decisions to limit unwanted births. Until the survival of at least one or two sons was assured, peasant parents usually would not even consider the use of contraception, let alone more permanent methods. It was only in the decade of the 1970s that there was a much more sustained attempt to introduce a population policy in China with the avowed aim of reducing the birth rate to 2 per cent. The two-child family was officially advocated and encouraged, and three children permitted in the cities, while in the countryside the three-child family was officially condoned although more births were allowable especially if all previous births had been girls. To achieve these goals, the government embarked on a series of national campaigns to persuade the population to adopt smaller families with Committees for Planned Birth Work established at every administrative level. In villages, the delivery of contraceptives was closely tied to the provision of basic health care in local clinics by bare-foot doctors, and all means of limiting fertility were to be provided for individual couples without charge. Within villages, women were divided into small groups each of whom was placed under the charge of a family planning worker who organised the meetings and met with each woman member individually in her home.

Whereas in the first two decades, family planning was largely voluntary, now there was some attempt to implement a birth quota system in which national and regional birth planning committees calculated desirable target numbers of births permissible in each administrative area, which were thus passed downwards through the administrative hierarchy until finally small groups based on residence or enterprise received their allocated number of births. However, although this collective birth plan seems to have operated in the cities and in some suburban communes, there were fewer accounts of its operation in villages. In rural areas, although the birth rate declined from 32 in 1970 to 20 per 1,000 in 1977, most estimates of the rural birth rates place them somewhere between 20 to 30 per 1,000 in the rural villages (see Table 8.1), and most village couples seem to have continued to reckon on upwards of three children with at least one to two sons. The traditional preference for more children and for more sons remained, and fertility rates and family size continued to reflect this preference so that households with the largest number of children almost invariably had a number of girls born before the much awaited son. However, if in practice there was little reduction in the number of children and particularly sons desired and born in the countryside, the collective birth plan marked an important precedent in policy in that the number of children born constituted a form of joint decision or controlled negotiation between state and parent. It was this first intervention by the state in the domestic arena of reproduction which paved the way for the appropriation of reproduction by the state when it attempted during the decade of the 1980s to become the exclusive arbiter in decisions to do with conception and contraception. Thus the peasant experience of reform came to include also enforced limitations on or even the abandonment of their recently realised age-old dreams for sons and the continuation of their family line as a result of the single-child family policy.

THE STATE AND SONS

One of the most momentous of the new and radical policies introduced into post-reform China was the single-child family policy, which was immediately distinguished by the degree of state intervention in decisions to do with conception and contraception which the Chinese government thought were too important to permit their delegation to the reproductive unit, the family: 'The population plan of the whole country is based on the reproductive activities of individual families and the family birth plan must be co-ordinated with the national population plan.'[12]

It is not an exaggeration to suggest that the single-child family policy represented an almost unique attempt by any state to acquire an exclusive measure of state control over reproduction or family planning and family size: 'You are in charge of the earth and the sky and now you still want to take charge of child bearing.'[13] The rationale for this new policy was that plans, and indeed ambitious plans, to promote China's development and modernisation were seen to be contingent not only on increased production but also on reducing population: unless the population to be fed, housed and clothed was reduced, the goals of any development strategy in China were bound to fail. In the late 1970s, the government was increasingly alarmed at the total sum of China's population (then more than 1 billion persons) and projected rates of population growth which, because of the age structure of China's population with some 65 per cent and 50 per cent of the population under thirty and twenty years of age respectively, were expected to become unprecedentedly high within the next generation. As a result of birth peaks between 1954 and 1957 and subsequently between 1967 and 1972, it was expected that some 20 million persons would enter marriageable and child-bearing age between 1979 and 1982 and again in 1987 through to 1996, which amounted to some 10 million more annually than was normal for other periods. Even if the government based its calculations on the then average birth rate of 2.3 children per couple, the total population would reach some 1.3 billion after twenty years and 1.5 billion after forty years.[14] Demographic projections and their correlation with material and social resources showed that land ratios, per capita grain rations and the demand for facilities to feed, clothe, house and educate such a growing population were formidable and a barrier to accumulating the necessary capital for economic development and modernisation.[15]

In 1978 the government did not alter its priority and emphasis on increasing production so much as redefine production to include also the reproduction of human beings. After the example of Engels:

> Social production itself is of a two-fold character: on the one hand, the production of the means of subsistence of food, of clothing, and shelter and the necessary tools; and on the other the production of human beings themselves, the propagation of the species.[16]

Current slogans thus directed cadres and the population to 'grasp the two kinds of production' and be aware of the consequences of allowing the population to increase out of step with China's productive capacity:

If we do not implement planned production control and let the population increase uncontrollably, rapid population growth is bound to put a heavy burden on the state and the people, cripple the national economy, adversely affect accumulation and State construction, the people's living standard and their health and slow down progress of the Four modernisations.[17]

On this basis, 'planned and proportionate development' not only called for the planned development of the production of material goods, but also for the planned production of human beings within national economic plans. This analysis, simple as it was, also conveniently offered an immediately comprehensible explanation for the now admitted lack of development in China in the past decades: had not the 'unchecked growth of population' and the resulting imbalance between the 'two kinds of production' been allowed to violate socialist principles of a planned economy? The five-year economic plans were henceforth to include twin goals for the development of material production and reproduction and therefore quotas or targets for population growth, while at the local level, in China's villages, the simultaneous implementation of these dualistic policies made quite different if not contradictory demands on the peasant household, which was also for the first time for some decades at one and the same time the most important unit of reproduction and production. Given the new demographic factors and new demands on peasant households to maximise family labour resources, the state thought it had no alternative, if it was to fulfil current national population targets, reducing rates of growth to 1 per cent by the end of 1979, 0.5 per cent in 1985 and zero population growth by the turn of the century, but to adopt the single rule: one child.

THE SINGLE SON

For peasants there would have to be a trade-off in dreams: if dreams of land and prosperity were to be realised, then dreams of sons would have to be truncated if not abandoned. There is little doubt that the single-child family policy has been the single most unpopular policy during the reform period, cutting short as it did age-old dreams of sons, family and future. However, the truncation or abandonment of age-old dreams did not take place without a struggle, and in the face of continuous peasant resistance, the government has had repeatedly to readjust the policy and the means by which it was implemented so that the experience of peasant households and villages in relation to this policy has primarily varied over time and region. Now that it is more than ten years since the government first attempted to implement the policy, it is possible to identify six phases in its implementation, each of which has affected the peasant household's experience of family planning during the period of reform.

In 1979 and 1980 the Chinese government suddenly and surprisingly introduced a one-child family policy at first on an experimental basis. It was unusual, largely because of its novel and universal injunction – one child per couple – and because of the number of attached economic incentives and penalties. The inclusion of quite punitive economic sanctions against those not adhering to official rules marked a unique departure from past policy practice, but during the first two years its implementation was marked by the degree of confusion inherent within the definition of the policy itself. The first published sets of rules and regulations uniformly advocated the birth of one child and categorically 'banned' the birth of a third child under any circumstances in both urban and rural China.[18] What was not so clear or so uniform, however, was the policy position on the birth of a second child, which included programmes to 'control' and 'regulate' second births in order to 'reduce' their number. Yet it was precisely the prohibitions against the birth of a second child which would determine the practice and the eventual success of the policy in permitting just one child per couple. The slogans ranged from 'no second child' to 'no more than two', and there was a range of circumstances, by no means uniform throughout China, under which a second child was to be permitted. In the absence of a single national family planning law, there were multiple regulations enacting the single-child family variously published by provinces and municipalities. Apparently, a family planning law was drafted for presentation to the Fifth National People's Congress in late 1980, but it did not appear largely 'due to the lack of consensus surrounding certain of its provisions'.[19] It is a fair guess that much of the dissent centred on the conditions under which a second child was to be permitted and the severity of the penalties to be attached to the birth of a second child.[20]

In the first two years a number of incentives were introduced, including the issue of cash and grain subsidies and benefits to do with health, housing and education. The penalties levied on the birth of a second or subsequent child were the reverse of the incentives; cash fines were to be exacted and sanctions operated in the distribution of grain, health care, education and housing. What distinguished the lists of incentives and disincentives published in 1979–80 was the discrepancies in their contents and the wide variation in the sources and extent of incentive funding and the circumstances in which penalties were exacted. This was particularly so in the countryside, where parents signing the single-child family pledge might receive rewards ranging from a small cash sum of a few tens of yuan to a thermos flask, a face flannel or a mere certificate of merit. Similarly, in some regions and cases, a cash fine of some hundreds or even thousands of yuan was imposed on peasants after the birth of a third or subsequent child, while in other regions or cases no penalties were exacted.[21] Reports suggest that local experiences ranged from the most stringent – those where a second pregnancy was not even permitted to proceed to term –

to those where the local authorities not only did not exact penalties but turned a blind eye or openly permitted second parity births. During the first two years, public campaigns to implement the policy were largely educational and designed to persuade the population voluntarily to accept the case for one child in the long-term national interest even if it directly countered short-term family interests.[22] The first single-child campaigns emphasised the dimensions of the population problem, and in the cities, especially among the higher educated, higher income and professional groups, there was some response, although even in the cities there was a general reluctance among those who had not yet had a son, while in the rural areas there was little serious attempt even to advocate the policy. Initially, the new policy was greeted with incredulity, and perpetual rumours suggested its imminent modification or demise. Indeed, twists and turns in official policies over the previous twenty-five years had generated a credibility problem for the government or a cynicism about whether it could hold any policy constant over time. It was only in September 1980 with the publication of an Open Letter on the Question of Controlling Chinese Population that the new policy was officially confirmed as permanent rather than temporary and experimental.[23] In my later interviews with family planning workers, they identified the publication of this letter as marking the beginning of a second phase of policy consolidation.

Although there was still no family planning law during this phase of consolidation (1981–82), the rules and regulations governing the one-child family policy were increasingly standardised, and defined more consistently the specific circumstances permitting a second child.[24] Exceptions to the one-child rule embraced a wide number of concessions permitting a second birth, including health defects, sterility and remarriage, with supplementary concessions to kinship and the continuation of the family line operating in the countryside. Here a second child was permitted if one son had been born for three consecutive generations, if both spouses were only children, if marriage was uxorilocal (the groom had moved into the bride's household) with the wife an only child, and if a household had only one son capable of begetting heirs. Additionally, households in mountainous regions which had economic difficulties were permitted to give birth to a second child. Although there was some attempt to standardise rewards and penalties attached to the policy, these were still largely dependent on the will and wealth of individual work units or neighbourhoods in which the couples were employed or resided. In the absence of a national policy or nationally allocated funds there was still a wide range in the value of rewards for single-child families and penalties for higher parity births.[25]

During this second phase the government seriously embarked on a national educational campaign to popularise the one-child policy, marshalling all aspects of the media in its support.[26] The government made considerable efforts to explain the population problem to the nation, to establish a direct link between family size and population totals, and to convince the present generation of parents that it was China's objective conditions rather than the Communist Party or the present leadership that prohibited the birth of more than one child. It also emphasised that it was the costs of educating and employing the younger generation and of providing basic needs for an ever-expanding population which reduced the resources available for accumulation, modernisation and increasing standards of rural livelihood. The State Family Planning Commission took specific responsibility for the nation-wide administration and implementation of the policy, and to persuade families to accept new norms and take practical steps to implement the policy. Each household was visited individually by members of the family planning committees of villages. Their task was to ascertain the couple's attitudes towards the new policy, their contraceptive practices and birth plans and to provide contraceptive services.[27] By the end of this period of consolidation, the single-child policy had been propagated in most regions of China – except for minority nationality areas – and by mid-1981 it was reckoned that some 12.5 million or so couples had taken out single-child family certificates.[28] Although the majority of these one-child certificated couples resided in the cities, the one-child policy was also operative in the rural areas.

During the decade of the 1970s, the birth rate in the rural areas was estimated to have declined significantly, from 2.3 per cent to 1.2 per cent,[29] and estimates of the proportion of couples with one child who were certificated as single-child families in villages (for which there were figures) ranged between 20 and 50 per cent. Reports from 1981 onwards also suggested that the birth rate was again rising in rural areas and that there were growing difficulties to be faced in implementing the single-child policy there. It was increasingly evident that family planning policies came into direct conflict with those of the responsibility production system, and that no system of incentives and disincentives was able satisfactorily to mediate this contradiction.[30] Economic sanctions constituted less of a deterrent to peasant households, which had access to many resources not available to urban households. Food supplies, for instance, could be produced on their land allocations, housing was privately owned, and health and educational facilities were not as well developed as in urban areas, and local village governments were not in the same position to reward and penalise peasant households. There was a single incentive which might have had some effect on the birth rate, and that was the introduction of a pension system similar to the one already operating in state factories in the cities and without which the labour of peasant children remained one of the only forms of insurance to which peasant elderly had access. Rural surveys during this period suggested that 45 per cent of women of child-bearing age still wanted three or more children and that for the large majority, sons constituted the most important pool of labour and a form of insurance in their old age. In a survey of peasant households published in 1982, a mere 2.2 per cent of peasant households wanted a daughter as an only child,[31] and again in a number of peasant household with two children recently surveyed, one-third of those with two sons wanted a third child, compared to 62 per cent of those with two daughters who wanted a son.[32] Son preference was the major factor in the countryside inhibiting the implementation of the single-child family policy.

The new single-child policy was not popular, and village leaders were themselves parents, kin and neighbours as well as family planning cadres, and where they did attempt to enforce rules strictly, there was evidence of local hostility in which it was not unknown for them to be attacked by irate peasant families. Indeed, it would have been hard to avoid tension between an older generation of cadres who had already had their children and a younger generation who were being asked to forfeit their right to decide their own family size. One enquiry into the birth rate of cadres found that 68 per cent of the cadres had three or more children, and of 494 cadres in one county 10 had 7, 53 had 6, 101 had 5, 164 had 4 and 166 had 3.[33] The cadres themselves were frequently accused of not setting an example, and in the face of local hostility it was not surprising to find that many preferred not to intervene in such a potentially unpopular area.

To counter this reluctance, the government attempted to link cadre responsibility and reward by attaching rewards and penalties to the operation of quotas so that cadres might be rewarded by as much as ¥100 for meeting birth quotas or, alternatively, be penalised by ¥10 for every unplanned birth. Even so by 1982, as a result of increasing problems in the implementation of the one-child policy, it seemed that the Chinese government had three alternative strategies at its disposal: the first was to continue to promote the single-child family policy despite all the problems, or alternatively, the government could modify either the new production or the reproduction policies with the aim of reducing the conflict between the two. In 1982, however, it seemed unlikely that the government would opt for either of the latter solutions, although it did ponder the problem of labour supply and granted permission to peasant households to hire labour as an alternative to reliance on family labour – a move which marked a major departure from past policies but perhaps more than any other factor confirmed the commitment of the government to the single-child family policy. There were also reports that some sections of the leadership thought that the one-child policy would never succeed in rural areas, and it would therefore be better to lower the targets and permit 1.5 or 2 children per couple by aiming for a 50 per cent acceptance rate in establishing one-child families in rural areas,[34] but by 1983, it was evident that the government had perceived the population problem and the rising birth rate in the countryside to be too serious to allow any relaxation of the single-child policy. Thus there began a third period: one marked by coercion.

The years of coercion (1983–84) were marked not so much by a change of policy as a change in the means to achieve its goals in that new penalties were introduced to increase peer and cadre pressure on parents contemplating out-of-plan births. In work or residential units, fellow workers were fined if one of their number transgressed quotas, and family planning cadres were also fined sometimes by as much as ¥100 if such births occurred.[35] Instances of enforced IUD insertions for women with one child, sterilisations for women with two children and abortions for unapproved pregnancies were increasingly reported in the media. In particular, the number of sterilisations performed within an administrative area became another criterion, alongside the number of single children, of success in family planning. During 1983 several provincial administrations outlined the main task of their family planning programmes as 'improving and furthering ligation and vasectomy work',[36] and administrative areas at all levels had quotas for sterilisation operations. Nationally the reported number of sterilisations showed a sharp rise: in February 1983, a month of peak campaigning, an estimated 8.86 million sterilisation operations took place in China.[37] For Hebei province it was reported that 1.77 million ligations and vasectomies, or 85.9 per cent of its annual quota, had been performed by the end of May.[38] Many of the media references to 'compulsory sterilisation' came from Guangdong province in the south of China where the birth rate at the end of 1982 – 24.99 per 1,000 – continued to be the highest of all provinces and municipalities[39] and where several family planning campaigns in 1983–84 had as their aim 'compulsory sterilisation for either party, husband or wife, of those couples who already had two children'. Internationally, the government, sensitive to the charge of coercion, continued to stress that it was China's consistent policy to encourage couples to practise birth control voluntarily, but admitted that forced abortions and sterilisations did occur in some regions.[40] The increasingly important question was whether there was any alternative to coercion if persuasion failed. It was this realisation which probably lay behind the admission made by some provincial leaders, that because the population issue was so important, they must take forceful measures if education failed. However, the apparent increase in female infanticide in rural China sparked a wave of national and international concern and contributed to the policy's growing unpopularity and impracticality within China[41] and led to international criticism and threats of withdrawing financial support for China's family planning programmes. It was these combined pressures, internal and external, which contributed to the modification of the one-child policy in the rural areas and a new phase of moderation (1985–86).

In 1984 policy documents began to accept that the unpopularity of the policy was such that there must 'be an enquiry into the views of the people' in order that the policy 'be reasonable', 'well received by the people' and 'practical for cadres to enforce'.[42] Although the single-child policy remained officially, there were substantial changes in its presentation and implementation. The contracepting rate rather than the single-child rate became the main measure of family planning achievement, and instead of stressing the uniformity and urgency of the single-child regulations, the authorities began to promote 'controlled relaxation' and the evolution of appropriate family planning rules to suit specific conditions and regions.[43] Most provincial governments, after investigating responses to the single-child family policy, subsequently issued supplementary regulations permitting more second parity births. These broadened the conditions permitting a second child in the countryside if either of the parents was an only child and in the cities if both parents were only children – as if the one-child rule should only prevail for a single generation. A second child was also newly permitted in the countryside where an only son gave birth to a daughter, where the continuation of the family line was threatened by the birth of a single daughter or where the husband had moved into the wife's household on marriage and the first child was a daughter.[44] Whereas previously a second child had been permitted only in cases where all these circumstances pertained, these modifications made major new concessions to the son preference and kinship ties in the countryside, thereby also officially acknowledging the unsubstitutability of daughters.

The second major modification of the policy was the authorisation of a second child where peasant couples found themselves in 'practical or financial' difficulties which, the most loosely defined of conditions, lent itself to a wide range of interpretations. Financial difficulties were defined, not according to individual couple circumstances, but according to regional natural endowments and economic and cultural development. In Sichuan province, for example, something of a pace-setter in family planning, the province was divided into five physical regions – urban, rural (suburbs and plains), hilly, mountainous and high mountainous regions, with each having regulations appropriate to its physical conditions: in urban areas, only one child was permitted; in plains and hilly areas, 50 per cent of households; and in mountainous and high mountainous regions, all couples were permitted a second child.[45] The regulations for other provinces were similar, and it seemed that while there was virtually no alteration in urban rules, in the countryside, despite the official emphasis on 'controlled relaxation', there was some verbal slippage 'generally permitting second births'. Indeed, informally throughout this period, in my interviews and conversations there was general recognition that there was *de facto* a two-child policy in operation in the countryside, an acknowledgement which placed the government in a new position of checkmate after 1987.

After a period of moderation, sharp rises in China's birth rate in 1987 led to renewed official demands for the stricter implementation of the one-child family rule in line with official fears that the population growth rate would 'get out of control' given the rise in birth rate to 21/2 per 1,000 in 1987 and a rise of 0.4 over the previous year, representing the sharpest annual increase over the previous five years.[46] The number of second and third births, although declining, still amounted to 50 per cent of all births (see Table 8.2), and in 1987 the total sum of China's population was reported to number 1.072 billion, or around 12 million more than at the end of 1986. If this trend was to continue, the Chinese government feared that the population would exceed its general target of 1.2 billion in the year 2000 by some 50–80 million. It was such projected trends which caused the media to warn again of an impending 'population crisis' which was caused by 'the defiance of millions of couples ignoring the one child rule' and the 'negligence of family planning cadres in implementing the one child rule'.[47] In the face of repeated references to an impending population crisis, the government perpetually called for the stricter implementation of the one-child policy, the reduction of exceptions to the policy and further penalties for offending parents and cadres including a new set of levies – on-the-spot fines. At the same time the policy permitting a second child after the birth of a daughter is reported to have been officially extended to all rural areas in the first half of 1988.[48] Simultaneously, a position of checkmate was born as calls for new policy strictures accompanied modification in the face of unprecedented difficulties in its implementation.[49] If the government wanted to impose strict family planning controls, it would have to come to some form of compromise with peasant households.

Since 1989 there have continued to be periodic calls for new single-child family campaigns to counter 'loss of control' of family planning.[50] The most immediate cause for concern is the third birth peak which, beginning in 1986 and expected to last until 1996, is characterised by the 35 per cent increase in the number of women between ages twenty and twenty-nine years and an increase of between 15 and 17 million babies born each year between 1991 and 1995.[51] With the birth rate at 20.98 per 1,000 and the death rate at 6.28 per 1,000, or more than 50,000 births outnumbering 16,000 deaths each day, trends in the population growth were expected to exacerbate the already heavy demands on scarce land, water, grain and housing resources. Although there is some dissension within China among demographers and state policy cadres as to the future of the one-child policy, the publication of the preliminary results of the fourth Chinese census held on 30 June 1990 was a daunting reminder of the population problem. These showed that China's population was in excess of 1.13 billion, with a birth rate of 20.98 per 1,000, and a natural growth rate of 1.47 per cent – little changed from the figures revealed by the previous census in 1982.[52] These preliminary results were depicted in the Chinese media as cause for both celebration and concern: celebration at the falling birth rate from 24 to 21 per 1,000 over the past fifteen years; concern at the increase in natural growth rates since 1982, from 14.5 to 14.7 per 1,000, which actually meant that China's population was still rising by approximately 17 million births each year.[53]

In the face of these figures, Party and Youth League members were once more exhorted to take the lead in implementing family planning policy. However, they could be forgiven for having some difficulty in discerning exactly what this is. It is freely admitted that while official rhetoric continues generally to advocate the one-child policy, the one-child rule only holds for urban residents and government employees. In February 1989 an annual meeting of the directors of the provincial family planning commissions suggested that there are four categories of official policies in the rural areas of China. First, six provinces (Guangdong, Hainan, Yunnan, Ningxia, Qinghai and Xinjiang) have a policy of allowing all rural couples to have a second child a few years after the first. Secondly, a very limited number of rural areas where the levels of economic development and population density are very high have not yet officially adopted the policy of allowing peasant couples whose first child was a daughter to have a second child after a certain interval. Thirdly, in some regions of these well-developed rural areas and in the rural areas of the other eighteen provinces, couples whose first child is a girl are permitted to have a second child after a number of years. And for a fourth category, not regionally bounded, minority nationalities were said to be permitted to have two or more births per couple.[54] In sum, in most rural areas, two children are now generally permitted to a greater or lesser degree, but it is also categorically stated that there should be no third births. Overall it seems that a compromise has been struck by a new rule: two children generally permitted, but absolutely no third births.

It remains to be seen whether renewed exhortation can effectively overcome peasant opposition and resistance to stringent family planning policies. In 1990 worried demographers and social workers, meeting to discuss population and economic growth in China's coastal areas, called upon the government to tighten its economic measures to encourage smaller families by providing one-child families with better community services and awarding them priority in obtaining education, housing and jobs.[55] The problem remains that these incentives are most operable in the cities and richer coastal regions where the decline in family size is most evident rather than in remote rural areas where the birth rate is still high, with farmers preferring to pay fines, often many thousands of yuan, rather than forgo additional children. Other recent suggestions to tighten the policy include the payment of accumulated one-child subsidies between birth and sixteen years as retirement pensions and that land contracts or employment be made dependent on adherence to family planning regulations. Given the difficulties in implementing and policing a one-child policy, it seems unlikely that it will again be advocated or imposed in the countryside; instead, there will be sustained efforts to exercise family planning policies in favour of the two-child family. In sum, peasant households in suburbs of large cities, on plains and on mountains have had different experiences of these policies given the readjustments in family planning policy according to place, its topography and level of economic development. Provincial figures for planned births and multiple births in 1988 showed a wide range in rates (see Table 8.3), and variations between villages located on plains, hills and mountains are also tolerated. In 1987, a study of four villages in rural Fujian and Heilongjiang provinces suggested that, whereas on paper a strong normative and putatively compulsory family planning policy existed, wide variations occurred in its interpretation and enforcement, with cadre authority increasingly weak with the lax enforcement of fines for unplanned births and a *de facto* two-child policy masked by unreliable data even in the highest-performing counties. In all four counties, the study concluded, family planning cadres had probably assessed the effective degree of their political and economic control and acted – or rather not acted – accordingly.[56]

In my own village studies since 1989, there has been a wide range of peasant experience of the family planning policies. In the suburbs of the largest city, Beijing, there was rarely a second child; in mid-level plain and low hill there was usually a second child; and in the remote mountainous and poor regions the number of children suggested that there had never been a family planning policy. In these latter villages, however, in some of the first women's meetings ever called, the women took great pains to point out to me that they willingly had fewer children now, three–four–five, compared to the six–seven–eight of their mothers and grandmothers. In some regions, the compromise, two but not three, was strictly adhered to. In 1989 my stay in a mountainous village in a county of the Beijing municipality (not the case study) was made miserable by the operation of a very strict rule that if two children were to be permitted then in no circumstances was a third birth to be permitted so that women pregnant with a third child were constantly harassed until they had been persuaded to have an abortion even at a very late stage, and, if it was so late, the infant was removed from the mother at birth. In this way no third births were registered in that county. There are continuing reports of early and late abortions forced on unwilling mothers of two or three children in the countryside, yet at the same time second and third births continue to be openly permitted in other regions. However, the compromise of two but not three appears to be increasingly accepted as official policy.

In assessing whether the government can operate its present policy of compromise, much is dependent on the degree to which continuing son preference can be countered. In this respect the phases in the implementation of the single-child family policy can very much be seen as part of a long-term contest of wills between family and state for control of family size which is likely to continue so long as parents refuse to abandon or truncate their dreams of sons and the continuity of the family line. While economic factors understandably play a role in defining family size, the State Family Planning Commission has always emphasised, in several of my interviews with them over recent years, that it was the issue of succession or the continuation of the family line which primarily underlay persistent peasant resistance to birth restrictions. If there was any doubt before reform that sons were preferred to daughters, the resistance to the single-child family policy has offered continuing proof that daughters not just cannot substitute for sons but indeed they may even be sacrificed for sons.

Chapter 9

Discontinuity
Daughters, discrimination and denial

Despite thirty years of revolution, on the eve of reform the age-old contrast remained: if sons were for continuity, daughters made for discontinuity; if sons were associated with certainty, daughters' lives and dreams were fashioned out of uncertainty. This contrast was to become even more pronounced during the reform years as a result of the single-child family policy. If sons were in any doubt that they were the preferred sex, the years of reform reinforced a singular message – that they were necessary, preferred and privileged. In contrast, daughters, during the revolutionary years, perhaps more than any other social category, received dual messages, simultaneously juxtaposing affirmation and denial of equality: if with the revolution, daughters were promised equity with sons as 'revolutionary successors', as 'family successors', they were represented as nowhere near the equal of sons.

DAUGHTER DISCRIMINATION

Within households daughters were born distanced from their natal family by the common practice of virilocal marriage – a practice whereby daughters were destined to become daughters-in-law and wives in other families. An early term used exclusively for female marriage meant 'going out', and numerous sayings emphasised this very important gender difference: 'a son is born facing in and a girl is born facing out', 'men rear sons just as they grow trees for shade', 'a daughter married is like water poured out the door', 'a daughter belongs to somebody else's family', 'investing in a girl is a loss' and 'a family with daughters is a dead-end family'. Temporary, daughters were in no position to compete with sons, who were permanent and long-term sources of support and certainty. For sons, permanent members of the family, 'taking in' wives reaffirmed their status from birth of permanence, continuity and certainty. Daughters were early taught that they ultimately belonged to another family, that their presence was transient and that their future lay elsewhere: they could neither substitute for sons nor compensate for their absence. All the evidence suggests that daughters were entirely cognisant of their transience 'passing through' households: 'We were successful as daughters if we made a good marriage and consolidated our position by bearing heirs.'[1] In my own fieldwork over the years, one of my most potent memories has been of the contrasting status accorded to sons and daughters constituting a message for daughters that was unmistakably clear. Although it is no longer the practice to reckon daughters of so little account that they are omitted from tallied lists of family members, in hundreds of household interviews, sons were enumerated before daughters whatever the birth order; many sons were the cause of congratulations and only daughters the occasion of com-miseration. On the unique occasion I can remember when the son was listed last, he had been adopted. Interestingly, the father felt more proprietorial towards his daughter-in-law for whom he had paid 'good money' than towards his son with whom he had no blood ties. It was only this very unusual reversal of sex order which had alerted me to question further. Family planning was not even considered to be a viable option until after the birth of a son, and family exchanges of daughters in marriage continued despite official advocation of free-choice marriage.

In households with several sons there was a degree of confidence and investment in the future of the domestic group that was just not charac-teristic of households with no sons and only daughters. In villages there was a close correlation between the number of sons per household and the building of new and additional houses. Those with sons built for a future; those without sons had no future. I can remember so very clearly the exact and stunning moment when I directly felt the differential value of sons and daughters in relation to the future of the household. During one of my first field experiences, I visited a succession of households in a southern Chinese village: those with sons were hustling and bustling, building houses, storerooms and new kitchens, anticipating and planning as they were for future expansion following marriage and births of children and grandchildren; in those with only daughters there was no housebuilding, no storeroom and no new kitchen, all signifying silence or a lack of anticipation, an absence of plans and the demise or foreshortening of the future. Here in one hot afternoon was the visible and audible evidence of the continuing efficacy of the old adages which likened daughters to 'goods without profits' or 'on which the future is lost'. The future was to be truly lost for a proportion of first-born daughters once the single-child policy was introduced during the reform years reaffirming the message of secondariness and unsubstitutability.

FEMALE INFANTICIDE

With the introduction of the one-child family policy the sex of the single child became a very important question: 'the question of having boys or girls is a common social problem that at present faces most families'.[2] In 1981 a survey from Hebei province had revealed that 95 per cent of the population wanted two or more children of whom one at least was to be a boy, and if only one child was to be permitted then a mere 2.2 per cent wanted a daughter.[3] Surveys and my own interviews in Beijing in 1983 revealed that parents of single daughters were more reluctant to support the policy, took longer to sign the single-child family certificate and constituted a majority of the couples defying the policy and proceeding with out-of-plan births.[4] In rural areas, there were reports of female infanticide, a practice not uncommon before 1949, although since that time there had only been occasional reports of female infanticide when sex ratios calculated at birth or in the first year had produced some puzzling discrepancies. In 1978 detailed population data for three counties in Zhejiang province suggested that the lower proportion of females born in 1978 should attract attention since this reflected the 'recurrence in recent years in some places of abandoning and killing infants, for the most part girls'.[4]

In 1980 it was noticeable that the new Marriage Law continued to incorporate prohibitions against infanticide as if it was relevant, but still in 1981 it came as something of a surprise to most foreign and Chinese observers when female infanticide became the subject of emotive headlines in the Chinese press. Then, the national youth newspaper ran the headlines 'Save our baby girls' because it deemed it necessary to draw attention to the 'numbers of baby girls abandoned and the sharp increase in female infanticide which had occurred in China in the 1980s'.[6] Once the media reported a sharp increase in female infanticide, the government charged the Women's Federation with initiating a nation-wide survey to investigate and document the scale of female infanticide and other forms of discrimination against female infants and their mothers. Some results were published which suggested that female infanticide was likely to occur where the birth of a daughter marked the end of the family line and, in the poorer inland regions of China, where there was a tradition of infanticide and where it was consequently scarcely thought of as a crime. In Anhui province, where the history of infanticide had given rise to large numbers of unmarried men over the age of forty years, a disproportionate number of newborn and young infants had died in the last few years. In some areas the ratio of female to male infants were reported to have dropped to a low 1 in 5, in one production team more than forty baby girls had been drowned in 1980 and 1981, and in another brigade, of the eight babies born in the first quarter of 1982, the three boys survived, three girls were drowned and a further two had been abandoned.[7] Further comparisons with nearby villages had revealed that these patterns were not unique. In one of the counties, the percentage of male over female infants had risen from 3.2 to 5.8 per cent within the scope of one year, so that in 1980 the percentage of males born was 53 per cent compared to 46 per cent female. In another county, the problem was shown to be yet more serious, for the percentage of males born had risen from 112.6 to 116.4 per cent between 1980 and 1981, so that in 1981 the percentage of males born was 58.2 per cent compared to 41.8 per cent female (see Table 9.1). A national newspaper drew attention to these trends in order to emphasise that the intolerable behaviour of drowning and forsaking baby girls is 'still rampant in some rural areas' and 'a major problem worthy of serious attention'.[8]

There were also reports in the media from Henan, Hebei and Hunan provinces where maltreatment and deaths of female infants occurred on some scale. In these inland provinces the sex ratios of the newborn showed a higher proportion of males, frequently as high as 111 to 113 to every 100 females.[9] These figures, above the national average of 108.5 to 100 estimated in 1981 by the State Statistical Bureau, do suggest a degree of female infanticide, female neglect or at least under-registration of female infants. The system of registration did not itself take account of babies dying within three days of birth, and in cases of acute disappointment, the registration of a baby girl seems to have signified that the parents or parent were relenting and accepting the child. However, any tendency to under-register female infants could only exaggerate and certainly not alone account for the higher ratio of males to females among the newborn in these areas. Investigations of the Women's Federation not only suggested that female infanticide was increasing, but also that there was a whole range of less tangible but none the less serious forms of prejudice and discrimination against female infants. The results of surveys in two rural communes on the outskirts of the capital, Beijing, undertaken by the Women's Federation, revealed that there had been no cases of female infanticide or untoward maternal deaths, but that a strong preference for sons still existed.[10] The birth of a son might be the occasion of much rejoicing by parents and kin, with the mother enjoying special foods and with the son the focus of joyful celebrations and feasting. In contrast, there had been occasions where disappointed relatives precipitately left the hospital on a girl's birth with no celebration or special foods. In hospitals, the degree of post-partum complications were found to be significantly higher among mothers of daughters, and this was attributed to their fall in spirits immediately after a disappointing birth.[11] Grandparents were particularly likely to show their disappointment, and in a few instances had taken a little time to be reconciled sufficiently to order milk for the granddaughter and special foods for the mother. Family relations, especially those between mothers and daughters-in-law, frequently deteriorated once it was known that the first-born was a daughter.[12]

It is difficult to ascertain the scale of female infanticide during the reform years. It has been periodically referred to as a problem in the Chinese press, and it is an open topic of conversation in China, where everybody has their story of either seeing for themselves or knowing somebody who has seen an abandoned female baby alive or dead. Since 1989, there have been reports that the male–female imbalance is such that there are now 2.2 per cent more male than female infants, with the result that in about twenty years there will be 40 million males in their twenties unable to find wives.[13] A number of foreign demographers have analysed Chinese statistics, and most conclude that recent Chinese surveys and censuses indicate high levels of female mortality at birth. Terence Hull, in examining recent trends in sex rates at birth in China (Table 9.2), suggests that the high sex ratios at birth indicate a substantial deficit of female births especially in the countryside and for second and third parity births.[14] His calculations suggest that 5,061.49 births are missing from a 1 per cent sample, and that for China as a whole, this calculation implies just over half a million missing female births for 1986. He suggests that these are due to female infanticide, gender-specific abortion and under-registration, with the first most likely to be playing a major role. Ainsley Coale considers the problem of excess female mortality in populations where discriminatory treatment offsets the natural lower mortality of females, and for China, he suggests 29 million missing females or 10 million or so below the 40 million estimated in the Chinese press.[15] Although there is some debate about the numbers and scale of the problem, there is no doubt that it is of such national concern that the Chinese government has unhesitatingly taken up the cause of daughters.

UPGRADING DAUGHTERS

Because it was one thing to turn a blind eye to lesser forms of daughter discrimination, but quite another to condone denial or loss of female life, both the Women's Federation and the government set out to persuade parents and the population at large that daughters were as valuable as sons. In one pamphlet, entitled 'It's as good to have a girl as a boy', the Beijing Women's Federation explained that the current wave of violence against mothers and female infants had made it necessary for them to emphasise equality.

> The question of how to regard having a boy or a girl is an important part of socialist morality and not to be ignored. These materials on the sameness of boys and girls and on protecting women and female infants should be widely studied to promote anti-feudal education and to teach people about the legal system. They set out to convince people that boys and girls are equal and that we should oppose actions which harm women and which lead to loss of life.[16]

The Women's Federation initiated an educational campaign to convince the population that females did not determine the sex of a child (a cause of some violence against mothers of daughters) and that daughters could participate in economic and political activities on a basis equal to sons and to both their own and to their family's advantage. Since daughters too care for their parents and sons-in-law can marry into households, their value should be equally recognised by parents. Booklets and pamphlets were full of stories in which grandparents were won round to accept female births, in which disappointed parents accepted daughters and in which reluctant husbands eventually supported their wives as mothers of first-born daughters against the opposition of other members of the family. Posters on village and urban walls almost all uniformly depicted infant girls as the single child alongside her smiling mother or parents. Cartoons illustrated the long-range problems which would result if daughters were devalued and infanticide occurred on any scale. In one, ten fond mothers watch proudly as ten sons play; years later, ten fond mothers are seen searching far and wide for ten daughters-in-law. Educational materials are also aimed at women, who are not only victims but also themselves frequently collude in the violence against infant girls. The Beijing Women's Federation, in its general introduction to the booklet 'It's as good to have a girl as a boy', also had a particular message for women:

> We also hope that young women who give birth to girls will not feel a loss of self-esteem, will value their own rights and life, will rely on various organisations and will struggle resolutely against backward, ignorant ideas, and stand up for their own rights.[17]

In addition to education, the Women's Federation also set out to acquaint women with their legal rights. One of the causes of female infanticide was seen to be a lack of understanding of the criminal nature of the offence and an absence of knowledge about legal rights and the new legal system. The provisions of the relevant laws, the new Marriage Law, the new Constitution and the new Criminal Law, were thus tightened and publicised.[18] Although the law might offer female protection, it was quite another matter to implement it so as to provide protection for women and children in practice. What was important was that there were legal institutions, personnel and individual support available to women to aid them in the exercise of these rights. Local women's organisations at the grassroots were reported as saying that their own experience had taught them that 'the rights and interests of women and children are best protected by enforcing the laws and regulations designed to help abused women and by acting as their legal advocates and helping them exercise these rights'.[19] The specific campaign to acquaint women with their legal rights was part of a revived interest in the rule of law and access to new legal institutions to provide women with a resource in the resolution of intra-familial disputes and particularly those which entailed some form of physical violence. Without access to legal institutions and support, individual women would find it difficult to acquire a power base and exercise sanctions alternative to those at the disposal of kin and elders.

In 1983–84, the Women's Federation attempted to establish a network of legal centres to advise female victims of violence, collect evidence and pursue the offenders through the courts.[20] In the capital, a 'Law Publicity Week' was organised by the Beijing Women's Federation with the purpose of 'helping women and those working for their interests to learn about the laws protecting the rights of women and children and how to use law as a weapon to protect these rights'.[21] Public forums were held on the laws for the protection of women and children, and law counselling centres were set up on street corners and in the parks, where legal advisers made themselves available to answer any queries and investigate any grievances. Away from the capital, in southern Jiangxi province, a one-month pro-gramme was held at the end of 1983 'to increase the knowledge of the law, commend good examples, criticise erroneous practices and offer legal counselling'. During publicity campaigns it was found that there were local cases where women had given away their first-born daughters in order that 'they might have a son to continue the family line'.[22]

It was the incidence of the visible and more extreme forms of violence against daughters which also led to new and broader political campaigns sponsored by the Women's Federation to counter all forms of discrimina-tion and violence against women. In an unusually strongly worded state-ment in September 1983, a Vice-President of the Women's Federation conceived of infanticide and violence against women as: 'only the visible manifestation of the visible patriarchal partiality that persists in spite of all the rule and laws written since liberation incorporating political and economic equality'.[23] Ironically, it was visible and extreme forms of violence which legitimised and validated an increased role of the Federation as defender and protector of women. It is no accident that in the following years more was learned about sexual discrimination in the family, in the village, in employment and in education than in the previous thirty years. The degree to which the Women's Federation had newly constituted itself as the defender and protector of women against violence was apparent in the reports of its Fifth National Congress in 1983.[24] In contrast to the Fourth National Congress of 1978, when the Women's Federation had rather solicited support for Party and government policies, this Congress emphasised gender-specific problems including female infanticide, and called for the protection of the rights and interests of women and children:

What demands attention is that remnant feudal ideas of regarding men as superior to women and traditional prejudices against women have re-emerged in recent years. For example, some localities and units have placed unreasonable demands and restrictions in recruiting or promoting women and women cadres. Some areas and units bluntly refuse to admit needed and qualified women; some neglect the labour protection of women in productive work. Parents interfering in their children's freedom of marriage, arranging marriage for money, marrying in order to extort money and other similar cases have become fairly commonplace.

What is intolerable is the fact that some ugly phenomena that had been wiped out long ago in new China have begun to recur. Criminal acts of drowning female infants, insulting women, persecuting mothers who gave birth to girls, and selling and harming women and children have occurred frequently. In some areas these have reached serious proportions.

We women must unite with others in society and resolutely struggle against all acts harming women and children and vigorously help the public security and judicial organs crack down on these criminal activities . . . and firmly protect the legitimate rights and interests of women and children.[25]

The main task of the Women's Federation in 1983 was primarily to associate itself with women's interests so that it could 'hope to deal effective blows at crimes cruelly injuring and murdering women and children, stop the drowning and abandoning of infant girls and eliminate all those ugly phenomena that should never exist in a socialist China'.[26] The proceedings of the Fifth Congress revalidated the gender-specific demands of the Women's Federation in its government-supported role as defender and protector of women, although the Chinese government was no stranger to the concept of female rights, which it had continuously and variously advocated during the revolution.

HALF OF HEAVEN

The revolution had promised women a privileged claim or entitlement to the future, summed up in sayings such as 'Even chicken feathers can fly to heaven' or 'half of heaven'. The sky was to be especially high for the female half of the peasant population whose very association with heaven was nothing short of revolutionary. The very construction of the popular revolutionary slogan 'half of heaven' constituted a rhetorical feat in that it challenged and invalidated the powerful cosmological tradition dividing female from male, yin from yang, earth from heaven and domestic inside from public outside. Confucian texts, folklore translations and prescriptive codes of behaviour inherited from generation to generation had long perpetuated the belief that women were as different from and inferior to men as earth was to heaven, with a correlative denial in female agency – to be a women had meant to submit, to respond and to have no part in public affairs. The slogan 'half of heaven', introduced by the Chinese government, was thus primarily designed to reverse the customary sexual division of labour whereby women were largely confined to the domestic inside. From earliest times, women had been taught that they should not concern themselves with public affairs. 'A wife's words should not travel beyond her apartments', 'a woman does not discuss affairs outside the home' and 'disorder does not come down from heaven, it is produced by women'. Women were denied participation in any of the significant government or local community or kin institutions and were prevented by the laws of inheritance from owning property in their own right. The few occupations open to women were domestically associated with magic or procreation, including midwives, marriage-brokers, prostitutes, courtesans, procuresses or spirit diviners.

Perhaps the most striking feature of social life to be challenged by the slogan was the segregation of the sexes based upon the cult of feminine chastity and ideal of segregation which had led to the increasing isolation of daughters and the seclusion of women in both richer and poorer households. The very word for woman, 'neiren', literally meant 'inside person'. Even among the peasantry where women customarily had more freedom of movement, the mobility of most village women was still restricted. They had not often been permitted to leave their courtyards for the first three years of marriage, and one traveller in nineteenth-century China found that women likened their existence to a 'frog in a well', and that tens of thousands of women had never been more than 2 miles from their villages and this was often only on the occasion of their marriage.[27] Common sayings, such as 'A man travels everywhere while a woman is confined to the kitchen' and 'An incompetent man can get about in nine counties but a competent woman can only get around her cooking stove', arose because appearances of women outside their household yards were rare. One working woman recalled that, when a family wanted to know more about a girl as prospective daughter-in-law, the highest praise and compliment from neighbours was 'We do not know, we have never seen her'.[28] A stranger within sent the women hurrying into an inner room, and this invisibility of person was taken to its extreme when an enquiry on the domestic threshold elicited the response given by the woman herself, 'No, there is nobody home'.[29] There are, of course, many recorded instances of women crossing or transgressing these boundaries, nevertheless imaging a heaven or future for women, who, like men, had a half or an equal place on the premise that 'anything a man could do a woman could also do' represented a revolutionary claim or entitlement for half the population.

During the revolution and influenced by this new rhetoric of equality, women took up new economic roles and occupied positions of political responsibility. The government encouraged the participation of women in social production as 'the most important link in the chain . . . leading the way to emancipation'[30] or the acquisition of new confidence, power and authority within both public and domestic arenas. In new collective representations of women, female role models were shown working in the fields and in the factories alongside men. Narratives showed women overcoming folk prejudice – 'A woman having a job is like flying a kite under a bed' or 'A woman in politics is like a hen trying to crow' – and attaining new positions in occupational and political decision-making bodies hitherto denied them. In public spaces and rhetoric, women were represented by new images and with new expectations that had altered their lives in ways likened to 'reversing heaven and earth'. Uniquely for the female half of the peasant population, however, this concept of heaven and of an equal place within it remained a relativised rather than hegemonic discourse, for alongside it, in opposition to and in competititon with it lay that other family discourse of discrimination which, as we have seen, also affected their experience of first revolution and then reform.

During the reform years, however, even the rhetoric of equality was punctured as infanticide drew attention to the thirty-year-old failure of the new language and rhetoric of equality to address the experience of women and deny continuing female secondariness. Women themselves could hardly believe that after all the rhetoric, slogans, policies and images of equality, female infants should now be so discriminated against as to lose their lives. Several mystified and perplexed mothers wrote to a national newspaper in 1983: 'We simply cannot understand why thirty-two years after China's liberation, we women are still weighed down by such backward feudal concepts.'[31] Henceforth the rhetoric of equality could not be taken at face value and neither could it be pretended that it reflected social practice. In conditions where parents were at all prepared to forfeit the lives of their daughters and deny them their place on earth, the rhetoric and celebratory language of equality or half of heaven was increasingly punctured and abandoned. The rhetoric of equality, attractive as it was, masked or disguised a female revolution that had been very much postponed and was certainly still incomplete or unfinished. Much of the shortfall between rhetoric and female experience has been attributed to the competing familial discourse and domestic practices which directly countered the message of the revolution. However, it can also be argued that revolutionary messages focusing on heaven, on the future and on delayed gratification may have been indifferently received by women as a result of their female-specific life-course experience which in turn gave rise to a female-specific concept of time relating present to future and future to present and thus estranging women from the very notion of heaven.

STRANGERS TO HEAVEN

Attractive as the alliteration is, the revolutionary slogan 'half of heaven' may not have been as comfortable conceptually for Chinese women as its popularisation or international appropriation suggested. In and out of China, gender-specific attention centred on the rhetorical feat associating female with heaven and on 'the half' entitlement of the female population.

While analysis was so concentrated on the half, attention detracted from the notion of heaven and its conceptual incompatibility, which fractured its very association with the female half and which may offer some explanation for the shortfalls in attaining the 'female half' of women's entitlement to knowledge and power. At a very simple level and given its association with yang, the male, the public and the outside, heaven was far from being an asexual or gender-free space. Attaining 'half of heaven' thus became synonymous with the appropriation of public male roles in production and politics with few concessions to female roles in biological reproduction or maintaining the household. As Iron Girls, women pene-trated male preserves hitherto denied them; there had been a recasting of sexual difference into sexual resemblance of which the male-styled unidress was perhaps the most potent symbol. It was as if the female body did not exist; the measures of success were male and access to public domain and identity came with the identification of values ascribed to the masculine yang.

In the binary of hierarchical oppositions, the domestic, dark, secretive, private yin spaces remained outside the definition of heaven (especially when it came to the allocation of resources), so that achievement and entitlement came to consist almost exclusively of the possibility for women to be permanent guests in a male-defined, -constructed and -hosted space. In a male-hosted space, the female as guest became by implication the invited or the outsider as defined by Simmel, for whom the stranger

> is fixed within a particular spatial circle, or within a group whose boundaries are similar to spatial boundaries. But his position in this group is determined essentially by the fact that he has not belonged to it from the beginning, that he imports qualities into it which do not, and cannot stem from the group itself . . . [His position is thus] composed of certain measures of nearness and distance.[32]

Subsequently, sociological literature on stranger–host relations centres on spatial and social distance, the acquisition of host qualities by the stranger within processes of accommodation, assimilation or incorporation and the resilience of stereotype and myth in mediating persistent socio-economic discrepancies between host and stranger.[33] The literature on Chinese gender relations is also primarily concerned with the appropriation of male roles, status, attitudes and behaviour by the female stranger in public places. The usual explanations given for shortfalls in assimilation have to do with continuing official and folk prejudice against and undermining of female appropriation, neglect of and lack of resource allocation to repro-duction and family discrimination and failure to invest in daughters. What these explanations have in common, however, is that they primarily attribute failure of accommodation, assimilation or incorporation to male host qualities, be they conscious, unconscious or even conspiratorial.

However, Simmel's original definition offers another set of explanations which have to do with the ambiguous qualities of the stranger combining both nearness and remoteness or concern and indifference, thus constructing the notion of the ambivalent if not willing stranger.

In China, what has constantly surprised participant and observer alike has been the reluctance of many women to take advantage of the unprecedented opportunities for the acquisition of new roles, statuses and attitudes afforded by the revolution; or, as a Chinese saying has it, they had proved 'unwilling to fly though the sky is high'.[34] Margery Wolf, in her book *Revolution Postponed*, observes that although peasant women were still excluded from most positions of decision-making in the villages, the significant point was that, because the rhetoric had constantly and persistently told women that they could do these things, they were less impressed by the fact that only men did them: 'Perhaps these important things of the men's world are not so important after all.'[35] This passage directly calls to mind the ambiguity, ambivalence or the combination of nearness and remoteness and the concern and indifference already referred to in Simmel's original notion of the stranger. In rural China, the female stranger was one who was not so intimately and personally concerned with the social life about her and who had a relative detachment which freed her from the self-consciousness, the concern for status and the divided loyalties of marginality, so that instead she retained a duality based on qualities imported. In this case, the distinctive quality imported and distinguishable from the male host may have been a female-specific experience and concept of time and, most particularly, of present in relation to the future, which had the effect of estranging women in China from the concept of heaven or a concept which distanced the present and privileged the future.

PRESENT TO FUTURE

The female-specific experience of time can be linked to women's unique experience of transience, uncertainty, rupture and discontinuity. If before marriage daughters experienced transience in the present, they also experienced uncertainty of future, with present and future divided by the anticipated rupture of marriage. The significance for daughters of the sudden change which virilocal marriage and the removal to another family normally entailed has been well studied. The movement of women as bearers or markers of property and status in marriage and the economic and socio-political significance of removal to another family occasioned by virilocal marriage has been well documented and not surprisingly identified as one of the most important obstacles to investment in daughters and the realising of or effecting female claims to 'half of heaven'. However, the moment of marriage has been primarily conceived as a movement of peasant women from one space (household and village) to another, so that women, uniquely during the revolution given lack of mobility, experienced both remoteness and nearness in their natal family and village and in their husband's family and village following marriage. This spatial dimension is an important factor with implications for women's experience of family and society, but it may be of equal importance to focus on the bearing and demarcation of time embodied in the female anticipation of and experience of marriage and women's consequent conceptualising of time, which may be an even more significant gender-specific marker.[36]

If, for males, time normally stretched endlessly and linearly from past, present to future in a sequence marked by continuity and certainty of narrative with quality of future seen to derive directly from investment in the present, for women it was different. For them time was broken or ruptured by marriage, making for discontinuity, separation and dislocation of present and future with no direct correlation necessarily perceived between investment in present and quality of future. Unlike sons, peasant daughters had long been, and continued to be, taught that their only future was to marry and that its quality was dependent on husbands (and another family): 'a husband he is heaven'. For women still, their 'rice was cooked' not so much at birth but at marriage marked by movement to and appropriation by another household. Sayings such as 'a daughter married is as water burst beyond its banks', 'marriage for daughters is as a slammed door', 'obey heaven and follow fate' and 'when you marry a chicken live with a chicken, when you marry a dog live with a dog' reminded women of their coming separation from the present and that their future lay somewhere else and was irrevocably linked, not to their present circumstances, but to those somewhere else – those of their husband and his family.

Before marriage, then, the present was shadowed by uncertainty or anticipation of discontinuity and dislocation: to compensate for the temporary nature of their positions, to mediate nearness and remoteness and to anticipate eventual estrangement from their natal family or an unknown or uncertain future, daughters dreamed, imaged or visualised a marriage and alternative future for themselves, the characteristics of which assumed qualities of romance, fantasy or at least limitless possibility. These dreams, bolstered by folk-tale and story-telling, not only went some way towards compensating or providing a refuge for their anxiety in the face of uncertainty and discontinuity, but also, prior to marriage, buoyed, enfolded and enclosed the present and even substituted for the present, giving it colour. Marriage not only separated or cut the present from the future for women, but after marriage, women uniquely lived the future as imaged, visualised or dreamed. This foreshortening or 'early arrival of dreams' – not shared, it seems, by males[37] – had important implications, for the future lived was seldom as good as that imaged, visualised or dreamed.

This unique female experience may have effected the removal of much of the mystery and efficacy associated with the invented collective heaven or future as imaged and striven for. As to the present, it too was uniquely shadowed for women. It was shadowed by discontinuity and uncertainty of future before marriage, and after marriage it was shadowed by the absence of familiar dreams imagining a future of limitless possibility to sustain or colour it and generate will or agency in its anticipation. This dislocation of time sequence or stretch due to enclosure of the present by the future and of the future by the present may have had unique implications for female constructions of both present and future, thus separating gender experience and conceptualisations of time.

Recent hints as to the signification of marriage for this female-specific experience of time can be found in short stories which draw attention to the generation and demise of female dreams before and after marriage and the subsequent 'down' of living the present without the image of a future to compensate and substitute for its shortcomings. In one short story, a thirty-year-old woman looks back over the previous decade contrasting the sweet dreams of limitless possibilities of twenty-year-olds centring on the meeting of a husband handsome, strong, rich and capable, with her dreams at the age of thirty years, which are in contrast 'just like beautiful bubbles, broken one after another and disappearing'. Now at thirty, albeit embraced by strong and tender arms, she usually had a 'sense of loss and solitude' and likened being thirty to 'ripe apples on a tree hanging on the branches heavily'. Did not, she ask, an 'age of heaviness' ensue for women deriving from a sense of loss and deprivation subsequent to marriage?[38] In another, more subtle short story the girls in a poor village customarily go to the 'other side of the river' to be married. One young girl who had been living in the shabby old village for seventeen years was about to make that fateful trip to 'the other side of the river' now that her father 'had found her a rich family'. For long it had been 'the other side of the river' which had constituted 'a sacred place in her mind', and the remainder of the story describes her disillusionment with 'the other side', an allegory for likening the impoverishment of life before marriage with that of the mind after marriage.[39]

Women's experience of the separation of the present from the future rather than sequential movement from one to the other contrasted with the continuity, certainty and commitment envisaged by males via the concept of heaven, and it was this contrast which may have transformed women into ambivalent strangers both disbelieving of and less inclined to will a better future. Their nearness and concern for the common future was also mediated by a distance and detachment generated by their unique experience of the future, which inhibited them from making a full subscription and commitment 'to these important things of men's affairs'. Although daughters may have most immediately felt both the remoteness and nearness in their natal and families of marriage in spatial terms as a result of their physical movement, it may be that it was their conceptualisation of time which became a more significant gender-specific marker in the long term differentiating female from male experiences and images of the revolution. This discussion of female-specific conceptions of time is not only important in contributing to a further understanding and re-analysis of female experiences and images of revolution, but it is also important because it marks the nearest parallel that I can think of in considering the movement from revolution to reform or from heaven to earth which, for all the population of China, was marked by rupture, discontinuity and uncertainty.

Conclusion

Chapter 10

Living the earth
Family aspirations

It is the main characteristic of rural reforms of the past ten years that they had less to do with the rhetoric of heaven than with resourcing the earth in the interests of raising inputs, incentives, productivity, incomes and lifestyle qualities. Both the promised lands of modernity and peasants' own experiences of development were various but firmly of the earth. Taking cognisance of the variety of experiences, it is still possible to identify a number of important features of reform which are common to these experiences. Along with the shift in focus from 'heaven to earth' or 'vision to reality', there has also been a shift from the future to the present and from image to experience. Concern with present rather than deferred needs largely focused on incentives, enrichment and gratification, all of which coincided in the interest in consumption, and interest in consumption is one of the most important of characteristics distinguishing reform from revolution. Indeed, the entire platform of reform was originally premised on the rationale or promise of improved and secure livelihood and quality lifestyle so that with reform, consumption became an end in itself.

CONSUMPTION

In societal terms consumption became the destination of production, and in familial and individual terms it became the reward for production. The initial and rapid delivery of these rewards in many regions of China encouraged the pursuit of the reform programme even in the face of otherwise unpopular policies. It is my own belief that the government could never have continued to push for so long that most unpopular policy of all, the single-child family programme, without a coincidental rise in levels of consumption which themselves became the criteria by which the reforms were judged: 'Economic reforms have very popular backing. The survey shows people perceive that reforms have improved living standards, boosted production and promoted the quality and variety of goods.'[1]

With reform, years of absent or minimal quantities and varieties of consumer goods ended, and the rapid expansion in and abundance of foods and consumer goods was early one of the most oft-cited characteristics demarcating reform from revolution. In the first years of reform it was the quantities and varieties of food in the home, shop and market which so impressed the long-time observer. My own appraisal of the reforms in their early years was very much influenced by an acknowledgement that the quantity of food and quality of diet had improved immeasurably for a goodly proportion of the population. Although peasant farmers had previously cultivated grain, grown vegetables and raised livestock, the production and marketing of these items have brought about major changes in diet while at the same time the proportion of rising cash income allocated to food is declining. In villages, one of my yardsticks for measuring sufficiency for years was whether the household consumed or sold the eggs of their few chickens – now that is only an appropriate yardstick in very poor regions. Although, as the village studies show, some poor households and villages are far from receiving sufficient food supplies, for the majority of peasant farmers annual per capita consumption of grain, meat, eggs, milk, fish, vegetables and fruit has improved immeasurably.[2]

Simultaneously, there is also a new interest in consumer goods and in their style, colour, material and brand name, all which have generated a new phenomenon – consumer desire. Eyes, and not just those on the advertising billboards, are firmly fixed on consumer objects to do with fashioning the individual and furnishing the home. One of the most visible of changes is in clothes; and fabric, colour, pattern and new fashions can excite attention and demand fostered by television, specialist magazines and shop displays. The home too – and one sure sign of improved reform livelihood is the scale and style of new rural housing – is also a focus of consumer attention, with new interests in furniture, soft furnishings and floor and wall coverings. New interior decoration magazines devoted to the art of furnishing suggest that sofas, wall cabinets and coffee tables are items in fashion which all require the space and income more characteristic of richer rural than urban homes. Children too have become an important new focus of consumption, with emphasis on children's clothes, toys and convenience foods. Finally, the interest in electrical goods is insatiable, with televisions, cassette recorders, refrigerators and washing machines topping the charts and not only in the cities. In suburban villages and even in far-off richer villages and markets, new clothes, sofas and elaborate sideboards and televisions or cassette players are not uncommon, and even in poorer villages I have seen televisions and cassettes in the richer households, albeit either running from yards of battery or awaiting the day of electrification.

Consumption itself has become a serious recreation and a sociable exercise with much noisy consultation, as those of you who have attempted to shop or even move on the main shopping pavements of the cities or busy rural market streets will know. A new item attracts crowds, queues, curiosity and much talk, frequently starting a fashion or craze. In the cities, many of the shoppers are peasants from the countryside distinguished by their surplus cash and bulk purchases. Indeed, it was the numbers of farmers shopping in the cities with cash in their pockets which first alerted the urban dwellers to the efficacy of the reform in the countryside. As a recent article on consumption noted, conspicuous consumption does not lag behind in rural areas; it is just different, in that farmers build houses, get married, buy electrical appliances, stage celebrations or make funeral arrangements and build graves and temples. Indeed, 'some people', it continued, 'spend money like water'.[3] What is noticeable, however, is that even among those who have little or no money to spend, items of consumption are of abiding interest, and are much discussed, and all but the poorest households are saving for some clearly identified item or occasion. In households or villages nothing excites as much interest and minute attention as novel consumer items, and it is this interest in commodities and lifestyles which has brought about a new relation between people and things, generating yearning and desire which was absent or certainly not so pronounced during the revolution. Persons have become classified not so much by their class background or 'work' or occupation as previously,[4] as by the objects or their evaluation so that identity has become associated with lifestyle rather than class label. Adorning the body and the home has drawn attention to the person and immediate environments in a proliferation of lifestyles that is born of income generation and generates a sense of individual and family difference.

INCOME AND LIFESTYLE

The second major change for peasant households during the reform years has been the introduction of new opportunities for income generation. My journeys during the first years of reform were punctuated and captivated by the new hum and liveliness of activity as families set about to expand their economic activities through cultivation, livestock raising, handicraft and entrepreneurial activities which spilled over into courtyards, streets and markets. The novelty of movement on all conceivable forms of home-made transport and business with stall, workshop and small factory all generating new goods and services created new wealth and new and greater choices for households and villages, which in turn have also brought new demands and new risks.[5] The generation of new demands on the peasant household has already been well documented, but what has received less attention is the new sense of risk and vulnerability felt by many peasant farmers. Many do not now fear new major twists and turns in government policy, although some say that there are still moments when they ponder the permanence of reform; rather, at a practical level, the new opportunities, choices and riches are seen to be vulnerable in that they are daily dependent on supplies of inputs and markets which are all frequently outside their experience, understanding and certainly control. While some enjoy risk-taking and become very practised, others find the new risks and responsibilities so onerous that they wish for a return to what was familiar and safe in the revolution. New religious acts of overt supplication to the gods for fortune and good luck can be directly linked to the increase in risk.[6] Perhaps material and market seem as far away as the gods – and certainly as capricious. In a thriving market town in Guangxi, I was recently struck by the preponderance of two items for sale – meat and incense; indeed, one could have been forgiven for thinking that these were the two staple items of consumption. Perhaps they were, for symbolically they both signified the two most common types of guanxi or relationships necessary to safeguard income and fortune: one for feasting and establishing guanxi in this world, and the other for appeasing and supplicating those in the other world.

The new lifestyle and consumer interest are both of the individual and of the family, or in rural China mainly of the individual family. In language there was a shift in emphasis from the 'we' of the collective to the 'we' of the family and, to a lesser extent, in the countryside 'I' of the individual. The 'we' of the revolution and of the collective had usually assumed a homogeneity of need, interest and attitude perhaps symbolised by the 'same big pot' from which all ate. The movement from the large 'we' of the revolution to the small 'we' or 'I' of reform has permitted the official recognition of differences in need, interest and attitude.[7] No longer were groups such as the 'masses' or the 'peasants' assumed to be homogeneous; rather, as farmers and entrepreneurs they were recognised as more heterogenous and exercising of agency. Economic and socio-political relations were also acknowledged to be much more complex and varied than previous representations registered. Official documents began to admit that different groups make quite different demands of reform and therefore will have different views and attitudes towards reform. Just as the new genre of 'wound' literature, centred on the scars of previous deprivations of the person during the Cultural Revolution, marked the literary rehabilitation of the self, so individual and family aspirations and ambitions acquired specificity of expression. To effect all these changes required a language less atrophied, a language of experience and the senses rather than the generalising and distancing of the outworn rhetoric. As writer Lu Wenfu noted on the eve of reform: 'Like everyone else I was excited beyond words, I could not remember how to find the words, I had forgotten the words.'[8] Once the words had been found, however, there was no returning to the substitution of image for experience, although

there have been periodic attempts especially post-Tian Anmen to eradi-
cate spiritual pollution and reimpose the rhetoric. Conversations reveal,
however, that the rhetoric no longer sustains or even holds most voices,
for what is distinctive about the new language of reform is that it commonly
addresses experience and therefore defies categorisation in the mutually
exclusive black–white, positive–negative or socialist–non-socialist dualities.

Unusually, the language of reform, representing the experience of
reform, admits both the positive and the negative. Indeed, the era of
reform is frequently referred to as the 'sweet and sour' decade embracing
both the 'sweet honey' and 'bitter wine' and inclusive of both benefits and
losses:

> Economically the decade has introduced the most dynamic and rapid
> growth since New China was founded in 1949, while living standards
> have risen faster than ever before. But many problems have also
> occurred in China's economic life, such as inflation, unfair income
> distribution and a drop in social morals.[9]

Although problems were admitted during the revolution, they were usually
couched in a rhetoric that only permitted the initiated to fathom their degree
and distribution. Now, during reform, not only have problems been openly
admitted, but they are also openly discussed and, most importantly, re-
searched. Enquiry into and analysis of social problems has been encouraged
and the studies and professions of sociology and anthropology rehabilitated
with a very specific brief to identify and investigate social problems.[10] The
problems associated with reform have been increasingly and officially
acknowledged as the honeymoon of the first years of reform has given way
to recognition that the reform process is difficult, slow and complex – much
more like the long, zigzag movements of the snake than the fast, fleeting
flight of the dragon[11] – with much debate about the scope or limits of
reform especially in relation to definitions of socialism and culture.

IDEAS ABOUT GOODS

As the rhetoric of the holistic and generalised collective dream faded, there
has been much discussion, some of it vexed, about the cultural and socialist
fabric that uniquely constitutes and identifies China. Even in the countryside there was an awareness that the origins of most of the new goods and
ideas lay outside of China in Japan, North America and Europe. The
cultural dilemma which has exercised those governing and influencing
China since the turn of the century is how to preserve Chinese culture even
while importing the secrets of Western wealth and power; or how to have
Western goods, and most specifically the benefits of its science and
technology, without the ideas associated with these goods about which
there has always been a certain ambivalence.

There are as many ideas about Western goods as goods themselves, and with Western goods come links and contacts with the foreign, and since much of what is distinctively Chinese is defined as different from 'outside', assimilation of 'the Western' arouses fears about losing Chineseness and questions about what is Chineseness. To retain Chineseness and thus maintain difference, the Chinese government has made a number of attempts in the past ten years to detach idea from object or Western culture from Western import. This is the substance of recent periodic campaigns against 'spiritual pollution' to outlaw Western influence and protect China's 'primary culture' or the 'essence of Chineseness' from imported culture.[12] The government has thus placed itself in an awkward position defending its import of things Western and at the same time denigrating the ideas associated with Western imports because they threaten what is distinctively Chinese and socialist or 'socialism with uniquely Chinese characteristics'. In examining the relation of socialism to revolution, the experience of socialism has been found wanting, but rather than abandon the term, it has been redefined during recent years to include reform, and most particularly the market. In the villages and households, however, peasants most often discuss these questions with reference to practical benefits and losses associated with their experience of revolution and reform. Regardless of the variety and range of reforms, all but a handful of villagers and householders interviewed spontaneously drew attention to their new autonomy, increased incomes and access to goods as the most important of their experiences associated with reform.

In an attempt to ascertain more generally peasant attitudes towards reform, there have been a number of surveys of peasant opinion. In one national survey of 10,938 farmers, published in 1988, 87.4 per cent were reported to be satisfied with rural reform, 0.8 per cent were dissatisfied and 11.8 per cent did not respond.[13] Most of the respondents were favourably disposed towards reform largely because of their increased autonomy and freedom to produce what they wished for a market. Those who were dissatisfied blamed 'the rise in prices for materials', low prices paid by the state to purchase farm produce, 'too much work required by contracts' and 'excessive farm quotas'. Most of the farmers thought that their life had improved as far as food, clothing, housing and daily necessities were concerned and was attributable to the responsibility system, although more than a quarter of the respondents attributed their improved life to the 'favour of the gods'. The 3.9 per cent who complained that their life had worsened blamed 'a lack of production experience after the contract system was adopted', 'the decreasing availability of household labour' and 'natural and man-made calamities', and many complained about lack of job choices outside of farming. When the farmers, who had become better off, were asked what they would first spend their money on, top priority was accorded to developing production, then building houses, improving their standard of living, children's marriages and purchasing household electric appliances and furniture. The survey showed that farmers felt that they were still over-burdened by excessive quotas imposed by the state in various forms. For instance, those surveyed had been required to hand over an average total of ¥109.4, or about quarter of their annual net income. Most of the farmers also complained about shortages of chemical fertiliser, diesel fuel, plastic film and farm tools. Most of their products they sold to the state, but they would like to sell more products in the free market.

Approximately two-thirds of the farmers surveyed agreed that it was necessary to establish village-based co-operatives to provide information, technical guidance and services in the areas of seed development, irrigation and mechanised land cultivation as well as ensuring proper implementation of contracts and welfare work in their villages. When it came to expressing opinions about rural officials, about 38 per cent of the farmers said that local cadres were 'working hard to help people get richer'; however, almost half of the remainder said that local cadres were 'only interested in how to get richer themselves', 'they took government allowances but didn't work', 'they didn't follow the Party's rural policy' and 'they abused their power in their own interests'. An overwhelming majority of the farmers agreed that education was useful in developing a market economy, and a third hoped that their children would receive secondary school education, with two-thirds hoping for a university education for their children. With regard to the increase in income differentials between peasant households, 70 per cent of the respondents thought that they 'should not be jealous', 5.6 per cent thought that the newly rich should be restricted and 4.9 per cent thought that people should 'stick together through thick and thin'. Although farmers thought greater riches would be inhibited due to lack of funds, technology and information, about half the respondents were optimistic about the future of reform, with 26.6 per cent 'not sure' and 2.5 per cent forecasting a decline in the lifestyle. Interestingly, about two-thirds of the farmers surveyed said they were still either 'doubtful' or 'uncertain' about whether the Party would maintain its current set of policies. Such a national survey, its variety of experiences and mix of attitudes and its publication in a national newspaper would have been unimaginable during the revolution.

FRAGMENTED ASPIRATIONS

As the rhetoric of the holistic and generalised collective dream faded, it has not just been replaced by differentiation in experience and of interest but also by the fragmentation and plurality of aspirations and dreams. Recently, during four separate working visits in villages in different regions of China, I have enquired of individuals and families their hopes of the future, their ideas of the good life or their dreams of heaven in an attempt to ascertain their aspirations. The responses to the question fall into several separate categories. First of all, very few responses had to do with production; yes, ideas of heaven did include big harvests and heaven was certainly irrigated, but by far the majority of responses had to do with rising incomes, usually expressed in terms of objects of consumption – fashioning the individual or furnishing the family home. Heaven was enjoying a new house, quality furniture, including sofas and sideboards, electrical goods such as colour television, refrigerator, sufficiency of food, a supply of good cigarettes and in a few cases a bathroom! The second category had to do with continuing the family, reflected in ambitions for children's education, their income-earning capacity and a good marriage (heaven was sometimes a good wife!) or in building new houses for sons with gardens, fruit trees and even flowers. A peaceful, tranquil old age surrounded by one's married sons and their children was an oft-discussed idyll. In the words of an old vegetable farmer, 'I will build up my family like a heaven' so that my family 'will be continuous like a stream', for 'to raise the family future is endless'.

In yet another range of responses, heaven was projected onto another place somewhere else – 'heaven is abroad' was a common response among rural technicians – and this perhaps best illustrates the new plurality with alternative images of the good life deriving from Europe, North America and Southeast Asia beamed out on television throughout China since the 'Open Door Policy'. For some in the villages, heaven is the city or at least a richer village. Finally, one person's most perceptive reply perhaps best sums up the new specificity and truncation of the dimensions of heaven, particularistic and specific to each individual and family: 'Heaven', he said 'is defined by the best you think is heaven.' His definition was unique in that it embraced the imaging agent – and no response could better symbolise the shift from the single monolithic, homogeneous, imposed and thus articulated concept of heaven to the new plurality, relativity and fragmentation of heaven based on the concept of small well-being or lifestyle – 'xiaokang'. However, while the substitution of the variety of differing voices for the single voice and rhetorical glaze reflects plurality and difference of experience, it has also left those of the earth without a definite and common idea of heaven and the present without the presence of certainty of future or even perhaps of a valued past.

FUTURE, PRESENT AND PAST

An important insight and field finding of the past two years, and really, I suppose, the source for the predominant theme of this book, is the widespread absence of a dream or a concept of the future as a point of reference in contemporary China. Although there was excitement at reform there was also a sense of loss or bereavement that has not so much to do with a wish to return to the past as with the onset of uncertainty, unpredictability and anxiety, as the present is increasingly suspended in time and place. As the present becomes increasingly mixed, combining gain and loss, and since 1984 the reforms too have fallen short of initial expectations, there is no sweetness of the future to compensate, no dream to sustain the disappointments of the present or certainty that tomorrow will be better than today. Again, this is not to suggest a state of uniformity throughout China. It can be argued that because of the female-specific conceptualisation of time, experience of revolution and reform or present and future continue to be gender-differentiated. If women were strangers to heaven or the revolution, then men had become newly estranged in the movement from revolution with certainty of future to reform or the present with uncertainty of future.

It is possible to place the case studies of my recent acquaintance on some kind of continuum. In one richer region, the future as long imagined has already arrived. In another richer region, the dream had gone sour with loss of land, scarce inputs, fewer sons, paralysing bitterness. In a poor region, the dream might be said to be still around the corner with hopes still high although admittedly centred on that most unpredictable of creatures – rabbits; in another very poor locality, futures were still for dreaming if one had the stamina and health; in another impoverished by drought, the dream was elsewhere, and in the fourth, of middling income, the present was good enough with a juggling of the earth's resources in a mixed local programme of hopeful readjustment. Nationally, however, China's leaders have admitted that their country 'has no clear idea of the future' (Deng Xiaoping)[14] or 'is a country without a concept' (Jiang Zemin),[15] and one of the most popular folksongs sung by a hero of Tian Anmen Square goes:

In the past, I had the illusion
the future would not be like the present,
But now I almost know what the future is like . . .
The things I used to think very simple,
I no longer understand . . .
I've tried hard to lift my spirits,
and woke up from a dream,
But now I've woken up,
I've found the world has changed so fast.[16]

Not just the future, but also the past, as viewed through the personal eyes of even the most committed, falls short, and sometimes tragically and damningly so, albeit in retrospect. This phenomenon is particularly acute for, but not confined to, city and intellectual. Several months before the events of Tian Anmen and with no foresight, I stood on the newly opened

Tian Anmen rostrum overlooking the square from where Mao Zedong and other leaders had long observed parade and crowd. I had just returned from a particularly depressing stay in an unhappy village within a few hours' journey from Beijing where revolution and now reform had gone sour, and my thoughts very much juxtaposed the enormous energy that the years of revolution had generated and the sense of watching, waiting and even wasting that I had experienced during the past week in the village. Was it all for very little, was it all an illusion: all those dreams, hopes and above all enormous physical and emotional energies which had been vested in the events of the decades of revolution and reform? While many would argue otherwise, and indeed my own views are mixed, a dominant theme in many interviews in China, as in contemporary Eastern Europe, has been the sadness and anger at the devaluation of the past at the hands of the present. A dedicated cadre in China echoes what cadres in Eastern Europe have said in recent months when he speaks of the sadness, but most all of the hurt, that all he had worked for over the years had just been thrown away:

> I used to have a dream for China – that one day this country I love would be united, and happy, and free. Sometimes I cling on to this dream, and just say to myself that it will just take a little longer, or maybe even a lot longer. But mostly these days and at the end of my career, I realise that the dream has gone. That is when I know that everything for which I stood is wrong, that this system is not appropriate for China now. That is when I wish all my children to go away, to get out before they ruin their lives. What a dreadful disappointment it has been. What a waste.[17]

In the face of much uncertainty and doubt rather than hope and worth, the absence of a heavenly dream and certainty of links relating present to future, there seems to be little prospect of generating will and agency beyond present reforms following the short, sharp burst of will in Beijing's Tian Anmen Square. One of the most common responses to my questioning about the future since the events of Tian Anmen Square has been a single reply: 'It all depends on the leadership.' Not only was the future seen to depend on what happened within the leadership, but more importantly the reply signified a complete denial of agency on the part of any other. Perhaps this is the most important legacy of Tian Anmen in capital and city, while throughout China attitudes towards Tian Anmen are dominated by the fear of disorder, a fear which is reinforced by past events of the Cultural Revolution and current events in the former Soviet Union and Eastern Europe. It is the fear of disorder which perhaps above all determines peasant attitudes towards events in the capital, whatever the official interpretation. Moreover, Tian Anmen for most villages and households in rural China is another world away and a less relevant frame for peasant experience of reform than their own immediate images of past, present and future.

There are many village and household images appropriate to the representation of peasant experience of reform, ranging from the prosperous and flourishing already living the future to the poor and floundering still a long journey from the future. Between, there is a predominant mood of living the present, of going about daily business as best one can, of holding the present in suspension and of watching and/or waiting – a mood which is perhaps best summed up in the final single image of my book. It is of a single household with two rooms, one to each side of a central kitchen. Visitors were received into one or other room and between the two (heaven and earth?) lay the centre – the 'h-earth' of the household. The one to the left, where I slept with other female members of the household, was meagrely furnished and more than half taken up with a kang, a large platform bed heated by a fire within and on which the colourful quilts of the two daughters of the household lay carefully folded. The walls were adorned with portraits of revolutionary leaders including Mao Zedong, a number of political posters and framed Communist Party certificates honouring the 'good' Party and community services of the cadre mother of the family. The other, to the right, where I lived by day could not have provided a greater contrast. It featured a bed, a comfortable sofa and a substantial marble-topped coffee table made by the local village factory of which the father of the family was the manager. Prominently displayed was a ghetto blaster, a colour television, a video-recorder and a bright green fridge-freezer. On the walls were a large, glossy calendar displaying a swimsuited female figure and a musical clock whose closeted bird sang 'Happy Birthday' every hour! Perhaps more than any other single image, this one household reflects the ambivalence, ambiguity and uncertainty of the links between peasants' experiences of development and their conceptualisations of time and change during the period of reform. It might be said to symbolise China's rural, betwixt-and-between revolution and reform – between the collective past and consumerist future and betwixt heavenly dreams of and earthly demands for development.

Appendix 1
Tables

Table 3.1 Household size and composition, 1987

Household no.	No. of persons	No. of generations	No. of children	No. of labourers	No. of dependants	Ratio of labourers to persons
1	5	2	3	4 (2+2)[c]	1	0.8
2	6	2	4	5 (2+3)	1	0.8
3	6	2	4	3 (2+1)	3	0.5
4	7	3	4	4 (2+2)	3 (1+2)[d]	0.6
5	5	2	4	3 (1+2)	2	0.6
6	3	2	2 (3–1)[a]	3 (1+2)	–	1.0
7	4	2	2	3 (2+1)	1	0.75
8	3	2	1	3 (2+1)	–	1.0
9	7	3	4 (2+2)[b]	5 (1+2+2)	2	0.7
10	4	2	2	4 (2+2)	–	1.0
11	4	2	2	2 (2+0)	2	0.5
12	5	3	1	4 (2+2)	1	0.8
13	4	3	3 (5–3)+1	3 (1+2)	1	0.75
Average	4.8					

Notes: a Total number of children minus daughters married out.
 b Total number of children of successive generations.
 c Total number of labourers of successive generations.
 d Includes dependants of both older and younger generations.

Table 3.2 Land resource of peasant households, 1987

Household no.	No. of persons	Arable land (mu)		Pasture lands (mu)				
		Per household	Per capita	Natural	Sown	Total	Per capita	Per head of cattle
1	5	17	3.4	34	3.5	37.5	7.5	9.4
2	6	18	3	40	5	45	7.5	45
3	6	19	3.2	40	5	45	7.5	22.5
4	7	23	3	45	7	52	7.4	17
5	5	17	3.4	34	3.5	37.5	7.5	37.5
6	3	10	3.3	21.5	1	22.5	7.5	22.5
7	4	12	3	18	2	20	5	7
8	3	11	3.7	21.5	1	22.5	7.5	7
9	7	17	2.4[a]	49.5	3	52.5	7.5	17
10	4	16	4	25	5	30	7.5	15
11	4	12	3	27	3	30	7.5	30
12	5	9	1.8[a]	21.5	1.5	22.5	4.5[a]	11
13	4	15	3.7[a]	34	3.5	37.5	9.3[a]	12.5
Average		15	3.1			40	7.2	15.6

Note: a Households where the allocation of responsibility lands has not kept pace with changes in family size.

Table 3.3 Crop cultivation of village group, 1986

Household no.	No. of labourers	Cultivated land (mu)	Value of fertiliser per mu (¥)	Production of Wheat		Production of maize (jin)	Production of beans (jin)	Crop output		
				Total (jin)	Per mu (jin)			Total (jin)	Per mu (jin)	Per labourer (jin)
1	4	17	12	4,000	235	600	200	4,800	282	1,200
2	5	18	4	1,300	72	500	170	1,970	109	394
3	3	19	16	2,500	132	400	600	3,500	184	1,167
4	4	23	11	5,000	217	400	300	5,700	248	1,425
5	3	17	9	2,200	129	210	600	3,010	177	1,003
6	3	10	7	2,000	200	200	280	2,480	248	827
7	3	12	13	2,600	217	1,000	200	3,800	317	1,267
8	3	11	5	2,000	182	500	400	2,900	264	967
9	5	17	9	3,050	179	500	300	3,850	226	770
10	4	16	9	2,300	144	500	500	3,300	206	825
11	2	12	7	2,000	167	500	150	2,670	223	1,335
12	4	9	8	1,600	178	200	150	1,950	217	488
13	3	15	4	3,000	200	400	200	3,600	240	1,200
Average per household		15.1		2,580		455	312	3,348		
Average per mu			8.8	171	171.2				221	

Table 3.4 Sideline activities of peasant households, 1987

Household no.	No. of persons	Chickens (nos)	Pigs (nos)	Cattle (nos)	Other sidelines
1	5	20	1	4	–
2	6	12	1	1	*
3	6	6	–	2	†
4	7	30	2	3	–
5	5	–	–	1	–
6	3	–	–	1	–
7	4	–	–	3	*
8	3	15	–	3	+
9	7	–	–	3	†/+
10	4	20	1	2	–
11	4	28	–	1	×
12	5	20	–	2	†/+
13	4	9	–	3	+/*
Average		12.3	–	2.2	

Notes: * Hire out labour (unskilled).
† Skilled carpentry and housebuilding.
+ Walnuts, dried persimmons.
× Food processing.

Table 3.5 Sources of household income: crops, 1986

Household no.	No. of persons	Production (mu)	Wheat Cash (¥)	Wheat Value (¥)	Maize Cash (¥)	Maize Value (¥)	Beans Cash (¥)	Beans Value (¥)	All crops Cash (¥)	All crops Value (¥)	Total	Total Per mu (¥)	Total Per person (¥)
1	5	17	300	500	30	60	–	60	330	620	950	56	190
2	6	18	50	220	–	75	–	50	50	345	385	21	64
3	6	19	75	460	–	60	120	60	195	580	775	41	129
4	7	23	300	700	–	60	–	90	300	850	1,150	50	164
5	5	17	50	390	–	40	120	60	170	490	660	39	132
6	3	10	60	540	–	30	70	–	130	570	700	70	233
7	4	12	70	450	30	120	40	30	140	600	740	62	185
8	3	11	250	200	15	60	60	60	325	320	645	59	215
9	7	17	100	520	–	75	–	90	100	685	785	46	112
10	4	16	75	400	–	75	45	105	120	580	700	43	121
11	4	12	75	340	–	75	–	45	75	460	535	45	134
12	5	9	50	280	4.5	25.5	15	30	69.5	335.5	405	45	81
13	4	15	125	500	30	30	–	60	155	590	745	50	186
Average per household	4.8	15	121.5	423	8.4	60.4	36.2	57	166	540	705.8	48	149.7

Table 3.6 Sources of household income: sidelines, 1986

Household no.	No. of persons	Eggs (¥)	Pigs (¥)	Cattle	Walnuts (¥)	Services or handicrafts (¥)	Hiring out labour (¥)	Total (¥)	Total per person (¥)
1	5	30	150	–	35	–	–	215	43
2	6	30	–	–	–	–	25	55	9.2
3	6	20	–	–	–	300	–	320	53.3
4	7	90	–	–	–	–	–	90	12.9
5	5	–	–	–	–	–	–	–	0
6	3	–	–	–	–	–	–	–	0
7	4	–	–	–	–	–	100	100	25
8	3	–	–	–	200	–	–	200	66.7
9	7	–	–	–	60	200	–	260	37.1
10	4	100	–	–	–	–	–	100	25
11	4	130	–	–	–	1,200	–	1,330	332.5
12	5	30	–	–	20	400	–	450	90
13	4	30	–	–	30	–	30	90	22.5

Notes: Average income from sidelines per household: ¥ 247.
Average income from sidelines per person: ¥ 60.

Table 3.7 Household income (¥): all sources, 1986

Household no.	No. of persons	Crops		Sidelines	Total income			Sidelines		Income	
		Cash	Kind	Cash	Cash & kind	Cash	% cash	% of total income	% of cash income	Total per person	Cash per person
1	5	330	620	215	1,165	545	47	39	18	233	109
2	6	50	345	55	450	105	26	52	12	75	18
3	6	195	580	320	1,095	515	47	62	29	183	86
4	7	300	850	90	1,240	390	31	23	7	177	56
5	5	170	490	–	660	170	26	–	–	132	34
6	3	130	570	–	700	130	19	–	–	233	43
7	4	140	600	100	840	240	29	42	12	210	60
8	3	325	320	200	845	525	62	38	24	282	175
9	7	100	685	260	1,045	360	34	72	25	149	51
10	4	120	580	100	800	220	27	45	12	200	55
11	4	75	460	1,330	1,865	1,405	75	71	95	466	351
12	5	69.5	335.5	450	855	520	61	86	53	171	104
13	4	155	590	90	835	245	29	37	11	209	61
Average per household: 166		155	540	247	953	413				209	93

Table 3.8 Expenses, savings and debts, 1986

Household no.	Total cash income (¥)	Main cash expenses			Total expenses (¥)	Surplus/ deficit (¥)	Savings (¥)	Debts (¥)
		Fertiliser (¥)	Daily living (¥)	Other (¥)				
1	545	200	200 (40)	–	400	+145	20	+200
2	105	78	50 (9)	600[a,c]	728	–623	–	–780
3	515	300	140 (23)	500[a]	940	–425	–	–500
4	390	250	300 (43)	500[a] + 700[b]	1,750	–1,360	–	–900
5	170	150	175 (38)	175[c]	500	–330	–	–360
6	130	70	100 (33)	30[c] + 500[d]	700	–570	–	–200
7	240	90	250 (62)	100[c]	440	–200	–	–100
8	525	60	200 (66)	350[a]	610	–85	100	–
9	360	150	300 (43)	40[c] + 1,100[d]	1,590	–1,230	–	–900
10	220	150	200 (50)	500[d]	850	–630	–	–500
11	1,405	80	300 (75)	100[c] + 1,300[b]	1,780	–375	–	–700
12	520	70	200 (40)	60[c] + 200[e]	530	–10	–	–200
13	245	70	200 (50)	30[c] + 30[e]	330	–85	–	–200
Average per household:	413	132	201 (44)	524	858	–444	9	–395

Notes: Figures in parentheses denote estimated daily living expenses.
a House (or repairs to house).
b Machine.
c Medical expenses.
d Marriage.
e Special food for child.

Table 3.9 Loans and indebtedness (¥), 1986

Household no.	Total debt	Sources of loan				Reason for debt				
		Bank	Kin	Friends	Neighbours	Medical	Capital assets	House	Wedding	Living
1	–									
2	-780	680	40		60	x		x		
3	-500	500						x		x
4	-900	500			400		x	x		
5	-360	300			60					
6	-200		200						x	
7	-100		100			x				
8	–									
9	-900		800	100					x	
10	-500	500							x	
11	-700	500		200			x			x
12	-200		200			x				x
13	-200	200								x

Table 3.10 School education of village children

Household no.	No. of children	Those who left school					Those at school					
		Graduates of middle school	Junior school		Primary school		Middle school	Junior school	Primary school	Late starters	Too small	Not known
			Graduates	Drop-outs	Graduates	Drop-outs						
1	3		1 (15)								1 (5)	
2	4	1 (22)				3 (20), (16), (14)					1 (8)	
3	4					1 (16)			3 (15), (12), (9)			
4	4				1 (15)	1 (20)						
5	4					3 (20), (17), (12)			2 (10), (8)		1 (6)	
6	2											
7	2		2 (30), (25)			1 (14)			1 (14)			
8	1		1 (21)									
9	2 + 2[a]					1 (23)					2 (6), (1)	2
10	2				1 (24)							
11	2											
12	1		2 (23), (19)						2 (12), (7)		1 (1)	
13	2 + 1[a]										1 (1.5)	
Total	36	1	6		2	10			8	6	7	2

Notes: Figures in parentheses represent age in years.
[a] Represents children of successive generations.

Table 3.11 Household size and composition in sample households

Household no.	(1) No. of persons	(2) No. of generations	(3) No. of children	(4) No. of labourers	(5) No. of dependants	Ratio (4)/(5)
1	5	2	3	3	2	0.60
2	3	2	1	2	1	0.60
3	4	2	2	4	–	1.00
4	4	2	3	4	–	1.00
5	4	2	2	2	2	0.50
6	3	2	1	3	–	1.00
7	5	3	2	5	–	1.00
8	2	1	–	2	–	1.00
9	6	2	4	4	2	0.60
10	4	2	2	2	2	0.50
11	4	2	2	3	1	0.75
12	5	2	3	3	2	0.60
13	5	2	3	3	2	0.60
14	7	2	5	6	1	0.80
15	7	3	4	3	4	0.40
16	6	3	3	4	2	0.60
17	4	2	2	2	2	0.50
18	5	2	3	2	3	0.40
19	4	2	2	2	2	0.50
20	6	3	3	3	3	0.50
21	6	2	3 + 1[a]	5	1	0.80
22	4	2	2	4	–	1.00

Note: a Daughter-in-law.

Table 3.12 Land resources in seven villages

Village		Arable land (mu) per person	Pasture land (mu) per person	Vegetable (mu)
Huanglung	Goats	1.20	5.00	0.13
Shaku		1.30	2.50	0.14
Xinwen	Fur	1.10	0.70	0.15
Taiping	rabbits	1.50	2.00	0.15
Daping	Meat	1.33	1.60	0.14
Lungwu	rabbits	1.25	1.45	0.01
Kanpu	Dairy cows/ goats	0.80	0.40	0.10

Table 3.13 Land resources of peasant households

Household no.	No. of persons	Arable land per household	Per capita	Pasture land per household	Per capita	Vegetable plot per household	Per capita	Total	Total per capita
1	5	7.0	1.4	15.0	3.0	0.6	0.12	22.6	4.5
2	3	2.7	0.9	15.0	5.0	0.3	0.10	18.0	6.0
3	4	8.5	2.1	8.0	2.0	0.56	0.14	17.06	4.3
4	4	7.0	1.8	10.0	2.5	0.7	0.18	17.7	4.4
5	4	3.1	0.8	12.0	3.0	0.17	0.04	15.27	3.8
6	3	2.1	0.7	3.0	1.0	0.4	0.13	5.5	1.8
7	5	5.0	1.0	5.0	1.0	–	–	0.0	2.0[a]
8	2	2.0	1.0	0.5	0.25	0.2	0.1	2.7	1.35
9	6	9.0	1.5	12.0	2.0	0.78	0.13	21.8	3.6
10	4	6.1	1.5	11.0	2.75	0.7	0.18	17.8	4.5
11	4	6.0	1.5	8.0	2.0	0.6	0.15	14.6	3.65
12	5	7.0	1.4	9.0	1.8	0.75	0.15	16.75	3.35
13	5	5.3	1.1	7.0	1.4	1.0	0.2	13.3	2.7
14	7	8.6	1.2	10.0	1.4	1.0	0.14	19.6	2.8
15	7	5.9	0.8	7.9	1.1	0.5	0.07	14.3	2.0
16	6	9.0	1.5	10.0	1.7	1.0	0.17	20.0	3.3
17	4	2.0	0.5	6.0	1.5	0.2	0.05	8.2	2.1
18	5	5.0	1.0	8.0	1.6	0.5	0.1	13.5	2.7
19	4	4.0	1.0	6.0	1.5	0.4	0.1	10.4	2.6
20	6	5.4	0.9	9.0	1.5	0.6	0.1	15.0	2.5
21	6	7.8	1.3	1.5	0.25	0.6	0.1	9.9	1.65
22	4	4.8	1.2	1.2	0.3	0.4	0.1	6.4	1.6

Notes: Broken lines represent village boundaries.
a Not including vegetable plot.

Table 3.14 The production of rice

Household no.	Arable land	Mu	Rice cultivation Total produce (jin)	Yield (jin/mu)	Tax (jin)	%	Use Consumption (jin)	Per capita (jin)
1	7.0	No paddy						
2	2.7	No paddy						
3	8.5	0.5	200	400	0	0	200	50
4	7.0			Insufficient labour				
5	3.1	1.0	600	600	0	0	600	150
6	2.1	1.1	600	545	120	(20)	480	160
7	5.0	3.0	1,800	600	250	(14)	1,550	310
8	2.0	1.0	550	550	120	(22)	430	215
9	9.0	3.6	2,880	800	800	(28)	2,080	347
10	6.1	2.4	1,640	683	420	(26)	1,220	305
11	6.0	2.5	2,000	800	300	(15)	1,700	425
12	7.0	3.0	2,400	800	700	(29)	1,700	340
13	5.3	2.4	2,000	833	530	(26)	1,470	294
14	8.6	3.4	2,500	735	900	(36)	1,600	229
15	5.9	2.3	1,700	739	350	(20)	1,350	193
16	9.0	5.0	4,000	800	1,000	(25)	3,000	500
17	2.0	0.8	640	800	20	(3)	620	155
18	5.0	2.0	1,600	800	200	(13)	1,600	280
19	4.0	1.6	1,100	688	185	(17)	915	229
20	5.4	2.0	1,600	800	200	(12)	1,400	233
21	7.8	4.8	3,500	729	700	(20)	2,800	467
22	4.8	3.2	2,800	875	370	(13)	2,430	607

Table 3.15 Dry crops cultivated by household[1]

Household no.	Mu	Total jin produced	Yield jin/mu	Consumption (jin)	Fodder (jin)	Use tax (jin)	Other
			Maize				
1	7.0	2,500	357	X	+	–	–
2	2.7	1,500	556	X	+	–	–
3	8.0	2,100	262.5	X	+	–	–
4	6.0	1,600	267	X	+	–	–
5	2.1	1,000	476	–	+	–	–
6	1.0	260	260	–	+	–	–
7	2.0	450	225	–	+	–	–
8	1.0	200	200	+	+	–	–
9	5.5	2,860	520	200	2,520	140	–
10	3.0	1,380	460	–	1,240	140	–
11	3.5	1,800	514	–	920	200	680*
12	4.0	1,600	400	440	960	200	–
13	3.8	1,700	447	440	900	360	–
14	5.2	2,200	423	500	1,300	400	–
15	3.6	1,500	417	–	1,220	280	–
16	4.0	1,600	400	200	1,000	400	–
17	1.2	600	500	560	–	40	–
18	3.0	1,800	600	1,600	–	200	–
19	2.4	1,200	500	–	1,000	200	–
20	3.4	1,940	571	–	1,740	200	–
21	3.0	1,200	400	–	800	400	–
22	1.6	1,000	625	–	739	261	–

Average grain consumption per annum per village

Huanglung	500–600 (maize)	Daping	450
Shaku	self-sufficient	Lungwu	self-sufficient
Xinwen	480	Kanpu	580–600
Taiping	500		

Notes: X Maize also exchanged for rice.
+ Use (amount unknown).
* 200 sale, 380 store.

Table 3.16 Farm livestock in sample households, by village

	Pigs	Average		Per household	Chickens (per household)	Ducks
			Goats			
Huanglung	345	2.5	400	5		
Shaku	180	2	385	7	20–30	
			Fur rabbits			
Xinwen	72	2	112	3–4	4–5	
Taiping	104	2	24	3	4	
			Meat rabbits			
Daping	455	2.2	120	17	4	+ ducks
Lungwu	600	2.3	100	5	5–5	+ ducks
			Dairy cattle			
Kanpu	1,050	3	16	1.6	2	+ ducks
			Goats			
			470	3		

Table 3.17 Farm livestock in sample households

Household No.	Pigs	Goats	Fur rabbits	Rabbits	Cows	Chickens
1	3	0				0
2	2	0				0
3	2	2				4
4	0	0				0
5	2		0			8
6	1		0			1
7	4		5			2
8	2		3			4
9	1		0			3
10	2		0			4
11	2		2			6
12	2		6			5
13	3			0		5
14	2			0		10
15	2			10		5
16	2			17		10
17	1			0		4
18	2			0		5
19	2			5		5
20	1+2			5		4
21	4	3			1	5 ducks
22	2	1			0	9

Table 3.18 Cost of keeping a pig in villages

	Purchase price (¥)	Feed, maize concentrate value (¥)	Health (¥)	Total raising cost (¥)	Selling price (¥)	Profit (¥)
Hunglong	50	150 (500 × 3)		200	180 (150 × 1.2)	20
Shaku	50	110	7	167	168 (140 × 1.2)	1
Xinwen	40 (25 × 1.2)	85 (300 × 2.6)	5	130	160	30
Taiping	40 (20 × 1.6)	60 (300 × 21)	3	103	143 (130 × 1.1)	30
Daping	48 (20 × 2.4)	70 + 10 (350 × 2)	5	133	143 (130 × 1.1)	10
Lungwu	50 (20 × 2.5)	80 + 30	2.5	162.5	195 (150 × 1.3)	32.5
Kanpu	50 (20 × 2.5)	87 + 20 (300 × 29)	5	162	200 (172 × 1.16)	38

Table 3.19 Cost of production (per pig) per household

Household no.	No. of pigs	Purchase price (¥)	Value of maize (¥)	Concentrate /¥	Medicine inoculation	Total	Selling price	Profit
1	3	0	Breeding of piglets					
2	2	50	75		1.5	156.5[a]	140	
3	2	45	78		1.3	124.5	200	75.5
4	0							
5	2	61	40		15	116	140	24
6	1	54	63		3	120		
7	4	60	60		5	125		
8	2	33	84		6	123		
9	1	50	Breeding					
10	2	28.5	70	50	6.5	155	175	20
11	2	30	60	25	3	118	150	32
12	2	62	59	27	3	151.5	150	1.5
13	3	25	60	20	5	110	157.5	47.5
14	2	60	100		5	165	185	20
15	2	48	100		6	154	180	26
16	2	50	50	25	5	130	150	30
17	1	50	95		3	148	Consume	
18	2	50	95		2.5	147.5	195	47.5
19	2	60	85.5		3	148.5	200	52.5
20	1+2	Breeding		165	22			
21	4	62.5	112	15	2.5	192	250	58
22	2	0	98		5	104	130	26

Note: a Extra costs to pigsty (¥30).

Table 3.20 Credit supplies for livestock by village

Village	No. of households	Households with credit		Average amount of loan (year) ¥	Interest rate	Repayment
		No.	%			
Huanglung						
Goats	133	80	60	200–1,000	Interest-free	3 years
Pigs	133	48	36	100	2.6	seasonal
Shaku						
Goats	90	54	60	7	2.6	1–3 years
Pigs	90	90	100	50	2.6	seasonal
Xinwen						
Pigs	39	13	33	600–900	2.6	1–8 years
Rabbits	39	8	20	70–100	Interest-free	1–1.5 years
Taiping						
Rabbits	52	2	4	40	2.6	1–3 years
Pigs	12	27	52	80	6.6	1–3 years
Daping						
Pigs	204	180	88	100–150	2.6	2–3 years
Rabbits	204	7	3	150	2.6	2–3 years
Lungwu						
Pigs	261	131	50	100	2.6	seasonal
Rabbits	261	19	7	200	2.6	1 year
Pigs	261	15	6	–	Interest-free	–
Kanpu						
Cows	340	10	3	2,500	2.6	7–10 years
Goats	340	70	20	100	2.6	1–3 years

Table 3.21 Application for loans in villages

Village	No. of households	Applications		Successful applicants	
		No.	%	No.	%
Huanglung					
Goats	138	133	96	80	61
Shaku					
Goats	90	90	100	55	61
Xinwen					
Fur rabbits	39	39	51	21	54
Fur rabbits, 1988	39	20	51	3	15
Taiping					
Fur rabbits	52	27	52	8	30
Daping					
Meat rabbits	204	170	93	7	4
All animals, 1988	204	130	64	60	44
Rabbits, 1987	42	40	95	5	12.5
Rabbits, 1988	42	42	100	4	9
Lungwu					
Meat rabbits	261	240	92	19	8
Meat rabbits, 1987	27	10	37	10	100
Meat rabbits, 1988	27	25	92	10	40
Kanpu					
Cows	340	100	29	10	10
Goats	340	100	29	50	50

Table 3.22 Project villages: income levels (year), 1987

		Gross income per capita			Net income per capita			Average production costs
		Average	Highest	Lowest	Average	Highest	Lowest	
Huanglung	Goats	200+	na	–	50	100	0	–
Shaku		230	400	120	40	70–80	0	190
Xinwen	Fur rabbits	135	150	80	–	na		–
Taiping		185	250	90	40–50	70–80	10	135
Village group		170	200	0	50	100	20	120
Daping	Meat rabbits	248	260	180	155	160	68	93
Lungwu		347	382	105	135	178	65	212
Village group		265	280	135	105	110	60	160
Kanpu	Cows	225	280	180	80	100	50	145

Table 3.23 Sample household income (¥)

Household no.	Total income		Sources					
	Per household	Per capita	Pigs, piglets	Crops	Vegetables	Chickens	Eggs	New livestock
1	200	40	200	–	20	–	–	–
2	200	67	140	40	–	–	–	–
3	512	128	200	–	–	–	–	312[a]
4	–	–	–	–	–	–	–	–
5	320	80	140	110	5	70	10	–
6	85	28	*	70	5	–	40	60[b]
7	249	50	*	144	–	–	60	90[b]
8	166	83	*	16	–	–	60	–
9	362	60	*	320	–	–	62	–
10	552	138	175	345	–	–	32	–
11	450	113	150	180	–	–	64	56[b]
12	439	88	150	240	–	49	–	–
13	328	66	157	30	50	19	72	–
14	460	66	200	110	–	–	–	150[c]
15	320	44	180	100	30	–	–	–
16	600	100	300	225	–	24	50	–
17	87	22	*	47	–	30	10	–
18	323	65	195	77	–	50	10	–
19	265	66	200	55	–	10	–	–
20	524	87	400	112	–	–	12	–
21	3,245	374	880	400	45	–	–	1,300[d]
22	715	179	430	250	15	20	–	–

Notes: a Goat milk.
b Rabbit fur.
c Hire out of oxen.
d ¥1,000 cow milk; ¥30 off-farm income.
* Pig-raising planned in 1988.

Table 3.24 Household cash expenditures (¥)

Household No.	Fertiliser	Chemicals	Seed	Livestock production	Farm implements	Hire of ox	Fuel***	School fees	Medical expenses	Daily necessities	Expenditure per household	Per capita
1*	100 (14)		30	186.5						30	473	95
2*	180 (66)		15	1.5				30		70	296	99
3	200 (23)			130					300	30	630	157
4	27 (4)			15							72	18
5	70 (23)	20	30	3			35/10	30	30	10	248	62
6	54 (26)	15	19	5			50/10		20	60	223	74
7	150 (30)	10	25	7			100/20		30	20	362	72
8	60 (30)	8	4	9			42/15		10	30	178	89
9	470 (52)	70	90	6.5			160	120	150	290	1,356	226
10	324 (53)	59	54	53			120	60	30	350	1,050	263
11	360 (60)	125	61	58	60		160	40	120	320	1,304	326
12	560 (80)	70	73.3	68	30		180	80	80	300	1,441	288
13	170 (32)	24	69	25				50	100	60	498	100
14	150 (18)	20	45	6			15	50	5	145	436	62
15	200 (34)	30	25	50				30	30	35	400	57
16	720 (80)	50	120	28				40	20	150	1,128	188
17	82 (41)	8	10	2.5	10			30	30	30	172	43
18	280 (56)	40	60	3	30	20		**	15	15	483	97
19	163 (41)	25	30	8	10			40	6	32	314	78
20	305 (56)	10	39.4	194	30			40	40	15	673	112
21	180 (23)	15	50	576	10	100	70	30	20	350	1,401	233
22	150 (31)		35	5	3	80	35		470	107	885	221

Notes: * Incomplete data.
    ** Exemption school fees.
   *** Coal/electricity.

Table 3.25 Average costs of production in two villages

	Daping village		Lungwu village	
	(¥)	*(%)*	*(¥)*	*(%)*
Fertiliser	157.5		250	
Seed	35		20	
Chemicals	8	44	10	60
Livestock raising	35		65	
Farm implements	20		20	
Grain processing	90		20	
Coal	60		50	
Medicines	40		60	
School fees	30	56	20	40
Daily necessities	112.5		100	
	588	100	615	100

Village	Value of fertiliser (¥)		
Huanglung	50–90 per year		
Shaku	120 per household		
Xinwen	35 per mu of rice; 11–12 per mu of maize		
	20–25 per mu of wheat; 30 per mu of rape		
Taiping	70 per mu		
Lungwu	70 per mu		
Kanpu	70 per mu		
Daping	*Costs calculated per mu per crop per year:*		
	Crop	Weight (jin)	Cost (¥)
	Rice	40	70
	Wheat	20	5.6
	Maize	150	57.0
	Rape	–	10.0
	Misc. grains	20	15.0

Table 3.26 School education of village children

Household no.	No. of children	Those who left school:				Those at school:			
		Graduates of middle school	Junior year	Primary school year	Not known	Middle school	Junior school	Primary school	No school
1	3			4 (15F)				2 (12F)	
2	1							2 (9M)	
3	2			5 (15M)				2 (9M)	
4	2			7 (22M)* (15M)*					12F
5	2							1 (7M)	3F
6	1				(19F)				
7	2	(16M)*	13F*						
8	–								
9	4	(19F)* (17F)*					13F		4M
10	2				22M	17M*			
11	2				20F			3 (9F) 5 (12M)	
12	3			(17M)*			8 (17M)	5 (13F)	
13	3			5 (20M)			6 (14M)	4 (10M)	
14	5		(21F)*	5 (17M) 5 (15F)				6 (16M)	

Table 3.26 Continued

Household no.	No. of children	Graduates of middle school	Junior year	Primary school year	Not known	Middle school	Junior school	Primary school	No school
		Those who left school:					Those at school:		
15	4							2 (9F)	4F 4M 1M
16	3		7 (21F) 7 (19F)				9 (16M)*		
17	2								5F 3F
18	3							5 (13F) 4 (10F) 2 (9F)	
19	2							4 (11F) 1 (8M)	
20	3							4 (11M) 2 (9M) 0 (7F)	
21	3	(25M)		5 (17M) 5 (18M)					
22	2			3 (15M)				5 (13F)	

Notes: Figures in brackets represent age in years.
M = male; F = female.
* Graduate.

Table 3.27 Savings, loans, debts

Household no.	Cash surplus/ deficit	Loan	Loan use		Debts friends/ relatives	Relief
1	−223	115		FS	500 jin*	20
2	−96	1,100	150	P	−	40
			150	F		
			800	M		
3	−108	2,400	2,300	T	100 G	
4	−72	60			300 jin	30 + 97**
5	+72	330	200	H	350 H	
					130 P	
6	−138	694	600	H		
			40	F		
			51	P		
7	−117	330	180	P	200 FM	
			150	R		
8	−13	150	150*		200 M	
9	−994	500		FP	230 C	
10	−498	250		FCS		
11	−854	200		FP	300 Bi	
12	−1,002	50		FF		
13	−169	90	90	P	100 MP	50
			20	F	15 P	
14	+24	80		P	116 CC	
15	−90	190		RP		
16	−528	1,400	1,300	R		
			100	P		
17	−85	131		PF		30
18	−160	100		P	150 F	120**
19	−49	300	130	R	50 F	
			120	P		
			50	F		
20	−149	200		R	50 F	
21	+844	500		C		
22	−170	300	100	M	350 Bu	40
			200	H		

Notes:
Bi	bicycle	M	medical expenses
Bu	buffalo	P	pigs
C	cows	R	rabbits
CC	chickens	S	seed
F	fertiliser	T	tractor
FF	fodder	*	including rabbit pen
G	grain	**	kind
H	house		

Table 3.28 Loans in the project villages

| | No. of households | Households with loans | | Average size loan | Source of loan | | Relief grants | |
		No.	%		Friends, relatives	Rural credit co-operative	No.	%
Huanglung	138	130	94	1,000	3–5,000	500–700	18	13
Shaku	90	90	100	320	100	220*	na	
Xinwen	39	39	100	70–900	70–300	70–900	8	20
Taiping	52	46	88	400	80*	320*	5	10
Daping	204	192	94	120	120*	250*	55	27
Lungwu	261	165	63	165–200	150*	100*	9	3
Kanpu	340	250	73	30–2,500	30–50*	100–2,500	10	3

Note: * Average size loan.

Table 3.29 Village A: income and profits, 1978–89

Year	Total income ¥ '000	Percentage change	Profits ¥ '000	Percentage change	Per capita income[b]	Percentage increase
1978	690.848		399.460		162	–
1979	715.484		410.070		222	37
1980[a]	1,804.454		759.826		383	73
1981	1,401.989	−22.3	628.779	−17.3	404	5
1982	2,304.887	+64.4	945.679	+50.4	498	23
1983	2,664.031	+15.6	952.808	+0.8	589	18
1984	3,321.671	+24.7	1,164.357	+22.2	646	10
1985	4,603.017	+38.6	1,479.152	+27.0	759	17
1986	5,353.306	+16.3	1,929.170	+30.4	991	31
1987	6,325.131	+18.2	2,158.118	+11.9	1,121	13
1988	8,254.249	+30.5	2,783.722	+29.0	1,380	23
1989	9,524.518	+15.4	3,349.085	+20.3	1,579	14

Notes: a Change in basis of statistics from 1980, therefore percentage changes not included for earlier years.
b These figures do not take account of rate of inflation.

Table 3.30 Village A: income, expenditure and profits, 1989

Income

Origins	Income ¥ m.	Profit ¥ m.	Percentage Income	Profits
Grains	0.66	0.44	6.9	13.1
Forestry	0.33	0.18	3.5	5.4
Animal husbandry	0.27	0.11	2.8	3.3
Farm machinery	0.40	0.26	4.2	7.8
Fishing	0.04	–	0.4	–
Industry	7.12	2.04	74.8	60.9
Land rents (enterprises)	0.35	–	3.7	–
Other	0.35	0.32	3.7	9.6
Total	9.52	3.35	100.0	100.1

Table 3.31 Village A: labour force distribution, 1989

Units	No. of workers	Male	Female	Average age
Agricultural				
Farm machinery	49	44	5	37
Land contractors	40	25	15	41
Forestry/orchard	96	46	50	34
Animal husbandry (including deer)	16	14	2	40
Industrial				
Colour printing	56	33	23	31
Electric porcelain	50	16	34	38
Bookbinding	25	11	14	33
Paper box	39	15	24	29
Fine chemicals	36	22	14	32
Weaving & dyeing	82	42	40	32
Clothing	172	41	131	31
Total	661	309	352	

Table 3.32 Village A: education of labour force, 1989

Unit	Total	Higher education	Middle school Senior	Middle school Junior	Primary
Agriculture					
Farm machinery	49		4	33	12
Land contractors	40		6	24	10
Forestry	96		11	62	23
Grain husbandry	16		3	10	3
Industrial					
Colour printing	56		11	36	9
Electric porcelain	50	1	7	25	17
Bookbinding	25		3	20	2
Paper box	39		6	26	7
Fine chemicals	36	5	8	20	3
Weaving & dyeing	82	1	11	65	5
Clothing	172		10	155	7
Total	661	7	80	476	98

Table 3.33 Sample income and expenditure: Beijing village households (¥), 1989

Household no.	No. of persons	No. of labourers (agricultural)	Income						Expenses			Per capita income
			Total (net)	Grains (net)	Pigs	Veg.	Other[a]	Expenses[b]	Production costs	Daily needs	Surplus[c]	
1	5	4 (2)	21,409	13,000	2,000	—	6,409	15,100	200[e]	2,500	10,000	4,282
2	4	2 (1)	7,000	—	—	—	7,000	7,000	—	3,000	6,500	1,750
3	3	1	8,000	—	—	—	8,000	1,300	—	1,300	5,000	2,666
4	4	2	6,005	—	—	—	6,005	2,096	—	2,096	3,000	1,501
5	3	2	4,300	—	—	—	4,300	2,750	—	2,750	1,000	1,433
6	4	2	21,000	12,000	—	—	9,000	4,000	—	4,000	15,000[d]	5,250

Notes: a Wages for enterprises unless otherwise indicated.
  b Includes expenses for daily needs (food, clothes), production costs, education, house improvements and furniture.
  c Includes cash sums over at the end of the year which were either used to purchase some item or accumulated as savings.
  d The household had lent ¥5,000 to help older sister with ¥60,000 medical expenses for her son.
  e Production costs for grain deducted before payments made.

Table 3.34 Village B: village income, 1989

Activity	Amount ¥ million	% of total
Grain	1.226	53.3
Other crops (vegetables)	0.200	8.7
Forestry	0.150	6.5
Animal husbandry	0.387	16.8
Industry	0.337	14.7
Total	2.300	100.0

Table 3.35 Village B: village income, 1978–89

Year	Total income ¥ million	Investment ¥ million	¥ per capita[a]	Annual percentage increase
1978	23.5	9.1	66	–
1979	36.3	12.9	99	50
1980	46.3	16.1	134	35
1981	53.8	18.4	160	19
1982	60.7	17.1	200	25
1983	90.9	12.5	267	34
1984	102.3	17.8	413	55
1985	115.1	21.9	450	9
1986	124.0	22.5	500	11
1987	133.0	24.2	520	4
1988	186.4	33.0	660	27
1989	230.0	66.7	750	14

Note: a Inflation not taken into account.

Table 3.36 Village B: grainlands and yields, 1978–89

Year	Grainland area (mu)	Percentage area	Yield (jin per mu)	Total yields (jin '000)
1978	4,319	79	389	1,683
1979[a]	4,790	88	601	2,878
1980	4,673	86	749	3,500
1981	4,511	83	818	3,690
1982	4,507	83	927	4,155
1983	3,898	72	1,067	4,159
1984	3,737	69	1,070	3,999
1985	3,628	67	1,081	3,922
1986	3,600	70	1,000	3,600
1987	3,709	68	1,020	3,783
1988	3,709	68	1,078	4,000
1989	3,883	71	1,122	4,360

Note: a One of the reasons the yields are high in the village after 1979 is that after this date the village adopted the practice of ploughing in the stalks and raising the organic content of the soil.

Table 3.37 Village B: land use

Crop	Area (mu)	% of total
Wheat	1,200	22.0
Maize	2,383	43.8
Millet	300	5.5
Vegetables	300	5.5
Mulberry	330	6.1
Fruit trees	500	9.2
Forestry	270	5.0
Oil crops, rapeseed, sunflowers	159	2.9
Total	5,442	100.0

Table 3.38 Village B: labour distribution, 1989

Activities	Households	Labour			Education			
		Total	Male	Female	Prof. Tech.	Senior (Middle)	Junior (Middle)	Primary
Agriculture	200	467	232	235	3	33	271	160
Grain	80	120	80	40	1	10	90	19
Sericulture	60	177	71	106	1	12	81	83
Vegetable	60	170	81	89	1	11	100	58
Orchard/forestry	50	60	50	10	–	–	40	20
Industry	50	137	83	54	3	41	91	2
Silk	10	38	–	38	1	20	17	–
Bricks/tiles	20	70	56	14	1	5	64	–
Concrete roof	5	12	12	–	–	4	8	–
Farm machinery	12	12	12	–	1	11	–	–
Food & oil processing	3	5	3	2	–	1	2	2
Animal husbandry	10	10	8	2	0	3	6	1
Dairying	5	5	4	1	–	2	3	–
Chickens	3	3	2	1	–	1	2	–
Breeding	2	2	2	–	–	–	1	1
Transportation	15	33	33	–	–	20	13	–
Services[a]	10	30	24	6	–	15	12	3
Labour households	335	737	430	307	6	112	433	186
Total households[b]	370							

Notes: a Services households refer to teachers, orchard, watchmen, accountants, doctors, electric technicians
b 35 non-labouring households.

Table 3.39 Village B: education, 1989

(a) Numbers in school

Education level	Total	Male	Female
Pre-school	155	75	80
Primary	226	110	116
Junior middle	51	35	16
Senior middle	35	20	15
Professional & technical	4	3	1
Total in school	316	168	148

(b) Education levels in village

Professional & technical	6	5	1
Senior middle	112	68	44
Junior middle	439	219	220
Primary	645	299	346
Total agricultural population	1,202	591	611

Table 3.40 Sample income and expenditure: Shanxi village households, 1989

Household no.	No. of persons	No. of labourers (agricultural)	Income					Expenses			Surplus[d] income	Per capita net income
			Total (gross)	Grains	Pigs, chickens	Veg.	Other[a]	Total expenses[c]	Production costs	Daily needs		
1	4	2 (2)	6,462	4,500	1,112	8–900	–	1,800	–	1,800	1,000	1,615
2	4	3 (3)	13,500	10,000	1,000	–	2,500	2,000	–	2,000	10,000	3,375
3	5	3 (3)	8,590	4,590	2,000	–	2,000	2,630	–	2,630	5,000	1,718
4	6	3 (3)	3,730	–	1,000	2,730	–	2,400	390	2,000	1,000	601
5	4	2 (1)	3–4,000	–	600	5–600	2,500	1,300	300	1,000	2,500	925
6	6	4 (4)	12,600	–	9,000	3,000	600	7,100+	4,100	3–4,000	5,000	1,666
7	4	3 (1)	13,000[b]	300	9,500	800	4,500	6,000+	4,000+	2,000	7,000	3,200
8	5	2 –	2,200	–	700	300	1,200	1,100	–	1,100	–	440

Notes: a In this village category 'other' includes sundry economic activities in the community such as film projection shows (household 2), hiring out a donkey (household 2), collection of grain (household 5), truck driving (household 4), grain processing (household 7), and remittances (household 8).
b This was thought to be a substantial underestimation.
c Includes cash expenses for daily needs (food, clothing, etc.), production costs, education, house improvements and furniture.
d Includes cash sums over at the end of the year which were either used to purchase some item or accumulated for savings.

Table 3.41 Village C: source of village income, 1989

Activity	Amount (¥ million)	% of total
Agricultural enterprises	1.557	92
Grain[a]	0.755	45
Cotton	0.384	23
Vegetables/fruit	0.210	12
Animals[b]	0.207	12
Other	0.001	0
Other enterprises (industry)[c]	0.140	8
Total	1.70	100

Notes: a Made up of wheat (¥0.04m) and maize (¥0.27m).
      b Made up of chickens, pigs, rabbits, cattle and eggs.
      c The non-agricultural sources of income include machine maintenance, welding
        machines, transportation, housebuilding and services or businesses such as
        selling agricultural machinery parts.

Table 3.42 Village C: source of village income, 1990

Activity	Amount (¥ million)	% of total
Agriculture	1.880	91
Cotton	0.768	37
Grain: Wheat	0.509	25
Maize	0.314	15
Other	0.040	2
Animals	0.249	12
Industry	0.150	7
Building	0.036	2
Business	0.028	1
Service	0.067	3
Other	0.019	1
Other	0.027	1
Total	2.057	99

Table 3.43 Village C: labour distribution, 1990[a]

Activities	Households	Total	Labour Male	Female	Senior	Education Junior	Primary
Agriculture	220	368	201	167	21	45	302
Animal husbandry	4	8	4	4	–	6	2
Chicken breeding	4	8	4	4	–	6	2
Industrial enterprises	20	31	29	2	7	21	3
Bricks/tiles	8	8	8	–	–	5	3
Farm machinery	12	23	21	2	7	16	–
Transportation	3	6	6	–	–	6	–
Services	3	12	10	2	5	7	–
Labour households/labourers	254	425	250	175	33	85	307
Total households	265						

Note: a There are some discrepancies in this table which need to be checked on a subsequent visit.

Table 3.44 Village C: per capita net income, 1978–90

Year	¥ per capita	Annual percentage change
1978	67	
1979	104	+55
1980	148	+42
1981	237	+60
1982	372	+57
1983	655[a]	+76
1984	750	+14
1985	754	+ 1
1986	654	−13
1987	705	+ 8
1988	750	+ 6
1989	864	+15
1990	1,000	+16

Note: a Year responsibility system came into operation.

Table 3.45 Village C: village income, 1978–90 (¥ 10,000)

Year	Total income	Agriculture	Industry	Other	Investment	Net income
1978	17.8	15.5	1.3	1.0	12.3	6.4
1979	27.1	24.9	0.5	1.7	12.3	10.1
1980	37.4	34.9	0.8	1.7	15.1	14.2
1981	52.8	48.0	2.9	1.9	21.2	21.8
1982	74.6	62.4	6.4	5.8	22.6	34.1
1983[a]	96.1	89.7	5.3	1.1	28.8	62.4
1984	106.6	99.7	6.0	0.9	26.7	73.7
1985	107.2	94.8	6.6	5.8	25.8	73.4
1986	99.5	89.4	6.7	3.4	26.0	63.7
1987	134.5	107.0	12.0	15.5	53.6[b]	71.6
1988	147.9	130.1	13.9	3.9	57.8	78.4
1989	170.1	156.0	14.1	–	65.6	90.8
1990	205.7	188.0	15.0	2.7	84.8	106.5

Notes: a Start of responsibility system.
  b Price increased for fertiliser and other raw materials.

Table 3.46 Village C: crops and yields, 1978–90

Year	Grains				Cotton		
	Area (mu)	% of total area	Yield kg per mu	Total yield '000 kg	Area (mu)	Yield kg per mu	Total yield '000 kg
1978	1,324	52	306	405	878	23	20.4
1979	1,324	52	467	620	872	30	26.5
1980	1,235	49	580	706	961	43	42.2
1981	1,240	49	910	880	1,064	50	53.4
1982	1,140	45	830	946	1,112	74	82.2
1983	1,252	50	858	1,075	1,276	76	97.6
1984	1,220	48	906	1,100	1,300	88	114.8
1985	1,150	45	940	1,081	1,210	72	87.5
1986	1,150	45	958	1,101	1,150	68	75.5
1987	1,250	50	826	1,032	980	77	76.0
1988	1,150	45	987	1,135	950	87	83.0
1989	1,150	45	990	1,139	1,100	75	82.5
1990	1,150	45	1,140	1,313	1,200	80	96.0

Table 3.47 Village C: education, 1991

	Total	Male	Female	% of total
Total population	1,065	540	525	100
Pre-school	123	59	64	11
In-school	106	74	32	10
Primary	48	35	13	5
Junior middle	46	31	15	4
Senior middle	12	8	4	1
Professional & technical	–	–	–	–
Post-school	669	369	300	63
Professional & technical	–	–	–	–
Senior middle	54	31	23	5
Junior middle	202	120	82	19
Primary	413	218	195	39
Illiterates	167	38	129	16

Table 3.48 Sample incomes and expenditure in Shandong Village A households

Household no.	No. of persons	No. of labourers (agricultural)	Income					Expenses				Per
			Total (gross)	Cotton	Grain	Pigs	Other[a]	Total expenses[b]	Production costs	Daily needs	Surplus[c] income	capita net income
1	7	3 (3)	9,325	3,500	375	1,500	3,950	4,580	2,280	2,300	4,745	1,000
2	4	4 (3)	7,570	3,100	1,600	2,400	470	3,962	1,942	2,000	3–4,000	1,400
3	6	5 (4)	11,006	2,500	2,946	560	5,000	9,615	2,415	7,200	2,000	1,437
4	6	5 (3)	6,532	4,500	532	1,500	–	5,328	2,328	3,000	2,000	700
5	4	3 (3)	7,735	3,060	325	1,350	3,000	3,100	2,100	1,000	4,000	1,408
6	6	3 (2)	13,475	–	2,600	1,875	9,000	6,880	1,160	5,220	6,000	1,969
7	4	3 (2)	25,526	1,616	2,400	510	21,000	10,532	8,372	2,160	11,000	4,288
8	4	4 (0)							–		40,000	10,000

Notes: a Includes tractor driving (1, 5), subsidies (2), vegetables (3), teaching salaries (4), tailoring (6), chickens (7), and profits from the machine shop (8).
b Includes cash sums for daily needs, production costs, education, house improvements and furniture.
c Includes cash sums over at the end of the year used for extraordinary expenditure or savings.

Table 3.49 Village D: village income, 1981–90 (¥ million)

Year	Total income (gross)	Agriculture	Industry	Other	Investment	Net income	¥ per capita	Annual percentage change
1981	3.02	1.25	1.57	0.20	4.68	1.59	387	
1982	3.30	1.24	1.88	0.18	4.84	1.81	460	19
1983	3.91	1.58	1.90	0.43	4.99	2.32	628[a]	37
1984	4.55	1.46	2.53	0.56	5.14	2.30	701	12
1985	6.85	1.26	5.02	0.57	5.25	3.05	902	29
1986	9.02	2.11	6.17	0.74	5.37	3.29	1,000	11
1987	9.10	1.36	7.10	0.64	5.52	3.51	1,000	0
1988	10.00	2.12	6.26	1.62	5.62	3.44	1,000	0
1989	11.00	2.61	7.10	1.29	5.87	4.01	1,000	0
1990	17.17	2.47	10.51	4.19	7.90	4.93	1,222	22

Note: a Responsibility system introduced.

Table 3.50 Village D: village income, 1990

Activity	Amount (¥ million)	% of total
Enterprises	10.50	61
Crops^a	2.47	14
Animal husbandry	0.67	4
Fishing	0.20	1
Other^b	3.33	20
Total	17.17	100

Notes: a Crops include maize ¥0.63 m, wheat ¥0.30 m, peanuts ¥0.19 m, and orchard ¥1.35 m.
b Other includes business income, trade and earnings from out of village.

Table 3.51 Village D: labour distribution

Activities	Households	Labour			Education				
		Total	Male	Female	Higher education	Middle Senior	Junior	Primary	Illiterate
Agriculture	130	200	69	131	–	5	70	95	30
Orchard	120	150	72	78	–	10	75	50	15
Enterprise (household)	22	22	22	–	–	5	12	5	–
Animal husbandry (part-time)	393	728	362	366	3	112	296	306	11
Industry (full-time)	191	250	152	98	–	48	150	49	3
Labour households	856	1,350	677	673	3	180	603	505	59
Total households	905								

Table 3.52 Village D: crop lands and yields, 1981–90[a]

	Grains				Peanuts		
Year	Land area (mu)	% of total area	Yield (kg/mu)	Total yield (kg 10,000)	Area (mu)	kg/mu	Total yield (kg 10,000)
1981	3,200	76	601	162.3	911	113	10.3
1982	3,200	76	619	167.0	920	118	10.9
1983	3,200	76	637	168.8	980	120	11.8
1984	3,200	76	629	166.8	1,100	131	14.4
1985	3,200	76	502	147.3	1,136	138	15.6
1986	3,200	76	654	199.4	600	124	7.4
1987	2,600	62	663	149.1	650	124	8.1
1988	2,600	62	676	152.1	600	124	7.4
1989	2,600	62	689	155.0	600	124	7.4
1990	2,600	62	735	165.3	600	134	8.0

Note: a The table gives a detailed breakdown of land utilisation; yields per mu have been calculated on the basis of this inter-cropping pattern.

Table 3.53 Village D: costs of production, 1989

	Cost per mu (¥)		
Input	Wheat	Maize	Peanuts
Fertiliser/chemicals	54.80	47.25	28.20
Seeds	6.82	10.20	60.00
Machines	13.70	7.00	10.40
Total	75.32	64.45	98.60

Table 3.54 Village D: education, 1990

	Total	Male	Female
Pre-school	462	228	234
In-school – total	350	173	177
Primary	200	96	104
Junior middle	115	56	59
Senior middle	35	21	14
Post-school – total	1,585	760	825
Professional & technical	3	3	–
Senior middle	185	90	95
Junior middle	753	368	385
Primary	644	299	345
Illiterate	645	335	310
Total population	3,042	1,496	1,546

Table 3.55 Sample incomes and expenditures in Shandong Village B households, 1990

Household no.	No. of persons	No. of labourers (agricultural)	Income					Total expenses[a]	Expenses			Per capita net income
			Total (gross)	Grain	Pigs	Veg.	Salaries		Production costs	Daily needs	Surplus[b]	
1	7	5 (2)	20,710	9,910	800	4,000	6,000	8–9,000	1,500	7,200–8,200	8–10,000	2,667
2	4	4 (1)	10,031	4,631	–	–	5,400	5,200	2,200	3,000	4–5,000	1,958
3	4	3 (1)	8,215	3,815	800	–	3,600	3,050	250	2,200	2,000	1,900
4	4	3 (1)	4,765	125	400	–	4,240	2,120	120	2,000	2,000	1,161
5	2	1 (1)	4,050	400	–	3,200	450	1,474	174	1,300	1,400	1,938
6	5	4 (–)	9,948	348	700	–	8,900	3,275	275	3,000	3,000	1,934
7	3	2 (–)	6,610	320	200	1,000	5,090	2,200	200	2,000	3,500	2,136
8	4	3 (–)	9,225	225	800	–	8,200	3,450	350	4,000	5,000	2,219

Notes: a Includes cash sums for daily needs, production costs, education, house improvements and furniture.
b Includes cash sums over at the end of the year used for savings for extraordinary items of expenditure.

Table 3.56 Village E: village and per capita income, 1978–90

Year	Total income	Income (¥ million) Agric.	Income (¥ million) Industry	Investment (¥ million) Agric.	Investment (¥ million) Industry	Profit (¥ million)	Per capita income (¥)	Annual percentage increase
1978	1.81	0.36	1.45	0.23	0.07	0.30	142	–
1979	2.68	0.36	2.32	0.25	0.26	0.42	198	39
1980	2.83	0.30	2.53	0.22	0.32	0.44	208	5
1981	2.17	0.31	1.86	0.21	0.17	0.53	247	19
1982	2.27	0.37	1.90	0.18	0.17	0.67	319	29
1983	3.39	0.47	2.92	0.33	0.15	0.98	456	43
1984	5.45	0.64	4.81	0.21	0.61	1.71	799	75
1985	11.64	0.49	11.15	0.28	1.19	1.74	829	4
1986	15.92	0.60	15.32	0.27	1.33	2.26	1,078	30
1987	32.93	0.56	32.37	0.28	3.12	2.41	1,167	8
1988	49.95	0.49	49.46	0.33	4.19	2.65	1,259	8
1989	51.55	0.78	50.77	0.47	4.60	2.92	1,339	6
1990	54.60	0.77	53.83	0.54	4.94	3.13	1,430	7

Table 3.57 Village E: labour distribution in detail, 1991

| Activities | Households | Labour | | | Education | | | | From outside village |
		Total	Male	Female	Higher	Middle Senior	Junior	Primary	
Agriculture		130	66	64	–	3	35	92	–
Grain		104	53	51	–	3	28	73	–
Mulberries		11	4	7	–	–	2	9	–
Pigs		3	2	1	–	–	2	1	–
Fish		4	4	–	–	–	2	2	–
Orchard		8	3	5	–	–	1	7	–
Industry (village)		804	388	416	12	67	393	332	46
Country factories		41	22	19	–	–	41	–	–
Township factories		112	39	73	–	2	52	58	–
Other village factories		48	31	17	–	3	44	1	–
Services		44	42	2	–	–	6	38	–
Business[a]		61	15	46	–	–	32	39	–
Other		48	33	15	–	–	42	6	–
Labour households	572	1,288	652	653	12	75	645	566	46
Total households	595								

Note: a Work out of the village.

Table 3.58 Village E: crops, 1978–90

| Year | Wheat & rice | | | Total kg ('000) |
	Grain land	% of land	kg/mu	
1978	1,665	97	1,013	168.73
1979	1,664	97	1,013	168.60
1980	1,665	97	817[a]	135.20[a]
1981	1,634	97	802	131.05
1982	1,605	97	966	154.99
1983	1,570	97	878	137.90
1984	1,505	97	849	126.78
1985	1,489	97	708[b]	105.44[b]
1986	1,454	96	708	102.96
1987	1,430	96	699	99.91
1988	1,421	96	748	106.26
1989	1,421	96	725	103.04
1990	1,405	96	746	104.77

Notes: a 1980–85: 3 crops a year (rice production disadvantaged if too short growing seasons).
　　　b 1985 onwards: double cropping.

Table 3.59 Village E: enterprise histories

Enterprise	Date of Founding	No. of labourers		Output (¥ 0'000)		Wages (¥)	
		Founding	Present	Founding	Present	Founding	Present
1 Dyeing chemicals	1977	15	400	6	2,954	450	2,011
2 Machinery factory	1975	7	180	3	1,371	420	2,765
3 Boat building	1985	19	80	31	238	930	1,968
4 Spare parts	1985	11	60	5	115	850	2,058
5 Iron casting	1958	10	25	4	133	360	2,000
6 Aluminium alloy	1986	8	30	12	133	1,250	2,000
7 Concrete pipe	1986	7	25	11	63	1,300	2,088
8 Engineering, mechanical	1989	4	10	7	118	2,100	1,810
9 Glove factory	1985	16	40	30	177	900	2,530
							1,400

Table 3.60 Village E: labour in village enterprises, 1990

Enterprise	Village labourers			Education				Out of village
	Total	Male	Female	Prof. technical	Senior middle	Junior middle	Primary	
1 Dyeing & chemicals	391	95	296	5	32	163	191	9
2 Machinery factory	175	140	35	3	22	107	43	5
3 Boat building	80	62	18	1	4	42	33	–
4 Spare parts	57	39	18	1	3	32	21	3
5 Iron casting	15	11	4	–	1	7	7	10
6 Aluminium alloy	25	16	9	11	2	17	5	5
7 Concrete pipe	16	12	4	–	–	3	13	9
8 Engineering, mechanical	10	8	2	1	2	4	3	–
9 Glove factory	35	5	30	–	1	18	16	5

Table 3.61 Village E: education

Education level	Nos.	Male	Female
Total population	106	52	54
Pre-school	330	172	158
In-school	272	141	131
Primary school	45	23	22
Junior middle	11	7	4
Senior middle	2	1	1
Higher education	130	66	64
Population in agriculture			
Higher education	–	–	–
Senior middle	3	3	–
Junior middle	35	22	13
Primary	92	41	51
Population illiterate	133	17	116

Table 3.62 Incomes and expenditures in sample households, Wuxi Village, 1990 (¥)

Household no.	No. of persons	No. of labourers (agricultural)	Income					Expenses			Surplus income[c]	Per capita net income
			Total (gross)	Grain	Pigs, animals	Veg.	Salaries[d]	Total expenses[b]	Production costs	Daily needs		
1	2	2 (2)	50,320	–	50,320	–	–	45,490	41,990	3,500	3,000	1,500
2	5	2 (–)	7,514	114	–	–	7,400	2,100	200	1,900	5,000	1,000
3	4	2 (2)	10,726	76	850	8,300[a]	1,500	4,970	3,670	1,300	2–3,000	6,200
4	5	2 (2)	35,112	31,342	3,770	–	–	22,944	18,794	4,150	12,000	2,600
5	4	2 (2)	4,614	414	600	3,600	–	2,421	761	1,660	2,000	5,000
6	2	2 (2)	20,340	19,440	900	–	–	9,280	7,480	1,800	10,000	5,000
7	4	3 –	13,500	–	1,500	–	12,000	4,685	1,285	3,400	6,000+	1,500
8	4	2 (1)	7,875	425	4,200	–	3,250	4,638	4,018	620	4,000	1,000

Notes: a Orchard.
b Includes cash sums for daily needs, production costs, education, house improvements and furniture.
c Includes cash sums over at the end of the year used for savings for extraordinary items of expenditure.
d This sample is atypical of the village in that the majority of the villagers have wages from enterprises.

Table 3.63 Minority nationalities, Yunnan and Guangxi villages

Anwang Admin. Vill.	Households	Population	Percentage
Han	391	2,111	65
Yi	178	1,021	30
Miao	29	156	5
Total	598	3,288	100
Zuodeng Township			
Zhuang	4,778	26,051	70
Yao	2,276	11,183	30
Han	–	53	–
Other	–	1	–
Total	7,054	37,288	100
Shiwan Admin. Vill.			
Yao	186	962	71
Zhuang	77	398	29
Total	263	1,360	100

Note: These examples demonstrate the high proportion of minority nationalities in the villages.

Table 3.64 Land utilisation: Yunnan and Guangxi villages

Location	Population	Arable	Flat	High	% high	Per capita arable/flat
Yunnan						
Anwang Ad.	3,288	3,085	1,479	1,809	59	0.9/0.45
Anwang Nat.	533	540	270	270	50	1.0/0.5
Guangxi						
Zuodeng T.	37,288	33,909	10,461	23,448	69	0.93/0.28
Longtao Ad.	1,556	1,096	311	785	71	0.7/0.2
Longtao Nat.	207	110	12	98	89	0.5/0.06
Shiwan Ad.	1,360	1,160	344	816	70	0.85/0.25
Longwan Nat.	305	221	34	187	85	0.72/0.11

Table 3.65 Yunnan village: household grain (jin)

No.	Persons	Mu	Maize	Per mu	Tax	Quota	Consumption	Per person	Months grain-short
1	5	8	3,000	375	284	28	2,688	537	–
2	10	8	3,000	375	397	30	2,573	257	4
3	2	2	600	300	90	8	502	251	–
4*	7	8	3,600	450	298	24	3,278	468	–
5	6	5	2,500	500	250[a]		2,250	375	2
6	6	6	1,500	250	280	70	1,150	192	4
7**	4	4	1,050	262	138	11	901	225	6
8***	4	5	not able to calculate						6

Notes: * Richest household in village.
       ** Poorest household in village.
      *** Both parents mentally incapacitated.
        a Figure includes quota.
(Many of the variations are due to the age composition of the household).

Table 3.66 Proportion of impoverished households: Yunnan and Guangxi villages

Location	Households	Poor households	Percentage	Proportion Very Poor
Yunnan				
Nanping T.	6,720	2,965	44	not known
Anwang Ad.	598	280	47	80
Anwang Nat.	97	54	56	15
Guangxi				
Zuodeng T.	7,057	5,267	75	3,960
Longtao Ad.	298	298	100	185
Longtao Nat.	37	37	100	27
Shiwan Ad.	263	263	100	80
Longwan Nat.	63	63	100	50

Table 3.67 Cash incomes: Yunnan and Guangxi villages

Location	Av. per capita (¥)	Highest (¥)	Lowest (¥)
Yunnan			
Nanping T.	223	10,000	0
Anwang Admin.	180	310	0
Anwang Nat.	150	227	0
Guangxi			
Zuodeng T.	188	–	
Zuodeng mtns	70–80	151	0
Longtao Admin.	142	171	0
Longtao Nat.	150	500	0
Shiwan Admin.	65	85	0
Longwan Nat.	70	100	0

Note: All figures include value of grain quota, tax, cash crops, animal husbandry and sideline income.

Table 3.68 Health profiles, Yunnan village

Household no.	Persons	Labourers	Dependants	Wealth	Comments
1	5	5	–	not poor	
2	10	6	4	not poor	
3	2	1	1	very poor	sick mother, unmarried
4	7	5	2	not poor	
5	6	2	4	poor	old mother, three children 3–7
6	6	4	2	poor	father chronic illness
7	4	2	2	very poor	mental incapacity (2)
8	4	3	1	very poor	mental incapacity (3)

Table 3.69 Per capita incomes: Yunnan households

In Anwang village the range in per capita household incomes was between ¥6 and ¥108.5 per annum.

Household no.	Persons	Grain	Pigs	Cattle	Rapeseed	Fruit	Plants	Other	Total (per capita)
1	5 np	2.6	150	–	38	2.4	20	–	213 (43)
2	10 np	6	560	260	55	4	–	200*	1085 (108)
3	2 vp	1.5	–	–	11	–	–	–	12.5 (6)
4	7 np	4.8	60	280	–	–	–	223**	568 (81)
5	6 p	40	–	380	–	–	–	80***	100 (17)
6	6 p	14	–	–	35	–	–	–	49 (8)
7	4 vp	2.2	–	–	–	–	–	42.5****	45 (11)
8	4 vp	–	–	–	–	–	–	–	4 (1)

Notes: p   Poor
         vp   Very poor
         np   Not poor
         *   Grain processing
         **   Wages cooking
         ***   Chickens
         ****   Bamboo weaving

Table 3.70 Major cash expenses: Yunnan households

In Anwang village the major cash expenses of a range of households included the following:

1 5 np   ¥30 fertiliser, ¥12 tools, ¥18 jars for wine payment for well building.
2 10 np ¥71 for fertiliser, costs of grain ¥283.5; school fees, 3 children ¥66.
3 2 vp   salt.
4 7 np   ¥100 fertiliser, school fees.
5 6 p   grain, salt oil, fertiliser ¥45, clothes ¥30–40 for children.
6 6 p   grain, ¥25 fertiliser, ¥10 salt and oil, ¥30 grain, school fees.
7 4 vp   grain ¥128, salt.
8 4 vp   salt, relief grain.

Table 3.71 Labour in townships and villages

Location	Pop.	Male (%)	Female (%)	Labour (%)	Male (%)	Female (%)
Yunnan						
Nanping	38,232			18,857 (49)	750 (50)	762 (50)
Anwang Ad.	3,288	1,634 (50)	1,654 (50)	1,512 (46)		
Anwang Nat.						
Hamlet (a)	168	86 (51)	82 (49)	80 (48)	30 (37)	50 (63)
Hamlet (b)	196	90 (46)	106 (54)	96 (49)	40 (42)	56 (58)
Guangxi						
Zuodeng	37,288	18,710 (50)	18,578 (50)	15,919 (43)	8,039 (50)	7,880 (50)
Longtao Ad.	1,556	755 (49)	801 (51)	596 (38)	256 (43)	340 (57)
Longtao	207	100 (48)	107 (52)	85 (41)	40 (47)	45 (53)
Shiwan	1,360	630 (46)	730 (54)	522 (38)	234 (45)	288 (55)
Longwan	305	142 (47)	163 (53)	132 (43)	57 (43)	75 (57)

Table 3.72 Domestic livestock distribution: Guangxi village, in Shiwan administrative village (263 households)

Animal	No.	Per house	No.without	%
Cattle	259	1	47	18
Goats	711	2.7	18	7
Pigs	690	2.6	31	12
Chickens	1,205	4.6	14	5

Note: A total of 7 households had no animals and 23 had chickens only.

Table 6.1 Peasant per capita income, 1978 and 1982[a]

	Percentage of Households	
	1978	*1982*
Earning more than ¥500	0.6	6.7
Earning between ¥500 and ¥200	27.4	66.5
Earning less than ¥200	72.5	26.8
	100.0	100.0

Note: a Based on a survey of 22,000 peasant households in 589 counties.
Source: Beijing Review, 16 May 1983, p. 7.

Table 6.2 Sample survey of peasant per capita income 1978–82 (¥)

	Sample survey	*Travers' adjustments*
1978	133.57	108.24
1979	160.17	127.76
1980	191.33	145.75
1981	223.44	165.94
1982	270.11	–

Sources: 'Sample survey of peasant household income', *Beijing Review*, 24 Oct. 1983, pp. 11–12; Travers, 'Post-1978 rural economic policy and peasant income in China', *China Quarterly*, 98, June 1984, pp. 241–60.

Table 6.3 Sources of peasant income, 1983

Types of household in order of wealth	*Proportion of total income from field cultivation (%)*
Specialised households	20.0
Well-off households	33.5
Poor peasant households	66.5

Source: Results of 1983 Survey of Rural Economy, *Renmin Ribao*, 1 Aug. 1983.

Table 6.4 Provincial per capita income, 1978–82

| | | Peasant income (¥) | | |
	Province	1978	1982	% rise
North	Hebei	114.0	236.0	109
	Liaoning	185.2	336.5	81.7
	Jilin	110.0	178.0	61.8
	Heilongjiang	110.0	250.5	25.7
East	Jiangxi	–	309.0	–
	Zhejiang	–	312.7	–
	Anhui	113.3	269.0	137.5
	Fujian	122.17	268.16	119.5
	Jiangxi	140.7	269.7	91.7
	Shandong	89.2	304.0	240.8
Central	Hubei	110.6	286.1	158.7
	Hunan	142.6	284.4	99.4
	Guangdong	220.9	381.8	72.8
	Guangxi	67.5	235.0	248.15
Southwest	Sichuan	–	233.7	–
	Guizhou	109.0	229.7	110.7
	Yunan	130.6	231.8	77.5
Northwest	Shaanxi	133.3	218.3	63.7
	Gansu	101.0	174.0	72.3
	Qinghai	–	221.92	–
	Ningxia	–	205.0	–
	Xinjiang	–	277.1	–

Source: Compiled from *Almanack of China's Economy*, 1983.

Table 6.5 Differentials in peasant incomes, Shaanxi province, 1983

Region	Average per capita income	% rise since 1978	% rise since 1982	Average growth rate over 5 years
Plains	303.1	130.0	13.6	14.2
Hills	293.0	200.0	41.5	25.0
Mountains	236.7	200.0	18.8	24.9

Source: Shaanxi Ribao, 28 May 1984.

Table 6.6 Macro-economic indicators and estimated incidence of absolute poverty*

Year	1980	1982	1984	1986	1988	1990
GNP:						
1978 = 100	116	132	167	203	251	274
Annual growth rate (%)	7.9	8.8	14.7	8.1	11.0	5.2
Per capita grain availability (kg):	338	367	401	368	368	400
Retail prices (% annual change):						
National average	6.0	1.9	2.8	6.0	18.5	2.1
Rural: all food	7.1	4.4	1.4	7.5	20.9	1.7
grain	7.1	3.5	−0.4	13.0	14.0	−3.3
Per capita income (¥):						
Urban	–	535	660	910	1,192	1,523
Rural	191	270	355	424	545	630
Urban[a]	–	467	550	633	632	685
Rural[b]	180	241	311	325	336	319
Employment (million people):						
Working age population[c]	–	567	602	641	670	697
Total employment	424	453	482	513	543	567
Rural economy[d]	318	339	360	380	401	420
Agriculture[d]	283	301	301	305	315	333
Non-agriculture[d]	35	38	59	75	86	87
Rural enterprise[e]	30	31	52	79	95	93
Estimated Incidence of absolute poverty:						
Registered urban (million people)	–	2	1	1	1	1
(% of urban population)	–	0.9	0.3	0.2	0.2	0.4
Rural (million people)	218	140	89	97	86	97
(% of rural population)	27.6	17.4	11.0	11.9	10.4	11.5
Total (million people)	–	142	90	97	86	98
(% of total population)	–	13.9	8.6	9.0	7.8	8.6

Notes: a   Deflated by the urban cost of living index.
  b   Deflated by the rural retail consumer price index.
  c   Officially defined as women ages 16–54 and men ages 16–59 (excluding military, prisoners and the disabled).
  d   Excludes urban staff and workers employed in rural agriculture and rural non-agriculture.
  e   Rural enterprise employment, including some part-time workers. A definitional change, to include all kinds of rural enterprise, explains part of the sharp increase in employment in 1984.

Source: State Statistical Bureau (1991a) for GNP, prices, income and employment, World Bank (1991b) for grain, and Annex 1 for poverty estimates; compiled by Alan Piazza and Lee Travers, in *China: Strategies for Reducing Poverty in the 1990s, A World Bank Country Study*, Washington, DC: World Bank, 1992, p. 4.

Table 6.7 Provincial indicators of social development

	Rural income (¥ per capita and % change)					1989 incidence of rural poverty		Illiteracy 1990
	1980	1984	1985	1989	Real increase 1980–89	Share of provincial households	Share of total poor population	
National average	191.3	355.3	397.6	601.5	75%	11.4%	100.0%	22.3%
North								
Beijing	290.5	664.1	775.1	1230.6	136%	0.2%	0.0%	11.0%
Tianjin	277.9	504.6	564.6	1020.3	104%	0.4%	0.0%	11.7%
Hebei	175.8	345.0	385.2	589.4	87%	13.0%	7.1%	21.9%
Henan	160.8	301.3	329.4	457.1	58%	16.5%	12.7%	22.9%
Shandong	194.3	404.2	408.1	630.6	81%	6.8%	5.0%	23.1%
Northeast								
Liaoning	273.0	477.4	467.8	740.2	51%	8.0%	1.9%	11.6%
Jilin	236.3	486.8	413.7	624.0	47%	12.2%	1.9%	14.3%
Heilongjiang	205.4	443.2	397.8	535.2	45%	18.3%	3.6%	15.0%
Northwest								
Inner Mongolia	181.3	336.1	360.4	477.5	47%	23.5%	3.6%	21.9%
Shanxi	155.8	350.5	358.2	513.9	84%	17.4%	4.1%	16.5%
Shaanxi	142.5	262.5	295.3	433.7	70%	20.3%	5.8%	25.3%
Ningxia	178.1	313.2	321.2	521.9	63%	18.99%	0.7%	32.2%
Gansu	153.3	221.1	255.2	365.9	33%	34.2%	6.7%	39.8%
Qinghai		264.2	343.0	457.5		23.7%	0.8%	40.6%
Xinjiang	198.0	362.7	394.3	545.6	53%	18.7%	1.6%	19.3%
Yangtze River								
Shanghai	397.4	785.1	805.9	1380.0	93%	0.0%	0.0%	13.4%
Jiangsu	217.9	447.9	492.6	875.7	124%	3.4%	1.9%	22.6%
Zhejiang	219.2	446.4	548.6	1010.7	157%	2.0%	0.8%	23.2%
Anhui	184.8	323.0	369.4	515.8	55%	7.7%	3.9%	34.4%
Jiangxi	180.9	334.4	377.3	558.6	72%	5.0%	1.6%	23.8%
Hubei	169.9	392.3	421.2	571.8	87%	6.0%	2.6%	22.2%
Hunan	219.7	348.2	395.3	558.3	42%	6.2%	3.5%	17.1%

Table 6.7 Continued

	Rural income (¥ per capita and % change)					1989 incidence of rural poverty		
	1980	1984	1985	1989	Real increase 1989–90	Share of provincial households	Share of total poor population	Illiteracy 1990
South								
Fujian	171.7	344.9	396.5	697.3	126%	1.8%	0.5%	22.8%
Guangdong	274.4	425.3	495.3	955.0	94%	0.9%	0.5%	15.2%
Hainan				674.3		3.3%	0.2%	21.3%
Southwest								
Guangxi	173.7	267.2	303.0	483.0	55%	15.4%	6.1%	16.5%
Sichuan	187.9	286.8	315.1	494.1	46%	11.2%	11.2%	21.4%
Guizhou	161.5	260.7	287.8	430.3	48%	17.8%	5.4%	36.4%
Yunnan	150.1	310.4	338.3	477.9	77%	19.0%	6.5%	37.5%
Tibet			353.0	397.3				67.6%

Source: SSB (1991a) for rural income and illiteracy, Annex 1 for incidence of rural poverty; compiled by Alan Piazza and Lee Travers, in *China: Strategies for Reducing Poverty in the 1990s, A World Bank Country Study*, Washington, DC: World Bank 1992, p. 37.

Table 6.8 Poverty relief in three villages

Location	House nos	Free grain	%	Cash	%	Clothes	%
Yunnan							
Anwang Nat.	97	7	7	2	2	3	3
Guangxi							
Longtao Admin.	298	185	62	–	–	86	29
Longwan Nat.	63	50	79	2	3	28	44

Table 6.9 Poverty alleviation loan history, Guangxi Village A

Year		House no.	Total amount (¥)	Per house (¥)	Purpose
1985		10	2,500	250	cattle
		39	1,392	36	animal husbandry
		6	1,200	200	house rebuilding
	Total	55	5,092	93	
1986		9	1,800	200	animal husbandry
		28	1,102	39	fruit trees
	Total	37	2,902	78	
1987		no loans			
1988		no loans			
1989		no loans			

Table 6.10 Poverty alleviation loan history, Guangxi Village B

Year		House no.	Total amount (¥)	Per house (¥)	Purpose
1985		13	3,250	250	pigs and cattle
		135	1,348	10	tung trees
		84	1,101	13	plum trees
	Total	232	5,699	25	
1986		7	1,400	200	cattle
		7	140	20	orange trees
		3	84	28	plum trees
	Total	17	1,624	95	
1987		no loans			
1988		no loans			
1989		no loans			

Table 6.11 Credit supplies for livestock, Sichuan village

Village	No. of households	Households with credit		Average amount of loan (year) ¥	Interest rate	Repayment
		No.	%			
Huanglung						
Goats	133	80	60	200–1,000	Interest-free	3 years
Pigs	133	48	36	100	2.6	seasonal
Shaku						
Goats	90	54	60	7	2.6	1–3 years
Pigs	90	90	100	50	2.6	seasonal
Xinwen						
Pigs	39	13	33	600–900	2.6	1–8 years
Rabbits	39	8	20	70–100	Interest-free	1–1.5 yrs
Taiping						
Rabbits	52	2	4	40	2.6	1–3 years
Pigs	12	27	52	80	2.6	1–3 years
Daping						
Pigs	204	180	88	100–150	2.6	2–3 years
Rabbits	204	7	3	150	2.6	2–3 years
Lungwu						
Pigs	261	131	50	100	2.6	seasonal
Rabbits	261	19	7	200	2.6	1 year
Pigs	261	15	6	–	Interest-free	–
Kanpu						
Cows	340	10	3	2,500	2.6	7–10 yrs
Goats	340	70	20	100	2.6	1–3 years

Table 6.12 Application for loans, Sichuan villages

Village	No. of households	Applications		Successful applicants	
		No.	%	No.	%
Huanglung					
Goats	*138*	*133*	*96*	*80*	*61*
Shaku					
Goats	90	90	100	55	61
Xinwen					
Fur rabbits	39	39	51	21	54
Fur rabbits 1988	39	20	51	3	15
Taiping					
Fur rabbits	52	27	52	8	30
Daping					
Meat rabbits	204	170	93	7	4
All animals 1988	204	130	64	60	44
Rabbits 1987	42	40	95	5	12.5
Rabbits 1988	42	42	100	4	9
Lungwu					
Meat rabbits	261	240	92	19	8
Meat rabbits 1987	27	10	37	10	100
Meat rabbits 1988	27	25	92	10	40
Kanpu					
Cows	340	100	29	10	10
Goats	340	100	29	50	50

Table 7.1 Size of family and income

No. of family members	Per capita household income (%)	
	Less than ¥100	More than ¥100
1–2	92	8
3–4	74	26
6–8	69	31

Source: Based on a survey of 296 peasant households in 1980 (reported in 'Analysis of reproduction of rural population', *Jingji Yanjiu*, 20 June 1984).

Table 7.2 Household size in China, 1987

No. of persons	1987	1982
1	5.5 ⎫	18.0
2	9.5 ⎬	
3	21.0	16.0
4	23.8	19.5
5 plus	40.2	46.4
No. of generations		
3 plus	18.5	
2	15.5	
1	65.9	

Source: Renmin Ribao, 5 Aug. 1988.

Table 8.1 Fertility and birth rates, 1971–81

	Total fertility rate		Birth rate	
	Rural	*Urban*	*Rural*	*Urban*
1971	6.011	2.882	31.86	21.30
1972	5.503	2.637	31.19	19.30
1973	5.008	2.387	29.36	17.35
1974	4.642	1.982	26.23	14.50
1975	3.951	1.782	24.17	14.71
1976	3.582	1.608	20.85	13.12
1977	3.116	1.574	19.70	13.38
1978	2.968	1.551	18.91	13.56
1979	3.045	1.373	18.43	13.67
1980	2.480	1.147	–	–
1981	2.910	1.390	21.55	18.24

Sources: Xiao Wenchang, Li Menghua and Wang Liyong, 'Changes in total fertility rate since 1950s', in China Population Information Centre, Analysis on China's National One-per-Thousand-Population Fertility Sampling Survey, Beijing, 1984, pp 58–62; *China Statistical Yearbook*, State Statistical Bureau, Beijing, 1983, p. 105.

Table 8.2 Proportions of households with one birth, 1970–87

No. of children	*1970*	*1977*	*1980*	*1986*	*1987*
1 child	20.7	30.9	41.8	51.2	51.7
2 children	17.1	24.6	26.6	31.5	31.5
3 (+) children	62.2	44.5	31.6	17.3	16.8
	100.0	100.0	100.0	100.0	100.0

Source: Zhongguo Renkou Bao (Chinese Population) 16 Dec. 1988; *Beijing Review*, 20 July 1987.

Table 8.3 Planned and multiple birth rates by province, 1988

Region	Year-end total population (million people)	Natural growth rate (per 1,000)	Planned birth rate (per 100)	Multiple birth rate (per 100)
Beijing	10.81	8.86	85.68	1.79
Tianjin	8.43	10.27	80.98	2.59
Hebei	57.95	14.82	50.25	9.33
Shanxi	27.55	13.86	50.23	17.10
Inner Mongolia	20.94	14.25	63.02	12.64
Liaoning	38.20	10.71	94.51	1.41
Jilin	23.73	12.72	87.41	2.41
Heilongjiang	34.66	12.71	71.78	6.83
Shanghai	12.62	6.40	97.77	1.12
Jiangsu	64.38	10.41	70.74	6.11
Zhejiang	41.70	9.19	79.85	2.64
Anhui	53.77	15.20	53.04	14.17
Fujian	28.45	14.71	36.93	17.84
Jiangxi	36.09	13.99	32.01	21.49
Shandong	80.61	11.50	63.98	12.87
Henan	80.94	15.59	53.46	17.01
Hubei	51.85	12.64	56.40	16.98
Hunan	58.90	16.50	40.32	13.44
Guangdong	59.28	15.83	42.21	24.08
Guangxi	40.88	15.82	69.29	29.97
Hainan	6.28	15.37	42.97	33.73
Sichuan	105.76	11.70	78.06	6.35
Guizhou	31.27	17.80	44.09	28.30
Yunnan	35.94	16.88	65.30	22.53
Tibet	2.12	17.18		
Shaanxi	31.35	14.93	46.36	23.78
Gansu	21.36	15.35	46.25	21.69
Qinghai	4.34	14.49	57.54	25.63
Ningxia	4.45	19.55	76.95	28.40
Xinjiang	14.26	13.73	14.33	45.43

Source: State Family Planning Commission Sample Survey, 1988, published 14 April in *Renmin Ribao* (People's Daily).

Table 9.1 Number of male and female infants born in some teams and communes in Huaiyuan County, Anhui province, 1987

		Number of births				
	Total	Male	%	Female	%	% of male over female
Shuangguo Commune	133	83	62.4	50	37.6	24.8
Lanqiao Commune	104	66	63.5	38	36.5	27.0
Langkang Commune	231	145	62.8	86	37.2	25.6
Heliu Commune	285	164	57.5	121	42.5	15.0
Shaowang Brigade	9	7	77.8	2	22.2	55.6
Lanmiao Commune (1 brigade)	8	7	87.5	1	12.5	75.0
Huayu Commune (1 brigade)	10	9	90.0	1	10.0	80.0
Total per county	10,768	6,266	58.2	4,502	41.8	16.4

Table 9.2 Number of births by sex, and sex ratios by birth by province

Province	Total	Male	Female	Sex ratio	Standard deviation
China	229,178	120,531	108,647	110.94	0.44
Beijing	1,585	833	752	110.77	5.33
Tianjin	1,452	733	719	101.95	5.57
Hebei	13,673	7,221	6,452	111.92	1.81
Shanxi	5,395	2,779	2,616	106.23	2.89
Inner Mongolia	3,900	2,011	1,889	106.46	3.40
Liaoning	6,793	3,548	3,245	109.34	2.57
Jilin	4,188	2,192	1,996	109.82	3.28
Heilongjiang	6,274	3,222	3,052	105.57	2.68
Shanghai	1,882	957	925	103.46	4.89
Jiangsu	10,134	5,452	4,682	116.45	2.11
Zhejiang	6,554	3,554	3,000	118.47	2.47
Anhui	9,764	5,270	4,494	117.27	2.15
Fujian	6,165	3,239	2,926	110.70	2.70
Jiangxi	8,437	4,409	4,028	109.46	2.31
Shandong	17,653	9,354	8,299	112.71	1.60
Henan	17,380	9,381	7,999	117.28	1.61
Hubei	12,007	6,265	5,742	109.11	1.94
Hunan	12,509	6,482	6,027	107.55	1.90
Guangdong	14,617	7,613	7,004	108.70	1.75
Guangxi	10,827	5,784	5,043	114.69	2.04
Sichuan	22,739	12,047	10,692	112.67	1.41
Guizhou	7,443	3,848	3,595	107.04	2.46
Yunnan	8,829	4,553	4,276	106.48	2.26
Tibet	693	362	331	109.37	8.06
Shaanxi	7,658	4,003	3,655	109.52	2.42
Gansu	4,658	2,405	2,253	106.75	3.11
Qinghai	1,072	542	530	102.26	6.48
Ningxia	1,071	548	523	104.78	6.48
Xinjiang	3,826	1,924	1,902	101.16	3.43

Source: State Family Planning Commission Sample Survey, 1988, published 14 April in *Renmin Ribao* (People's Daily).

Appendix 2
Field methods

For many years now my fieldwork experiences in China have been of the short-term variety, lasting anything from one to several weeks. The most efficient and fruitful means of undertaking short-term field investigation in China is very much dependent on the subject of enquiry, the amount of documentary material available to the researcher and the type of access and time allowed for in the field itself. For close on thirty years and until quite recently, virtually no sociological surveys or fieldwork studies had been carried out in China either by Chinese of foreign social scientists. While Chinese sociologists have been undertaking some quite large-scale surveys and a very few foreign scholars have been successful in obtaining visas for longer-term fieldwork, most foreign anthropologists and sociologists wanting to do fieldwork in China have had to be content with limited forms of access frequently confined to three or four weeks. In these circumstances, fieldworkers face two questions: how to make the best use of such a short period of time in the field, and how to weigh up the various constraints and decide which are acceptable and which may seriously impair the value of the research itself. In addition to the time constraint, a second major factor to take into account in any field investigation is the existence of a clearly defined ideology representing social structures and social processes as they 'ought to be', how certain socio-political and economic institutions ought to function, and how political, social and economic relations ought to be constructed. It is thus more difficult to identify rapidly what actually is, as opposed to what ought to be. In terms of subject matter, it may therefore only be feasible to research the less intimate and politically sensitive areas for which data are relatively easily attainable and less subject to normative constraints. However, this does not necessarily preclude obtaining basic data which the researcher can use as the basis for more sensitive interpretation, argument and hypotheses.

During each of my own short periods in the field in China to investigate quite a wide range of specific topics, I have found a well-prepared village and household set of structured interviews with a scope and a focus appropriate to the subject and location and allowing for national and local context, to be the most effective means of completing a study, be it centred on a particular social, political or economic institution, relation or policy. The subjects of my field investigations have included production, employment and income, marriage, family and kin groups or reproduction and family-planning policies, socialisation and education, food production and consumption, poverty alleviation, village land and enterprises and formal and informal village economic and political institutions. In each county, township, village and household, sets of interviews provided case studies, which could be set alongside general or other case study data from documentary sources. In all cases, though, household interviews were preceded by documentary preparation before entering the field, and by field interviews once in China. Indeed, I like to think of the field investigation as the icing on a very substantial cake of documentary work and long-term experience. In any event, the documentary research comprises an essential first phase of a three-staged research process. At the end of the first stage, the researcher has acquired the necessary background documentation on the topic, a number of hypotheses, a set of questions for the field, and some idea of the types and characteristics of the preferred or designated field locations. It is quite frequently the case that the questions for the field are redefined with increasing acquaintance with documentary sources, and are not necessarily those that would have been anticipated at the outset of the project.

The second stage of the research process, which is also the first in the field, familiarises the researcher with the norms and practices of the location and provides a context for household interviews. This may be quite a simple procedure, achieved by arranging interviews to test the proposed household survey with cadres of the higher government administrative levels, mass and other appropriate organisations, and village and township leaders, or it may be more complicated if the topic of research involves resource flows and the distribution of goods and information. Frequently, after initial acquaintance with the region, questions may have to be altered, eliminated and added to the interview schedule. The initial interviews also permit acquaintance with regional and local variations in the use of national terms and definitions which seem to me to be increasing as a result of the new reforms. Over the years I have come across quite striking differences in the calculation of income, definitions and political nomenclature, and quite different meanings attributed to commonly used terms such as 'specialised'. The initial interviews also enable the researcher to identify the questions where there are likely to be strong local or national norms affecting the response of informants, and the measures to expect in households so that if answers of figures for a particular household seem unusual or extraordinary, it is possible to recognise such differences and question more closely. Finally, a comparison of the data obtained from higher administrative cadres or mass organisations with those for the household may show quite interesting normative discrepancies between official representations, expectations and estimates and the data obtained in the households. On many occasions, it is these discrepancies and differences which contribute to the search for explanation, interpretation and argument.

The third stage of the research process, and the second within China, comprises interviews in households, the location and structure of which are usually negotiable. Although in the early years the location was normally negotiated according to several general parameters, more recently the location has been designated by a project or institution. In such cases it is necessary to establish why, and on what criteria, the location had been chosen. Two factors are particularly relevant to the choice of field site. One is the size of the unit, especially if it is to be an all-inclusive study, and the other is the appropriate reception and co-operation of local cadres. I have always maintained that it is better to study a complete unit, and that despite the temptation to study one location in greater depth, it is better to choose two to three sites for investigation on the grounds that the co-operation of the local cadres will be forthcoming in at least one or two. This factor will substantially affect the ease of the enquiry, if not the very dimensions and quality of the survey itself. In terms of locations, certain constraints seem to be acceptable, so long as no exaggerated claims are made for the survey and it is prefaced by a clear explanation of these constraints and the characteristics of the location. In such a large, diverse and under-studied country as China, it can be argued that no region, township or village is representative, and any local data systematically collected and clearly labelled are of inestimable value.

When it comes to the selection of the households themselves, then any constraints are less acceptable, and the selection of households can pose problems. Very often on the first visit to the site, the local cadres have pre-selected the households, and a very complicated process of negotiation can sometimes be necessary to overcome the bias of this pre-selection. One way of surmounting this was to negotiate to visit every household within, say, a village, a village subdivision or a street or housing block, and generally I have preferred to take this approach and visit every household within a smaller unit. When I have had to settle for visiting a selection of households I have generally laid out the criteria for choice very carefully in terms of composition, income level or economic activity and carefully checked these parameters with village data. In this respect, I have retained some control over the choice of households; it is also another argument in favour of household interviews, rather than those with individuals, who will almost always be brought to the researcher, which then deprives the researcher of the choice and opportunity to map and observe within the households themselves. Within the household, interviews follow a single, tightly structured set of questions, designed to acquire both basic demographic information and data specific to the research topic. House-hold interviews first aim to build up details of households in terms of composition, family size and structure, ages, occupations, income and proximity to kin. These questions are generally straightforward once the household (hu) is defined and differentiated from the family (jia). More-over, the introduction of the household members to the visitor is a good way both to clarify household composition and to establish some degree of rapid rapport between researcher and informants. Specific questions are then quite tightly structured to allow for maximum information from a minimum number of questions in as straightforward a terminology as possible so as to facilitate ready comprehension and comparable data from each area or household. However, some additional open-ended questions allow for the discussion of observed subjects or objects of unforeseen interest – perhaps an unusual residence form, a food habit, an adoption or an extraordinary expenditure, activity or item.

The constraints of rapid appraisal mean that the interview design has to incorporate as many safeguards as possible so as to reduce errors or misconceptions to a minimum, as this kind of data cannot usually be checked once the researcher leaves the field. In this respect, interviewing in households in China has had certain advantages in that there has been a common vocabulary incorporating well-defined categories, clear definitions and common institutional characteristics of villages, teams, communes, households, occupations and forms of employment so that some of the definitional problems which complicate rapid research in other societies are less common. However, common terms can also cover a multitude of practices. More recently, I have noticed a decline in the use of common definitions and greater variations in the meaning attributed to terms in common usage. This is one of the many changes affecting and complicating research processes in post-reform China. In the past, too, one reason why it was possible to collect data on very personal matters was that there was less cause for secrecy, given taxes were paid by the collective, and fewer differentials within villages, where 'everybody knew everybody else's affairs'. However, more recent experiences suggest that while these conditions may still hold in the poorest regions, in the richer, well-developed regions of China, research on economic activities of individual households is a much more time-consuming exercise, given that peasant households are now much more complex, autonomous and diverse economic units less inclined to reveal the details of their economic activities, incomes and savings.

Interview data can be checked where there is appropriate documenta-tion such as land contracts and official calculations of remuneration according to output, of taxes and of local welfare levies. More informally, one way of checking grain stores, housing, space, items of consumption and even marriage costs and payments is to ask at the end of the interview to see the house, where all these items are pointed out and discussed at some length. Where there are strong official and local norms governing socio-economic or political relations, certain techniques, such as questioning about both general habits and specific occasions can be incorporated into the survey and be quite effective in getting beyond the generalisations and identifying discrepancies between social norms and social practice. One of the most common ways I have employed to break through collectively constructed representations is to make more specific enquiries about individual events that day, week, or month, and relationships, which has proved quite effective in penetrating generalisations and reducing discrepancies. One memorable example had to do with the then new free and private markets which, because they had just been re-established, still caused some anxiety among informants as to whether they should really use them since they did constitute the private sector and hence smacked of bourgeois practice. Informants might simultaneously 'never' or 'only very rarely' shop at these markets, yet have purchased articles there that very morning! Even so some questions – for example, those to do with the interests and activities of individual family members – have had to be dropped because they could only be inappropriately foreshortened in the context of the rapid survey. Where strong norms favour common family sharing and management in the village, appropriate questions have had to be reserved for other occasions when there was sufficient time to deconstruct the questions into many constituent parts so as to enable a more complex and nuanced picture to emerge.

Despite safeguards, however, there are still areas of enquiry which can only be properly investigated during extended periods of observation. More difficult to obtain are data on the distribution of familial funds, including consumption within a household. While it was possible, by means of rapid investigation, to disaggregate the household in terms of inputs, it was not so possible to break down intra-familial distribution. When it comes to the analysis of resource flows, 'management' is not the same as 'control', and it has been very difficult to think of ways in which both the households and individuals could be simultaneously taken as units of measurement, evaluation and analysis in areas such as nutritional status, consumption of food and other individual items which require long-term observation of the formal and informal mechanisms of allocation of family resources. More difficult, too, is enquiry into areas in which there are rules and regulations that are implemented by the very cadres responsible for help in conducting the research.

The question of the role of local cadres is complicated. On the one hand, their agreement is essential to access and their co-operation can facilitate the research process and greatly add to its quality. The degree to which their presence and co-operation affects the relationship between researcher and informant will probably very much depend on the subject of research.

On only two or three occasions have I found there to be any problem in collecting straightforward local data. On one occasion, access to every single household, 'which were all the same anyway', had to be negotiated with recourse to considerable diplomatic capacities, and on another more recent field visit, there was a general attempt to down-play the riches in a wealthy village. On yet a third occasion, the cadres unpopular in the village avoided involvement in my visit. On all the other occasions, the local cadres assigned to me have been very co-operative, and their help has been invaluable both in the collection of data and as informants themselves subject to ethnographic investigation. Indeed, some sensitive questions are more open to cadre influence than others, and one such subject in my own field has been family planning, in which the sensitivities of cadre–household relations have led to interviews with the cadres in charge of family planning in ten to fifteen households rather than in households.

Perhaps no single factor symbolises the recent reforms and changes in rural China so much as the fact that there is now so much competition for the time and attention of cadres and householders that research is now that much more difficult to organise and facilitate. This is not only a problem for foreigners, but also for host institutions and Chinese sociologists. In the countryside, in the busy agricultural season, it is now practically impossible physically to locate local cadres and house-holders and to take up their time in a relaxed manner, for time is now money. Another longer-term problem is language, and indeed, unless the researcher has sufficient understanding of the language to keep a check on the phrasing and word order, a bias may unwittingly influence or invalidate the findings even with the help of the most objective and helpful of interpreters. The use of interpreting gives the researcher time to write down answers, think of the implications of the answer for further question-ing, check any quantifiable data and check generally observed items of interest within the household. It is for these reasons, too, that while I have cause to be grateful for the assistance of others, I have never been tempted to delegate any part of the research to them, partly because there has been no time to train assistants sufficiently or to guarantee the systematic nature and accuracy of the enquiry given the necessity to check every piece of calculation at the time of the enquiry. Moreover, questioning in each household yields items of interest, often unexpected, which contribute to an understanding of the research topic specifically and Chinese society generally.

Finally, there is the important question of how best to utilise the data obtained from the field – can it stand alone as the basis for argument or the testing of hypotheses? Although limitations on field investigation in China call for narrower definitions of the scope and scale of the field project and the unusual acceptance of certain constraints by anthro-pologists, with thorough preparation and great efficiency in research effort, short periods of field investigation can add immeasurably to ongoing research on most aspects of Chinese society. Even so, given limitations on field research, case studies are probably best used, given the scale and diversity of local conditions in China, as additional, more detailed data to add to other data already gleaned from documentary materials. Only now, in 1992, with an accumulated number of case studies over many years, have I felt able to use them as the primary source material for this book.

Notes

1 IMAGING HEAVEN: COLLECTIVE DREAMS

1 See, for example: J. Clifford and G. Marens (eds) (1986) *Writing Culture: The Poetics and Politics of Ethnography*. Berkeley, University of California Press; R. Fardon (ed.) (1990) *Localizing Strategies: Regional Traditions of Ethnographic Writing*, Edinburgh, Scottish Academic Press and Washington, DC, Smithsonian Institute; and R. Inden (1990) *Imagining India*, Oxford, Blackwell.
2 For a discussion of these questions in relation to studies of the Soviet Union, see Caroline Humphrey (1983) *Karl Marx Collective: Economy, Society and Religion in a Siberian Collective Farm*, Cambridge, Cambridge University Press.
3 See M. Bloch (ed.) (1985) *Political Language and Oratory in Traditional Society*, London, Academic Press; and D. Parkin (ed.) (1982) *Semantic Anthropology*, London, Academic Press (ASA Monograph 22); for a specific reference to development, see D. Parkin (1985) 'The rhetoric of responsibility: bureaucratic communication in a Kenyan farming area', in Bloch, *Political Language*.
4 For an elaboration of the complex notions of heaven in Chinese cosmology, see John B. Henderson (1986) *The Development and Decline of Chinese Cosmology*, New York, Columbia University Press.
5 Concepts of heaven also had a shadow side largely ignored in recent years or sometimes projected onto negatively defined social categories.
6 See P. Bordieu (1977) *Outline of a Theory of Practice*, Cambridge, Cambridge University Press (1971); and (1990) *The Logic of Practice*, Cambridge, Polity Press; for an early specific reference to the process of development, see F.G. Bailey, 'The peasant view of the bad life', in T. Shanin (ed.) *Peasants and Peasant Societies*, Harmondsworth, Penguin, Modern Sociology Readings; J. Fabian (1983) *Time and the Other*, New York, Columbia University Press; and (1991) *Time and the Work of Anthropology*, Chur, Switzerland, Harwood Academic Publishers.
7 For a summary of Chinese concepts of time, see Joseph Needham (1964) 'Time and Eastern man', The Henry Myers Lecture, Royal Anthropological Institute, London.
8 Nora Waln (1933) *The House of Exile*, London, The Cresset Press, pp. 38–9.
9 See Richard Newnham (1980) *About Chinese*, Harmondsworth, Penguin Books.
10 Waln, *The House of Exile*, p. 42.
11 Mark Gayn (1967) 'Mao Tse-tung reassessed', in F. Schurmann and O. Schell (eds) *Communist China*, London, Pelican.

12 For a psychological study of these processes, see Robert J. Lifton (1961) *Thought Reform and the Psychology of Totalism*, Harmondsworth, Penguin Books.
13 See Helen Sui (1983) 'Mao's harvest: voices from China's new generation', *China Update*, March, pp. 11–13.
14 Julia Kristever (1977) *About Chinese Women*, London, Marion Boyars, p. 165.
15 C. Lévi-Strauss (1953) 'Social structure', in A.L. Kroeber (ed.) *Anthropology Today*, Chicago, University of Chicago Press, p. 517.
16 See R. Fardon (1985) *Power and Knowledge: Anthropological and Sociological Apparatus*, Edinburgh, Scottish Academic Press; for a specific reference to development, see M. Hobart (1992) 'Introduction', in M. Hobart (ed.) *A Critique of Development: The Growth of Ignorance*, London, Routledge.
17 See William Hinton (1966) *Fanshen: A Documentary of Revolution in a Chinese Village*, New York, Monthly Review Press; (1984) *Shenfan*, London, Picador.
18 For an explanation of the assumptions underlying the 'mass line' and other participatory forms, see James R. Townsend (1967) *Political Participation in Communist China*, Berkeley, University of California Press.
19 *Honan Daily*, 2 Nov. 1955, reprinted in *Socialist Upsurge in China's Countryside*, Peking, Foreign Languages Press (1957).
20 In an interview a young woman reports that her father knows that it is foolish to await the early arrival of dreams. See R. Mahoney (1990) *The Early Arrival of Dreams*, London, MacDonald; for autobiographical accounts of the shift in eyes, see Yue Daiyuan and Carolyn Wakeman (1985) *To the Storm*, Berkeley, University of California Press; and Liang Heng and Judith Shapiro (1983) *Son of the Revolution*, New York, Alfred A. Knopf.
21 For a debate on the economic variables, see contributions to N. Maxwell and B. McFarlane (eds) (1984) *China's Changed Road to Development*, Oxford, Pergamon Press.
22 For a memorable fictional account, see Gu Hua (1983) *A Small Town Called Hibiscus*, Beijing, Panda Books; for a memorable anthropological account, see J. Unger and A. Chan (1984) *Chen Village*, Berkeley, University of California Press.
23 See discussion in Hobart, *A Critique of Development*, with reference to R. Bhasker (1979) *The Possibility of Naturalism: A Philosophical Critique of the Contemporary Human Sciences*, Sussex, Harvester.
24 Headlines in *Renmin Ribao* (People's Daily), 18 Nov. 1987.
25 *Survey of World Broadcasts*, BBC, 21 Sept. 1978 (FE 5922/B11/1–5).

2 STATE POLICIES: REVOLUTION, RESPONSIBILITY AND REFORM

1 See Chao Kuo-chun (1960) *Agrarian Policy of the Communist Party, 1921–1959*, London, China Institute of Pacific Relations; V.D. Lippit (1974) *Land Reform and Economic Development in China*, New York, International Arts and Science Press; P. Schran (1969) *The Development of Chinese Agriculture, 1950–59*, Chicago, University of Illinois Press.
2 For an elaboration of this thesis, see Elisabeth Croll (1983) *The Politics of Marriage*, Cambridge, Cambridge University Press; and (1983) *The Family Rice Bowl*, London, Zed Press.
3 For articles on the rural responsibility system, see 'Quota fixing at household level', *Survey of World Broadcasts (SWB)*, 28 Dec. 1979; 'Discussion on the systems of responsibility for output quotas by production teams in rural people's communes', *Jingji Yanjiu* (Economic Research), 20 Oct. 1980; 'Fixing output

quotas for individual households', ibid., 20 Jan. 1981; 'Communist Party Central Committee discusses agriculture' *NCNA* (*New China News Agency*), 19 May 1981; 'Prospects for development of double-contract system', *Renmin Ribao* (People's Daily), 9 March 1982.

4 *NCNA*, 19 May 1981.
5 'Results of 1983 survey of rural economy', *Renmin Ribao*, 1 Aug. 1983; 'New achievements in rural economy', *Beijing Review*, 5 Sept. 1983; 'Rural economic reforms', *Hongqi* (Red Flag), 23 Nov. 1984.
6 'Results of 1983 survey of rural economy', *Renmin Ribao*, 1 Aug. 1983.
7 Ibid.
8 For excerpts from and commentaries on Document No. 1, 1984, see *SWB*. 23 Feb. 1984, 25 Feb. 1984 and 16 May 1984.
9 *Xinhua News*, 5 Aug. 1984; 'Jilin implements contract purchasing of grain', *SWB*, 21 March 1985; 'Heilongjiang decision on replacing unified purchase of grain with contracts', ibid., 28 March 1985.
10 *Jingji Yanjiu*, 20 Aug. 1984; Zhao Ziyang (1985) 'Reorganising agriculture and loosening price control', *Xinhua News*, 30 Jan.
11 *NCNA*, 16 June 1981.
12 See Elisabeth Croll (1982) 'The promotion of domestic sideline production in rural China, 1978–79', in Jack Gray and Gordon White (eds) *China's New Development Strategy*, London, Academic Press.
13 *Renmin Ribao*, 8 Oct. 1981.
14 K.R. Walker (1986) 'Chinese agriculture during the period of readjustment, 1979–83', *China Quarterly*, Dec., p. 789.
15 *NCNA*, 14 June 1980, 16 Aug. 1980, 30 Aug. 1980.
16 Ibid.
17 'Home processing industry in Shenzhen', *Nanfang Ribao* (Southern Daily), Guangzhou, 15 June 1980.
18 Zhao Ziyang, op. cit., *Renmin Ribao*, 1 Aug. 1983.
19 Zhao Ziyang (1985) 'Reorganising agriculture and loosening price control', *SWB*, 2 Feb.; *Xinhua News*, 30 Jan. 1985.
20 *Renmin Ribao*, 1 Aug. 1983.
21 'Developing specialised households is a major policy', *Renmin Ribao*, 23 Jan. 1984.
22 'Anhui regulations on specialised households', *SWB*, 28 April 1984.
23 'Expansion of rural production', *SWB*, 1 Feb. 1984.
24 Du Runshung on 'Rural development plans', *Xinhua News*, 13 March 1984.
25 *Tongji* (Statistics), 17 June 1984, pp. 12–13.
26 Ibid.
27 Croll, *The Family Rice Bowl*, pp. 297–304.
28 *SWB*, 16 July 1981.
29 'Role of women in four modernizations', *Hongqi*, 1 March 1978.
30 'Survey of five guarantee households', *SWB*, 15 May 1985.
31 This section on political structures is based on extensive interviews in villages in Henan province, Feb. 1987; also, 'More township governments and villagers' committees established', *Beijing Review*, 12 March 1984; 'People's communes no longer govern', ibid., 7 Jan. 1985.
32 'More township governments'. *Beijing Review*, 12 March 1984.
33 'Reform of the rural grassroots political power structure', *Renmin Ribao*, 14 Nov. 1986.
34 'More township governments', *Beijing Review*, 12 March 1984; A.R. Khan (1984) 'The responsibility system and institutional change', in K. Griffin (ed.)

Institutional Reform and Economic Development in the Chinese Countryside, London, Macmillan, pp. 76–131; 'Rural specialised households in Heilongjiang', *SWB*, 21 Jan. 1984; *Hongqi*, 28 March 1984.

35 See 'Peasants' economic co-ordination societies', *Renmin Ribao*, 11 July 1985; Dai Yannian (1986) 'Beefing up the rural co-operative system', *Beijing Review*, 23 June.

36 Ibid.

37 *Renmin Ribao*, 11 July 1985.

38 Ibid.

39 Dai Yannian, 'Beefing up the rural co-operative system'.

40 *NCNA*, 9 March 1982.

41 Dai Yannian, 'Beefing up the rural co-operative system'.

4 RESOURCE MANAGEMENT: LAND, SERVICE AND ENTERPRISE

1 Du Runsheng, *Xinhua News*, 30 Oct. 1987.

2 Li Yining, *Xinhua News*, 23 Nov. 1988.

3 Gua Shutian and Liu Chunbin (1989) 'Probe into urbanisation of rural areas', *Beijing Review*, 22 May; *Xinhua News*, 14 March 1988; *Survey of World Broadcasts* (*SWB*), 20 May 1988.

4 *Xinhua News*, 10 April 1988.

5 'Peasants worried about the future allow soil to deteriorate', *Nongmin Ribao* (Farmer's Daily), 11 Dec. 1987.

6 Ibid.

7 *Renmin Ribao* (People's Daily), 23 Nov. 1988; 'Report on forum on agriculture', *Beijing Review*, 1 May 1989.

8 *Xinhua News*, 17 Sept. 1987; see also *SWB* reports, 7 Nov. 1988; 26 Nov. 1988; 30 Nov. 1988; *Beijing Review*, 5 Dec. 1988.

9 He Kang (1989) 'China's agriculture', *Beijing Review*, 1 May.

10 *Xinhua News*, 16 Jan. 1988.

11 E.g., *Xinhua News*, 15 April 1989.

12 'Farmers active in commercial sector', *Beijing Review*, 11 May 1987.

13 Ibid.

14 Report on National Agricultural Conference, *Renmin Ribao*, 6 Feb. 1988.

15 *Xinhua News*, 8 Nov. 1988.

16 Henan provincial radio, 3 March 1988; *SWB*, 8 March 1988.

17 Editorial, *Nongmin Ribao*, 15 Dec. 1987.

18 'Trial rules aid rural enterprises', *Beijing Review*, 4 July 1988.

19 *SWB*, 3 May 1989.

20 'Rural private economy', *Beijing Review*, 27 Feb. 1989; 'Collective and private sectors in China', *Beijing Review*, 29 June 1988; 'Individual and private businesses encouraged', *Nongmin Ribao*, 28 Dec. 1987; 'Private businesses produce millions', *Beijing Review*, 21 March 1988.

5 INFORMATION NETWORKED: CADRE, KNOWLEDGE AND AGENCY

1 J. Gittings (1984) 'From blossoms to bricks', *China Now*, Summer, pp. 3–6.

2 'Rural population policy', *Survey of World Broadcasts* (*SWB*), 18 Feb. 1982;

'Population and education in planning work', *Renmin Ribao* (People's Daily), editorial, 29 Sept. 1981.
3 'Survey of relations between rural cadres and the masses', *SWB*, Beijing, 13 July 1988.
4 Ibid.
5 See J.R. Townsend (1969) *Political Participation in Communist China*, Berkeley, University of California Press.
6 Gu Hua (1983) *A Small Town Called Hibiscus*, Beijing, Panda Books.
7 Ibid. pp. 146–9.
8 *A Small Town Called Hibiscus*, pp. 68–71.
9 Marsh Marshall (1985) *Organisations and Growth in Rural China*, London, The Macmillan Press, p. 9.
10 *Xinhua News*, 1 May 1989; ibid., 2 Nov. 1988.
11 'Drive to end illiteracy planned', *China Daily*, Beijing, 12 Sept. 1989; 'Ten million no longer illiterate', *Beijing Review*, 14 Sept. 1987; 'The anti-illiteracy campaign goes on', *Beijing Review*, 10 Sept. 1990.
12 Lu Xueyi (1987) 'Dampened farmer initiative', *Xinhua News*, 4 Dec.
13 'Farmer criticises government for unilaterally scrapping land contract', *Xinhua News*, 19 May 1988.
14 'Shanghai's rural intelligentsia', *Beijing Review*, 25 Jan. 1988.
15 'Peasant takes on county government', *Beijing Review*, 12 Sept. 1988.
16 See Elisabeth Croll (1981) *The Politics of Marriage*, Cambridge, Cambridge University Press.
17 Dai Yannian (1988) 'Dealing with unfair income gaps', *Beijing Review*, 15 Aug.

6 INCOME GENERATION: RICHES, POVERTY AND PROJECTS

1 L. Travers (1984) 'Post-1978 rural economic policy and peasant income in China', *China Quarterly*, 98, June.
2 See Central Committee's Document No. 1, 1984; 'Making peasants rich', *Shanxi Ribao*, 4 Feb. 1984, translated in *Survey of World Broadcasts (SWB)*, 8 Feb. 1984.
3 *Beijing Ribao*, 16 May 1983, p. 7.
4 'Sample survey of peasant household income', *Beijing Ribao*, 24 Oct. 1983, pp. 11–12; Travers, 'Post-1978 rural economic policy . . . '., pp. 241–60.
5 Ibid.
6 See 'Report on 1983 economy', *SWB*, 1 May 1984.
7 *SWB*, 6 April 1985.
8 Ibid.
9 'Results of 1983 survey of rural economy', *Renmin Ribao*, 1 Aug. 1983.
10 'Questions and answers on rural work', *Shanxi Ribao*, 11 Feb. 1984, translated in *SWB*, 24 Feb. 1984.
11 *Renmin Ribao*, 19 April 1989.
12 *Compiled Almanack of China's Economy*, 1983.
13 *SWB*, 27 April 1985.
14 'Report on Anhui's rural economy', *Nongye Jishu Jingji* (Journal of Agricultural Technical Economy), 1982.
15 *Shaanxi Ribao*, 28 May 1984.
16 *New China News Agency (NCNA)*, 9 March 1982
17 'Dealing with unfair income gaps', *Beijing Review*, 15 Aug. 1988.
18 Cited in *Ban Yue Tan*, 25 Nov. 1987; in *SWB*, 8 Dec. 1987.
19 Report in *Xinhua News*, 30 Oct. 1987.

20 *Renmin Ribao*, 26 June 1984.
21 World Bank (1992) *China: Strategies for Reducing Poverty in the 1990s*, Washington, DC, p. 4.
22 *Liaowang* (Outlook), Beijing, 30 June 1984.
23 'Survey of five guarantee households', *SWB*, 4 Feb. 1984.
24 See William Hinton, reported in Orville Schell, 'A reporter at large (China)', *New Yorker*, 23 Jan. 1984, pp. 43–86; and John Gittings (1984) 'From blossoms to bricks', *China Now*, Summer, pp. 3–6.
25 *Outline of Economic Development in China's Poor Areas* (1989) Office of Leading Group for Economic Development in Poor Areas Under the State Council, Beijing, Agricultural Publishing House.
26 World Bank, *China*, p. ix.
27 Ibid., pp. 14–15.
28 Ibid., p. 37.
29 'International agricultural aid', *Beijing Review*, 25 Jan. 1988.
30 *Xinhua News*, 23 March 1988.
31 Ibid., 14 Dec. 1987.
32 *Beijing Review*, 18 Jan. 1988; *Xinhua News*, 9 May 1988, 26 Feb. 1989, 22 Feb. 1989, 27 Feb. 1989; Canton Radio, 1 March 1989; *SWB*, 4 March 1989.
33 *Beijing Review*, 14 Dec. 1987

7 AGGREGATION: LABOUR, FAMILY AND KIN

1 See Elisabeth Croll (1981) *Politics of Marriage in Contemporary China*, Cambridge, Cambridge University Press.
2 'Analysis of reproduction of rural population', *Jingji Yanjiu* (Economic Research), 20 June 1982.
3 'Survey of rural economy, 1983', *Renmin Ribao* (People's Daily), 1 Aug. 1983.
4 Interviews in China, 1983–84.
5 Liu Fanrong (1983) 'A hill family goes all out', *Women of China*, July, p. 2; Xiu Ling (1983) 'Once poor Yanbei is prospering', *Women of China*, Jan.
6 *Xinhua News*, 26 Dec. 1988; *Liaowang* (Outlook), 24, 1988.
7 *Guangming Ribao*, 4 March 1988; *Xinhua News*, 23 March 1988.
8 Ibid.
9 *Liaowang*.
10 *Xinhua News*, 10 July 1988; 'Putting an end to child labour', *Beijing Review*, 25 July 1988.
11 *Xinhua News*, 31 Aug. 1988; 'Dropout rate alerts educators', *Beijing Review*, 16 Jan. 1989.
12 *Xinhua News*, 2 June 1988.
13 Kan Kequing (1980) 'Problems facing women in China', *Survey of World Broadcasts (SWB)*, 31 Oct.
14 Ma Ping (1983) 'A challenging leader', *Women of China*, April.
15 Xu Dixin (1981) 'On the agricultural responsibility system', *Nongye Jingji* (Rural Economics), 11: 6.
16 Liu Fanrong, 'A hill family'.
17 Xiao Ming (1983) 'What the responsibility brings', *Women of China*, 1 Nov.
18 See Elisabeth Croll (1979) *Women in Rural Development: The People's Republic of China*, Geneva, International Labour Office.
19 Xiu Ling, 'Once poor Yanbei is prospering', pp. 18–19.
20 Elisabeth Croll (1983) 'Production versus reproduction: a threat to China's development strategy', *World Development*, 11 (6).

21 Croll, *Politics of Marriage*.
22 Zhengzhou Radio, Henan; *SWB*, 26 Jan. 1989.
23 *Xinhua News*, 8 March 1988; 'China works to eliminate illegal marriage', *Beijing Review*, 8 May 1989.
24 Shaanxi Radio, 11 Feb. 1989.
25 Lanzhou Radio, Gansu, 2 Feb. 1988; *SWB*, 6 Feb. 1988.
26 *Xinhua News*, 5 Aug. 1988.
27 Harbin Radio, 28 Feb. 1988; *SWB*, 4 March 1988; *Xinhua News*, 2 March 1989.
28 Xinhua News, 15 April 1989; Nanjing Radio, 6 Nov. 1987; *SWB*, 20 Nov. 1987.
29 C.K. Yang (1959) *Communist Society: The Family and the Village*, Cambridge, MA: MIT Press; I.B. Taeuber (1970) 'The families of Chinese farmers', in M. Freedman (ed.) *Family and Kinship in Chinese Society*, Stanford, CA, Stanford University Press; Croll, *Politics of Marriage*.
30 M. Cohen (1976) *House United, House Divided, The Chinese Family in Taiwan*, New York, Columbia University Press, p. 59; Fei Hsiao Tung (1946) 'Peasantry and gentry', *American Journal of Sociology*, 52: 1–17; M. Freedman (1963) 'The Chinese Domestic Family: Models', Vle Congres International des Sciences Anthropologiques et Ethnologiques, Paris, vol. 2, pt 1, pp. 97–100; Croll, *Politics of Marriage*.
31 Yang, *Communist Society*, p. 9.
32 'Chinese families getting smaller', *SWB*, 6 April 1984.
33 'Nuclear families dominate countryside, Shehui', quoted in *Beijing Review*, 7 Jan. 1985.
34 'The new situation of China's families', *Renmin Ribao*, 5 Aug. 1988.
35 *China Daily*, 31 Oct. 1990.
36 Academy of Social Sciences (1984) 'Attitudes of young people in China to family formation', Paris, UNESCO.
37 Wu Ming (1982) 'Some older women in China's countryside', *Women in China*, 1 May.
38 Elisabeth Croll (1977) 'Chiang village: A household survey', *China Quarterly*, Dec. pp. 786–814.
39 N. Gonzalez (1983) 'Household and family in Kaixiangong: a reexamination', *China Quarterly*, March, pp. 76–89.
40 'Shanxi calls for support for specialised households', *SWB*, 15 Feb. 1984; *Renmin Ribao*, 23 Jan. 1984; 'CCP Document No. 1 in the Countryside', *SWB*, 16 May 1984.
41 'Ending clan fights', *Nanfang Ribao* (Southern Daily), 5 Nov. 1981; 'Clan strife', *SWB*, 5 Nov. 1981; ibid., 19 Nov. 1981; ibid., 23 March 1982; ibid., 5 April 1982.
42 Guangzhou Radio, 9 May 1989; *SWB*, 13 May 1989.
43 Rubie Watson (1981) 'Class difference and affinal relations in south China', *MAN*, 16, pp. 593–615; Rubie Watson (1985) *Inequality Among Brothers: Class and Kinship in South China*, Cambridge, Cambridge University Press.
44 'Questions and answers on rural work', *Shaanxi Ribao* (Shaanxi Daily), 11 Feb. 1984; in *SWB*, 24 Feb. 1984.
45 'Marriage law and socialist morality', *SWB*, 4 Feb. 1982; ibid., 14 Dec. 1984; 'Arranged marriages', *Xinhua News*, 8 March 1985.
46 Lin Yueh Hwa (1948) *The Golden Wing*, London, Routledge & Kegan Paul.
47 Cohen, *House United, House Divided*.
48 'A common family', *China Reconstructs*, Sept. 1978.
49 'Rural women come into their own', *Beijing Review*, 9 March 1987.
50 Li Zhenying (1983) 'On a chicken farm', *Women in China*, 1 July, p. 2.
51 Xiao Ming, 'What the responsibility brings'.
52 Ibid.

8 CONTINUITY: SONS, SUCCESSORS AND THE SINGLE CHILD

1 Margery Wolf (1972) *Women and the Family in Taiwan*, Stanford, CA: Stanford University Press.
2 Olga Lang (1946) *Chinese Family and Society*, Newhaven, CT, Yale University Press, p. 149; L.C. Smythe (1935) 'The composition of the Chinese family', *Nanking Journal*, 5, pp. 12, 14.
3 J.L. Buck (1937) *Land Utilization in China*, Nanking, University of Nanking, pp. 385–6; S.D. Gamble (1954) *Ting Hsien, A North China Rural Community*, Stanford, CA, Stanford University Press, pp. 21–59.
4 M.B. Treudley (1971) *Men and Women of Chung Ho,* Ch'ang, Taipei, table 11.
5 C.K. Yang (1959) *Chinese Communist Society: The Family and the Village*, Cambridge, MA, MIT Press, p. 18.
6 M. Yang (1945) *A Chinese Village*, New York, Columbia University Press, p. 11.
7 Chen Ta (1940) *Emigrant Communities in South China*, New York, p. 125.
8 Han Suyin (1973) 'Population growth and birth control in China, *Eastern Horizon*, 12 (5); 8–16.
9 Lim Kahti (1959) 'Obstetrics and gynaecology in the past ten years', *Chinese Medical Journal*, 79 (5), Nov.: 375–83.
10 Judith Banister (1987) *China's Changing Population*, Stanford, CA, Stanford University Press, p. 106.
11 Han Suyin 'Population growth', 9.
12 Liu Zheng (1980) 'There must be a population plan', *Renmin Ribao* (People's Daily), 2 June.
13 'Take urgent action to reduce the birth rate', *Tianjin Ribao*, 4 Aug. 1979.
14 For a lengthy discussion in English on the characteristics of China's population, see Liu Zheng, Song Jian *et al.* (1981) *China's Population and Prospects*, Beijing, New World Press.
15 'One married couple, one child seen as a necessity', *Zhongshan Daxue Xuebao-Zhexue Shehui Ban* (Zhongshan University Journal), 4, 1980.
16 Engels quoted in Liu Zheng (1979) 'Problems of China's population growth', in *Jingji Yanjiu* (Economic Research), 20 May.
17 Editorial, *Renmin Ribao*, 8 July 1978.
18 For example, see 'Sichuan regulations on family planning', *Survey of World Broadcasts* (*SWB*), 16 March 1979.
19 *Xinhua* (New China News Agency), 13 Sept. 1980.
20 See 'Sichuan regulations'; Saith Ashwani (1981) 'Economic incentives for the one-child family in rural China', *China Quarterly*, Sept.
21 'Problems in family planning', *Renmin Ribao*, 11 April 1980.
22 See Gui Shixin,'Population control and economic policy' (1980) *Zhexue Shehui Kexue Ban* (Philosophy and Social Science), Shanghai Teaching College, 25 April; Chen Muhua (1979) 'Population control', *Renmin Ribao*, 11 Aug.; 'Population situation: theory studies from an economic angle', *Jingji Yanjiu*, 20 May 1979; 'Population control and economic planning', *Renmin Ribao*, 2 June 1980; Li Shiyi (1982) 'Development trends in Chinese population growth', *Beijing Review*, 11 Jan.
23 See Elisabeth Croll (1985) 'The single child family in Beijing: a first hand report', in Elisabeth Croll, Delia Davin and Penny Kane, *China's One Child Family Policy*, London, Macmillan.
24 'Shanghai planned parenthood regulations', *Jiefang Ribao* (Liberation Daily), 10 Aug. 1981, in *SWB*, Aug. 1981; 'Central Committee and State Council urge better family planning', *New China News Agency*, 13 March 1982; 'Shanxi

Notes 307

planned parenthood regulations', *Shanxi Ribao* (Shanxi Daily), 17 Nov. 1982, in *SWB*, 16 Dec. 1982.

25 See, for example, 'A survey of single-child families in Hefei, Anhui province', by the Population Research Office, Anhui University, 1980; 'One child family becoming norm in Beijing West District', *Renkou Yanjiu* (Population Research), 1 Jan. 1981.
26 For full discussions of arguments in support of the policy, see Gui Shixin, 'Population control'.
27 For example, see 'Family planning in Tianjin', *Tianjin Ribao* (Tianjin Daily), 22 July 1979; 'Family planning in Shanghai', *Wenhui Bao*, Shanghai, 18 Jan. 1980.
28 'Beijing Centre for Communications and Family Planning', *Renkou Lilun Xuanchang* (Essays in Population Theory), 40.
29 Xu Xuehan (1982) 'Resolutely implement the policy on rural population', *Renmin Ribao*, 5 Feb.
30 For full discussion on this theme, See Elisabeth Croll (1983) 'Production versus reproduction: a threat to China's development strategy', *World Development*, 11 (6): 467–81.
31 'Analysis of reproduction of rural population', *Jingji Yanjiu*, 20 June 1982.
32 Ibid.
33 'Problems of family planning work in Zhejiang province', *Renmin Ribao*, 11 April 1980.
34 Xu Xuehan (1982) 'Resolutely implement the policy on rural population', *Renmin Ribao*, 5 Feb.
35 Data from interviews in Beijing, June 1983.
36 *Hebei Ribao* (Hebei Daily), 19 Jan. 1983; 'Hunan provincial service', *SWB*, 10 Sept. 1983.
37 Interviews, Beijing, 1985.
38 Ibid.
39 Guangdong Provincial Radio, 22 April 1983, 8 July 1983; 'Family planning achievements in Shandong province, *SWB*, 2 Nov. 1983; *Liaoning Ribao* (Liaoning Daily), 21 May 1983.
40 Reuter's report, *Guardian*, 16 June 1983.
41 For discussion on female infanticide, see Chapter 9.
42 Central Document No. 7, 1984; for themes, see *SWB*, 24 July 1984.
43 National Conference on Population Planning, *Xinhua News*, 11 Oct. 1986; 'Encouragement but not compulsion for one-child families', 8 June 1985, e.g., Guangxi Province Regulations, ibid., 2 Aug. 1986.
44 Shaanxi Provincial Regulations, *SWB*, 2 Aug. 1986.
45 Interview, Sichuan Family Planning Association, Nov. 1984.
46 Reuters report, Beijing, 14 Jan. 1988.
47 Ibid.; Reuters report, 21 Jan. 1988; 'Family planning in Hunan province', 19 May 1987; 'Shandong family planning policy', *Renmin Ribao*, 2 Aug. 1988.
48 Zeng Yi (1989) 'Is the Chinese family planning program tightening up?', *Population and Development Review*, 15 (2), June: 336.
49 'New population circumstances cause unprecedented difficulties', *Renmin Ribao*, 14 Jan. 1988.
50 *Xinhua News*, 1 March 1989.
51 *Xinhua News*, 31 Oct. 1990.
52 *Xinhua News*, 30 Oct. 1990.
53 *Xinhua News*, 8 Nov. 1990.
54 Zeng Yi, 'Is the Chinese family planning program tightening up?', p. 335.
55 *Xinhua News*, 30 Oct. 1990.

56 Joan Kaufman, Zhang Zhirong, Qiao Kinjian and Zhang Yang (1989) 'Family planning policy and practice in China: a study in four rural counties', *Population and Development Review*, 15 (4), Dec.: 707–29.

9 DISCONTINUITY: DAUGHTERS, DISCRIMINATION AND DENIAL

1 Barbara Ward (1954) 'A Hong Kong fishing village', *Journal of Oriental Studies*, 1 (1): 195–214.
2 Editor's Note, *Gongren Ribao* (Workers' Daily), 4 Aug. 1982.
3 'Analysis of reproduction of rural population', *Jingji Yanjiu* (Economic Research), 20 June 1982.
4 See Elisabeth Croll, (1984) 'The single-child family in Beijing, a first hand report', in E. Croll, D. Davin and P. Kane, *The Single Child Family in China*, London, Macmillan Press.
5 'Report from three counties in Zhejiang province', *Renkou Yanjiu* (Population Research), 3, 1981: 32–7.
6 Yang Fan (1982) 'Save our baby girls', *Zhongguo Qingnian* (China Youth), 9 Nov.
7 'Problems caused by boy–girl ratio imbalance', *Renmin Ribao* (People's Daily), 7 April 1983.
8 Ibid.
9 *Xinhua News*, 17 April 1983.
10 See Croll, 'The single-child family in Beijing'.
11 See Beijing Women's Federation (1983) 'It's as good to have a girl as a boy', Beijing, Jan.
12 See Croll, 'The single-child family in Beijing'.
13 'Population imbalance grows', *Beijing Review*, 27 March 1989; 'Population imbalance', *China Daily*, 5 Oct. 1989.
14 Terence Hull (1990) 'Recent trends in sex ratios at birth in China', *Population and Development Review*, 16 (1), March.
15 A. Coale (1991) 'Excess female mortality and the balance of the sexes in the population: an estimate of the number of "missing females"', *Population and Development Review*, 17 (3), Sept.
16 Beijing Women's Federation, 'It's as good to have a girl as a boy'.
17 Ibid.
18 Ibid.
19 'Female infanticide punishable by law', *Beijing Review*, 25 April 1983.
20 *Zhongguo Funu* (Women of China), 1 Jan. 1984, p. 1.
21 Report on 'Law Publicity Week', *Zhongguo Funu*, 1 Jan. 1984, p. 2.
22 'A program upholding rights of women and children', *Zhongguo Funu*, 1 April 1984, pp. 12–13.
23 Ge Dewei (1983) 'Traditional values keep women in outdated roles', *China Daily*, 24 Aug.
24 Reports on 1983 Congress; see *Survey of World Broadcasts* (*SWB*), 15 Sept. 1983, 23 Sept. 1983.
25 Ibid.
26 Ibid.
27 A.H. Smith (1900) *Village Life in China*, London, p. 262.
28 I. Pruitt (1967) *A Daughter of Han: An Autobiography of a Working Woman*, Stanford, CA, Stanford University Press, p. 29.

29 I. Crook and D. Crook (1966) *The First Years of Yangyi Commune*, London, Routledge & Kegan Paul, p. 211.
30 *Documents of the Women's Movement in China*, All China Democratic Women's Federation, Peking, 1949.
31 'Why female infanticide still exists in socialist China', *Women of China*, May 1983, p. 1.
32 G. Simmel, (1950) 'The stranger', first published 1908, translated in K. Wolff, *The Sociology of Georg Simmel*, Glencoe, IL: The Free Press, pp. 402–8.
33 For a summary of the discussions on Simmel's notion of the stranger, see D.N. Levine, 'Simmel at a distance: on the history and systematics of the sociology of the stranger', and W.A. Schak, 'Introduction', in W. Schak and W.P. Skinner (eds), *Strangers in African Societies*, Los Angeles, University of California Press, 1979.
34 Liao Suhua (1963) 'In what respects should we be self-conscious?', *Zhongguo Funu*, 1 Oct.
35 Margery Wolf (1985) *Revolution Postponed*, Stanford, CA, Stanford University Press, p. 137.
36 Reference to Bordieu's 'time spots' and versions of time might be relevant here: see P. Bordieu (1990) *The Logic of Practice*, London, Polity Press; and (1977) *Outline of a Theory of Practice*, Cambridge, Cambridge University Press. For a discussion of conceptualisations of time from the perspective of motherhood and reproduction, see Julia Kristeva (1981) 'Women's time', *Signs*, 7 (1), Autumn: 13–35.
37 In an interview, a young woman reports that her father knows that it is foolish to await the early arrival of dreams; See R. Mahoney (1990) *The Early Arrival of Dreams*, London, Macdonald.
38 Cui Ling (1990) *The Age of Maturity for Women*, translated in *Women of China*, Nov.
39 'The other side of the river', translated in *Women of China*, May 1991.

10 LIVING THE EARTH: FAMILY ASPIRATIONS

1 Xin Lin (1989) 'Popular support for the reforms', *Beijing Review*, 22 May.
2 'Projected changes in Chinese consumption', *Beijing Review*, 3 Oct. 1988.
3 'Matters for deep thinking', *Zhongguo Qingnian* (Chinese Youth), May 1989.
4 S.H. Potter and J.M. Potter (1990) *China's Peasants*, Cambridge, Cambridge University Press, chap. 9.
5 Bai Nanfeng (1987) 'Social environment in China's economic reform: its changes and choices', *Jingji Yanjiu* (Economic Research), 20 Dec., trans. *Survey of World Broadcasts* (*SWB*), 5 Feb. 1988.
6 S. Feuchtwang (1991) *The Imperial Metaphor: Popular Religion in China*, London, Routledge.
7 'Different interest groups under socialism', *Beijing Review*, 30 Nov. 1987.
8 *The World of Dreams*, Beijing, Panda Books, 1986, p. 15.
9 Liu Guoguan, 'A sweet and sour decade', *Beijing Review*, 2 Jan. 1989.
10 See S. Rossi (1985) *Sociology and Anthropology in the People's Republic of China*, Washington, DC, Academic Publishers.
11 Li Haibo (1989) 'From Dragon to Snake Year', *Beijing Review*, 6 Feb.
12 'Whither should Chinese culture go? and Chinese and Western cultural exchange', *Wenshi Zhishi* (Knowledge of Culture and History), 1, 1987.
13 'Farmers like economic reform', *Renmin Ribao* (People's Daily), 12 April 1988; also report in *Beijing Review*, 4 July 1988.

14 Interviews reported by Louise Branson, *Sunday Times*, 27 May 1990.
15 Ibid.
16 Cui Jian, trans. Simon Long, BBC, Beijing.
17 Interview reported by Simon Winchester, *Guardian*, 17 April 1990.

Index

abortion 196
accountants in villages 31, 32
accumulation by households 163, 177
administrative village 30, 31
affinal kinship 176
aggregate families 173–7
aid agencies 152–3, 154, 157
ancestors 175, 181
Anhui, infanticide 200
animals *see* livestock
army/militia expenditure 67
aspirations *see* dreams

back-carrying of materials 43, 88–9
bank loans 103
beans 37, 44, 65
Beijing: family planning 196, 200;
  villages 52–7, 110, 112, 172
betrothal *see* marriage
birth rates 184–5, 190–1, 193–4, 288,
  289; female–male proportion 200–2,
  290–1
boat building 273
bookbinding industry 55
books 126, 128
brick manufacture 63
building materials manufacture 63, 73
burial grounds 98

cadres: authority 112–13, 116–18; birth
  rates 191; bribery 118; co-operation
  in research 294, 296–7; income of 84,
  90; and information 118–34; pensions
  112; public opinion of 221; relations
  with villagers 94, 112–15, 116–34;
  state 123
carrying of materials 43, 88–9
cash aid 146

cash crops 23, 58, 59, 66, 104
cash deficit/surplus of households 41,
  57, 81
cash income *see* income
cattle 38, 41–2, 45, 46, 48–9, 50, 54, 62,
  83–4, 89
cereals 37, 53, 65, 75, 276; consumption
  37, 44, 71, 82, 238, 239, 276; for
  fodder 38, 44, 239; food-grain lands
  67, 70–1, 75–6, 98, 99, 101; income
  from 58, 60–1, 66, 71; inputs 53, 60,
  61, 71, 76, 77; intercropping 65,
  66–7; prices 60, 104, 145; processing
  63; quotas 37, 39, 44, 53, 60, 67, 71,
  77, 82; as relief 146, 147; shortage of
  82, 103–4; yields 37–8, 44, 58, 61, 76,
  82, 238, 239
Changchih 58
change agents 119–34
Chanping: village land 101
chemicals industry in villages 55, 79, 273
chickens *see* poultry
children: care in households 20, 28–9;
  infanticide 192, 199–202; labour
  165–6, 168, 183–4; mortality rates
  182–3; nurseries 19, 29, 112; *see also*
  daughters; education; sons
clan groups 175–6
clothing: expenditure on 40, 51; fashion
  216; as relief 146
clothing factories 55
co-operatives 33–5
Coale, Ainsley 202
Cohen, Myron 177
collectives/collectivisation 12–13,
  17–20, 77–8, 97, 100
commercial households 54
commodity economy 26, 30, 31, 35